— Second Edition —

THE NEW STYLE IN ELECTION CAMPAIGNS

ROBERT AGRANOFF
Northern Illinois University

Holbrook Press, Inc., Boston

To my wife, Zola

Library of Congress Cataloging in Publication Data

Agranoff, Robert, comp.
    The new style in election campaigns.

    Includes bibliographical references and index.
       1. Campaign management—United States—Addresses, essays, lectures.
2. Electioneering—United States—Addresses, essays, lectures. I. Title.
JK2281.A6   1976   329'.01   76-877
ISBN 0-205-05469-2

CONTENTS

Preface   *v*

✓ 1 / **INTRODUCTION**   *1*

The New Style of Campaigning: The Decline of Party and
the Rise of Candidate-Centered Technology, *Robert
Agranoff*   *3*

2 / **PROFESSIONAL CAMPAIGN MANAGEMENT**   *49*

✓ 1. The Role of the Political Consultant, *Sanford L.
Weiner*   *59*

2. How the "I Dare You!" Candidate Won, *Harry N. D.
Fisher*   *79*

✓ 3. The Agency Knack of Political Packaging, *Walter Troy
Spencer*   *87*

4. Advance Men Ensure Campaigners Against Silent Mikes,
Short Stories, *Jonathan Cottin*   *104*

✓ 5. The Role of Political Parties in the New Campaigning,
Robert Agranoff   *123*

3 / **INFORMATION SYSTEMS AND THE CAMPAIGN**   *143*

6. Information Technology and the Political Campaigner,
Robert L. Chartrand   *153*

7. The Computer's Role in Getting Out the Vote, *Rex
Hardesty*   *188*

8. Aggregate Election Data in the Campaign: Limitations,
Pitfalls, and Uses, *Charles H. Backstrom and Robert
Agranoff*   *198*

9. Basic Information Systems—P.I.P.S., *Vincent P. Barabba*   224

10. Meaningful Uses of Polls in Politics, *Charles W. Roll, Jr., and Albert H. Cantril*   237

4 / CAMPAIGN MEDIA IN THE AGE OF TELEVISION   *259*

11. The Emerging Conventions of Campaign Television, *Stanley Kelley, Jr.*   277

12. Political Advertising: Making It Look Like News, *Congressional Quarterly*   285

13. Radio Use in the Television Era, *Jules Witcover*   296

14. Campaign Consultants: Pushing Sincerity in 1974, *Congressional Quarterly*   300

15. Candidate Exposure in Uncontrolled Media, *Robert MacNeil*   310

16. On the Bus: Covering Presidential Campaigns, *Timothy Crouse*   320

17. Contrasts in Presidential Campaign Commercials, *L. Patrick Devlin*   334

18. The Inside of the Outside, *Tony Schwartz*   344

5 / ETHICS AND REFORM IN THE NEW-STYLE ERA   *359*

19. Financing National Politics, *David W. Adamany*   379

20. Campaign Finance Reform: What Is Happening in the Individual States? *Herbert E. Alexander*   415

21. A Memo to the Ervin Committee, *Stephen Hess*   424

22. Watergate and the Electoral Process, *Herbert E. Alexander*   428

Index   *461*

PREFACE

Something of overwhelming visibility and significance occurred between the publication of the first and second editions of this book, which crystallized its concerns. The occurrence was, of course, the series of events that came to be known as Watergate, and among other concerns it called major attention to the fact that political party organizations have given way in the campaign to candidate-centered professional-technological operations. Besides the illegal activities, obstruction of justice, impeachment proceedings, and use of the immense power of political office, Watergate underscored the fact that modern campaigning is an individualized candidate enterprise, which is generally beyond the resource base, control, or technological ability of those political institutions we have come to expect to play a major role in electioneering and its attendant political functions, i.e., the political party. This revelation, which actually had been upon us for some years, led to other important questions, such as the meaningfulness of parties as representative agencies, their efficacy in providing relatively equal access to office regardless of wealth or position, their control over the key candidate selection process, the degree of meaningful controls over free-agent party candidates who command direct attention with voters via media, and others. Watergate helped to surface concerns related to candidate-centered technology, and these have now become public policy-reform issues.

Like the first edition, this book is designed to introduce the reader to the important technical, organizational, and communication changes that have occurred in the American electoral process over the past few decades. In addition, this edition deals with the public policy/reform issues which emanate from the practices of modern electioneering. Organized around the theme of the declining effectiveness of political party organizations, the book makes clear how candidates for office now mobilize their own electorates with the use of new professional cadres who specialize in management, information, and media. The book is hardly designed to be a handbook for gaining victory with the new style of campaigning; rather, it is hoped that the reader will gather insights into the process of contemporary campaigns, and perhaps overcome certain misconceptions surrounding the role of political parties, professional consultants, polls, computers, and television in the campaign process.

This edition was designed to be used in conjunction with standard texts in the field. It especially should be useful for courses in American government, state and local government, political parties, public opinion, electoral behavior, communications, and the growing number of "field experience in campaigns" or "campaigns and elections" courses. It also is designed so that it can be a companion book of readings to the editor's single-authored book, *The Management of Election Campaigns,* also published by Holbrook Press.

Some of the readings are from sources and writers not ordinarily associated with political science and politics. They are included here because these authors represent the new men of politics, and it was felt that through them, the style of the new politics could best be communicated. The language and flavor of the PR man, the adman, and the filmmaker is as interesting today as was the language of the ward boss of an earlier era.

The introductory essay is designed to give the reader an overview of the new style of campaigning and to raise some concerns that are implicit throughout the readings. The selections in the four sections that follow the introductory essay, "Professional Campaign Management," "Information Systems and the Campaign," "Campaign Media in the Age of Television," and "Campaign Ethics and Reform in the New Style Era," are by no means exhaustive of the issues or modes of campaigning, but they represent central aspects of campaigning, and are informative and interesting. These readings are integrated with section introductions that apply the conceptual framework contained in the introductory essay. There may appear to be overlap or unusual organization in certain places, due to the somewhat artificial organization imposed. For example, direct mail is actually a medium, yet it is so closely bound up with information technology that it was necessary to make it an important part of the second section rather than the third. So it is with polls and media strategy, polls and management, and management and media.

The original chapters on election data in the campaign are worthy of special mention. Their inclusion in an introductory book is designed not only to introduce the topic, but also to promote better understanding and use of this almost universally employed but poorly understood means of campaign information. It is likely that more readers, particularly those involved in a practical campaign endeavor, will encounter this subject, the use of aggregate electoral data, than any other discussed in this volume. Other aspects of the new style in campaigning are too involved to be discussed in this book. The reader may wish to consult other works, such as Charles Backstrom's and Gerald Hursh's *Survey Research*.

As others have stated, a second edition is nice. The response to the first edition by persons in the field is most gratifying. Many persons have given me valuable feedback between the two editions, including Bill Crotty, Doug Dobson, Jim Davis, and Dale Enoch. I would like particularly to acknowledge the critical assistance and many constructive suggestions I received over the years from the late Fred Damaske of St. Louis University, who knew the field so well and understood the problems of the teaching political scientist. Again, special thanks to Charles Backstrom, who, because of his ability, practically stands alone as a practical politics/policy advisor among political scientists. Several persons contributed to the preparation of the manuscript, including Zola Agranoff, Sister Mary Brian Bole, Bill Alexander, Bobbi Cooper, and Lisa Parts. Paul Conway of Holbrook Press has provided valuable feedback on the first edition and in the preparation of this volume. I appreciate the opportunity to print the papers of contributors.

Finally, my wife Zola, to whom this book is again dedicated, offered more support, more understanding, and more assistance.

PART ONE

INTRODUCTION

THE NEW STYLE OF CAMPAIGNING: THE DECLINE OF PARTY AND THE RISE OF CANDIDATE-CENTERED TECHNOLOGY

Robert Agranoff

The Committee for the Re-election of the President had the responsibility to get the President re-elected; the Republican National Committee had the responsibility for other candidates. We very definitely did not want Nixon to be perceived as the Republican candidate for President, but as Richard Nixon running for re-election, or the President running for re-election.[1]

Peter H. Dailey, President,
The November Group,
1972 Nixon advertising agency

On the basis of the evidence presented by party workers, it is possible to present a few hypotheses as to the motivation of voters. The appeals made to party history and party heroes in any election campaign clearly indicate that the politicians regard party tradition as an important control. Boss Kelly wants to know how many people he can count on to be loyal to his party year after year. The Republican bosses want to know who will stick to their party in spite of the disastrous reverses in recent elections. If the precinct captain is an efficient one, he will know pretty well who the traditional voters are in his bailiwick.[2]

Harold F. Gosnell,
Machine Politics: Chicago Model

VIDEO	AUDIO
MINIATURE SOLDIERS, SHIPS, AND PLANES BEING SWEPT OFF A BOARD	*Drum Roll. Voice-over: The McGovern Defense plan: He would cut the Marines by one-third . . . the Air Force by one-third. He'd cut Navy*

Personnel by one-fourth. He would cut interceptor planes by one-half . . . the Navy fleet by one-half . . . and carriers from sixteen to six.

Senator Hubert Humphrey had this to say about the McGovern proposals: "It isn't just cutting into the fat. It isn't just cutting into manpower. It's cutting into the very security of this country."

PRESIDENT NIXON
ABOARD A NAVAL
VESSEL

Music. Faded. "Hail to the Chief." Voice-over: President Nixon doesn't believe we should play games with our national security.

He believes in a strong America to negotiate for peace from strength.

Democrats for Nixon spot advertisement.[3]

Tinker's commercials for Governor Nelson A. Rockefeller followed a carefully designed strategy. Beginning in July, they emphasized the administration's record. . . . Tinker's people emphasized his narcotics law ("With these tools the junkie destroys his life"), his new medical bill ("We hope you never need it"), his highway program ("If you look at all these roads . . . end to end, they'd stretch all the way to Hawaii"), his efforts to combat air pollution ("Just breathe for twenty-four hours and you get what you get from two packs of cigarettes every day"), and his aid to higher education.[4]

Richard Donnelly,
"How TV Turned a Race Around"

The examples cited, ranging from a study of Chicago politics in the 1930s to the 1972 presidential campaign illustrate the four most important changes in modes of campaign communication. First, the candidate, rather than the party, tends to be the chief focus of today's campaign communication. Nowhere in the Nixon or Rockefeller commercials was it mentioned that they were Republicans; they chose to link the issues of their administration with their name, not their party. Moreover, campaign activities are organized on behalf of the candidate rather than through the party. New York State Republican Chairman Charles T. Lanigan expressed his frustration over this situation in Rockefeller's last campaign for the Governorship: "County Republican organizations, some understaffed, some underfinanced—fighting it out in the backroom of a downtown poor-grade hotel for their headquarters—would witness the Rockefeller organization coming in and renting a storefront on the best street in town, with shining lights and telephones, and then seeing their people, who had been volunteers for years, suddenly being put on the payroll."[5] The acquisition of campaign resources, the campaign organization, strategy formulation, and media selection have become the province of the candidate instead of the party organization.

Secondly, in the new modes of campaigning, the party professional has given way to a different type of professional—the advertising and public relations man, the management specialist, the media specialist, the pollster—who performs services for candidates based on the skills he has acquired in non-political fields. As the modern campaign has become a large-scale enterprise, the campaigner has employed practices long used in large-scale organizations: systematic long-range planning, budgeting, market research, cost control, advertising, and public relations. Since there was no existing body of party professionals possessing these skills, candidates began to employ professionals from other spheres, thus forming a new breed of political professionals.

Thirdly, these new professionals have brought to the campaign their habit of obtaining systematic research about products, markets, and audiences prior to making important decisions, and have made electorates the new objects of their research. Rockefeller's polling organization indicated early in the campaign that he was personally unpopular and far behind any candidate who might oppose him. The polls indicated that few New Yorkers were aware of his programs for highways, pollution, education, and drug abuse. His specialists took this research and carefully designed and placed media spots based on the viewing and listening habits of various groups interested in different issues. To support such research efforts, the computer has become a valuable campaign worker. Thus the audience survey, the poll, and other aspects of systematic elections research have replaced the party worker as the primary method of gathering campaign information.

Fourthly, the new style of campaigning includes communication through a variety of media. Party organization no longer has a near monopoly on campaign communication. The candidate organization, the news event, the computer-generated letter, and, most importantly, the electronic media are the prevalent means of getting messages across in the modern campaign. The rise of the candidate volunteer and the electronic media has enabled the candidate to bypass the party and appeal directly to electors. Rockefeller had fewer worries about the upstate Republican county organizations that did not like him or his spending, because these county parties have given way in importance to the nine media markets of New York State. The most popular of the media, television, has become the surrogate party worker, the vehicle for conveying candidate style, image, and issues.

The cases of the Nixon and Rockefeller candidacies, using new styles of campaigning, are not unique in American electoral politics. More and more, the personal style, the image, the candidate personality is prevailing over party in the tone of American politics. New styles have produced successful politicians—John F., Robert, and Ted Kennedy; John V. Lindsay; Barry Goldwater; Edmund Muskie; Eugene McCarthy; George McGovern, to name a few—who possess characteristics quite different from the products of the old party organizations. New styles have brought forth candidacies from those who have achieved celebrity status in some other field and transferred it to politics—Nelson Rockefeller, Ronald Reagan, George Romney, John Glenn, and Shirley Temple Black.

In addition to these more dramatic examples of the new "stars" of American politics, an increasing number of lesser-known contemporary politicians have circumvented the old mode of party campaigning and are using personalism to seek elective office. For example, in 1975, not one but three candidates took on Chicago Mayor Daley himself and his venerable "machine" in the Democratic mayoral primary. The most notable of these candidate-centered efforts was that of reform alderman William Singer, who first gained national attention by leading the move to oust organization Democrats from the 1972 Democratic National Convention. Singer announced his candidacy sixteen months in advance of the primary and proceeded to walk the streets of virtually every city neighborhood contacting voters in bowling alleys, supermarkets, and at transit stops, met with hundreds of group and community leaders, and visited over 500 city schools. Singer attacked Daley on the issues of the poor performance of city schools, inattention to neighborhood development because of overemphasis on the downtown area, and the corruption and scandals surrounding the present administration. But in typical new style fashion, Singer had more than issues. He had a full-time staff of 45, 10 district headquarters spread about the city, about 2,000 regular and highly committed volunteers, and coverage of nearly all 3211 precincts during the voter canvass and on election day. Moreover, Singer spent about $250,000 on polls-based television advertising, with commercials prepared by David Garth, a New York consultant.[6] The Singer approach and techniques, although unsuccessful in this case—Mayor Daley was nominated and subsequently elected to a fifth term—is becoming an increasingly frequent means of displaying party independence.

Americans have embarked on a political era in which independence is the hallmark of party politics. Electors are more independent of party labels and party loyalties. Issue positions are formulated by elected officials acting as independent agents. Candidacies and strategies tend to be independent of the party. American governors, for example, have found new independence in their "professionalism" in office. That is, as they have undertaken innovative fiscal, personnel, organizational, and programmatic steps to modernize their governments, they have tended to develop a personal "governmental competence" image rather than a party political one.[7] The new style and technology of campaigning blends well with this independence. Indeed, it simultaneously supports it and produces it. Changes in the habits of the American voters, the rapid growth in the size of constituencies, new means of communication, and the application of new technologies have caused a virtual revolution in campaigning, which, in turn, is accelerating the change in the entire political fabric of America.

Electioneering is no longer centered in the party organization; it has entered the era labeled by Frank Sorauf as "the candidate-centered campaign." The party, as Sorauf claims, no longer plays the main role as the organizing intermediary in the campaign; as the style of campaigning shifts to mass media, advertising, and public relations, "[c]andidates increasingly mobilize their own electorates."[8] No longer is the important campaign weapon the activity of large numbers of party precinct workers producing a cohesive vote for the straight party ticket.

The old techniques are employed, to be sure, but they are systematically organized by, and are conducted on behalf of, a single candidate. As Robert Pitchell observed as early as 1958, professional campaign management firms efficiently organize traditional precinct activities on an *ad hoc* basis with utmost speed and efficiency.[9] George McGovern's 1972 Wisconsin primary victory was put together by a McGovern coordinator, 35 McGovern field offices and 3,000 McGovern volunteers. McGovern canvassers identified definite McGovern supporters as "number ones" on their index cards. Those leaning to McGovern or still undecided were listed as "number twos," while persons supporting another candidate were filed away as "number threes." On election day the "number ones" and "number twos" were "pulled" to the polls by the same workers, by telephoning and, in some cases, providing transportation. In addition, the workers distributed 600,000 McGovern sample ballots.[10] Voter contact programs like the McGovern effort are likely to be planned by computer, and candidate loyalists are assigned by areas of priority rather than by the neighborhoods in which they live.

More importantly, the candidate is now likely to put together his own team of researchers, strategists, handlers, arrangers, and expediters. The use of political consultants is normal practice for most high-visibility offices. A survey of the 208 candidates running in statewide constituencies in 1972–73 revealed that 168 of them employed the services of at least one hired consultant: 61 of 67 Senate candidates, 38 of 42 gubernatorial candidates, 30 of 37 attorney general candidates, 20 of 32 state treasurer candidates, and 19 of 31 secretary of state candidates.[11] A recent *National Journal* study of U.S. Senate candidates indicated that of the 67 candidates with opposition, 62 employed advertising firms, 30 hired professional media consultants, 24 used national polling firms, and 20 acquired the services of a campaign management and public relations firm. Only 5 Senate candidates had no professional consultants working in their campaign.[12] Rhode Island Senator Claiborne Pell's 1972 re-election team of consultants represents a prototype of the modern candidate putting together a full team of consultants. Pell's team and their roles included: (a) Charles Guggenheim, to produce two five-minute films and a dozen thirty- and sixty-second spots; (b) Tony Schwartz, to create radio spots; (c) Matt Reese, to provide assistance on organizational development, precinct and block work, and get-out-the-vote; (d) Tom McCoy, to organize fund-raising activities; (e) Valentine, Sherman, to prepare canvass lists and house-to-house cards; and (f) Patrick Cadell, to produce issue analysis and voting predictions.[13] All of these consultants were out-of-state consultants for hire, and while the extensiveness of the Pell package is not found everywhere, more and more candidates are using one or more of these outside entrepreneurs.

At one time, employment of the outside consultant was considered to be relegated to areas where political parties were considered extremely weak or the candidate felt he needed such outside help to defeat the party. The most famous case remains Pennsylvania Governor Milton Shapp's first and successful try for the Democratic gubernatorial nomination against the party organization's candidate. Shapp was then a political unknown, and he hired super-consultant Joseph Napolitan to put together a three-to-four million dollar campaign that included polling, television films, radio and newspaper advertising, and direct mail. After the primary victory over the organization, Napolitan underscored his ignoring of the party by stating that, "When it comes to Pennsylvania politics, I hardly know a soul."[14]

This Shapp effort was in early 1966, and it received much attention then because it appeared unique. Today, the candidate-centered campaign and the political consulting business, and attendant techniques, work hand in hand, and their presence is widespread—national, state, local, primary, general, strong party, and weak party. The number of professional campaign consulting firms in the U.S. is estimated at about 300, not to speak of the hundreds of ad agencies, mail houses, and printing firms involved in campaigns. And more and more professional consultants are being employed by candidates for such less visible offices as the U.S. House, state constitutional offices, mayor, and state and local legislative offices.[15]

Nowhere have the new trends in campaigning crystallized more than in the campaign-related events surrounding Watergate in 1972. To many, the Nixon campaign and its abuses stood as a monument to the evils of the candidate-centered campaign and its new techniques. The campaign stood alone in the Republican framework, virtually ignoring other candidates in any hortatory or organizational sense. Its major operatives were not seasoned party workers, and this was said to have led to the many ethical and legal violations in the campaign. The power of incumbency was said to have been abused for campaign purposes. The large amount of money available to the Committee for the Re-election of the President made it possible to engage in illegal surveillance activities, which the campaigners would never have undertaken if there had been a shortage of funds. Nixon campaigners also solicited contributions from corporations and did not disclose them; both are violations of the election code. When the contributors pleaded guilty to these offenses, they claimed that solicitation was made with extortion-like tactics. Unfavorable government treatment was suggested if they did not contribute, and favors were promised if they cooperated. And the Watergate events led to a Watergate era. Financial abuses of Democratic candidates were also revealed, plus other illegal campaign operations. All of these events have accelerated a wave of reform—nationally and in the states—relating to campaign financing and spending, media use, and the relationship between candidate and party, which is predicated on redressing the conditions that made these campaign activities possible.

Campaign reforms effective beginning with the 1976 election were designed to promote fairness and equity in an era when roughly equal and competitive parties meant relatively little in the face of big money campaigns, multi-media approaches, expertise for hire, and cross-over voting. If the latter trends continue, they will solidify the revolution in campaigning, accelerate the demise of political parties in the electoral process, and create what many political observers have called a "new politics." Penn Kimball describes this new politics as "the contemporary contest for power, characterized by primary reliance on personal organizations in preference to party machinery, emphasis on consolidating voters rather than dividing them along traditional lines of class or region, projection of political style above issues and exploitation of the full range of modern techniques of mass communication."[16]

THE RISE OF THE NEW POLITICS

The new politics has arisen because of changes in the American political scene that have weakened traditional party structures and strengthened personalism. Once-powerful party organizations that mobilized a pre-existing bloc of voters behind a party ticket have given way to a new politics dominated by personal cliques, based on "stars" of politics who employ new means to mobilize a more fluid electorate.

The Decline of Party Organization

The primary factor in the rise of a new campaigning is the atrophy of political party organizations. Since the latter part of the nineteenth century, there has been a gradual decline in the control exercised by party organizations over the most important aspects of the electoral process—candidate selections, issue positions, setting of strategies, and allocation of campaign resources. This decline in party control and the accessibility of mass media have combined to hasten the decline of local party activism in elections.

Since the era of the direct primary, party organizations have steadily lost control over the candidate selection process. Prior to the primary era, leader-controlled methods of candidate selection—slate-making, caucuses, and conventions—guaranteed a tightly controlled party group. The primary election opened up this process to voters. Candidates can now marshal their own personnel and resources, use polls to demonstrate their strength, and circumvent the door-to-door activity of party workers by using mass media to make an assault on the electorate. This process has developed competing sources of power and political resources in many state parties, which has led to disintegration of the highly structured pre-primary party. As V. O. Key, Jr., maintained, party hierarchies cannot survive the repeatedly successful assaults on their attempts to propose slates of candidates, and the results are "competing centers of power—informal hierarchies based on localities, regions, groups, personal followings."[17]

The following example of Connecticut is not an unusual scenario for the new politics. In 1974, Ella Grasso's Congressional seat became "open" when she ran for governor. The two Democratic contenders were Stanley Pac, mayor of New Britain, and Anthony Moffet, a Ralph Nader associate and former Director of the Office of Students and Youth in HEW. Pac had the support of most of the party leaders in the district and the State Democratic Central Committee, and he relied on the Democratic organization to deliver the nomination to him in the primary. Moffet mounted his own candidate-centered campaign, which included coverage of virtually all 48 towns in the district, and involved more than 1500 volunteers and over 100,000 telephone calls, plus their own media assault. Moffet defeated Pac, and his successful effort was made possible through the interrelated processes of weakening parties and new political techniques.[18]

The loss of organizational control over the candidate selection process is nowhere more clear than in the Presidential nominating process, in which primaries are not the exclusive source of decision making. Presidential aspirants now stimulate news coverage of their activities, seek nationwide television coverage of states with primaries, and use private and public polls to demonstrate their standing among the electorate, in order to place early pressure on state party leaders and delegates to support them. Where the delegate selection process is open, contenders use their personal organizations to mobilize already committed supporters to become delegates. Recent party reforms, combined with changes in the state laws concerning the selection of national party convention delegates, have meant that about two-thirds of those delegates are chosen through Presidential primaries. And the trend in both primary and non-primary states is for earlier designation of candidate preference and candidate mobilization of delegates. In 1972, for example, it was estimated that 2600 of the 3000 Democratic convention delegates were selected before the (early June) California primary. These patterns have forced Presidential aspirants to engage in earlier and more extensive delegate organizing and voter persuading efforts than earlier practices of lining up less committed key party leaders.

Thus, the 1972 McGovern effort in nonprimary states was based on getting more of his rank-and-file supporters to the local party caucuses than those of other candidates; his workers studied turnouts and found that only about 5 percent of the party voters normally turned out, and they strived for 6 percent or more of their own supporters. In the primary states, they used a combination of the old party techniques, only candidate-oriented, such as voter identification and voter turnout, plus mass media appeals. McGovern's use of media in the California primary included spots that ran for the last five weeks before the primary, increasing in tempo as the election approached, and two half-hour productions that together were shown eighty-five times in all twelve California media markets. McGovern's spots outnumbered Humphrey's by three-to-one in the Los Angeles area and four-to-one in the San Francisco area.[19]

Nelson Rockefeller adopted a different strategy in 1968 when he tried to stop Richard Nixon's nomination by using his own strong standing in the polls to show voters and delegates that he was the most electable. He ran full-page newspaper ads in 36 cities, one-minute prime-time spots on all 3 major networks covering 200 local stations, and a half-hour prime-time program in 36 market areas. Rockefeller also increased his political staff by over 60, while retaining the services of the Tinker agency for advertising, a four-journalist speechwriting team, and a campaign management firm to recruit regional managers and state specialists. He also transferred twenty press aides and clerical workers from his State of New York staff to the campaign payroll to work on non-paid media.[20] These new patterns of delegate hunting reflect the decline of party-leader control over Presidential nominations; control is steadily shifting to the public and to individual delegates who are precommitted to candidates. Nelson Polsby suggests that the national party conventions are overrated as decision-making bodies. He points out that all but four of the convention nominations since 1928 have occurred on the first ballot, thus suggesting that the selection process occurs elsewhere.[21]

The new party reform rules, which were ostensibly to strengthen and make parties more representative, have served to reinforce candidate centeredness. For example, the rule that required candidate identification on the primary ballot meant that party organizations in 1972 were, in effect, out of the convention process. The uncommitted party delegation, which would be open to persuasion from any one of the candidates, has disappeared. This, of course, means the candidate has to run earlier and rely almost exclusively on his own efforts. The process also encourages a withdrawal of elected officials from the nominating process, which makes it more difficult to put the party back together for the general election. Moreover, some activists like John Stewart have argued that the process has reinforced intense concern for the candidate and lessened concern for the party itself, to the point where supporters care more about beating the party leaders and winning the nomination than about electing the candidates. And Stewart claims McGovern did little to discourage this trend by threatening to run as an independent or to support someone other than the Democratic nominee if the nomination was "stolen" from him.[22]

As party organizations have lost their ability to control the candidate selection process, their tenuous hold on the issue positions taken by candidates has declined even further. Today's candidates ordinarily have a predetermined set of issues that they make known early, and these issues are often carried forth from their initial quest for nomination. In the era of the candidate-centered campaign, the evil of the party organization is often an issue in the campaign. Milton Shapp's primary slogan was "The Man versus The Machine." Once elected, officials are no longer as dependent on the party organization for renomination and re-election, and thus they no longer fear being "dumped" for disloyalty. Members of the party-in-the-government are more free to select issue positions for personal reasons, such as their own val-

ues, constituency pressures that are contrary to official party position, or calculation of their re-election effect. Instead of the party
organizations' declarations of issue positions in the campaign, the
point has been reached where powerful candidates within the
party structure can and do insist on the party taking the positions
that they wish to advocate.

The 1972 Republican Party platform was finely honed by
Nixon's White House staff, even to the point where long-held positions had to give way to re-election interests. Because Nixon was
making a serious effort to enlist labor support, the long-standing
right-to-work element of the labor plank was dropped. Many platform Committee members complained that it was "a political decision contrary to the sentiments of most of the delegates" and they
objected to "being *told* that they had to take it," but it stood.[23]
Likewise, the Democratic issues of 1972, in particular their tilt on
foreign policy, the economy, and social welfare issues, were, in
large part, a product of the different coalition of party liberals,
minorities, youth, and women's rights people that supported Mc-
Govern's nomination. Alaska Governor Jay Hammond's successful
primary victory over former Interior Secretary Walter Hickel in
1974 was based on, of all things for a Republican, questioning the
benefits of the pipeline boom and the royalties on oil leases. He
actually questioned economic growth and development. Hammond carried the issue with him into the general election, arguing
that the state's leaders have labored under the impression that all
growth is good, but, if the benefits of development do not clearly
outweigh the costs, "you ought to leave it in the ground, on the
stump or in the water."[24] Hammond's self-developed issue strategy came at a time when Alaskans were beginning to associate
rising prices, scarce housing, heavy traffic, and out-of-staters taking high paying jobs with the pipeline project, and it probably
contributed to his general election victory over former Governor
Egan.

Nowhere has the independence of candidates been more consistently demonstrated than in the development of candidate campaign organizations. The candidate organization as we know it
today was developed and perfected by the Kennedy campaigns. As
Theodore Sorenson describes John F. Kennedy's 1960 Presidential
effort:

> The organization was based on the Kennedy-O'Brien maxim that
> "There is no such thing as too much campaign activity, properly

directed." The object was to involve as many people as possible. On a national, state and local basis, Kennedy supporters created special groups for Kennedy. A nationwide telephone campaign of women "Calling for Kennedy" was kicked off by Jacqueline's placing a conference call to eleven ladies in eleven states. Each state had its own publicity chairman, announcing each new group's formation to small as well as large newspapers.

The Kennedy-O'Brien approach also called for detailed party organization—not merely in the key states but in every state—not merely in the big cities but in every county possible—not merely of the party regulars but of every volunteer. No one who volunteered in or out of Washington was ignored; some assignment was found for all. Volunteers, as pointed out by the "O'Brien Manual," and particularly women volunteers, are the backbone of any successful Democratic campaign organization.[25]

Undoubtedly the most famous candidate-oriented organization was Nixon's 1972 Committee to Re-elect the President. CREEP, as it became known by its popular acronym, was organized entirely independently of the Republican National Committee. It had a number of divisions, including public relations (press relations, press advance, candidate surrogate advance), media (including its own advertising agency), direct mail (including seven computer centers and four district mail centers), information (including affiliated polling groups), state operations (including ten regional headquarters, 250 telephone centers in twenty-three states, and hundreds of paid fieldworkers), group divisions (youth, labor, ethnic, minorities, and many others), a vote security division, and, of course, the most famous security division, whose operatives were apprehended breaking into Democratic headquarters in the Watergate complex.[26] CREEP had a headquarters staff of 355, plus over 300 regular volunteers. In addition to the regular Nixon organization, there was the White House staff, Democrats for Nixon, and the Finance Committee for the Re-election of the President. Under chairman Maurice Stans, the Finance Committee had its own extensive structure, including several co-chairmen, three vice-chairmen, several committee officers, nine regional chairmen, and fifty-three (including territories) state chairmen.[27] Nixon campaign organization staffers were convinced that there were few party regulars in the precincts who could perform the necessary direct contact chores, so they appointed their own precinct captains, and where there were reliable party organization workers, they were brought under CREEP control.

The McGovern campaign had its own candidate-centered structure, with its own divisions, affiliated firms, and field organization.

Its structure is more difficult to describe, inasmuch as it changed so often, and the organizational roles were not as rigid.[28] In general, there was an official McGovern campaign structure in the states, which was designed to include party regulars, and a "citizens'" structure comprised of the hard-core McGovern supporters. A great deal of the ongoing operations, with the exception of budgets, scheduling, and media, were left up to the state organizations, coordinated by McGovern state coordinators. McGovern's New York State organization included over 250 storefront headquarters and between fifty and sixty thousand volunteers. The New York organization claimed to have added over one million voters to the registration rolls and to have distributed over fifteen million pieces of literature.[29] All of these electioneering activities, as is becoming the practice, were organized by, and conducted on behalf of, the candidates, performing the chores once ascribed to the party organizations.

And the incumbent, particularly the holder of executive office, has the resources of office to call on, ranging from strategic and organizational assistance to use of the office as a public forum. Nixon involved almost all of his top aides in the campaign, including Haldeman (strategy); Erlichman (domestic issues, party liaison, strategy); Kissinger (foreign affairs and national security issues); Malek (liaison with CREEP); Colson (special interest groups and fund-raising); Klein (speechwriting and media liaison); Dent (speechwriting and political briefings); and Ziegler (news relations).[30] Nixon also employed a set of thirty-five national government officials as candidate "surrogates" to make tough, politically useful statements that the public might consider shocking if they came from the President.[31] While the Nixon array of governmental employees was most extensive, it is not unusual for the incumbent official to directly or indirectly use his staff for campaign purposes. Thus, in an interesting twist of historical irony, lower-level party patronage workers as a campaign resource have been eliminated in most parts of the country, but higher-level mass communication, political organization, and technical experts remain on the public payroll, and remain available to serve the incumbent candidate.

Interest groups have also joined candidate groups in performing electioneering chores once assumed to be the province of the party. Hubert Humphrey was able to use his long-standing contacts with labor to help him in the 1972 primaries. In Pennsylvania, for example, labor volunteers and labor money was responsible for between two hundred and three hundred thousand phone calls and over five hundred thousand pieces of computerized mail. Despite McGovern's problems with organized labor, many union leaders decided to circumvent the AFL-CIO's policy of official neutrality and established labor committees in forty-two states, staffed by workers from individual unions that supported him. These committees performed their usual functions of canvassing, voter registration, voter education, and voter turnout, electioneering that the AFL-CIO Committee on Political Education (COPE) normally performs.[32] Labor's electioneering activities are the most visible. A number of other interest groups, including teachers' associations, the American Medical Association, and business groups, are now also engaging in these "party" activities.

In the era when political party organizations were dominant, strategies were more party oriented. The strategy for individual candidates was based on the office seeker as a part of a party "team," which mobilized a predetermined group of party voters, primarily on the strength of personal appeals. From this basic strategy came substrategies predicated on building permanent organizations and mobilizing voters from basic demographic groupings—women, youth, veterans, business, labor, etc. A second strategic component was based on persuasion of independent or non-party-identified citizens, with substrategies employing special independent groups and use of prestigious persons in the community. The basic planning agency was the political party organization.[33]

As candidates have become more independent of the party organization, so have campaign strategies. A high-ranking staff member of the Republican National Committee expressed his pleasure after the election that, in 1972, they were included in the organizational decision-making process as they hadn't been in previous years. Interestingly, he said they had *asked* for a role in the 1972 campaign and got one. John Mitchell and Jeb Magruder apparently met with them in early 1971 and told them what decisions had been made in the White House.[34] But it was with only eight weeks remaining in the campaign that the Nixon people actually called state and national party leaders in to tell them what campaign plans were for "the coming months." Party leaders were called to Washington to hear the strategy and techniques outlined for them.[35] Different coalitions formed for the purpose of winning a nomination often dictate a different strategy with regard to issue and group appeals. Moderate Southern Democrats now include black leaders and black voters in their primary election coalition and thus deviate from their party brethren in regard to the use of civil rights as a strategy. Issue differences are often the basis of candidacies that are independent of party organizations, causing different electoral strategies. The Goldwater strategy in 1964 was based on issue differences with traditional Republican party strategy. It was related to Goldwater's premise that there was a "hidden conservative vote" that stayed home on election day, but would come out to vote if a conservative was the candidate. Unlike more conventional strategies, no appeals were made to identifiable regions or groups. From this premise came the unconventional regional strategy that "little campaigning would be needed to win the South, no amount of campaigning could win electoral votes in New England and on the East Coast, but that votes could be won in the Midwest and on the West Coast."[36] Goldwater was neither ideologically in sympathy with, or organizationally indebted to, the establishment that had controlled the national party organization. He therefore felt no compulsion to adopt a traditional party strategy.

Campaigning, as David Leuthold maintains, is largely the process of acquiring and using the political resources that can secure votes.[37] Party organization was once the most powerful resource in the campaign. The organization's door-to-door workers were needed by candidates to turn out voters for the ticket. Many of the workers were part of a vast patronage army whose livelihood depended on loyalty to the organization and success in election day activities.

The powerful campaign resources called upon by party organizations are not as available as they once were. The incentive of patronage has been eliminated by law in some areas and has become less appealing in others.[38] Contemporary party organizations no longer offer the only political cues to voters. Moreover, weakened party organizations now appear to contact fewer and fewer voters.[39] Party is not only weak but it is less fashionable, as the news media, opinion leaders, and independent-thinking candidates articulate values that are not supportive of the party.

The prime resources necessary in a contemporary political campaign have changed and, as presently constituted, are beyond the ability of most modern party organizations to deliver. As face-to-face media give way to mass media, and the technological sophistication of campaigning increases, candidates are turning elsewhere for technical assistance and funds, for access to the mass media depends not on party, but on skills and money.

As group identity and appeals diminish in importance, other appeals increase, and they can be implemented by special development and special channeling of messages. If workers are needed, a core of personal loyalists is available to do the job. Contemporary party organizations no longer have the monopoly they once had on political workers. Party organizations have become, in a word, weak. The modern candidate has filled the breach of the weakened party through acquisition and distribution of his own resources.

The Decline of Party Voting

The new campaigning has emerged as a result of movement in the electorate away from the strong party loyalties they once demonstrated. Party loyalty has traditionally been measured by political scientists through the concept of party identification, a psychological measurement considered to be the central factor in explaining the behavior of the American electorate. As the authors of *The American Voter* explain, party identification is "a psychological identification which can persist without legal recognition or evidence of formal membership and even without a record of formal support. Most Americans have this sense of attachment with one party or the other. And for the individual who does, the strength and direction of party identification are facts of central importance in accounting for attitude and behavior."[40] In this landmark study of Presidential voting in the 1950s, the authors found that most voters with a party identification voted consistently with that party, and the stronger the feeling of party identification, the more likely they were to support that party consistently.[41]

Party loyalty, as measured by party identification, has been one of the most durable of political phenomena. Strong candidate attachments have waned as office seekers have been replaced by others. Issues have gone beyond the point of saliency as problems are solved, but most voters continue to align themselves psychologically with one of the two major parties. A compendium of different sample surveys by the Survey Research Center at the University of Michigan indicates that party identification has been relatively stable since the 1950s. The Center's pre- and post-election surveys indicate only a slight overall movement in the direction of weaker partisanship, and a small increase in the number of independents. Specifically, the 1952–1972 changes are: Strong Democrat, 22 to 15 percent; Strong Republican, 13 to 10 percent; Weak Democrat, 25 to 26 percent; Weak Republican, 14 to 13 percent; Democrat leaning Independent, 10 to 11 percent; Republican leaning Independent, 7 to 11 percent; Independent, 5 to 13 percent.[42] But the basic conclusion remains that party loyalty as measured by psychological identification persists.

However, a significant trend in relation to the new campaigning is that party identification seems to be less powerful as a predictor of the vote. Recent research on voting behavior appears to underscore an early finding identified by Campbell, Gurin, and Miller in *The Voter Decides,* that conflicting motivational patterns are more likely to cause voters, including party identifiers, to split their votes.[43] Early indicators of this lack of power of party identification were postulated by Matthews and Prothro in their study of participation by blacks in the South. They developed a scale of "party image," and found that persons who identified with a party, but had a poor image of that party, were more likely to split their vote.[44] The most prominent grouping in this category consisted of whites who identified themselves as Democrats but perceived the national Democratic party as pro-civil rights. This was the group most likely to vote Republican in Presidential elections. Political scientist and campaign consultant Walter DeVries has studied the rise of ticket-splitting as an aggregate data measure of party voting. DeVries claims that professed partisanship or independence is not nearly so important as what he calls behavioral partisanship or independence. Thus, to DeVries, the only operational test of independence is a split ticket, and of strong partisanship, a straight ticket. He indicates that the number of straight ticket voters has declined from 90 percent at one point in our history. In recent years, DeVries cites evidence that up to half of the electorate, including sizeable blocs of Republican and Democratic party identifiers, split their tickets in certain contests.[45] A Gallup poll seems to confirm DeVries' analysis. It reports that 54 percent of the American voters said they split their tickets, 43 percent said they voted a straight ticket, and 3 percent said they didn't know.[46]

The Survey Research Center's study of the 1968 election indicates the researchers' awareness of the limitations of their own measure in predicting the vote. There was an unusually high degree of vote switching; almost one Goldwater voter in five turned to Humphrey or Wallace, three in ten white Johnson voters switched to Nixon or Wallace, and a full 40 percent of Nixon's votes came from 1964 Johnson voters.[47] Yet, they report that party identification changed only slightly from 1964 to 1968, which makes the authors of the SRC study call into question the predictive value of party identification relative to other determinants of the vote.[48] They conclude that as soon as conditions permit, the "drag" or inertia of habitual party loyalties can be weakened by issue domains of great concern to the voter. They report this phenomenon in relation to Wallace voters and the issues of civil rights and law and order.[49]

A similar pattern continued through the 1972 elections. Overall strength of party identification dropped only a few percentage points from the previous election, with a lesser number of strong partisan identifiers of both parties and a greater number of weak party identifiers. Also, the number of very weak partisans leaning to independence grew slightly. What is more significant is the vote cast by partisans in 1972. Seventeen percent of those calling themselves strong Democrats and 30 percent of those calling themselves not-so-strong or independent-leaning Democrats voted for Nixon. McGovern's vote was mostly from Democrats, but he picked up about 10 percent of the Republican identifier votes. Independents split 34 percent for Nixon and 17 percent for McGovern (the remainder, non-voters). In 1972, the proportion of voters claiming to be ticket splitters by voting in both party columns, by the strength of their party identification was: strong party identifiers, 15 percent; weak party identifiers, 27 percent; independents who lean to one party, 61 percent; and independents, 76 percent.[50] Thus, independence from the political parties appears to have continued in voting behavior, if not in party identification.

A final dimension of the change in partisanship of Americans is the pulling power of candidate factors. Candidate factors include a number of dimensions that relate to the person running for office, as opposed to his party, chiefly: personality and personal characteristics; the ability to do the job, or "competence" for the office; and candidate-issue positions. Obviously, if party is declining in importance, something else must be motivating voters, and it appears that candidate factors now loom large in the formula. In *The Voter Decides*, the authors found that party allegiance was not as important a determinant of the Eisenhower vote in 1952 and 1956 as it was in the 1948 election; indeed, one-fourth of the Eisenhower majority was composed of Democratic identifiers.[51] In the Survey Research Center's study of the 1960

Presidential election, it was found that a particular candidate attribute—Kennedy's Catholicism—had a significant impact, both for and against, on the normal vote of partisans.[52] In the SRC's study of the 1964 Presidential election, the authors place heavy emphasis on explaining the Johnson landslide as negative voter image of Goldwater as a candidate, especially the "policy" image of the candidate and, to a lesser degree, in the "personality" component of his image.[53]

Not surprisingly, similar factors were at work in the 1972 election, with McGovern suffering a "net personal minus." Despite the Democratic candidate's peace identification, voters thought Nixon would be more capable of achieving peace in Vietnam, including over one-third of the Democratic identifiers. McGovern also lost the confidence of his fellow partisans in terms of trust and personality. More Democrats named Nixon as the one having the more appropriate personality to conduct the office of President, and an equal number of Democrats "trusted Nixon more" as "trusted McGovern more." Also, after Senator McGovern dropped Missouri Senator Thomas Eagleton from the ticket as the Vice-Presidential candidate, 60 percent of the Democrats surveyed said McGovern handled the Eagleton affair poorly, and 60 percent of that group intended to vote for Nixon. Among the 40 percent who said he handled it well, McGovern gained an 85 to 15 percent split in his favor.[54] Thus, the personal attributes of the candidate and the issue-related identification with the candidate are key factors in determining the vote—especially in terms of pulling one away from normal partisanship.

The decline of party voting has had its effects on electoral outcomes. In what he calls "The Onward March of Party Decomposition," Walter Dean Burnham cites the fact that split outcomes in party victories (by Congressional districts) between Presidential and Congressional races has increased from around 5 percent or less of the districts before 1910 to around one-third of the districts since 1964. Likewise the spread between the percentage of the vote for President and Congress has increased steadily since 1920.[55] The 1972 election proved to be the first election in which a President won with over 60 percent of the vote while his party failed to add seats in the House and Senate.

A related outcome is that overall party competition has increased between 1920 and 1970. James Sundquist's analysis of that period reveals that the most Democratic and most Republican states show a decline in majority party strength and an increase in minority party strength in voting for Governor, U.S. Senator, and Congress. These differences are not all due to the declining regularity of partisan voters, of course. Some changes must be attributed to partisan conversion, the net replacement of one generation of voters with another, and the net effects of in-migration and out-migration.[56] For whatever reason, increased competition between the parties has meant that more candidates have a chance to win and undoubtedly wage a more aggressive and more diversified campaign.

Thus, the decline in party voting and increased party competition in the United States have obviously worked hand-in-hand with the new techniques. The mobilization of voters based on fixed loyalties behind a straight ticket was more suitable to the face-to-face campaigning of party organizations. As American electors become more amenable to issue and candidate-personality appeals or a combination of them, candidates formulate individualistic appeals to be delivered through carefully chosen media. The candidate will use his personal organization as a medium, but is likely to concentrate on mass communications devices, in which the messages and visual images are developed with a particularistic criterion in mind, basically single-candidate oriented. In turn, the new techniques, with their individualistic appeals, have weakened traditional party loyalties. Candidates seem disinclined to sell party, as well as themselves, through the new channels. Voters seem less inclined to buy party through any channel.

The New Experts of Politics

As political party organizations became less important in mobilizing voters, and voters became less inclined to vote a straight party ticket, candidates began to turn to persons who possessed the requisite skills to market candidates through other media. The process began in the 1920s with the governmental affairs component of business public relations. The PR counselor was called upon to create programs to develop public support and thereby bolster access and influence with governmental bodies. Then, publicity men began to work for political party organizations, primarily the national committees. Their primary task was the formulation and execution of propaganda programs that built a favorable party image. As candidate groups became more important in the scheme of party campaigning, they began to employ the skills and techniques of public relations firms, with the active encouragement of party national committee publicity men.[57]

It was only a short step from occasional consulting in a campaign to the development of a full-fledged campaign management firm. One of the earliest and most famous was Campaigns, Incorporated, run by Clem Whitaker and his wife, Leone Baxter. Whitaker began as a California newspaper man; he established a news bureau that supplied state capital news to over eighty newspapers. He then became a professional lobbyist for various groups or coalitions interested in certain issues. In 1933, Whitaker was retained as a publicity man by the supporters of a referendum issue. He met Leone Baxter on this successful campaign and then established their firm, with a subsidiary advertising agency. From this point they began to handle candidates and develop a wide range of campaign services, including research, planning, budgeting, media development, creation of a candidate volunteer organization, and enlistment of the support of key groups.[58] Today, a number of firms operate along the same lines, offering the candidate complete management of the campaign, and operating very much as political party organizations once did.

In a more typical but less visible pattern of development, candidates for high office began to perceive the inability of party organizations to deliver the campaign services necessary to appeal to a more fluid electorate through different media. Candidates first turned to advertising men to create and produce messages suited for radio, television, and newspaper audiences. They quickly found that advertising men relied on market research to analyze audiences and test messages. It was only a short step to the employment of the political pollster, a recently developed profession based on market research and academic voting behavior research. Pollsters gave candidates all sorts of valuable information about the electorate: different groupings had different images of the candidate; issues previously not considered were on the minds of voters; issues of concern to candidates did not concern voters; and different groups could be reached by different means. Findings like these stimulated candidates to employ even more specialists: specialists in direct mail to target specific messages to identified voters, journalists to formulate news releases, television documentary producers to develop the images desired, voting behavior researchers to target specific groups of voters by precinct. As these experts were employed, the campaign became larger in scale and more expensive, requiring management skills and technology, which further professionalized the campaign.

At one time in the history of political consultants' involvement in campaigns, the outside specialist was often depicted as some sort of secret weapon behind the scenes that automatically made the long shot or sure loser into a winner. Then observers began to realize that these specialists were also used in the campaigns of sure winners and in losing campaigns. Now the consultant is realistically looked upon as one among many factors in organizing a campaign.

The new politics has thus engendered a variety of experts applying their arts where party organizations once operated. Technologies developed elsewhere are being used in the campaign, and a new technology of the political campaign has emerged. It runs the gamut from the famous Spencer-Roberts of California, which handles an entire campaign with its advertising and research affiliates, to Market Opinion Research, which applies computerized management systems to printing firms that translate voter canvass information on computer tapes into letters that interchange words and paragraphs. The following is a selected list of the various specialists that are now employed in campaigns.

Management	*Information*	*Media*
Campaign Management Consultant	Marketing Researcher	Journalist
Campaign Handler	Public Opinion Pollster	Media Advance Person
Public Relations Counselor	Political Scientist	Radio and TV Writer
Advertising Agent	Social Psychologist	Radio and TV Producer
Advance Person	Computer Scientist	Film Documentary Producer
Fund Raiser	Psychologist	Radio- and TV-time Buyer
Management Scientist	Computer Programmer	Newspaper-space Buyer
Industrial Engineer	Demographer	Television Coach
Telephone Campaign Organizer	Statistician	Radio and TV Actors
Accountant		Graphic Designer
Election Legal Counselor		Direct Mail Advertiser
		Computer Printing Specialist
		Speech Coach
		Speechwriter

The Electronic Media

The most prominent element in the new campaigning is the use of new media. One need not be a follower of Marshall McLuhan to realize that politics has adapted itself rapidly to electronic media. Electronic communication has been part of campaigning from the earliest days of radio, when President Coolidge spent $120,000 for a series of radio addresses over 500 stations in his 1924 Presidential campaign,[59] to the peak of candidate broadcast outlays in the Presidential campaign of 1968, when Nixon spent almost twelve million dollars and Humphrey six million dollars for radio and television, using speeches, commercials, documentaries, telethons, and free news coverage.[60] Legal limits on broadcast spending, plus increased emphasis on getting nonpaid electronic news coverage, had its effect on 1972 broadcast spending: Nixon spent only 4.4 million and McGovern spent 9.6 million on air time. Candidates at every level now use some form of electronic communication; together, all candidates in 1972 spent $59,600,000 on radio and television, a 1 percent increase over 1968.[61]

The air waves and the computer are performing many of the voter contact activities that campaign workers once undertook. Radio, television, and the computer letter are replacing in importance the campaign poster, button, and bumper sticker that once symbolized the American political campaign. The mass media are readily accessible to the campaigner. At present, the only requirement (. . . as long as you belong to one of the two major parties . . .) is possession of sufficient financial resources to buy time and space and to secure the expertise for creative and production work. In a period of declining availability of party workers, quick access to electronic media is an increasingly desirable alternative to building an extensive organization in a short period of time. As the party stimulus in voting decreases in importance, short-term candidate and issue factors become more important, making the electronic media the most available vehicle for such messages.

The impact of these media is massive, in the sense of reaching large blocks of voters in large constituencies. Few political media experts consider the media "mass" in the sense of an undifferentiated audience. Rather, the same groups appealed to in older types of campaigning—the old, young, union members, well-educated, uninformed, liberals, conservatives—are differentiated, and special messages are delivered to them through time slots and address files. Groups of differentiated voters are targeted in much the same fashion as groups of consumers are targeted by commercial advertisers. The modern campaign tries to avoid forcing politics directly on voters; it attempts to make the campaign proximal to the everyday life of the citizen. Television spots and special programs are designed to intersect with normal viewing habits. Radio is used to inject political messages while the voter is driving to work, eating a meal, or performing household chores. Direct mail appeals are interspersed with personal correspondence and the household bills. Throughout, candidates attempt to stimulate the news media to "piggyback" their appeals with citizen news acquisition.

The typical media-oriented campaign today, with its general themes, slogans, and symbols, is formulated on careful research of the viewing, listening, and reading habits of the audience, and on political opinions from polls. From the results presented by the research division of the campaign management team, the media division takes over and formulates a media plan that includes themes, unified messages, and color schemes for everything from the literature hand-outs to the backdrop at the televised rally. When the candidate addresses the cheering throng, the press specialist takes care that the newspapers receive printed copies of the text, radio stations receive recordings, and television stations receive videotapes for newscasts. Meanwhile, time buyers follow the media plan and purchase time and space—most frequently spot announcements interspersed with commercial messages on radio and TV, and large blocs of transit advertising cards, billboards, and newspaper ads so that the creative division can translate theme, symbol, and slogan into visual and verbal messages. The practice of broadcasting an entire speech may be used, but less often than in earlier years because surveys have indicated that the audience for speeches is small. A compromise between the program and the spot is often presented, a five-minute film documentary on the candidate which preempts a portion of a popular program. Occasionally the candidate answers questions formulated by a carefully selected panel of citizen-supporters.

The workings of the media are as likely to dictate campaign events as are the workings of the party. The electronic media and the airplane have combined to make possible the "media event," which has become a significant component of major office campaigns. Simply stated, the media event is the candidate "doing something," as opposed to merely "saying something," that can get news coverage—however, the candidate "does something" in a number of different media markets in the same day, on a flying tour. The media event was first recognized in the middle years of campaign television, when news crews filmed and ran coverage of Robert Kennedy at plant gates, John Lindsay on New York ghetto street corners, or Eugene McCarthy informally talking to a group of students. There then began a conscious effort to stimulate such coverage. George McGovern's scheduling was built around the creation of media events, such as going through a factory talking to workers in one place, then flying on and visiting a hospital, talking to patients and the administrators about their problems, in another location, and then on to another market to visit the home of a member of the working poor who was struggling to keep up with her property tax payments to keep her home. In the New Hampshire primary campaign, McGovern ordinarily flew in through Boston, the most important television outlet for New Hampshire, and a media event there was scheduled for blanketing to the neighboring state, while the other candidates overflew Boston directly to their first stop in New Hampshire. In Florida, it meant constant flying back and forth, particularly, campaigning every day in both Miami and Tampa.[62]

Foremost in media campaigning is the candidate image, in which the campaign organization stresses human qualities of the candidate, his association with key issues and his competence for the job. Electronic media have become the vehicle for candidates to appeal to electorates as party organizations once were. Party organizations were better suited to use their manpower or to mobilize a preexisting sentiment, party orientation. Electronic media are better suited to use advertising to *manufacture* sentiment, candidate, and issue orientation.

The High Cost of the New Campaigning

It is now a well-established fact that the contemporary campaign is an expensive enterprise. The Citizens Research Foundation, which regularly estimates political spending in the U.S., places the 1972 total for all levels at $425 million, a 42 percent increase over 1968.[63] Reported expenditure for the 1972 Presidential nomination and election contest was $137 million.[64] It is now commonplace for a statewide campaign to exceed one million dollars in cost; some senatorial and gubernatorial contests have exceeded five million dollars. Congressional contests now regularly exceed $100,000. It is not unusual for a state legislative contest to range from $10,000 to $20,000.

Aside from the much larger size of contemporary constituencies and the general increase in price levels, the high cost of modern campaigning is directly linked to the direction it has taken.

The services associated with the new style and technology have shifted campaigning to more expensive modes of voter communication. Use of political consultants, polls, and mass media has accelerated the growth rate in the price of campaigning. The services now required by candidates are not generally available from the political party organization, necessitating the purchase of services from one or a series of entrepreneurial firms. These firms operate on the same model as other American business enterprises —overhead, labor, development cost, profit margin—and thus must build these factors into their price structure. Also, as campaign media have shifted in emphasis from the party worker to radio, television, and direct mail, an additional element has skyrocketed costs—access. Fractions of a page of newspaper advertising, minutes or seconds of radio and television time, computer time, printing, and postage are expensive; and, until political candidates are given free access to the various means of communication by law, they must purchase the prevailing modes of contacting with voters.[65]

Determination of costs for the new campaigning is somewhat easier than it was for the old, particularly since campaign finance reform legislation is bringing a great deal more information in the open. Required disclosure of expenditures through a central campaign committee (prior to 1976, it was legal to channel monies through a series of committees) plus the long-standing required report of broadcast expenditures to the Federal Communications Commission should facilitate the examination of the costs of the new campaigning. State campaign reporting requirements vary, but the trend is similarly to require meaningful disclosure. However, there will always be problems in understanding the full picture. Campaign consultants are as reluctant to disclose their fees as older-style operatives were to disclose campaign finances. Even with improved disclosure after the 1971 Federal Election Reform Act, difficulties in cost determination remained because dodges through committees continued, there were no limits on direct mail spending, and the costs of media production were not limited. Any estimate of costs therefore must be based on various available sources and by using available examples.

The personal organization is expensive to maintain. The candidate-centered volunteer organization does not have the built-in advantage of being able to acquire precommitted party workers. It takes money to identify supporters and build a personal organization. Campaign money, as Joseph Schlesinger maintains, "represents 'instant' organization by helping to expand activities rapidly," and it is required in contemporary campaigning to develop an organization quickly.[66] For example, the Nixon field organization in Illinois in 1972 had an organizing staff of sixty paid employees and was budgeted at $800,000. Postprimary election field operations in California for the McGovern campaign that year were budgeted at 1.4 million dollars. One means of purchasing rapid expansion is to secure the services of a campaign management firm that knows the constituency politically and has a reserve of volunteers it can call upon to perform various services. This has been the hallmark of the well-established campaign management firms in California, such as Spencer-Roberts, Baus and Ross, Hal Evry, and Cerell Associates. The Kennedy style of recruiting volunteers has been to move in the old hands from previous campaigns, plant advertisements in the newspapers, and open up numerous neighborhood store-front headquarters. The advantage here is the speed with which large numbers of persons can be brought into the campaign. Building a volunteer organization in this fashion is quite expensive. The best estimate for this portion of Robert Kennedy's 85-day primary campaign is about one million dollars.[67] Richard Viguerie used direct mail to build a volunteer organization for Max Rafferty's 1968 primary contest with former California Senator Thomas Kuchel. Two mailings to the 2,000,000 registered Republican voters yielded a volunteer and contributor list of over 83,000 persons. The cost was $300,000.[68]

Use of the news media, in a nonadvertisement or uncontrolled media situation, is a contemporary campaign practice that is often assumed to be "free exposure," while in actuality only the air time or press space is free. All the ancillary factors in the candidates' "creating" the news are costly. A topnotch writer is ordinarily salaried at $20,000 to $30,000 per year. The costs of physically reproducing a news release have increased since the days when the headquarters duplicating machine produced a press release and the audio portion was sent by telephone to radio stations. If the release is to be videotaped, studio costs, production costs, and telephone and transportation costs are built in. A single television news release can easily cost $1,000. The McGovern people perfected this technique in the California primary by hiring a TV camera crew to cover every McGovern appearance, which were fed into a rented TV production truck for dubbing, editing, and distribution, at a cost of about $2,000 per day.[69]

In order to increase the number of media events in a given campaign period, the candidate often airplane-hops from media-market to media-market, thereby increasing travel expenses. In order to maximize the impact of the media event, the proper arrangements must be made so that the crowd is sufficiently large and demonstrative to give the impression of widespread support. This requires the services of advance persons. It is not unusual for a Presidential candidate to have thirty to sixty advance persons in the field at a given time, with as many as five advancing a single large event. Most advance persons work either as volunteers or for extremely low wages, but if there is a significant amount of traveling involved, their expenses can easily exceed $1,000 per week.

The cost of campaign consultants is the most difficult to determine because most refuse to disclose their fees. California consultant Hal Evry is less reticent than most. He once reported the following cost structure: $60,000 for a state senate race and $100,000 for a congressional race. Mr. Evry keeps 20 percent of this as his fee; the remainder is for campaign expenses.[70] An anonymous Democratic political consultant reported to the *Congressional Quarterly* in 1970 that his firm of twelve persons would require about $80,000 for a congressional candidate. He claimed his firm had to clear $1,200 a day to meet salary and travel expenses. His personal services were billed at $500 per day.[71] Former Senator Albert Gore was approached before the 1970 campaign by a consulting firm that offered to organize the operation and shape campaign themes for $175,000. The cost of an outside campaign handler, that is, a person who travels from state to state (within a single party) to organize a single campaign, work on strategy development, and identify issues, can run as much as $25,000 or $2,000 per week plus expenses.[72] The costs of a media consultant, exclusive of time and production costs, are estimated at $10,000 to $25,000 in a major media campaign.[73]

The cost of obtaining campaign information is easier to determine. Polling rates are generally stated on a per-interview basis. Nineteen seventy-four rates were quoted as between $20 and $30 per interview, and they continue to increase. It is not unusual for a statewide candidate to poll 1,000 persons at least two times; thus, the cost can easily exceed $50,000. In 1968, Nixon's polling operation cost $364,102 and Humphrey's was $261,521. Election data analysis is sometimes performed within the campaign, and if computers are used it becomes costly. Firms that perform these services charge $2,500 per congressional district and add another $1,000 if census data are added. Firms tha specialize in direct mail charge from $10,000 to $20,000 per congressional district for development and file-maintenance of voter lists. Addressing from these lists costs about $15 per thousand, exclusive of printing, paper, and postage costs. Kevin White retained consultant John Marttila to direct canvassing for his 1971 Boston mayorality campaign. Marttila employed 6,000 volunteers to canvass 90 percent of the city's 152,000 voting households and develop a computerized list of 130,000 likely supporters, at a total estimated cost of $500,000. Governor George Wallace of Alabama has retained the direct-mail services of the Richard A. Viguerie Company to raise funds and develop an organization for a 1976 run for the Presidency. In the first five months of 1974 alone, Wallace paid Viguerie $396,407 for printing, mailing, postage, computer processing and programming, raw computer time, and other expenses.

The highest cost in modern campaigning at all levels is the purchase of media—television, radio, billboards, newspaper advertising, and literature. Since financial allocations were first reported by Alexander Heard in 1956, media and advertising expenses have amounted to about half of all campaign expenditures.[74] Political broadcasting time is becoming a larger and larger proportion of this total. In 1968, it was about 20 percent of all political expenditures at all levels. In 1972, the proportion dropped to about 15 percent, although there was a slight dollar increase. The drop in proportional spending was undoubtedly due to the overall media limitations in effect then, in which only 60 percent could be spent on broadcast media. Production and promotional costs must also be added to the purchase of time. While it is not unknown for production costs to match or exceed time costs, they normally run around 20 percent of time costs. Thus, when one considers the four to five million usually spent for media promotion, production costs, plus purchase of time, the total for 1972 is closer to 75 million dollars, easily making it the largest single campaign item.[75]

Advertising agencies that handle political campaigns generally charge a standard 15 percent of all time and space billings plus travel expenses and creative costs, which is the same rate generally charged nonpolitical clients. Under this system, advertising media, from newspapers to TV, allow a 15 percent discount on advertising placed through agencies. The agency then charges the amount the client would have paid anyway, and keeps the discount money as its fee. In large-scale campaigns the fee is negotiable, owing to the large volume of business a political candidate brings to an agency in a short period of time. The November Group was created as an in-house agency, among other reasons, to save this agency fee. Most high-level campaigns employ the services of agencies for creative purposes, for production arrangements, and for time buying. Agencies are also involved in many congressional campaigns, for which their charges are almost always 15 percent.

The higher the level of the race, the greater the media cost, although spending limits plus a greater emphasis on nonpaid media have coalesced to level spending in the large constituency races. Political broadcast spending in the 1972 Presidential contest totalled $14 million, a decline attributed to broadcast spending limits and a corresponding emphasis on different techniques, plus relatively low Republican primary spending because there was an incumbent President. Senatorial candidates spent $6.4 million in 1972 (a reduction from 10 million from 1970) and House candidates spent $7.4 million (an increase from 6.1 million in 1970). Gubernatorial candidates, who do not come under federal regulations, spent $16.4 million in 1970, when more of the large state races were held and $9.7 million in 1972.[76] Media spending in the 1972 California primary campaign was between $460,000 and $500,000 for McGovern and was about $225,000 for Humphrey. McGovern's general election media purchases for New York State alone were $900,000. The cost of Nelson Rockefeller's re-election campaign for Governor of New York in 1966 is estimated at $6,000,000, one-third of which was spent for paid time. He reportedly ran 208 commercials on a single station, with a billing of $237,000.[77] It is not unusual for total media billings in the average statewide campaign to exceed one million dollars in the larger states and one-half million dollars in the smaller states.

Television rates vary with the size of the audience in any given time slot. Political candidates must pay the same rates as commercial advertisers even though their audience tends to be smaller than the audience they are replacing. Political time purchases once cost more per time slot than commercial purchases because many commercial customers purchase larger blocs of time over longer periods and receive discounts. Stations are now required to charge political candidates at the lowest available rates. One network station in Chicago has a rate structure that ranges from $20 to $2,000 for thirty-second periods. Smaller stations in large cities charge considerably less. Rates for stations in medium-sized cities are also less. For example, one such station in Michigan has a rate structure that ranges from $12 to $210 per thirty-second spot. Network TV spot announcements in the 1968 Presidential contest cost an average of $23,193 each. The three television networks ran a total of thirty-six hours and thirty-five minutes in programs paid for by Presidential candidates and supporters during the primary and general elections. The average cost of these programs was $2,112 per minute.[78] Program time ranges from about $1,800 for one half-hour on a small station to $75,000 for a half-hour of network prime time.

Radio rates vary with the size of the audience and the size of the territory covered by the signal. Small rural stations charge as little as one dollar per ten-second spot if purchased in large blocs and the time is not specified. Big-city stations charge anywhere from $200 per minute for "drive time" (prime) down to $50 per minute. A thirty-second spot is often priced at 80 percent of the one-minute charge and a ten-second spot at 50 percent. Network program radio time averaged $263 per minute in the 1968 Presidential campaign. Network spot announcements averaged $645 per announcement.[79]

Newspaper advertising varies with the circulation, the placement within the newspaper, and the column inches used. Costs for a full page in a big-city newspaper can run as high as $9,000 per page, although the normal rate is closer to $4,000 per page. Small-town dailies average $2.30 per column inch, or $430 per page. The cost for advertising in weeklies is about half the daily cost. Special newspapers, such as ethnic, religious, or union publications, are even less. Newspaper advertising is generally a larger part of the advertising budget in lower-level campaigns, where television is either too expensive or uneconomical. In congressional districts where television coverage is difficult, the newspaper costs can reach $10,000. With extensive television usage, newspaper space costs are usually lowered to $2,000 or $3,000. Newspaper space costs for recent Presidential races has run about $500,000, a great deal of which goes for promotion of media broadcasts.

Other media costs vary so greatly with the amount and size of the campaign that general estimates are difficult. Billboards average about $55 per month. In a statewide campaign, it is not unusual for billboard and poster costs to range from $25,000 to $50,000. A congressional campaign can get by with $3,000 to $6,000. Buttons, brochures, gadgets, and other campaign paraphernalia cost the Nixon-Agnew campaign an all-time high of $1,124,626; however, they are becoming a smaller proportion of the budget in high-level campaigns. In the smaller constituency campaigns, where media and advertising is not as extensively used, these items still make up a greater share of the total costs.

Media production costs are difficult to estimate in the abstract. The only meaningful rule-of-thumb is to assess production costs as a percentage of time and space; television averages from 20 to 30 percent of the time cost, radio 15 percent of the time cost, and newspaper 25 percent of the space cost. In commercial advertising, costs average less (5 to 10 percent) because the productions are run more often. Production costs for a major media campaign average $100,000 exclusive of the consultant's fee. Production costs have been known to exceed time costs; the late Governor John Burns of Hawaii spent $152,000 for production and just over $100,000 for time in his 1970 primary contest.[80] A congressional candidate who uses four different television commercials will spend about $12,000 to produce them. Production of Nixon's election eve telethon in 1968 cost $27,000, mostly for costs of set building and interconnection of the various stations. Media production costs for the Humphrey-Muskie campaign totalled $1,105,559.

Other media costs include travel and time buying. Media travel for the 1968 Humphrey campaign was $450,000; time buying charges were $332,202. The press expense for the Nixon-Agnew campaign, which included travel and hotel accommodations for their press entourage, was $491,954.

Even when there are no advertising or electioneering expenses, the cost of campaigning can be quite high. McGovern campaign manager Gary Hart reports that they were spending about $158,000 per month by fifteen months before the election, of which $53,000 went to direct mail expenses. He reports the February to October 1971 budget to be: national operations, $172,308 (staff, travel, overhead); field operations, $85,419 (staff, travel); candidate activities, $29,787 (scheduling and advance staff, staff and candidate travel); political intelligence and research, $13,175 (staff); advertising and promotion, $44,637 (materials, design); fund-raising activities, $4,934; direct mail, $162,021 (production and computer costs).[81]

The shift in emphasis from party-oriented to media-oriented electioneering has played a major part in the rise of campaign costs. No longer is a few thousand dollars for headquarters expenses and brochures sufficient to implement a campaign. The scale of modern campaigns extends to the financial as well as the operational. The budget estimates that follow represent in round figures realistic expenditures in the 1970s for a $100,000 congressional campaign and a $1,000,000 state-wide campaign.

	Congressional	Statewide
Headquarters	$ 10,000	$ 95,000
Personnel	15,000	127,000
Candidate and Staff Travel Expenses	1,500	46,500
Special Events	500	8,500
Research (Polling and Election Data)	14,500	75,000
Direct Mail	11,000	90,000
Television	30,500	375,000
Radio	3,000	40,500
Newspaper	2,500	15,500
Outdoor Advertising and Transit	5,000	42,000
Agency Fee		25,000
Literature and Stickers	4,000	25,000
Telephone Banks	2,500	35,000
	$100,000	$1,000,000

Strategies in the New Campaigning

The most exciting reading in the new politics is the glamorous postelection account of how highly paid political consultants used polls and computers to formulate a systematic and integrated plan, and then used television to create the political image of a candidate. These postelection newspaper and magazine success stories always tell the reader that the new politics strategy of the winner was efficient, mechanical, and, of course, accurate. The hapless loser is depicted as a bumbling soul whose ill-planned and haphazardly executed old-style noncampaign was the cause of his defeat. The reader is left with the assumption that all a candidate needs to do to win is to acquire the strategic genius that necessarily accompanies the new campaigning, and the experts will complete the details of writing the plan, formulating the messages, and creating the image.[82]

The notions that there is a strategic magic formula that accompanies adoption of the new politics and that hiring the right consultants equals victory are false. Political consultants have yet to develop a chemistry of campaigning. As in the old politics, strategy building more nearly resembles alchemy. The contingencies of each situation, limitations on knowledge, and great numbers of variables make the development of universal rules of campaigning very difficult to formulate.

Strategies are based on the setting of the campaign and how the strategists perceive their situation and act upon it. Setting refers to the geographic-economic-social-political context within which a single candidacy must operate. Among the many factors that can be included in the setting of a constituency are: party patterns and voting habits, candidate characteristics and candidate images, key issues, geography, district size, population density, economic and occupational characteristics, racial and ethnic characteristics, transportation and communication patterns, population changes, other contests in the election, ballot position, group support and opposition, the particular office sought, the electoral system, the temper of the times, unique organizational problems, and the potential pool of political resources.[83] The essence of strategy building, then, is to understand the particular context within which the contest operates and then to make plans to manipulate and modify these contextual factors.[84] What is different about contemporary campaigns is that there is a greater emphasis on systematically examining a range of factors affecting the setting on a more comprehensive basis through such means as polling, demographic research, audience research, secondary data analysis, and many other means of examining the constutuency. The factors revealed are less likely to suggest a party strategy, that is, stressing partisanship and running with a party ticket. This allows the modern campaign strategist to avoid guesswork and to undertake the activities necessary to win, regardless of party interests or capabilities.

New campaign strategies are rarely executed with the neat precision commonly associated with the more successful ones. Polls, computers, and television take a considerable amount of lead time to develop and acquire, necessitating integrated planning and budgeting. But campaigns using these techniques remain a series of improvisations, adjustments to crises, reactions to unplanned events, and exceptions to the rule, just like the older modes of campaigning. Unfortunately, analyses of campaign strategies are usually inferred by *post hoc* observers, who do not have access to the planning stages of the campaign and must rely on specific tactics for their reports. The unfolding of events often has the appearance of supporting a carefully planned strategy, when, actually, the events may be unplanned reactions to unexpected happenings.[85]

Nor can one easily claim that the new politics always wins. First, campaigns that encompass the new techniques always include elements of the old methods. No new-politics strategist would ignore the valuable resource of party organization when it is available. Adlai E. Stevenson, III, in his 1974 Senate campaign, did not shun the vote-mobilizing ability of the Chicago Democratic organization, even though his own campaign was largely television oriented. New style campaigns are almost always this blend of the old and the new. Secondly, the scoreboard of the new politics reveals a mixed picture of wins and losses if one examines all cases. For example, in a recent series of campaigns for governor and senator, nine national media consultants worked in thirty-eight campaigns; the score was ten winners for the Democratic consultants and five for the Republicans. In terms of broadcast spending, nineteen gubernatorial winners outspent their opponents, but there were also sixteen losers who outspent their opponents.[86] This suggests that professional image makers do not always have the formula for victory, and that other factors are at work. Thirdly, political scientists have explained so little about the impact of various campaign efforts on the outcome of the election that it is difficult to document the increment that these techniques contribute to winning or losing. Candidates and academic survey organizations are just beginning to assess the impact of the new campaigning on the outcome by taking postelection polls. Fourthly, just as most new-style campaigns encompass some old techniques, party-oriented campaigns generally use some facets of the new. Chicago Mayor Richard Daley relies heavily on his Democratic Party organization in city campaigns, but he does not shun polls, newspaper, radio, or television advertising. Most contemporary campaigns for higher office use at least advertising and television, and an increasing number are incorporating information systems into their own overall planning.

What, then, is the basic strategic premise of the new campaigning? It is not different from the conventional in that politicians like to win, and that winning is the process of acquiring a favorable distribution and wise allocation of resources. Based on Nixon's incumbency, his overall lead, and generally negative images of McGovern, Jeb Magruder, Deputy Campaign Director, articulated the following 1972 strategy:

> Basically, our strategy, which we really did not change to any great extent from the beginning in '71 when we started contemplating the campaign, called for a heavy use of surrogates in place of the President. We found this was very effective. We cooperated with the Democrats for Nixon in their emphasis on what we thought were

McGovern's deficiencies. We made moderate use of advertising and a very heavy use of direct mail, and used telephoning only for identification and get-out-the-vote purposes. We did absolutely no persuasive work because we felt that it was not necessary; we saw our problem as simply getting our vote identified and getting it out. So our people did not go in and try to pitch the President's record or anything of that kind; they mainly tried to identify all pro-Nixon voters, and then we tried to get them to the polls.[87]

As Nelson Polsby maintains, from the desire to win and from the findings about the behavior of voters, one can deduce a series of propositions that would describe the strategic moves of the contestants in an election.[88]

In each situation candidates attempt to acquire a favorable balance of resources in four areas: acquisition of sufficient finances to support the strategy, the support of party leaders, key interest group support, and electoral support.[89] One might assume—incorrectly—that the strategy of the old campaigning was entirely based on party and group, and the new on money and electorate. Rather, the support of party leaders and group leaders was once more critical than it currently is, and money and appeals to the electorate can be used to circumvent the lack of such support. The converse is also true; in an era when party was strong and group identity was more predictive, there was less need for money and swaying electorates when the important resource was party organization. Candidates who pursue new politics campaigns still prefer to have parties and groups with them rather than against them. Kennedy campaigning—John, Robert, and Ted—has always been an admixture of polls, computers, and television on the one hand, and the courting of party chieftains, union leaders, and ethnic and civil rights leaders on the other. Situational changes have merely altered the balance.

Although they are not always articulated in this fashion, the basic theoretical underpinnings of campaign planning strategies in the new politics are derived from the findings of social research. Studies of campaigning have indicated three basic processes at work: reinforcement of the committed, activation of the indifferent and conversion of the doubtful.[90] Strategists use studies of the geography and demography of the vote to discover which forces are at work among subgroups of the population. They then formulate campaign messages and select a medium to transmit them based on the campaign process discovered.

This type of strategy building in the new campaigning can be illustrated by citing a lengthy example of how media use is planned in a campaign. In one Congressional campaign, a Democrat (Berg) defeated a five-term Midwest Republican Congressman (Able). Berg's poll, a private venture, revealed the following information:

> The incumbent, Able, could be identified by only 35 percent of the voters sampled; 15 percent could name one single accomplishment of his.
>
> Though 40 percent of the voters favored the Democratic challenger, Berg, only 10 percent of this group could name him, and 90 percent of this group identified themselves as Democrats.
>
> The most important issue identified without previous stimulation was economic conditions—unemployment, inflation, and taxes; and 60 percent of the undecided voters selected this as one of the three most important issues. Over 80 percent of this group responded that they thought the incumbent (Republican) President was doing a poor job of managing the economy.
>
> Of the undecided voters, 80 percent selected television as the medium from which they received their most reliable political information. Most of this group selected talk shows, newscasts, and editorials as the most influential source.
>
> Of the voters sampled, 30 percent were laborers, and 60 percent of this group favored the Democratic candidate. The other 40 percent were Republican identifiers; about half of the Republican laborers were for the incumbent and half were undecided.

The next step was to use voting statistics and census information to find out where the laboring people, Democrats, and swing voters resided. Television audience surveys were used to give the strategist information on what types of occupational, income, and educational groups make up specific program audiences, and these voter types were matched with similar voter types, revealed by the poll. A media plan was formulated based upon the poll data:

> Since so few voters know the name of the incumbent, why not exploit this? Messages were formulated to underscore the fact he was unknown. The slogan was to be based on his perceived lack of accomplishment—"Do you know your representative in Washington? If you don't, you are with most of the voters in this district. What hasn't Congressman Able done to become nameless? Berg can get something done in Washington."
>
> Billboards and ten-second television spots containing the short slogan and the name would be used to reinforce voters already favoring Berg. Billboards were purchased at busy intersections and shopping centers in working-class areas. Spots were placed during programs with low-education and low-income audiences.
>
> To reinforce partisanship, literature specifically labeling Berg as a Democrat would be distributed house-to-house three times in those precincts known to be 67 percent or more Democratic.
>
> Direct mail appeals, exposing the anti-labor record of the incumbent and revealing the pro-labor position of the challenger would be

sent to all union homes in the district to reinforce support and convert union Republicans.

Conversion of the undecideds would be approached by having Berg appear on television, stressing the sad state of the economy under the President and the incumbent's support of these policies. This was planned as videotaped press releases and one short complete coverage program that would preempt the first five minutes of all three network late-night talk shows. Regular newspaper releases and radio appearances as the candidate traveled to the various small towns of the district would stress similar themes.

There is no neat formula for linking motivational forces with the campaign processes, nor is a single medium always best suited for a specific strategic component. In general, partisanship, which is a preexisting sentiment, is most often reinforced. The prevailing party reinforcers are the party organization, billboards, direct mail, and face-to-face contacts. Television and radio are considered the best means of developing candidate-image appeals, candidate-issue appeals and issue appeals. Longer television and radio spots, films and programs are used for developing candidate personality. News releases, news panels, and talk-show formats are used to develop candidate-issue appeals and issue appeals. On occasion, direct-mail appeals are sent to undecideds and independents to activate latent feelings towards the candidate and issues. Short television and radio spots are used to reinforce candidate support and to activate latent candidate support.

The specific motivational forces that strategists select and the campaign processes they choose are necessarily a mixture. It is always a matter of the proper mix between candidate, issue, and party factors, and reinforcement, conversion, or activation of latency. Since the smallest number are usually converted, the strategist plans his margin from a foundation of those who are already committed and those who are likely supporters.[91] Up to three-fourths of the electorate already know which candidate they will support at the time the nominees are selected.[92] This group is made up primarily, but not exclusively, of party identifiers. The task at hand is to reinforce those who are committed, so that the opponent's conversion attempts do not succeed in activating latent supporters and do not convert a small number of those predisposed to the opposition. The latter two processes represent the margin with which the strategists must work.

Recent research indicating the declining predictability of the effect of party identification on the vote has increased the margin with which the strategist can work. Candidate and issue factors are becoming more important, and the new politics strategist has moved in to fill the party breach. His strategies are based on the marketing of a single candidate in a single race. The personality, the image, and the issues the candidate chooses to emphasize are selected with a great deal of independence from any party strategy. Each office seeker has not only an independent strategy but also an electorate different from that of fellow partisans on the ticket.[93] These seemingly pedestrian notions are the most important strategic considerations, and they pervade the strategic, tactical, organizational, and communication processes employed in modern campaigns.

The contemporary practice of candidates mobilizing their own electorates means that a series of non-party-oriented strategic practices occur that are rarely stated in the textbook literature on American politics. Candidates are less likely to use mass media to make party appeals to vote a straight ticket, as they once did. Indeed, they are more likely to make ticket-splitting appeals for themselves. Media plans are designed to stress the personality and issues of a single candidate. Campaign workers and campaign organizations are designed to support a single candidate's strategy. Workers are more likely to be recruited without regard to their party identification and to work in a single campaign. The specialists who are employed generally consult one client per ticket-constituency; that is, they work for a single candidate in a single race running on a single party ticket in any state or locality. Issues are individually selected, and the most visible ones may deviate from those of the candidate's fellow office seekers. In sum, candidates formulate singular strategies.

In the era of the new campaigning, it is thus difficult to speak of political party strategies except as the sum of candidate strategies. The list of partisans whose strategies deviate from their parties, such as Goodell in New York, Hammond in Alaska, Shapp in Pennsylvania, plus Goldwater, McCarthy, and McGovern is getting too long to label them as unique. More and more, candidates for office use the mass media as the forum for their individually calculated strategies, honing an image and forging carefully selected issue positions, which may differ from other candidates of the same party.

CONCLUSION

Throughout this essay and the pages that follow it should become clear that the new campaign era has given rise to a number of important concerns and issues. Is the financial cost of gaining access to office beyond the means of both most individuals and our political party organizations? Are the high offices now reserved for the wealthy or the already known celebrities? Are the newer techniques available to all, or are they reserved for those who can afford to buy them? What is the potential for abuse in the new techniques? Is campaign advertising distorted to brainwash voters? Do polls and computer technology manipulate voters into behaving in a fashion contrary to their inclinations? What effect has the American practice of requiring candidates to gain access to mass media through advertising had? Has the hired consultant, who appears much less attached to the party, displaced party leadership in the campaign process? What effect has the candidates' independence in electioneering had on other important facets of party? These questions are implicit in the three sections that follow and are taken up systematically in the concluding section, particularly those relating to the ethics of techniques, access to broadcasting, and reform of election finance.

The rise of candidate-centered technology in the electoral process has created a problem for American parties that is less visible but equally significant to more popular concern for the ability of party to represent people. In what some people call an "anti-party era," where party psychological loyalty is diminishing, party voting behavior is on the decline, elected officials in government display increasing independence, and party appears to be less of an agent of people's wishes, parties are similarly losing their grip over their preeminent function, the selection and election of candidates. The newer modes, with the candidates securing the needed vehicles, techniques, and technologists for themselves, both have brought on this weakening of party and are reflective of it.

NOTES

1. Quoted in Ernest R. May and Janet Fraser, *Campaign '72: The Managers Speak* (Cambridge: Harvard Univ. Press, 1973), p. 223.

2. Harold F. Gosnell, *Machine Politics: Chicago Model,* 2nd ed. (Chicago: Univ. of Chicago Press, 1968), pp. 91–92.

3. Reported in Thomas E. Patterson and Robert D. McClure, *Political Advertising: Voter Reaction to Televised Political Commercials* (Princeton, N.J.: Citizens' Research Foundation, 1973), p. 15.

4. Richard Donnelly, "How TV Turned a Race Around," *Television Magazine* 23 (December 1966):39.

5. *National Journal* 4 (October 28, 1972):1676.

6. Edward S. Gilbreth, "Singer Camp Confident of Upset," *Chicago Daily News,* January 27, 1975, pp. 5-6.

7. *Congressional Quarterly Weekly Report* 27 (August 17, 1974):2220.

8. Frank J. Sorauf, *Political Parties in the American System* (Boston: Little, Brown Company, 1964), p. 108.

9. Robert J. Pitchell, "The Influence of Professional Campaign Management Firms in Partisan Elections in California," *Western Political Quarterly* 11 (June 1958):281-82.

10. *National Journal* 4 (April 29, 1972):715.

11. Joseph Gaziano, "The Role of Advertising Specialists in State-Wide Campaigns in the 1972 and 1973 General Elections." (Ph.D. dissertation, Northern Illinois Univ., 1975).

12. "Professional Managers, Consultants Play Major Roles in 1970 Political Races," *National Journal* 2 (September 26, 1970):2084-85.

13. Warren Weaver, "Rivals for Rhode Island Senate Seat are Using Expert Consultants," *New York Times,* October 20, 1972, p. 21.

14. Quoted in *Wall Street Journal,* September 15, 1966, p. 1. See also, Carl Lieberman, "The Defeat of an Organization Candidate: Shapp versus Casey," *Social Science* 43 (October 1968):210-16.

15. "Campaign Management: Expertise Brings Dollars," *Congressional Quarterly Weekly Report* 23 (May 1, 1970):1183-91.

16. Penn Kimball, *Bobby Kennedy and the New Politics* (Englewood Cliffs, N.J.: Prentice-Hall, 1968), pp. 1-2.

17. V. O. Key, Jr., *American State Politics: An Introduction* (New York: Alfred A. Knopf, 1956), p. 167.

18. Robert Walters, " 'Organization' Candidates are in Trouble," *National Journal* 6 (October 19, 1974):1587.

19. Andrew J. Glass, "Effective Media Campaign Paced Way for McGovern Win in California," *National Journal* 4 (June 10, 1972):966, 972.

20. Stephen C. Shaddeg, *Winning's A Lot More Fun* (New York: Macmillan, 1969), pp. 182-83.

21. Nelson W. Polsby, "Strategic Considerations," in Milton C. Cummings, Jr., ed., *The National Election of 1964* (Washington, D.C.: The Brookings Institution, 1966), pp. 108-9.

22. John G. Stewart, *One Last Chance: The Democratic Party, 1974-76* (New York: Praeger, 1974), p. 65.

23. *National Journal* 4 (September 2, 1972):1393.

24. *National Journal* 6 (October 5, 1974):1510.

25. Theodore C. Sorenson, *Kennedy* (New York: Bantam Books edition, 1966), p. 197.

26. Linda Charlton, "The Re-election Team: 'We are Organized,' " *New York Times,* October 10, 1972, p. 25.

27. For further information on the Nixon campaign organization, see: *National Journal* 4 (May 27, 1972):882-90; *National Journal* 4 (September 2, 1972):1381-93; *National Journal* 4 (October 14, 1972):1607-16.

28. For a discussion of the McGovern organization, see Gordon L. Weil, *The Long Shot* (New York: Norton, 1973), ch. 7.

29. For further information on the McGovern campaign organization, see: *National Journal* 4 (April 29, 1972):715; *National Journal* 4 (October 7, 1972):1306; and *National Journal* 4 (October 7, 1972):1568.

30. Dom Bonafede, "Nixon Strategy Calls for Low Key Campaign with Strong Emphasis on Performance," *National Journal* 4 (April 22, 1972):677.

31. See "Surrogates: Nixon Cabinet on Campaign Trail," *Congressional Quarterly Weekly Report* 25 (September 2, 1972):2224–26.

32. *National Journal* 4 (October 7, 1972):1568.

33. For descriptions of party strategies, see Avery Leiserson, *Parties and Politics* (New York: Alfred A. Knopf, 1958), p. 254; and Austin Ranney and Willmoore Kendall, *Democracy and the American Party System* (New York: Harcourt, Brace & Co., 1956), pp. 346–48.

34. May and Fraser, *Campaign '72*, pp. 68–69, 223.

35. *New York Times*, September 13, 1972, p. 32.

36. Karl A. Lamb and Paul A. Smith, *Campaign Decision-Making: The Presidential Election of 1964* (Belmont, Calif.: Wadsworth Publishing Co., 1968), p. 95.

37. David A. Leuthold, *Electioneering in a Democracy: Campaigns for Congress* (New York: John Wiley & Sons, 1968), p. 1.

38. Sorauf, *Political Parties*, pp. 90–97.

39. E.g., Samuel J. Eldersveld, *Political Parties: A Behavioral Analysis* (Chicago: Rand McNally & Co., 1964), pp. 350–51.

40. Angus Campbell *et al.*, *The American Voter* (New York: John Wiley & Sons, 1960), p. 121.

41. *Ibid.*, pp. 124–26.

42. John P. Robinson, Jerrold G. Rusk, and Kendia B. Head, *Measures of Political Attitudes* (Ann Arbor, Mich.: Survey Research Center, 1968), p. 496.

43. Angus Campbell, Gerald Gurin, and Warren E. Miller, *The Voter Decides* (Evanston, Ill.: Row, Peterson and Co., 1954), pp. 162–63.

44. Donald R. Matthews and James W. Prothro, "The Concept of Party Image and Its Importance for the Southern Electorate," in M. Kent Jennings and L. Harmon Zeigler, eds., *The Electoral Process* (Englewood Cliffs, N.J.: Prentice-Hall, 1966), pp. 139–74.

45. Walter DeVries and Lance Tarrance, Jr., *The Ticket Splitter: A New Force in American Politics* (Grand Rapids, Mich.: William B. Eerdmans Publishing Co., 1972), pp. 22, 51.

46. *Gallup Opinion Index*, December 1968, p. 7.

47. Philip E. Converse *et al.*, "Continuity and Change in American Politics: Parties and Issues in the 1968 Election," *American Political Science Review* 63 (December 1969):1084.

48. *Ibid.*, p. 1085.

49. *Ibid.*, p. 1097–99.

50. 1972 Election Study, Survey Research Center, Univ. of Michigan. Made available through the Inter-University Consortium for Political Research.

51. Campbell *et al.*, *The Voter Decides*, p. 109.

52. Philip E. Converse *et al.*, "Stability and Change in 1960: A Reinstating Election," *American Political Science Review* 60 (June 1961):275-79.

53. Philip E. Converse, Aage R. Clausen, and Warren E. Miller, "Electoral Myth and Reality: The 1964 Election," *American Political Science Review* 59 (June 1965):331.

54. Warren E. Miller, "Reflections on the 1972 Election" (lecture at Northern Illinois Univ., December 18, 1972); for more on McGovern defections, see Robert D. Cantor, *Voting Behavior and Presidential Elections* (Itasca, Ill.: F. E. Peacock, 1975), pp. 74-76.

55. Walter Dean Burnham, *Critical Elections and the Mainsprings of American Politics* (New York: Norton, 1970), pp. 106-19.

56. James L. Sundquist, *Dynamics of the Party System* (Washington: The Brookings Institution, 1973), pp. 334-35.

57. For a historical account of the use of public relations in campaigns, see Stanley Kelley, Jr., *Professional Public Relations and Political Power* (Baltimore: Johns Hopkins Press, 1956), pp. 26-38.

58. For a detailed account of the activities of Whitaker and Baxter, see Pitchell, "Influence of Campaign Management Firms," pp. 286-94.

59. Richard L. Worsnop, "Television and Politics," *Editorial Research Reports* 54 (May 15, 1968):369.

60. "Nixon Broadcast Costs are Twice Those of Humphrey," *Congressional Quarterly Weekly Report* 22 (September 12, 1969):1701.

61. "Broadcast Spending: Presidential, Senate Costs Drop," *Congressional Quarterly Weekly Report* 26 (May 12, 1973):1134.

62. Weil, *Long Shot*, pp. 42-43, 57, 60.

63. Herbert E. Alexander, *Financing the 1972 Election* (Lexington, Mass.: D. C. Heath, 1976), in press.

64. *Ibid.*

65. General campaign finance practices and campaign finance reforms are discussed in Part 4.

66. Joseph Schlesinger, "Political Party Organization," in James G. March, ed., *Handbook of Organizations* (Chicago: Rand McNally Co., 1965), p. 785.

67. Herbert E. Alexander, *Financing the 1968 Election* (Lexington, Mass: D. C. Heath, 1971), p. 33.

68. Richard Viguerie, "Candidates Timing Raises Havoc with Fund Raiser's Need for Time," *Fund Raising Management* (November-December, 1969):27-30.

69. Hank Parkinson, *Winning Political Campaigns with Publicity* (Wichita, Kan.: Campaign Associates Press, 1973), p. 123.

70. Frank J. Prial, "Professional Managers Play an Expanding Role in Election Campaigns," *Wall Street Journal*, September 15, 1966, p. 24.

71. "Campaign Management," p. 1185.

72. "Professional Managers," p. 2083.

73. *Ibid.*, p. 2078.

74. Alexander Heard, *The Costs of Democracy* (Garden City, N.Y.: Doubleday, 1962), pp. 344–45.

75. Herbert E. Alexander, "Political Broadcasting in 1968," *Television Quarterly* 9 (Spring 1970):42.

76. "Broadcast Spending," pp. 1134–35.

77. James M. Perry, *The New Politics: The Expanding Technology of Political Manipulation* (New York: Clarkson N. Potter, 1968), p. 135.

78. "Nixon Broadcast Costs," p. 1702; for 1972 information, see *Broadcasting* (November 13, 1972).

79. *Ibid.*

80. Thomas Coffin, *Catch a Wave* (Honolulu: Univ. of Hawaii Press, 1973), pp. 162–63.

81. Gary Hart, *Right From the Start: A Chronicle of the McGovern Campaign* (New York: Quadrangle, 1973), p. 73.

82. Some examples of these accounts are: Donnelley, "TV Turned a Race Around"; Joseph Lewis, *What Makes Reagan Run?* (New York: McGraw-Hill, 1968); Perry, *The New Politics;* Richard B. Stolley, " 'Hopeless' Case of Milton Shapp," *Life Magazine* (May 27, 1966).

83. Robert Agranoff, *The Management of Election Campaigns* (Boston: Holbrook, 1976), ch. 6; Lewis A. Froman, *Congressmen and Their Constituencies* (Chicago: Rand McNally & Co., 1963), pp. 51–52; Charles O. Jones, "The Role of the Campaign in Congressional Politics," in Jennings and Zeigler, eds., *The Electoral Process*, pp. 29–30.

84. David Paletz, "The Neglected Context of Congressional Campaigns," *Polity* 2 (1971):197.

85. For a thorough analysis of the strategies of both major parties in a Presidential election, see John Kessel, *The Goldwater Coalition* (Indianapolis: Bobbs Merrill, 1968).

86. "Washington Tensions Increase as Both Parties Claim Election Gains," *National Journal* 2 (November 7, 1970):2432.

87. May and Fraser, *Campaign '72*, p. 193.

88. Polsby, "Strategic Considerations," p. 82.

89. Stanley Kelley, Jr., *Political Campaigning: Problems in Creating an Informed Electorate* (Washington, D.C.: The Brookings Institution, 1960), p. 5.

90. Paul F. Lazarsfeld, Bernard Berelson, and Hazel Gaudet, *The People's Choice: How the Voter Makes Up His Mind in a Presidential Election* (New York: Duell, Sloan and Pearce, 1944), p. 101.

91. Lewis A. Froman, "A Realistic Approach to Campaign Strategies and Tactics," in Jennings and Zeigler, *The Electoral Process*, p. 7.

92. Campbell, *The American Voter*, p. 78.

93. Sorauf, *Political Parties*, p. 108.

PART TWO

PROFESSIONAL CAMPAIGN MANAGEMENT

In 1956, Stanley Kelley, Jr., predicted in his famous *Professional Public Relations and Political Power* that, if the public relations man reaches the point where he can participate in the more basic campaign policy decisions—selection of issues and group appeals, expenditure of funds, selection and use of media—it will go far toward making him a leading influence in shaping the public image of parties and candidates.[1] In the 1970s, that prophecy has come true. Professional campaign managers have moved from occasional consultant status to major policy-making roles in campaigns. The key decision makers in most contemporary major-office campaigns are no longer party chieftains but political consultants.

A major-office candidate, who can afford it and is so inclined, can retain the services of a campaign management consultant, a pollster, a computer firm, an advertising agency, a filmmaker, a journalist, a media time buyer, a direct mail firm, and a speech-writer.

Campaign consultation has burgeoned into a national enterprise of considerable significance. David Rosenbloom's national survey of campaign management firms revealed that in 1972 there were close to 100 public relations firms offering complete campaign management services, 60 firms that called themselves professional campaign management firms and did the bulk of their work in political campaigns, and about 200 other companies offering professional campaign management services as a part of their business.[2] Rosenbloom has also traced the rapid growth of these firms' campaign involvement: they show an overall growth rate of 650 percent from 1952 to 1970, ranging from a 300 percent increase in usage in local races to an 842 percent increase at the Congressional level. The most rapid growth was in the 1960s, with the number of campaigns undertaken by such firms increasing from 188, in 1960, to 658, in 1968.[3] It is not unlikely that, by the end of the 1970s, practically every major-office candidate will employ the services of professional political consultants.

The contemporary campaign manager is quite different from his counterpart of an earlier political era. He may visit his client's state or district only occasionally, preferring instead to closet himself with poll data, computerized studies of voting patterns, media audience surveys, and demographic profiles. The new manager prefers working with candidates for whom he can control many factors in the campaign, rather than with politicians who are set in their ways and thereby impede resource allocation and image creation. He is not necessarily wedded to the candidate's party, and if he is, the affiliation is loose. He comes at a high price. The management fee for a single state-wide campaign has been known to go as high as $200,000.

The role of organizing intermediary in the campaign, once played by the political party, has been assumed by the professional campaign handler. The style and techniques used by the modern manager are quite different from those used in the party-oriented campaigns. Robert Pitchell, in his early study of campaign management firms, lists four key differences. First, the old-style politician uses a permanent political organization that does most of its effective work in the inter-campaign period. The campaign management firms organize particular campaigns on an *ad hoc* basis and must accomplish their missions with utmost speed and efficiency. Secondly, the old-style politician uses personal contact and individual favors as his basic association with the electorate. The management firm depends heavily on mass media through the use of advertising and public relations. Thirdly, the professional politician deals primarily or even exclusively in personal power and patronage. The campaign management consultant generally does not deal in these things himself. Between campaigns, he reverts to private advertising or public relations work. Fourthly, the work of the campaign consultant is generally unpublicized. Although in operation for a considerable period of time the consultant has not been given the widespread publicity th: the political boss once received.[4]

If the professional manager has replaced the party chieft: what management activities does he perform? The consultant c. relieve the candidate of everything but campaigning. Management consultant Joe Napolitan said of his involvement in the Shapp campaign, "When I first got here, Milt Shapp was running around worrying about the size of the lettering on bumper stickers and getting typewriter ribbons for secretaries. I had the job of convincing him to forget that stuff because I'd been hired to do it."[5] Mr. Napolitan and his colleagues offer the candidate expertise in the style and technology of campaigning, based on their knowledge and experience. Most consultants have been through the campaign process dozens of times. As a professional, the consultant provides the continuity and the experience that amateurs think they have but really do not. His expertise is primarily in the following areas: information, planning, management, handling, and media-appeals and advertising.

INFORMATION

One of the first things a professional consultant undertakes is to gather all the requisite information to plan and implement a campaign. The information used is a combination of "soft," or political, judgments by the candidate and his staff about the opponent, prevalent issues, and the nature of the constituency and "hard" information gathered through a "benchmark" poll and demographic and voting studies. In the absence of polling, the other studies are combined with media audience surveys. Other information services include voter targeting, electronic data processing, and issues research.

PLANNING

Hard and soft information is combined into the comprehensive campaign plan. While campaigning is often a series of reactions to unplanned events, the professional consultant tries to reduce the number of such happenings by structuring as many events as possible from his client's viewpoint. The late Clem Whitaker of Campaigns, Inc., explained that, at the outset of every campaign he was retained to manage, his staff would seclude themselves for about three days and draw up a campaign plan that included issue development, mapping of strategy, media selection and determination of their relative importance, and budgeting. Then they would write a campaign plan for the opponent, trying to surmise the important moves in the campaign.[6]

A contemporary campaign plan is written many months before the election, outlining in considerable detail what a candidate has to do to get ready for a campaign and how to go about it. It will weigh candidate assets and liabilities, candidate images, and his record, and his means of maximizing gain based on these factors. Often it deals with strategies in various phases of the campaign: first, speaking out on various issues as an unannounced candidate, building up an organization, and lining up key individual and group support; second, the transformation of these contacts into an organization and a step-by-step plan to extend the organization throughout the constituency and to develop and maintain cordial relations with the party organization; third, for the actual campaign period the development of a table of organization, issue research needed, media plans, press relations plans, voter contact plans, finance and operations, and other important facets of the campaign.[7] Often the consultant will present dozens of sample forms, checklists, volunteer instructions, and sample appeals along with the plan.

Planning in a media-oriented campaign is usually carefully outlined from election day backward to the day of the plan, with each event or activity and the preceding steps carefully integrated into the entire scheme of the campaign. Media use requires certain carefully worked-out time steps. If a TV spot is to be run ten days before the election, it should be taped about four weeks earlier, written about two weeks before taping, and planned with the candidate about two weeks before writing; the time should be bought at least five months before running, general media plans should be established at least six months before election day, and campaign plans should be set at least six weeks before that. Campaign managers are now beginning to use complex budgeting and systematic resource allocation techniques as well as complex management systems like operations research and Critical Path Method. CPM is a management planning technique similar to the one used in building the Polaris missile and many engineering and construction projects, which step-by-step and day-by-day integrates organization, finance, candidate scheduling, and media activities of the campaign.[8]

MANAGEMENT

The extent of management involvement in a campaign varies with the nature of the firm and the campaign. In the very largest-scale campaigns, such as Presidential or large statewide campaigns, overall top management remains in-house, and the management team interacts with and coordinates the work of outside consultants. The most prevalent pattern is for an advertising firm to manage the entire media and communications segment of a campaign. Increasingly, the management involvement is more complete. Bailey, Deardourff, and Bowen is one of a growing number of political consulting operations—a full service advertising agency that is also involved in management consulting. The firm will not manage a campaign on a day-to-day basis, but it serves as a campaign employment agency. It claims it will find a good manager and polling organization and will recommend a direct-mail house. It will write a campaign plan for the candidate and a step-by-step manual that runs up to 150 pages in length. The firm provides all of the advertising services for the candidate.[9] Another well-known firm is Matt Reese and Associates. Reese offers research and planning services, but he will also accept operational responsibility for portions of the campaign. He specializes in organizational development, voter registration, voter identification, and election-day activities. Reese uses his own trained supervisors and procedure manuals to mobilize campaign volunteers to do the actual work. In the words of one political scientist, one can now "rent-a-party."

Spencer-Roberts is representative of consulting firms offering more complete management services. Its personnel usually will settle on several "touchstones" that they consider to be essential to any campaign plan, and devise three or four key projects tailored to the particular problems of the individual campaign. They like to play to their client's strength, looking for undecided voters among demographic groups that are generally favorable to the candidate. Spencer-Roberts schedules the opening of campaign headquarters, the distribution of printed brochures, and the development and purchase of advertising in all media; it conducts polls, vote history, and demographic studies through its own subsidiary; coordinates the volunteer and organizational efforts; and handles the candidate.[10]

HANDLING OF THE CANDIDATE

Many professional managers are involved in the handling of the candidate on the campaign trail. Basically, the professional consultant ensures that the candidate is following the campaign plan as designed and that his performance on the stump projects the image that has been established. A little-known case of a professional management firm handling of a famous candidate was Spencer-Robert's handling of Ronald Reagan in his first bid for the California Governorship.

There were two major problems to overcome: party disunity and Reagan's lack of experience. Reagan had the image of a right-winger, and there were charges of extremism. Moderate Republicans would find it difficult to work for and support a candidate so closely identified with Goldwater. In addition, Reagan had never held a public office, but was seeking the Governorship of the most populous and one of the most complex states.

Spencer-Roberts handled Reagan by capitalizing on what it perceived as his personal assets—his personality, skill as a public speaker, and good looks in a state that admires youth and vigor. They tried to present him as a moderate, responsible, "decent guy." The announcement of Reagan's candidacy took on the characteristics of a Hollywood spectacular and involved a series of carefully planned events: a massive news conference, a reception for 6,000 supporters, a dinner with community leaders, and a statewide thirty-minute television special. To meet the problem of inexperience, they tried to build the image of "citizen-politician." A favorite saying of Reagan was, "I think it is time for ordinary citizens like you and me to bring some common-sense thinking to all these problems that have been created in California in the past eight years by professional politicians." Reagan's handling of the extremist charge was to ignore it whenever possible. Spencer-Roberts hired a team of psychologists to perform in-depth analysis on issues and Reagan's position on the issues. They concluded that Reagan should back away from extremism and the "white-back-lash" vote and stress morality, taxes, and government spending. For the Reagan campaign, Spencer-Roberts steered clear of sophisticated and creative television production. They put Reagan in front of the camera and let him talk, for fear that fancy production techniques would bring the cry of "Hollywood" against him.[11]

Among the more prevalent handling activities managed for the candidate are scheduling, speechwriting, advancing, event planning, and group contacts.[12]

MEDIA-APPEALS AND ADVERTISING

Advertising is a long-established industry in which there are many specialties unknown to most politicians. The account executive, the writer, the time buyer, the sound man, and filmmaker possess skills that are necessary in putting together a media-oriented campaign. Most candidates for major office, therefore, use the services of advertising firms to create and produce media appeals and to secure time and space.

The extent of involvement of an advertising firm varies from campaign to campaign. In some, the agency receives some general issue positions, campaign themes, and media allocations from the campaign management, and it only creates and produces advertising. The growing trend, however, is to involve the advertising agency at a much earlier stage and to make it an integral part of the campaign management. The account executive becomes a key decision maker in the campaign, as he participates in formulating the media plan, poll design, development of issues, images, and campaign themes, as well as media handling.

In "The Role of the Political Consultant," Sanford Weiner traces the short history of the professional campaign management field through its four phases, from the early years of media campaigning to the recent Watergate-era hard-times period, and suggests new technical and political roles for professional campaign consultants in the post-Watergate period. Sanford Weiner is president of Weiner and Company, a San Francisco-based national campaign management firm, and has served as president of the American Association of Political Consultants.

"How the 'I Dare You!' Candidate Won," by Harry N. D. Fisher, describes how a public relations firm took John Danforth, a young, attractive candidate from a well-known family in Missouri, and shaped his image, developed a campaign theme, and handled him. Harry Fisher is the public relations director of Stemler, Barton, Fisher, and Payne, a St. Louis advertising agency. Mr. Fisher also handled Danforth's 1970 campaign for the U.S. Senate against Stuart Symington.

"The Agency Knack of Political Packaging," by Walter Troy Spencer, deals with the role of advertising agencies in campaigns, with emphasis on Presidential campaigns. It was written in the preconvention stage of the 1968 Presidential campaign, when the prospective nominees were lining up delegates and advertising firms. Walter Spencer is a free-lance writer who specializes in advertising and media.

In "Advance Men Ensure Campaigners Against Silent Mikes, Short Stories," Jonathan Cottin explores the emerging campaign management function of advancing candidates. In the era of candidate-organized media campaigns, the candidates themselves must ensure crowds and stimulate news coverage, as did the 1972 Democratic candidates covered by Cottin. Mr. Cottin is a staff writer for the *National Journal.*

"The Role of Political Parties in the New Campaigning," by Robert Agranoff, suggests a new role for the political party organization in a period of declining party influence in campaign management. Agranoff relates how a state party organization attempted to bring the new technology to a large number of candidates in small constituencies, and then indicates how political parties might offer campaign services more in tune with new trends.

NOTES

1. Stanley Kelley, Jr., *Professional Public Relations and Political Power* (Baltimore: Johns Hopkins, 1956), p. 211.

2. David Lee Rosenbloom, *The Election Men* (New York: Quadrangle, 1973), p. 50.

3. David Lee Rosenbloom, "Managers in Politics." (Ph.D. Dissertation, Massachusetts Institute of Technology, 1970), p. 52.

4. Robert J. Pitchell, "The Influence of Professional Campaign Management Firms in Partisan Elections in California," *Western Political Quarterly* 11, no. 2 (June 1958):281–82.

5. Quoted in *Wall Street Journal,* September 15, 1966, p. 1.

6. Clem Whitaker, "The Public Relations of Election Campaigns," *Public Relations Journal* 2 (July 1946):10.

7. Rosenbloom, *The Election Men,* p. 40.

8. William H. Wilcox and James O'Brien, "How to Win Campaigns: Critical Path Method," *National Civic Review* 61 (May 1967):265–69; see also " '72 Campaign Trends: More Computers, Fewer TV Spots," *Congressional Quarterly Weekly Report* (April 15, 1972):856–59.

9. "Professional Managers, Consultants Play Major Roles in 1970 Races," *National Journal* 2 (September 26, 1970):2078.

10. For a recent account of California management firms, see Nancy Boyarsky, "The Image Makers: Behind the Mystique of the Powerful but Unseen Manipulators of the California Political Process," *California Journal* 5 (May 1974):144–55.

11. For accounts of Spencer Roberts' handling of candidate Ronald Reagan, see: Walt Anderson, "Spencer-Roberts: Dynamic Duo of California Politics," *Los Angeles Times West,* December 11, 1966, pp. 20–27; Edmund G. Brown, *Reagan and Reality* (New York: Praeger, 1970); Joseph Lewis, *What Makes Reagan Run?* (New York: McGraw-Hill, 1968); H. Theodore Radke, "An Image of Ronald Reagan: The Role of Spencer Roberts in The Campaign," *New Scholar* 1 (April 1969):122–33.

12. See Jonathan Cottin and Andrew J. Glass, "Democrats Depend on Speech Writers for Their Ideological Images," *National Journal* 4 (February 2, 1972):350–59; Barry Wagner, "Writing for Political Candidates," *Writer's Digest* 52 (November 1972):34–35.

THE ROLE OF THE POLITICAL CONSULTANT

Sanford L. Weiner

I am honored to be asked to speak about the future of political consultants and the future of politics in this country. I suppose one of the reasons I was asked is that I have survived 17 years in the business. To be considered a senior political consultant at 45 says something about the impermanence of our profession.

It is also somewhat ironic that Democrats are being honored. My career began representing conservative Republicans, but my clientele has become increasingly Democratic and liberal over the years. California—my home base—has been regarded as a political oddity by many of you, but now it must be recognized that much of our "strangeness" has spread across the nation. The fact that no one in California cares that my firm represents both Democrats and Republicans is symbolic, not only of current California politics, but symbolic of politics around the nation as well. Strict partisanship just isn't that important anymore.

The role of the political consultant in 1975, and beyond, will exactly parallel the future and atmosphere of all politics in our country. As political consultants, we are not an isolated segment of America's political system. We are an integral part and force within that system. If our political system is now suspect or in a state of ill repute, then so are we. If the political system is now considered intolerable, then we are intolerable. If the political

From Sanford L. Weiner, "The Role of The Political Consultant" (An address before the American Association of Political Consultants, Washington, D.C., January 1975). Reprinted by permission of the author.

system is to regain the confidence of the American people we will have to play a vital role in helping to rebuild that confidence.

The key question is, do we have a role to play, and if so, specifically what should it be? During our meetings of the past incredible year, our increasing sadness and despair reached a point where survival in this profession truly became a crucial problem. There are fewer or us now. Some gave up voluntarily. Some were forced to give up financially.

So let us discuss whether we have a well-managed, media-oriented funeral for political consultants in 1975, or whether or not we collectively have the courage for renewal, rebirth, and rebuilding along with the needs of our entire political system.

PHASES OF PROFESSIONAL DEVELOPMENT

Before expressing my views on our future role—if any—I think it is important to briefly trace what our role has been. It is also important to know what we have done well and what we have done badly. Our country still has a young political system, and certainly our profession is young in years. American democracy has developed flaws which suddenly appear acute. Our profession shows cracks that can permanently break us apart.

About 6 blocks from my office in San Francisco is the home of the first established professional political management firm in the nation. That was only 30 years ago. The founders of that firm recognized a need for professional communications relating to political matters in California. They began formulating special techniques which conveyed political messages as opposed to commercial messages. A key reason for the need for such services was the then peculiar nature of California politics. Because of the transient nature of the California population and the Hiram Johnson tradition of nonpartisanship, our political parties lacked strong leaders. There was no ward boss system, and very little patronage, and no real political party control or influence. The only way of communicating political views was by mass media. Thus, our profession was born.

From then on, our profession went through four general phases. These phases closely paralleled the political climate and attitude of the nation. During the period of the late 1940's and early 1950's, television was just beginning to prove its potency. Early experiments utilizing television on behalf of candidates and causes were beginning to show dramatic results. At the time that I began my career, filming a candidate in any format and showing his name on television drew instant attention and, for the most part, drew positive voting results. Television was the new discovery which was to simplify campaigning, while allowing candidates to reach mass audiences.

During this first phase most of us were not called political consultants. We were political campaign managers.

Those of us who were practitioners during this first phase had to be diversified by necessity. They were, incidentally, some of my happiest days. To spend a given day sitting in a drafty headquarters, typing news releases, organizing committees, creating newspaper ads on scratch pads, scheduling the candidate, calling a half dozen people for money, deciding not to pay oneself because the campaign had to pay a printing bill, all had a very special excitement. Learning about television, discovering the magic of film, were all part of this early excitement. Few of us were specialists. We openly managed campaigns, and we had to do everything.

Those were happy times in the profession, and relatively happy times in the political atmosphere of the country. While there has always been suspicion of politicians and those around them, and doubt in the public's mind about the integrity of many of our office holders, there was also a feeling in the 40's and the 50's that even though "they might be a little corrupt," those in government were basically on the side of the people. Campaigns were looked upon as slugging matches, and the fights themselves created their own intrigue. People were interested in the political process; they got excited about the candidates of their choice and campaign managers were able to show their talents. The potent role of the political press also became more evident. More and more newspapers throughout the country began to recognize the need for reporters who understood politics, who had the energy and drive to probe into the activities of candidates and campaigns, and who had the determination to find out what was really happening.

The rapport between political campaign managers and the political press became a very meaningful thing. Frequent phone calls, drinks late at night, in-depth discussions on the problems of the campaign—all had a two-way value. The political reporters were able to report and interpret accurately the progress, the views, and the circumstances of the campaigns. The candidates and the managers felt little restraint in offering as much information as possible. The end result was a now enviable combination of good stories and good coverage. Political managers were proud of their jobs. Political reporters were proud of their work. The publishers of newspapers allowed the political reporters the time and facilities to do their job.

That was all in phase one. It constituted the beginnings of our profession. It set the format for what was to come later. And in many respects, those were the good old days. We cannot go back to those times, but there were significant portions of that phase which we were perhaps too quick to dissolve.

The second significant stage of our profession began in the late 50's and early 60's. Television had proven its worth, and many professionals began specializing in political television production. It became more and more apparent that political advertising had significant differences from commercial advertising. In addition to the political film specialists, the political advertising specialists came along who would not only concern themselves with television, but with radio, outdoor, and direct mail advertising as well. As media became more important to political campaigns, so did the need for higher budgets. As the rates of television time climbed, so did the costs of producing political commercials. Costs of postage and printing and other related necessities also skyrocketed.

This was also a period when we considered media as the all-important factor in winning a political campaign, and when we de-emphasized the need for volunteer activity and basic campaign organization. We all got caught up in our own fascination with our ability to motivate electronically, and were so engrossed with our successful results, that we forgot basic lessons about the human element in politics and in campaigns. The public was responding so well, mainly because the television commercial was the closest many had ever been to a major candidate, that we collectively decided that this was probably the permanent route to success.

It was also during this second phase that government itself began to more and more neglect the human element of politics. Government discovered that it, too, could be an electronic image. As we moved from the headquarters to the projection room, governmental leaders more and more called the cameras in as a substitute for going home.

In retrospect, all of us had found a short-cut and were participating in a grand experiment. We also all soon discovered a vital personality trait which could be exploited: "charisma." A handsome profile, twinkling eyes, a toothy smile, all suddenly became basic criteria for a successful campaign. All of us sized up prospective candidates in terms of not what they knew, not what they felt, but how would they look on television. The press, quickly took note of this new form of politics, and joined with us in exploiting candidate charisma, and the public responded enthusiastically to the "charismatic" candidate.

We all took part in this significant phase. I can personally take the credit—or the blame—for one of the more dramatic examples of this type of campaigning. A semi-retired, but still handsome, silver-haired movie actor and I sat up one night discussing the premise that if charisma was the most potent factor in winning elections, then why shouldn't a handsome, good-guy movie star with twinkling eyes be the epitome of all that was happening. We decided the idea was worth pursuing. Starting with a campaign war chest of $1,000, and despite the derision of other politicians in California, a year later George Murphy became a U.S. senator— much to everyone's surprise, especially mine. A few years later, at the start of another era, and after having learned some other lessons, we turned the technique around and defeated one of the most famous movie stars of all, Shirley Temple, with the credibility of Paul N. McCloskey. But we had participated in a new trend. Another movie star, Ronald Reagan, embellished the technique, and has just concluded an eight year term as governor of my home state.

Highlights of this second phase included media excitement and media techniques, which the public liked and responded to, but which eventually fell victim to overuse and overexposure.

The third phase of our profession, and the role we played, pertained to what might be called the "war" years. While social problems associated with race and discrimination had previously polarized parts of the nation, the mid 60's began to show polarization regarding the Vietnam war. The war years brought significant changes to the political process. Our government didn't know what to do about it, and still doesn't; the press began to realize its full discovery potential, along with its ability to editorialize as well as report; we more and more came to be called political consultants rather than campaign managers because of the specialty aspects that had developed within the business, and the public, more and more, began to increase its doubts about everyone concerned.

As professionals, we re-discovered volunteers in the political campaign. I don't think we can pretend that we re-created the idea, because thousands of people, particularly the young, were motivated to translate their anti-war passions into action. It therefore became a more important role of the political consultant to discover meaningful ways of utilizing the new breed of volunteer in terms of meaningful programs and activities that would help various candidates get elected.

It was also during the phase that another new magical political wand was brought into being. As television was the miracle weapon in the preceding years, the computer became a new instrument of political communication. Computerized lists, computerized mailings, the ability to mass produce letters that identified people by their own names, all had attractive aspects and we all looked upon ourselves as parents of new digital babies. Again, the public responded phenomenally.

During this phase, political television formats became more sophisticated, changing from the original basic and blunt concepts to a new style of so-called "newsreels." Even then, the public was beginning to demand a higher degree of credibility in political communication. The newsreel style of commercials appeared to answer that need. The candidates casually talking on the street corner with people in an ad-lib situation; the candidate sitting in a living room engaged in an informal discussion of critical issues, answering questions; the candidate walking along the beach with his coat thrown over his shoulder meditating on the problems that faced the country; and the candidate and his family caught in a spontaneous moment while picnicking in the park. The basic idea was that these commercials were not supposed to look like commercials. To the uninformed, they might look like part of a news program. Movement and action were a definite part of the technique, and it proved so successful that we all ended up using it. As a matter of fact, looking at our collective films over the last 2 years, we're still using it. Unfortunately, we all got the word too late that the public no longer finds our attempts at naturalness very natural.

It was also during this phase that the effective use of polling and polling techniques became an integral part of our profession. While polling had taken place previously, we began to rely more and more on polling techniques as a way of not only measuring public opinion, but determining the strengths and weaknesses of our candidates and our opponents in order to formulate game plans and programs.

It was also during this period that barriers began to rise between the press, the political consultant, government, and the public. The press became more critical of the over-all media approach. We became more and more defensive. Government became more and more inaccessible. The public started saying the "hell with all of you."

Political parties which had been on a downhill trend throughout all of these phases, became more fractionalized, less and less effective, and more ignored by government leaders, by the press, by political consultants, and certainly by the public. Through it all, the public was concluding that no one was on its side, and that public statements by government leaders and politicians were not to be believed. By and large, the public was right.

Phase four of our collective careers really began about three years ago. Before Watergate, the public was expressing its distrust of government, politicians, and all of us associated with the system. We really didn't have to spend money on polls to learn the extent of public disillusionment. All one had to do was talk to friends, go to a party, attend a meeting, and listen to what the people were saying. As the war terminated, the public continued to retreat from political participation even as its distrust and suspicion increased. During this period, the government became even more aloof, the press concentrated more heavily on political technique as opposed to political substance, and political consultants spent a lot of time worrying. The public grew weary of the political dialogue, mainly because all sounded the same. Political messages acknowledged the fact that the public was cynical, turned off, and didn't believe anything. But the public wanted more than acknowledgment of its feelings. It wanted someone, somewhere, to do something about the situation. But nothing happened. That is nothing, until Watergate.

Watergate served as the spark that ignited our most historic and devastating political explosion. Watergate was the dramatic symbol of all the accumulated evils that the public had imagined about our political system. Watergate was horrid proof that politicians were crooked, that government and the people in government were arrogant and abusive, and above all, that those in government were there only for selfish rewards, and not out of any desire to serve the people. The public was shocked by the intensity of Watergate, but it wasn't entirely surprised by its disclosures.

While Watergate was symbolic of all the wrongs of our political process, its smoke and odor covered everyone involved in the system, innocent as well as guilty. If a Haldeman and an Ehrlichman were political advisors to the President, their activities, in the public's mind, became synonymous with all of those who advise people in government and politicians.

To say that the role of the political consultant was dramatically changed by Watergate would be a gross understatement. For the past year and a half, we all had to live in defense of our profession as the Watergate convictions mounted.

For the political consultant, there have been drastic changes during this terrible period. We can call this last phase the period of reform, purity, godliness, holiness, and hypocrisy.

As soon as the first Watergate volcano erupted, office holders around the nation immediately set out to cleanse the system under the guise of campaign reform. While many were well-intended, and while I certainly will not disagree with the need for reform, the cold, hard fact is that a vast amount of legislation and law was created in panic and in haste in an effort to make government and politicians appear suddenly honest and clean. In many respects, the over-reaction to Watergate will prove just as dangerous to the system in the new few years, as was the lack of any action prior to Watergate. While it is not my intent here to state which formats of campaign reform I would advocate, or which ones I think are wrong, I do believe that the over-reaction has produced a great deal of legislation that is incumbent protective, that will discourage good people from participating in the process and from entering public life, and will bog down government in endless litigation.

While noting the problems of over-reaction, I must again say that we are all partially to blame. How many of us advised our candidates and office holders to strike out in the cause of campaign reform? Most of us did. How many of us urged our clients to suggest immediate remedies that would instantly cleanse the political process? Most of us did. Our polls said it was the crying need, and who would dare oppose purity?

It would also seem as if we had all had the same script writer for everyone's campaigns. It became a contest of who was the most honest. It became a horse race as to who would propose and enact laws the fastest. How many of us volunteered our services to local, state, or federal legislative bodies to suggest practical reforms that would work instead of theoretical laws that would hinder? Very few.

Consequently, during this last phase of political activity, the political consultant became by necessity a collector of ever-changing reform laws. He had to acquire new talents for accounting and filling out forms, and had to procure the best attorneys available to try to interpret legislation that was in many cases ambiguous and clouded with loopholes.

I have watched, as I'm sure all of you have, those whom we have helped elect fall into the purity-in-government trap. I happen to be immensely proud of many of the good people I have helped who now sit in Congress or the Senate. Many were "long-shots," and young challengers who defeated better known candidates or incumbents. I am proud, not only because of the campaigns that helped them achieve election, but of the records that they have established in Washington. So it is with a great deal of sadness, and with an admitted lack of purity in my heart, that I realize that under California's new laws, for example, people like them will probably not be elected any more. It is also with some guilt that I realize that we sat back and allowed this over-reaction to take place.

NEW ROLES FOR POLITICAL CONSULTANTS

What is our role now? What is our role in the future? I have reviewed our history because I believe it offers some clues to what lies ahead.

I refuse to believe that our political system has totally disintegrated. I refuse to believe that the public will not respond to politics as it should be. I refuse to believe that the basic parts of our system that have survived through the years are totally wrong. And, I therefore refuse to believe that the role of the political consultant is over. It will only be over if we continue to hide our heads in our accounts receivable; continue to cluster in an atmosphere of despair; refuse to come to grips with the realistic aspects of politics in America as it is today, and fail to face up to what must be our realistic role in the system.

Let me try to visualize our role in two categories. First, from the technical view in terms of day-to-day operations, services we must provide and ways that we might go about it. And second, where I believe our responsibilities lie over and above our technical knowledge.

On the technical side, we must first adapt to the post-Watergate syndrome. We have the responsibility on behalf of our clients and candidates to keep ourselves totally informed and up-to-date on existing and new campaign laws as they are created. With that knowledge, we have the difficult responsibility of keeping our candidates, clients and committees in total compliance with these laws.

In California, for instance, it is now almost impossible to run for any major office without professional help in the area of campaign law compliance. Our new laws are so complicated that we now spend close to 30% of staff time in making sure that the proper forms are filed properly at the proper time. In addition to that, we have found it necessary to retain a firm of politically oriented lawyers to oversee our own staff work on behalf of our clients. The average candidate, committee, campaign treasurer or finance chairman cannot possibly be aware of his legal responsibilities under the laws that now prevail in my home state. Frankly, it was never my intention to direct an accounting organization. I'm basically a campaigner. But these are the facts we must live with. These types of laws will spread more and more throughout the country during the coming year. We used to have to worry about getting clients out of trouble. Now our chief concern is keeping clients from inadvertently getting into trouble.

You don't need me to tell you that there is a diminishing amount of money available for political campaigns and causes. We have all felt that sting and again must accept it as part of the reality of political life today. The days of the grand budgets and fees are over. By law and by interest, the large donors are also a memory of the past. As consultants, therefore, we must improve techniques for raising lesser amounts of money from a greater number of people. We have barely scratched the surface in terms of small-donor fund raising techniques. It's easier to accomplish for higher offices such as the presidency, but so far most of us are lacking in skills of this type for lower offices. Our creative abilities in terms of direct mail and people-to-people solicitation must be expanded and improved, and will be an increasingly important part of our services.

Throughout the short history of our profession, I doubt if we have fully realized the critical role we have played in the candidate selection process. We would all like to think we only have worked for candidates we believed in, and who represented our own individual political thinking. By and large, I think we have all tried to do that when possible. Unfortunately, as with any profession, economics enter the picture. We have all, from time to time, represented clients whom we didn't particularly love, but who could help pay the overhead. Admitting that, which I think we should, we have to guard against a danger that I can foresee occurring fairly soon. Because of voter apathy, distaste for politics and the new campaign restrictions, I firmly believe that fewer good men and women will offer themselves as candidates.

As a result, many less talented and less scrupulous candidates will attempt to fill the void. Difficult economic times, as we are experiencing now, are likely to encourage this process unless we are careful. As professionals, who care about the system and our government, we have a duty and a responsibility to screen would-be candidates more carefully than ever, and weed out those who would attempt to take advantage of the situation.

A significant role yet to be played by political consultants relates to the smaller political races on the local government level. We have paid too much attention to the "big ones." While much of the glory, and sometimes much of the money, is focused on the national races, on senate races and on gubernatorial races, I believe a significant future role might very well be in more of the congressional, state legislative, and municipal-type campaigns. In my experience, some of these so-called smaller races have been the most exciting of all. I think too many of us, for reasons of pride and assumed economics, have turned our backs on these smaller races. In truth, these races are composed of people and candidates who truly desire professional help, are sometimes more willing to experiment with new approaches and can be the ingredient for a more stable economic professional base and a more consistent flow of business. And I might add, during the period when there is a cry for leadership and a desperate need for better candidates, our encouragement and professional help on these lower levels will, in the long run, produce a much better choice when it comes time to select those who will run for higher office.

Another new role of the political consultant which is worthy of our exploration is in the area of openly working with government officials—many of whom we helped to elect. Part of the reason that government exists in a vacuum is because of its own attitude, but another reason is because of a surprising lack of information about what really is on the minds of the people. The members of this group either conduct or oversee or receive more than 100 polls per year, covering almost every region of the country, on a state-wide and local level, discovering attitudes on national and local affairs, and receiving responses on specific concerns. Occasionally, we share that information with one another and frequently are amazed at the results. Think what it might mean to our higher governmental officials or to the major party leaders if a way could be devised to make them privy to this information once our vital use of it was concluded. While many of our office holders receive some minor information from newsletter polls and the like, and while everyone reads general judgments from Gallup or Harris periodically, think what might happen if our governmental leaders received a steady flow of cross-country information covering the range of subjects that we all explore. I think they, too, might be astonished to know what the people around the country were feeling. This is one area where we can professionally be of service to the political system and to our country.

I believe another significant responsibility of the conscientious political consultant in the years ahead should involve re-establishment of some of the old type of rapport with the political press of this country. The press has a responsibility to monitor us, to follow our campaigns, to comment on the techniques being used, the money being spent, and to criticize us when it thinks we've done wrong. But that responsibility is a two-way street. We have the right to openly challenge our friends of the press when we think they are wrong. More programmed meetings should be arranged throughout the country between us and political writers and commentators to seek ways to improve political coverage and the public's understanding of campaigns. I am not talking about those few professional writers who have been at it a long time, who know how to get the information when needed, and who can recognize a gimmick from a legitimate story. Unfortunately, they are the rare exceptions. Most ask that the candidate talk about the issues and tell them where they stand, but we all know what happens when we produce a well-documented issue paper which spells out the candidate's views and plans. By and large, it is still thrown in the wastebasket. But when we take that same candidate, and send him scuba diving to discover how polluted the ocean might be, almost drowning him in the process, then we make the front page.

Political consultants and the press are among the major communicators of the nation. And yet we, and the press, have a serious communication gap. On top of that, more newspaper publishers are deciding that less money should be spent on political coverage on the assumption the public isn't interested. Their theory is wonderful. If the public is apathetic, then less coverage and less political activity will somehow make everyone more interested. The truth of the matter is that they don't want to expend the money to get the job done. Newspapers such as the *New York Times, The Los Angeles Times,* and *The Washington Post* are beginning to stand more and more alone in terms of adequate staffs to cover elections properly. Unfortunately, a majority of Americans don't have the privilege of reading these newspapers. We have a role to play here. Individually and collectively, we must strive to persuade newspaper owners to provide the public more information to know what's happening in the political arena.

Rapport with, and coverage by, newspapermen is only part of the problem. The electronic media, and most particularly the networks, seem to be living in their own political world, which has very little relationship with either government, the public, the consultant or with anyone. Again, I am not speaking about the qualified commentator or reporter who takes the trouble to call, to visit a political area, to properly investigate, and to properly report.

But I am continually amazed at the sporadic coverage that comes across our airways on both the national and local level. Last November, for instance, I watched sweet faces give election returns from throughout the country, standing in front of vast scoreboards and reciting data spewed out by a computer. Senators were called congressmen. Congressmen were called senators. The pronunciation of candidates' names was atrocious. Winners were declared and undeclared. We have all had the experience of seeing races that we were involved with, covered electronically, without anyone from a network or a station bothering to take the trouble to talk to anyone who was involved on either side of the campaign. The stations need our expertise. We need the stations to properly let the public know what is happening in our races. This might be, perhaps, one of the most important roles we can play during the coming years. While we complain about apathy, we have by negligence and by living in our own isolation booths, helped perpetuate public apathy. We, as consultants, have a duty to give out factual information. The networks and their subsidiaries have the same duty.

CANDID MESSAGES

Fundamentally, I think our most important role pertains to substance in the survival of the political system, and the responsibility that we must accept.

No matter what our current specialty may be—television producers, organizers, managers, direct mail specialists, get-out-the-vote specialists, phone bank operators, fund raisers, and so forth, all covered by the term political consultant—the one common denominator is communication.

We are all political communicators. What we say in a brochure, what is shown on a commercial, what a person says in a telephone message, what a volunteer says on a doorstep, all constitute various forms of political communication.

The public receives its total political communication from what our office holders say, what our campaigns say, what our candidates say, and what the press says. The fact that we now have an apathetic public that doesn't even care to vote says that somewhere along the line we have failed.

As I have indicated before, Watergate gets all the blame. But that's really a cop-out. During the past two years there were too many candidates who looked and sounded the same. Our overall political communication looked and sounded the same, and the public found nothing to get interested or excited about.

We all said that our candidate was the most honest, or that our candidate would cure inflation, and the public said "bunk."

If the premise was valid that Watergate had turned everyone off on politics, then why in at least eight congressional races that I know about throughout the country did 70% and 80% of the voters turn out to cast their ballots? And why did a majority of those campaigns have a multitude of volunteers who energetically worked for months to try to get their candidate elected? The answer is that in those races candidates represented a cause that related to the concerns of their area. Their campaigns and their messages came through in a way that said to the public "this is important to you," and most of the candidates in those races created an excitement of their own.

This is where I think the heartbeat lies in our total political problem and in the key role that we as consultants can play if we so desire.

When we all discovered that the public wanted honesty, truth and candor we told it we were giving honesty, truth, and candor. We greatly underestimated their intelligence. The point that we all missed was a desire for real candor.

Can we stand here today convinced that the public believes that in the space of a year our office holders, our government, and our candidates have made the political process as clean as a vacuum tube? By asking for candor, the public tried to tell us that it wanted candidates and office holders who will tell them what they want to do, and do it, and also tell them what they can't do. The public wants office holders and candidates who show guts and action—not computerized rhetoric. The public wants office holders and candidates who show that they can relate to everyday problems and do something about them!

As political communicators, our key role and challenge is to create and help those who we represent create political messages that relate to practical problems, practical hopes, and also relate the practical facts of political life.

Let me try to illustrate examples of what I'm trying to say. During this past election we represented a candidate for secretary of state in California whose main issue was the elimination of pay toilets in public restrooms. She worked for 3 years in the state legislature to achieve the passage of that bill. Her entire campaign was based on the premise that while everyone was talking about multi-million dollar budgets, and immediate solutions to the state's complicated problems, she, at least, was going to bring specific results in an area which could help someone a little bit in everyday life. She became known as the "pay toilet" lady. The political pols laughed. The political press said she was a candidate without substance. Everyone laughed except the public which decided that there at least was something they could relate to and someone who wasn't offering pie in the sky solutions. She maintained that message throughout her entire campaign. She had two major Democratic primary opponents, one who spent better than $500,000 and another who spent better than $200,000. Her total primary expenditure was $62,000, of which $36,000 was spent on media. She had one 30-second commercial with a total production cost of $1,400 which was filmed inside the ladies' room of the San Francisco International Airport. She not only won the primary, but in the general election, with a total expenditure of $105,000, including $36,000 for media, she led the entire Democratic ticket and was the top vote getter with better than 1,300,000 votes. She had a message that related. She had a message that was believable. She had a message that the public understood. Her message said that there was at least one thing that one office holder could do to help.

As one who hopes our next President will be a Democrat, I believe that this need for political messages that relate is of particular importance to Democrats. The symbolism of a George Wallace is more than just imagery that appeals to the Archie Bunkers of the country. He has managed through a very direct appeal to relate his thoughts to the fundamental and everyday problems of many Americans. As political consultants, I think we have a great deal to learn from the Wallace appeal. And incidentally, our research and other polls that I have seen show his strength to be much broader-based than many people are willing to concede. His message even has an appeal to a surprisingly large number of minorities throughout the country. He has been able to project himself on the side of the people, convincing them that he understands their day-to-day economic struggle. Now I am not a Wallace fan per se, but as a political communicator, I have to admit that he has made great strides in making his political messages believable and candid.

A couple of weeks ago I had the privilege of listening to one potential Democratic presidential candidate explain at length how he was going to reduce inflation. He was very expansive on economic theory. He had charts and graphs. He talked with great authority about certain layers of government that could be curtailed and how that money could be used in other layers of government for social benefit, and he talked, and he talked, and he talked. If I had recorded his dialogue, I might have been able to figure out what he was trying to say after studying it for a day or two. But, there isn't a housewife in America who would have understood a thing he had to say.

I believe a great deal of the distrust of government, of office holders, and of candidates results from lack of candid communication, and from our collective inability to relate in a meaningful manner to the public.

The re-building of our system requires that type of candid message that relates to people's everyday problems and concerns. Instead of telling voters how honest we all are, let's try being frank.

There wasn't a lot wrong with the politics of leaders like Harry Truman. I wonder how many of us would have had the courage or the wisdom to advise a Harry Truman to call a columnist a "son-of-a-bitch" because he criticized his daughter. He did it, and the public loved it because it showed he was for real.

While admitting that many parts of campaign reform are needed and necessary, and that full disclosures and reasonable limitations are certainly proper, I wonder how many of us would currently advise an office holder or candidate to openly stand up and say, "In order to do a job for you, it is necessary for me to meet with my fellow legislators and make trades, concessions and deals." In truth, isn't that the way the system works? Isn't that the way the system has always worked? And isn't that the way the system will always work? Why don't we quit kidding around and let the public know bluntly and honestly how things get done! The public will respond to those who use candor in the truest sense, not in its most hypocritical sense. The public wants office holders who will try to accomplish things that will help, even if that help is limited.

These are rugged times, not a hoax perpetrated by the press, not scare tactics produced by over anxious politicians, but truthfully troubled economic and political times.

The American housewife cannot relate to economic theory, to statistics, or to the gross national product. This has nothing to do with her intelligence. But she can relate to the fact that the cost of bread has increased as much as 30% in many areas over the last 2 years, that the cost of milk has increased 20% to 30% over the same period, that the cost of eggs has in some cases doubled, that her husband has lost his job or is afraid that he might, and that even though the family income has risen over the last five years she and her budget cannot make it through the last two weeks of the month. She and her husband want to know how they are going to pay for their children's education and her husband wants to know how in the hell he is going to pay his mortgage. They cry for answers and help. They plead for leadership. They beg for communication.

But everytime this distressed family tries to listen to government, to our office holders, to our candidates, or tries to watch or read the news, everytime they try to get interested, we seem to do everything possible to turn them away. They hear the government talking about cutting governmental spending, which seems unreal.

They hear government talk about increasing the cost of gasoline, which is somehow supposed to solve an international problem that will get us more gasoline. They hear office holders say they are concerned about soaring prices and soaring unemployment rates. That's not news; the family's concerned, too. And then we show them arty commercials of our candidate walking on the beach, saying that he is going to bring honesty back into politics. And then we wonder why people don't vote or participate anymore.

Those of us who advise candidates, those of us who have the job of putting candidates' ideas into mass media messages, must forget the politics of consensus and have the courage to advise our candidates to "tell them what's on your mind—what's really on your mind. Tell them what you can do, and what you can't." There isn't one of us who hasn't practiced the art of waffling, dodging and avoiding with meaningless rhetoric. The public just won't tolerate that anymore. We must answer their desire for this type of courage or the system and all of us in the system will continue to disintegrate.

PROFESSIONAL PRIDE

In order for our profession to survive we have to go several steps further in terms of our own candor and pride. Because of the pressures of the current holier-than-thou atmosphere, because of pressures from the press, we have resorted to hiding from what we do. As I am proud of our political system, and most of the people in it, I also am proud of my professional abilities and those of my associates.

There is nothing wrong with political technique in campaigning. It's been a part of our history from the very beginning. There are a lot of damn good office holders who wouldn't be in this city today if it hadn't been for solid professional and well-constructed political technique. Why should we be afraid to say so?

Let's stand up and say we are proud to be professionals. Let's fully admit that, particularly in an era of public apathy, that we must find means of calling attention to our candidates and our causes so that the public can get acquainted with them and hopefully get excited once again. Let us all share the secret that most of these political messages cost money! Let's talk with pride about the research that we undertake to give us an understanding of the electorate. Let's let it be known that because of our professional talents and experience that we, each year, save thousands of dollars on behalf of our clients who would ordinarily waste that money on meaningless expenditures because of their own lack of experience. Let's fully admit that we thoughtfully produce campaign game plans which in turn produce political campaigns that are finely tuned and coordinated.

In short, while we seek to produce political messages that relate to the public and will revitalize our political system, we, at the same time, should openly and proudly proclaim what our profession is, and what it has and can accomplish.

I don't want to leave the impression that the role of the political consultant during 1975 and in future years will be the sole salvation of our political system. Our importance is not that significant. And while I have openly criticized mistakes that we all have made, I also don't want to let us forget the accomplishments that our young profession has made over these past 30 years.

FUTURE ROLE

The role of the political consultant isn't over. Put in proper perspective, our real role might just be beginning. It is a new era of politics and we not only have to adjust to it, we have to become a more integral part of it and hopefully take more of a leadership role as it progresses.

No law will ever change the closeness of the relationship between the political consultant and the candidate. But we have the responsibility of using that relationship carefully.

Our main role in the next few years is renewed political communication. We have the talent to do it. Now we are up against the problem of communicating what is most important of all—what's good about our system, what can make it better, what should be retained from the past, and what additions can be made to make it work better.

Our future really depends upon our own attitude about it. Like most of you, I would not trade my profession for anything. In our short history, no one has ever walked away rich. I doubt that any of us ever will. Most people don't realize that we have chosen this field because we love the process, and while we are paid advocates, the vast array of talent we represent could make far more money in other fields. We love this profession because we feel we are a part of history. We love it because we get decisions every June and every November on the quality of our work. We love it because of the thrill of being where the action is. We love it because we of all people know that politics—that dirty word—affects everyone in this country every day. And, we love the thrill of winning.

With all of the ups and downs, during good times and bad, and even during a period such as we're enduring right now, I still love the campaign. The key to it all is pride. With our help, and the help of others, the over-reaction that has occurred will dissipate and the pendulum will swing back. We'll probably all be the better for it. There is an instinctive pride that we all maintain in being professionals. The pride of knowing our job better than anyone else. The pride of always learning how to do it better. The excitement of knowing that every campaign is different than any previous campaign. And probably most importantly, the pride of knowing and having the respect and friendship of other professionals who have endured and thrilled and even suffered from the same type of experience.

Let us never forget our pride. Let us not let our political system disintegrate further because we failed to speak up in its behalf—or in our behalf. Let us always remember that even though things are out of whack at the moment, we are a group of people who can help put them back together again. That, in truth, is our role for the future.

—2—

HOW THE "I DARE YOU!"
CANDIDATE WON

Harry N. D. Fisher

On November 5, 1968, John C. Danforth was elected attorney general of Missouri with a 73,000 majority. Danforth was the first Republican to be elected statewide in Missouri in 22 years, the first Republican to be sent to the state capital in 28 years, the first Republican to be elected attorney general of the state in 40 years. And except for President Nixon, with a 14,000 vote plurality, Danforth was the only Republican elected statewide in Missouri in 1968. The result was little short of miraculous; and, considering that Danforth is an ordained Episcopal clergyman, some people think it *was* miraculous.

This was Jack Danforth's first try for public office. Worse, this very young man had returned to his native state a scant two years before. His family was known in Missouri, but he wasn't. His being a board member of the Danforth Foundation might be of some help. His membership on the boards of the Episcopal Church Foundation and Union Theological Seminary would do him more good in the East than in the Midwest. His life membership in the National Association for the Advancement of Colored People would probably do him some harm.

He was facing opposition in the primary from an entrenched member of the "old guard" Republican faction; and his general election opponent—if Jack were fortunate enough to get through

From Harry N. D. Fisher, "How the 'I Dare You!' Candidate Won," *Public Relations Journal* (April 1969):26–29. Copyright © 1969 by Public Relations Society of America. Reprinted by permission.

the primary—would be either an incumbent who had won in a landslide four years previously, or a highly respected former Federal prosecuting attorney.

Jack Danforth's grandfather, a native of Missouri, founded Ralston Purina Company and wrote a book. Jack's father is former president and chairman of the Ralston Purina board; Jack's brother Don is the company's executive vice-president; Jack himself, before his election to office, was on the company's board of directors. Another brother, Bill, is vice-chancellor in charge of medical affairs at Washington University. Sister Dorothy is married to Jefferson Miller, vice-president of a leading St. Louis bank.

The 32-year-old father of four daughters, Danforth is young enough to step lively. He is also brilliant. An honors graduate of Princeton University, he was granted graduate degrees from Yale in divinity and law on the same day. He has practiced law with leading firms in New York City and St. Louis, while simultaneously serving Episcopal churches in both cities as assistant or associate rector.

Jack Danforth has the courage of his convictions. His was the first angry reply to Chicago Mayor Daley's order to police to shoot to kill arsonists and to shoot to wound looters.

Danforth was personally grieved upon the assassination of his fellow board member at Morehouse College, Martin Luther King, but he had the good sense not to over-react to the shooting. Indeed, but he kept his head during turbulent 1968 when many others about him seemed to be losing theirs.

"Birth, wealth and education ranked him among the aristocrats. . . . To these finer qualities he added a loftiness of character which lifted him above his fellows and made him their master. His personality was so impressive, his reputation so unspotted, and his policy so sagacious and so generally successful that the demos supported him implicitly."

The above quote is from James R. Joy's book, *Grecian History;* the reference is to Pericles.

Coupled with the foregoing assets, Danforth has three powerful prerequisites for personal success: memory, concentration and the will to win. He also is tall (6'3") and lean and craggy enough to remind more than one person of another prairie lawyer, Abraham Lincoln. In his speeches, the resemblance to Lincoln is more than incidental even as to cadences.

There are, moreover, limits (set by law if not by one's own

resources) on the amounts of money that can be spent in a campaign. Some candidates evade these limits by allowing proliferation of their campaign committees, or by spending vastly greater sums prior to the 90-day reporting period. That is not Jack Danforth's way, however. From the moment that he decided to make the race for office, his advisers and friends had the burden of working within a limited budget and a limited period within which to spend it.

At the outset, the decision was made to spend $60,000—most of the money then available and less than half of the total lawful budget of some $145,000—for media. Extra money up to the $145,000 limit was reserved for printing, filming and other production, office overhead, travel and staff expenses.

The staff closest to the candidate included his campaign manager, the advertising and public relations agency for which I served as account executive and my partner George Stemmler as account supervisor, a professor of law to provide research and position papers, a committee chairman, a campaign executive director to handle speaking and travel arrangements and other logistical matters, a chief of volunteers, a Kansas City press representative, a secretary, a driver and general handyman, and necessary clerical and office helpers. On the periphery of the inner circle of this staff were numerous heads-up volunteers who provided invaluable service.

The Danforth campaign made use of several committees, not to evade the election laws, but to make it easier for Democrats and Independents to join in. Thus there was the "parent corporation" (the Danforth for Attorney General Committee) and five subsidiaries: Danforth Clubs, Citizens for Danforth, Doctors for Danforth, Lawyers Committee for Danforth and the Metropolitan Kansas City Lawyers Committee for Danforth for Attorney General. Hundreds of persons throughout Missouri generously allowed use of their names and contributed time, talent, and money.

We also assembled a fine team of photographers and Shelby Storck's TV production company.

All suppliers, like everyone else on the team, had to perform accurately under deadline pressures. Taken as an entire unit, the Danforth team has the potential to stampede a convention, as in fact it did stampede the Missouri State Republican Convention in Kansas City in June, 1968.

Danforth announced his candidacy in mid-March.

I DARE YOU

In April we chose the campaign theme: I DARE YOU. A book of that title had been written by Jack Danforth's grandfather as a challenge to the youth of the Twenties. The book is still selling reasonably well; and it is fondly remembered, particularly among churchgoing people and in small town and rural areas.

We liked the title because it was catchy, strong, short and had real bite, because it meant Danforth to a lot of people, because it was beamed to youth—half of the U.S. population is now under 25 years of age—and above all because of its flexibility. It could be used over and over again, in a variety of contexts.

For example, in one of the more important speeches of the campaign—in St. Louis in July—Danforth drew a close parallel between the events leading up to the national calamity of 1861 to 1865 and the disorders of the present. He gave what he believed were the reasons the Union had to be preserved then, and why, all the more, the Union must be preserved now. He closed with these words:

"I dare you and all citizens of Missouri to join with me in achieving respect for law in our state, to help root from the hearts and minds of our people all semblance of bigotry, and to create through law a society where neighbors can live with neighbors in dignity and harmony and peace."

Our photographers had captured Jack in all kinds of situations. From the more than 500 still photographs taken, we selected a half dozen definitive campaign pictures.

The basic head-and-shoulders shot was featured in the poster-type brochure, photostated up in size for meetings, still farther up in size for major rallies, down in size to fit inside a standard envelope, and still smaller to fit on a mass-mailing postcard.

The "dare" theme was carried out by copy reading: "I DARE YOU to elect a man who will put law above special interests, personal honesty above professional politics, and public service above private gain."

There was method in these tautologies. At this early date in the campaign it was well to say something everyone would agree with but no opponent could shoot at. At the same time, the dare seemed to say something nasty about all of Jack's opponents.

Of course the Danforth platform had substance, too, with scores of individual issues developed throughout the summer and fall down to the cut-off date in mid-October. Jack's less general challenge that appeared on his brochure and elsewhere read: "I

DARE YOU to approach the problems of crime and disorder thoughtfully and not emotionally; to support a plan giving Missouri the soundest and most up-to-date methods of law enforcement and criminal procedure, and dealing effectively with juvenile delinquency; to support law enforcement officers by giving them adequate pay and benefits; to elect an Attorney General who will not only perform the statutory duties of his office efficiently, but who will also provide leadership in the name of the law; and to show by your words and actions that ours is a system of law, and that law must be obeyed by all the people."

A DIFFERENT APPROACH

In mid-April, the Storck group brought in some "interesting" black-and-white footage on Jack Danforth. At SBF&P we had already reached a similar conclusion: the strongest way to present Jack Danforth to the Missouri electorate was in black-and-white. Other candidates were going through the whole color spectrum— red, blue, orange, even yellow. *Our* billboards, brochures, bumper stickers, and television commercials would be different.

While our creative group was working on the brochure and billboards, and Storck was off filming Danforth, media director Frank Chipperfield was doing some of the most important work of all, talking to the media reps.

THE PERFECT SCHEDULE

It is here that the Danforth campaign got close to being scientific. Armed with his own carefully kept charts on total audience, age of audience, sex of audience, and viewing habits of audience, Chipperfield constructed the perfect schedule. We ordered and paid for that schedule before any other candidate. Even after the law had been complied with as regards pre-emptions and equal-time offers, 95 percent of our original purchases were still there.

The TV schedule for Danforth consisted of a total of 376 plays of 18 different spot announcements—60's, 30's, and 10's— plus six plays of a five-minute program. We first bought the spots, trusting to late-arriving funds to buy the program schedule. Some of the spots were for general use. Most, however, were custom-tailored to the urban audience, the rural audience, the young audience or the women.

All of the spots were concentrated into a saturation effort in the final two weeks of the general election campaign, with the peak being in the final two days. On November 4th, Danforth spots were shown 61 times on 12 Missouri TV stations. If that same sort of schedule were maintained statewide daily for a year, it would cost nearly $3,000,000. Nationwide, that would represent an annual advertising schedule approaching $50,000,000—the kind of money spent by General Motors and Procter & Gamble.

It was pretty much the same story for outdoor posters. Locations are critical to the value of outdoor boards. We asked for the best locations in the St. Louis and Kansas City regions, and by buying early, did well. We printed enough extra paper to leave running room just in case something else good showed up, as in fact it did.

In August, as we turned our guns toward the general election day, we pre-printed several thousand sheets of legal-sized news release paper boldly bearing the words NEWS FROM DANFORTH and I DARE YOU.

We had been kicking out a heavy schedule of news releases all along—at least once a week, usually two or three. To avoid clogging our clerical force, releases were beamed to coded lists—A being wire services, major dailies, radio, TV and the inner circle, B being metropolitan weeklies and minor dailies, and C being outstate weeklies.

From late August on, the pace of news releases quickened into one, two and sometimes even three releases *per day*. Such frenetic activity was not calculated for mere effect: we had a tremendously active candidate to deal with, and he was saying and doing important things. One of his activities, a tour of all Missouri's prisons, obtained sensationally good press.

The newspaper, radio and television news coverage carried our little attorney general campaign quite well, right up to the point where the paid advertising schedule kicked in; and that's saying a great deal considering that in 1968 we had competition from assassinations, riots, national conventions and major national and international stories, not to mention other candidates.

THE PRESS CAME FIRST

Of course such wonderful editorial coverage was not achieved accidentally. We personally introduced Jack to many editors; and Jack was under obligation when traveling without us to call on editors and reporters. We followed an old maxim: the press comes first.

This liberal policy toward the press paid handsome dividends in the form of interviews and news conferences, features, page one articles and—particularly precious—editorials. The final editorial tally was Danforth 27, his opponent 1.

As fast as the newspapers could print editorials we reprinted them. A St. Louis *Post-Dispatch* editorial one afternoon in late June was photostated up to giant size and flown to the state Republican convention in Kansas City for prominent display the next evening. A *Globe-Democrat* feature that appeared Saturday morning, October 26, was pasted into an editorial montage that afternoon, printed that night, and a half million copies were in the hands of readers throughout the state by Monday afternoon.

THE 13 ELEMENTS OF "LUCK"

How do you market a minority party candidate?

1. Start with an attractive candidate who is willing to work.
2. Obtain expert assistance. TV and print production, media analysis and purchasing, speechwriting and position paper research, press relations and campaign management, all done with an exquisite sense of timing, are too important and too difficult to be handled by amateurs.
3. Assemble and mobilize the best team you can get, and let everyone know ahead of time of the stern requirements for accuracy and speed.
4. Set up a long-range plan. Budget limits and other considerations may require that you take calculated risks against the plan—like buying media for a general election on the assumption that you can win the primary without paid advertising. You don't win elections by having groups and individuals jumping on separate horses to go riding off in all directions.
5. Check your long-range plan against developments frequently. Twice weekly is not too often, once weekly is absolutely minimal.
6. Establish a power base, the broader the better, and cultivate it.
7. Budget your money. The budget may be open-ended on the high side. There are, nevertheless, priorities that must be established, and commitments that must be made early, if expenditures are to have their maximum effect.
8. Since no campaign has truly unlimited resources, concentrate the resources that are available.
9. Remember that the press is at least as important as, and probably more important than, the advertising.
10. Public relations and advertising should be completely coordinated.
11. Merchandise your publicity! Academicians may say that testimonials are logically indefensible, but don't you believe it!

12. Don't get caught short. Decide at the outset that the unexpected can and probably will happen. Have the contingency funds, or the extra paper, or those extra hours, ready.
13. Dare to be different, dare to be strong.

These conclusions, based on John Danforth's election, may be helpful to public relations men who become involved in political campaigns.

—3—

THE AGENCY KNACK OF POLITICAL PACKAGING

Walter Troy Spencer

Hail to B. B. D. & O.
It told the nation how to go;
It managed by advertisement
To sell us a new President.

Eisenhower hits the spot
One full general, that's a lot.

Feeling sluggish, feeling sick?
Take a dose of Ike and Dick.

Philip Morris, Lucky Strike,
Alka Seltzer, I like Ike.

Marya Mannes,
"Sales Campaign" (1952)*

If Miss Marya Mannes was wryly shocked at the reliance of presidential candidates on advertising 16 years ago, she must be knocked speechless by the situation in this election year.

The major candidates all have agencies supporting them. Experts estimate that television and radio revenues from political advertising this year will rise to a record total of well over $50 million, up from the estimated $35 million to $38 million spent in the 1964 campaigns.

Television is now established as the undisputedly crucial communications factor in the race. Observers estimate that the average

*Reprinted with permission of the publisher from *Subverse: Rhymes for our Times* by Marya Mannes and Robert Osborn (George Braziller, Inc., New York, 1959). Copyright © 1959 by Marya Mannes and Robert Osborn.

From Walter Troy Spencer, "The Agency Knack of Political Packaging," *Television Magazine* 25 (August 1968). Copyright © 1968 by *Television Magazine*. *Television* is now incorporated in the weekly *Broadcasting*. Reprinted by permission.

political candidate from local to national office this year will allocate up to 75% of his ad budget to television. It may be even greater for presidential aspirants.

John Poister, senior vice president and director of planning at Fuller & Smith & Ross, Richard Nixon's agency, estimates that 90% of the buys made for the Republican candidate will be in radio and television, even though the agency also is using "some newspaper, a little magazine and outdoor advertising." He adds: "if anything, the amount of television advertising will be too low.

"Everyone thought TV made the election in 1960. I think it's even more important now," Poister says. "This year it's going to come on like Buster's gang. It will be overwhelming."

Arie Kopelman, vice president and account supervisor at Doyle Dane Bernbach, Hubert Humphrey's agency says: "There is no question television will play the major role in the communications aspect of the campaign," although this early in the race he declines to estimate what percentage of the Vice President's advertising dollar will go into the medium.

No agency executive will hazard anything beyond the roughest guess at what any presidential candidate's billings will add up to by the time Nov. 5 rolls around.

"There is no way of knowing or predicting what the costs will run at this point, since we can only suspect, without really knowing who our competition is going to be, much less what platform of issues he's going to run on," says Poister, who is serving as management supervisor on the Nixon account. "The total billing could run anywhere from $4 million to $15 million," he noted, adding: "We won't even have a master plan for media and creative strategy drafted until after the Democratic convention, and even then it will be subject to change depending upon campaign developments."

Before Senator Robert Kennedy's assassination, executives at his agency, Papert, Koenig, Lois, were privately estimating that billings for him would run from $15 million to $18 million if he went all the way to the fall election.

One of the most publicized side issues of the spring's primary elections, of course, was the amount of advertising and promotion money allegedly poured into the Democratic presidential race by Kennedy. The Twentieth Century Fund has a five-man Commission on Campaign Costs in the Electronic Era, under former FCC Chairman Newton Minow, studying what it describes as "ever-increasing use of television and radio in political campaigns (that) may be fundamentally altering the nature of the political process in America and may raise important issues of public policy."

In this presidential election year, political advertising has become such a staple of the industry that the American Association of Advertising Agencies recently issued a 31-page "Manual of Political Campaign Advertising," complete with a "Code of Ethics for Political Campaign Advertising," adopted by the AAAA's board of directors last February.

Yet while television and advertising have become indispensable to the American political process, after almost 20 years of practice, controversy over the ethics and techniques of campaign "selling" creates more heated national debate than ever.

Fair game for both professional and amateur, from the floor of Congress to cocktail-party chatter, are such issues as the morality— if not outright threat to the democratic process—involved in "packaging" a politician for sale to his constituency like so much detergent or toothpaste and the likelihood of all but "buying" the nation with sufficient purchase of TV time.

One television network (CBS) even broadcast a candid one-hour documentary last spring dramatizing the problem. The *CBS Reports* "Campaign American Style" presented a case study in the increasingly common practice of packaging a public image for a major local candidate, right down to market research, such as selecting the issues upon which he would campaign. ("Sometimes I find myself rebelling against their advice even though I know it's good advice, because I resent the fact that they're trying to . . . market me as a product rather than recognizing the fact that I'm an intelligent human being seeking a very responsible public office." So said the subject of the CBS study, Sol Wachtler. He was referring to the public-relations firm of Harshe-Rotman & Druck, which was paid $75,000 to mold his unsuccessful $700,000 campaign last fall to be elected to the $30,000-a-year job of county executive in the New York City suburb of Nassau County, New York.)

The sophistication of major agencies handling presidential candidates and the strong personalities of the candidates themselves are such that the Wachtler kind of blatant packaging is precluded. But even on the presidential level, it is likely that as the political fighting heats up this fall there will again be sharp schisms of opinion over how far taste and ethics may be stretched in ad techniques used to "sell" a man who will govern his fellow citizens. It has happened before. One of the sharpest arguments in

1964 was precipitated by Doyle Dane Bernbach's (then Johnson's agency) creation of an anti-Goldwater spot in which a little girl counting daisy petals in a field faded into an atom bomb countdown.

The division even within the ad industry over propriety begins with the hard line of agency head Carl Ally, who handled Senator Eugene McCarthy's early primary campaigns. (There is some disagreement over why Ally and McCarthy parted in the middle of the Indiana campaign. Ally says his agency is too small to stand the strain of taking on a major political account; he had only volunteered his personal services, "like plumbers, barbers or anyone else who wanted to help out of personal conviction." Others say there was a dispute over both Ally's creative approach and media buys.)

Ally says: "Maybe I'm wrong; maybe we ought to put candidates up in two-for-a-quarter packages and sell them over the counter, but I think an agency should only say, 'If you've got $100,000, I'll show you how to spend it.' An agency should serve as a 'go-fer,' taking a five-minute lift-out from a speech, having it dubbed, making a media plan so that it can reach an audience without the candidate having to bother with that crap. If an agency goes beyond that, I think it is wrong. Generating the material for a political client is not an agency's business. The agency should only put it in a form that is usable. An agency is not running for President; a candidate is."

Executives of other major candidates echo the sentiment to varying degrees.

Poister, of Nixon's agency, says: "The agency has utterly no business in the area of Nixon's position on issues and his platform. What we'll do is what he will allow us to do. He doesn't want to be packaged and he doesn't want phony gimmicks. All the footage used so far has been taken from location shooting, with no special effects and no overt effort to present it in any special way." (In the primaries, Nixon was handled by the agency of Feeley & Wheeler, and spots used were simple lift-outs—running from 20 seconds to five minutes—from a 30-minute documentary tape of a Nixon speech in New Hampshire. Harry Treleaven, a former J. Walter Thompson vice president who served as creative director in the primary campaign, has moved along with the account to Fuller & Smith & Ross.)

Kopelman of Doyle Dane, who is serving as account supervisor on the Humphrey campaign, also dismisses the idea of "packaging" his client, although, ironically, this is the 29-year-old Kopelman's first political account after having spent all his advertising career in package goods, first for three years at Procter & Gamble and then on such accounts as Heinz ketchup at Doyle Dane.

"Mr. Humphrey has his own ideas," says Kopelman. "He will exercise the same control over his ad campaign as any other client would. If he has a suggestion, we'll darn well listen to it. If we have a different opinion, however, we feel it our obligation to tell him and fight it out. He's the expert on what is said. We're the experts on how it is said."

Al Gardner, Papert, Koenig, Lois account executive, who handled Kennedy's 1964 senatorial campaign and was account executive on his presidential campaign until the assassination, says: "If PKL has a point of view about political advertising, it is that our job is to be as quiet and unobtrusive as possible. As against product presentation, our job is to put the candidate on camera, talking straight and simple in a good light. No music, no dissolves, just the candidate standing up there.

"The agency should leave politics to the politicians. You don't write copy strategy; you don't put words in your client's mouth. In cases where agencies become issues counselors, they're treading on dangerous ice," says Gardner.

"What the agency does is if a brilliant young lawyer on the politician's staff writes a good position paper, that may be the beginning of an ad. Here the copy doctors go to work. The agency becomes tape and film editors and makes judgments on the look, sound and flow of the material to mold the content of a commercial, because there are certain things a copywriter understands about a 60-second commercial better than anyone else.

"What we should be doing is creating better knowledge, not better propaganda, because there *is* an enormous potential for ill that lies in the mass media today. I sincerely hope that we don't play a crucial role in the election of a candidate. You have to have basic faith in the electorate," says Gardner.

Humphrey's Kopelman concurs with a favorite quote of his agency's president, William Bernbach: 'Nothing will make a bad product fail faster than good advertising'—it is the same thing in political advertising. The information is so intense in a short campaign that if it is misleading, people will get onto the candidate quickly.

The AAAA, in its manual on political campaign advertising notes: "A candidate for the U.S. Senate is not the same as a new detergent. Most agencies which have accepted political assignments do not look upon their clients in this manner. Usually they are already committed to the candidate and his views. And that commitment is normally accompanied by a belief in the importance of the issues involved."

While agency personnel are in agreement in their denunciation of out-and-out hucksterism in hustling a candidate like a box of soap flakes, even the most pious admit that the type of strategy to a certain extent must be stretched to fit the personality of the individual candidate and illustrate the issues involved. In this interpretation of what constitutes good taste in political advertising—plus the pressures expected from a more competitive-than-ever television ad campaign—observers think some controversy over campaigns can be expected again this year.

VARIED APPROACHES

For one thing, the political advertising experts agree that some political personalities lend themselves much more readily than others to a straightforward campaign in which the client is merely put "on camera, talking straight and simple in a good light."

David McCall, president of LaRoche, McCaffrey and McCall, which handled the successful campaign of John Lindsay for mayor of New York City, says: "It's easier for someone like Fred Papert and me when we have an attractive vivid personality to sell. If you've got a good candidate it is much more interesting to watch the candidate in action than see a slick one-minute commercial."

Gardner, of Papert, Koenig, Lois, agrees. "Whenever possible we simply used Kennedy talking to people. It provided better rapport, understanding and more passion. The agency's major creative input was simply to find people and situations for Kennedy. The commercials were at their best when he was challenged by people who were neutral, or even hostile. Then he got his Irish up and came across more convincingly than when the audience was just there to stare at his curly locks."

Selling the Mass

As the opposite to this straight-forward approach, McCall cited the commercials created by Jack Tinker & Partners for Nelson Rockefeller in his 1966 bid for reelection to the governorship of New

York State—a campaign that was heavily criticized by Rockefeller's opponents both for content and amount of money spent, but which many political observers credit with providing the edge Rockefeller needed. "They had to take a shapeless, amorphous mass and sell it to the voters," said McCall, noting that the agency had a client who wasn't personally too popular with the voters at that time, so rather than concentrating on him, the agency seized upon issues in the form of claimed accomplishments of his administration and illustrated them with slick advertising techniques.

Tinker, re-hired by Rockefeller in his bid for the Republican presidential nomination this summer, used very similar techniques again. It is here, in the advertising illustration of political issues, that disagreement on ethics and taste can most frequently pop up. Tinker partner Gene Case, who headed the copy-writing operation on both Rockefeller drives, has defended the technique: "Personally, I've never been upset by an attempt to take the facts and present them in as enjoyable a way, and as tastefully, as possible. I don't think that's selling the candidate as soap."

Much of Doyle Dane's 1964 Johnson campaign followed a similar tack: "A lot of time was spent mentioning Goldwater statements," recalls Kopelman.

Agency representatives maintain that it is still far too early to broadly predict what general advertising formula will be followed by the candidates—"We have to be ready to move in any direction, depending on the political climate," says Kopelman. "All we know is that we will take whatever direction we consider best to get our man across in the face of the opposition."

Kopelman notes the "variety of strategies available: the candidate talking directly, question-and-answer sessions, voice-overs, focus on issues." Most observers expect a little of everything, and Nixon's Poister sees the agencies trying some entirely new things.

"The old formulas are not going to hold up," says Poister. "With the tremendous use of TV you are going to see after the conventions, if the saturation I expect takes place in September and October—both on the presidential and the local levels—the creative concepts have to be absolutely unique. Otherwise the mental tune-out will be great."

Poister sees few "stand-up political speeches," but some lift-outs from speeches, as well as question-and-answer audience sessions and specific versions of commercials on major issues for various parts of the country. "People in Pittsburgh want to know how national issues will affect them locally."

Get the Specifics

He also sees more "creativity" in issue commercials. "Politicians have a tendency to overgeneralize, but people seem to want specifics, and commercials have a way of homing in on one specific issue at a time," Poister says.

"Can you imagine a political issue presented in something like the style of the Excedrin commercials—I don't mean humorously, but with the ingenuity—a means of presenting something in a completely different light to get people to think about it."

Poister sees the use of "every time segment imaginable day and night. A lot depends on availabilities, although I doubt if there'll be too many half-hours, simply because of the start of a new season, if nothing else."

"The long political speech, presented in paid air time, seems to be a thing of the past," says the Four-A's manual on political campaign advertising. "In national, state and big-city campaigning particularly, the trend has been toward brief professionally executed and professionally placed spots on radio and television."

The standard agency estimate is that about two-thirds of this year's political-broadcast spending will go into spot.

Kennedy's primary advertising, according to Gardner of Papert, Koenig, Lois, was more a matter of careful buying than fancy production or money. "Despite the poor-mouthing that was done, by election eve McCarthy would end up with more programs on the air than we did," said Gardner. "In Oregon, he outspent us. But his money often came in late in each state and there wasn't a chance for much planning.

"The media function in a political campaign is the fastest moving and most important. Media becomes terribly competitive. We knew as much about Senator McCarthy's media planning as he did.

Move Fast and Nag

"The job Bill Murphy (PKL vice president, media and television programs) did in media planning and buying was unequalled. Where in product advertising you aim for a specific group of people over a year's time, in political advertising you try to block all positions and stay competitive on an hour-by-hour basis. You have to plan, move fast and get in there with the stations, nagging and haggling."

Kennedy's agency used surprisingly little material. "Seventy-five percent of our material was on video tape, partly because of the speed and partly because there is the sense of reality about tape that blends well with the sense of straightforward direct personal involvement Kennedy was projecting."

Fifteen percent of the television material used by Kennedy was from film footage shot in late March and early April by Charles Guggenheim Productions, plus a 1964 film biography of Kennedy that Guggenheim had shot for the New York state senatorial race. "Essentially it was the same show updated. We just added new revisions to use in each of the primary states and showed it a number of times prior to the last week of the campaign."

There also was a half-hour documentary on Kennedy shot in Indiana as a volunteer effort by television-turned-movie director John Frankenheimer. It was used as an election-eve show in each state.

For the spots, "despite what people said about Kennedy changing his stand on issues in different states, most of the material stood up through the campaign," said Gardner. "The majority of the material we used in Indiana and Nebraska, we also were using clear through until the last few days in California. We concentrated on four central issues on the air: The problem of the cities—riots, law and order, etc.; Vietnam; decentralization of federal control, and the problem of welfare versus jobs.

"All of the buying was done very deftly. Negotiating was particularly careful on the half-hour show. In the entire campaign, we never had a half-hour show following another political program. We used no 15-minute shows.

"The vast majority of the programs were under-five-minute spots, and they certainly got the vaster portion of the audience. Almost the worst prime-time 20-second spot got more audience than the best half-hour program."

Half-hour shows were used by Kennedy, and will continue to be used by other candidates, according to Gardner, because "the quality of impression in a half-hour is more intense. You can see a lot more of the candidate, expect more detail. People are likely to think about a spot: 'Well, he stated the problem, but he didn't give me the solution, but then I guess he didn't have the time to.'

"On the other hand, from a hard-headed point of view, people who tune in a half-hour are people who probably are going to vote for the candidate anyway."

Mother Love

Says McCall of LaRoche, McCaffrey and McCall: "My God, you almost have to be the candidate's mother to sit through a half-hour political show. You draw only the most devout supporters, and I've never seen a really good half-hour one done."

In the end, says Gardner, the reason agencies continue to buy half-hours, as well as almost every other available form, is "the unspoken feeling that runs through every political campaign that if there's a possibility anything may do you some good, let's do it."

Although the candidates obviously have found agencies a good investment, what is a political campaign like from an agency's viewpoint?

For one thing, there are obvious disadvantages. Some of them are listed by the AAAA in its political campaign advertising manual:

> Political campaigns can be disruptive to normal agency operations, because people are often pulled off their regular assignments to handle a short-term but intensive advertising campaign.
>
> A political campaign might create controversy among agency personnel, causing internal dissension and complaints, and among clients.
>
> An agency may have trouble collecting from political clients. ("Get cash in advance" is the watchword.)

McCall, who says his agency has turned down a number of candidates since its successful Lindsay campaign, recently told a group of New York Young Republicans:

GREAT CREATIVE BURDEN

"No good advertising agency is terribly well served financially by total commitment to a political campaign. Any campaign represents a major disruption of an agency's staff. Inevitably, the senior people in the agency find their time siphoned to an unfair degree into the campaign. The creative load is very great. The time pressures and last-minute buying is totally unlike the ordinary advertising account. Even the biggest political expenditures are small compared to major advertisers' expenditures. And instead of a marriage of year-in, year-out budgets and relationships, the agency finds itself in a torrid affair with a demanding mistress who wants it day and night and then in the second week of November has gone off with another man for four years."

Agency heads usually wave flags about civic responsibility, be-lief in the candidate they've taken on, etc., as justification for handling political accounts. In addition, Gardner of Papert, Koenig, Lois notes: "I think advertising people generally like poli-tics and campaigns. The adrenalin flows very freely and you can put in 100-hour weeks without any trouble. There now seems to be a sub-colony of politically oriented radio and TV production people. We had some people working for us on the Kennedy pri-mary campaign that had worked for us in the '64 senatorial race and I hadn't seen since. I sometimes wonder where they go be-tween elections."

Says Nixon's Poister: "I think a lot of people secretly love it. It's a challenge to work above their own capacities."

It's also pride and excitement: "When my wife or a copywriter or an overloaded traffic man gets disgusted or depressed," says Gardner, "I find myself turning to them with the prod of saying, 'After all, what you are involved in is the election of a President of the United States.' "

The agencies make most of the participation in key jobs on a campaign team voluntary. "We aren't assigning people to the Humphrey account because it would show very quickly if we did," said Doyle, Dane's Kopelman. "The hours and pressures are ex-hausting. They'd give in very quickly if they were just doing it as a job."

No Outsiders Needed

Doyle Dane is the only agency staffing its political account solely from within the agency. "In an agency as creative as ours, we don't have to go outside for people," says Kopelman.

The Nixon account is, and until the assassination the Kennedy account was, staffed on the "anchor and loan" plan established by the AAAA in 1956 under which one agency (Fuller & Smith & Ross for Nixon; Papert, Koenig, Lois for Kennedy) provides the facilities and central organization, and volunteer workers from other agencies are recruited. Depending upon the affluence of the volunteers, they may either work for nothing, get paid on a per-diem basis, or in the standard anchor-and-loan plan, the anchor agency reimburses the loan agency, which continues to carry the loaned volunteer on its regular payroll.

At this point, Poister estimates that the Nixon account has about 35 people assigned to it full time, about 12 of them from outside the agency. There also are four part-time outsiders in media buying and another five in the creative section. As the campaign heats up (if Nixon wins the nomination), the Nixon ad staff will increase. "If things really get tough, we could have 100 people in here before the election is over," says Poister. "Although I hope not that many, because we'd run out of physical space, for one thing. But as the size of the staff goes up, the percentage of outside workers will increase tremendously."

At the height of the Kennedy primary campaign, Papert, Koenig, had about 40 full-time people on the account, half of them from outside the agency, plus another 30 part-timers, including typists, billers and estimators, most of them from outside the agency.

THE NEED FOR CARE

Account manager Gardner said: "Because of the crucial nature of traffic and forwarding, we needed regular agency procedure not to drop the ball." On the other hand, most of the copy writers below chief Fred Papert were from outside the agency, including a couple of major executives of other agencies. "The entire TV production team was staffed from outside except for one producer who served as a link between us and them," said Gardner. "It was really an amalgam."

Interestingly, with all its creative people, in addition to handling Humphrey, internally, Doyle Dane has been counted to have volunteers working outside the agency at various times during the spring for McCarthy, Kennedy and Rockefeller. "Not everyone at Doyle Dane wears a Humphrey button," concedes account supervisor Kopelman. "With over 1,500 employees here not everyone drives a Volkswagen or flies American Airlines all the time either. We're not a bunch of robots."

By staffing their account internally, Doyle Dane has an advantage in that "all the key people don't have to get to know each other," according to Kopelman, but at the same time, there's a disadvantage in that it requires "a tremendous reorganization of company resources. Because of the large amount of money being spent in a short time, the account requires a tremendous number of people. But come Nov. 5, that's the end and we'll have to be ready to redistribute our people, so it requires long thinking on how to do this without disrupting the whole operation for a short-term account."

An anchor-and-loan team obviously is easier to set up and disband after the election, since there are fewer people to redistribute within the agency, but this system provides initial problems in organization.

"There obviously are problems in cohesiveness," says Gardner of Papert, Koenig, "the kinds of problems you have anywhere putting strangers together. Sometimes they don't mesh or can't do the job they were hired for. But there are factors that tend to solve these problems. Things don't always get done in the best way, but they get done."

As long as the agency provides a central, disciplined office, however, notes Nixon's Poister, and as long as a volunteer is good at his professional specialty, "it makes up for the fact that he doesn't know all the minutiae of agency function. If he writes well, a copywriter doesn't really need to know how the agency operates."

THE PRO'S COOLNESS

Agency executives agree that the key to taking on any personnel for a political campaign, volunteer or from within the agency, is their professionalism. "You have to get people who won't break and run," says Poister. "It takes a very strong push to work creatively under fire on a major political campaign. They can't throw up their standards just to get the job done. If you get people that have been in the business any length of time, they know the anguish and travail to expect in a political campaign and they are sort of prepared for it emotionally."

Poister adds that in addition to coolness, flexibility is another prerequisite for the staff of a political campaign. "You might hire a guy with a lot of broadcast experience to be a TV buyer, but the next week he may end up working on billboards because that's where the momentary crush is."

Agency executives list pressure as the greatest single factor distinguishing a political campaign from any other advertising drive. "It makes ordinary business look like heaven," says McCall.

"The whole world is compressed in a political campaign," says Gardner. "Twenty-four hours seems an eon. You do an ad in one day that would take seven working days on a normal account."

Poister likens a political account to the fact that "in 60 days you are doing the equivalent of what Procter & Gamble might spend a year and $50 million or $60 million on introducing a single new brand."

Says Kopelman: "Everyone in the advertising business is used to deadlines, but not every day. Where in a standard account you have peaks and valleys, a political race has steadily increasing pressure: there are 100-yard dashes in a regular account. We're sprinting a mile."

All agency executives talk of 20-hour days, 100-plus hour weeks for everyone working a political account, from the top down.

To keep up with the sprint, political advertisers agree on two general characteristics of a campaign staff: effective communications and flexibility.

"When in Doubt, Act"

"For all the talk about the Kennedy machine, it seemed very much a myth when you were in the middle of it," said Gardner. "Its basic characteristic was chaos. Information just can't be distributed in the normal way. It has to be disseminated almost instantly, sometimes at the expense of organization. It's not very orderly because when things are moving quickly, you get whole areas of duplication, you may have seven people doing the same thing. If you stop and wait for someone to get answers for you, the question may go away. This is an advantage in that it provides an amazing amount of freedom up and down the line for people to act with very little red tape. The basic slogan is: 'When in doubt, act.'

"Of course, with very little time to test and evaluate ideas, there are going to be errors made. And there is a disadvantage in that some frustrations will arise because the politicians are also making intuitive decisions and if you clash over something, there is no chance for mediation or arbitration of the situation."

McCall cites similar problems on a local level with the Lindsay mayoral race. "With no normal lines of communication, you run the risk of having 20 people at the political headquarters calling up 20 people at the agency with the same question." To head this off, his team held meetings every morning and issued daily status reports on every phase of the campaign "even if there wasn't anything to report for the day. It saved us."

To maintain proper communications on the Humphrey campaign, Kopelman has two red "hotline" telephones on his desk, one of them tied directly to Washington. Also "we're in Washington roughly two days a week and they're up here frequently."

Kopelman says: "we have virtually instant communications because you have to be very, very tight in this area, plus you have to be so flexible that one phone call can change the whole ad strategy. The Vice President can come out with a new statement that may make the current ads you're working on ancient history."

In an attempt to impose some organization on the inescapable disarray of a political campaign, Poister has charted the Nixon effort into four basic functions: political policies, which are solely the function of the Nixon advisory staff and are handed down to the agency; information, which is fed in from a number of areas, such things as polls and research surveys, reports on activity of the opposition candidate and observations on important local issues in key states; campaign operations, which are defined as tactics of the daily fight—advertising strategy, media buys; finance and administration.

BLUEPRINT TO ELECTION TIME

Poister also set up a 29-week planning diagram for the campaign, stretching from the beginning of May until the election. It was broken down into the major divisions of client, agency contact, media, research, creative. By the first of July, some sections already had gotten out of phase with progress in others.

"Well," said Poister with resignation, "it's just a basic battle plan, and battles don't always go as planned."

Except for the previously cited requirements of flexibility and coolness under pressure, political advertising seems to require few specialized skills of staff members. There are no unusual tricks, for example, required of a good creative team. Quite the contrary, Gardner found on the Kennedy account. "The best copywriter we had was a girl who was politically naive," he said. "She'd go to the politicians and say: 'Explain this to me so I can understand it.' Then she'd reduce the issue or situation to language which would explain it to the average citizen."

As far as actual duties on a political ad team, Gardner finds "they are identical to any account, except that the timing margin is different and the work load shifts rapidly." One hour the stress is on the creative team, the next on media people, next on traffic. This again calls for flexibility among personnel.

"In a stress situation, a media supervisor sometimes may have to function as an account executive; if we suddenly have a call to do a documentary, we may have to pull in everyone with documentary writing experience and one of us with a documentary background might take off our departmental hat and set down to make a documentary," said Poister. "Everyone must be available so that we can take the best equipped people and throw them into the breach for any situation."

WHERE DIFFERENCES MIGHT BE

Structuring of a political advertising staff is remarkably like that of almost any other ad campaign, except at the very top and bottom. At the top, there generally seems to be one administrative level, above the normal account executive, and it is diffused among top agency people.

Thus on the Kennedy campaign, ultimate responsibility was spread three ways—among Gardner, over the account executive; Papert in charge of the creative team, and Murphy overseeing media planning.

Supervision of the Humphrey drive also is jointly maintained, with Kopelman over the account executive and Bernbach serving as creative director over a team of art directors headed by Ken Duskin and a copywriting team spearheaded by Paul Green and David Hertzbun.

On the Nixon campaign, C. R. Giegerich, creative chief and executive vice president of Fuller & Smith & Ross, splits responsibility with Poister. In addition, the Nixon drive employs two major coordinators, one a liaison for all broadcast communications and the other an administrative assistant under Poister who serves as a liaison with all other departments. These are jobs that Poister says "would not normally be used on an account."

On the other end, traffic and expediting departments are somewhat more heavily staffed on a political campaign because of the often crushing and last-minute loads there. "Communications are horrendous between the agency and all 50 states at once," notes Poister. "You can imagine the tremendous load it puts on the account service people and think of the poor media people on the phones calling 20 stations at one time for last-minute availabilities."

Gardner says: "On a political campaign, basically, the whole agency is a big traffic operation. It's easy for me to decide what I want on the air and where, but it's up to the traffic people to get it there."

He cited California in the primaries, where there were 30 television stations, and Indiana, where there were 25. "Material often wasn't completed until the 22d hour and not delivered until the 23d," he said.

"Most stations waved rules on 48-hour previewing of commercials. In Indiana, a circuit court judge, issued an injunction on the showing of a commercial on a technicality the night before the election. We spent the evening finding a higher judge, who at 10:30 issued a stay of the order. Then we had to send telegrams to the stations to pull a repeat of an 8 o'clock show and put the originally scheduled one back in."

On the whole, while political advertising adds excitement and a certain amount of disorganization to agency routine, executives agree that it cannot be allowed to seriously disrupt regular business. "This is a two-way street," says Doyle Dane's Kopelman. "We can't slight a client we've had for years for a six-month client"—even if he may be the future President of the country. "That's not fair to our stockholders. Serving a political candidate doesn't mean losing money. If you (do) it right, you can have the best of both worlds."

—4—

ADVANCE MEN ENSURE CAMPAIGNERS AGAINST SILENT MIKES, SHORT STORIES

Jonathan Cottin

If politics is the art of the possible, then the goal of political advance work is to make anything possible, and the rewards often are long-lasting.

Examples abound in President Nixon's White House, where his closest advisers formerly were his advance men. They include John D. Ehrlichman, assistant to the President for domestic affairs; H. R. Haldeman, assistant to the President; and Dwight L. Chapin, Mr. Nixon's deputy assistant.

The rapid rise in their political fortunes reflects, in part, Mr. Nixon's high regard for good advance work.

In the Democratic Party, those who would have Mr. Nixon's job also have come to appreciate a good advance. And, in the last few weeks before the party's nominating convention in Miami Beach, Presidential candidates pressed their scheduling and advancing staffs to make each public appearance a rousing success. The staffs were expected to deliver enthusiastic crowds and large contingents of reporters and cameramen to relay the proceedings to the voters.

Seasoned advance staffers say the political sciences of scheduling and advancing are oriented primarily toward avoiding disaster.

To an advance man, disaster can come in many forms: failure

to arrange a bus for the traveling press; a loudspeaker system that goes dead just as the candidate launches into his most important address of the campaign; a small crowd; a late arrival because the trip was not accurately timed beforehand.

To the scheduler, who decides what stops his candidate will make, disaster is all of those and more: an appearance in a town with no media outlets or in a city where the population is overwhelmingly enrolled in the opposition party—virtually guaranteeing a small turnout.

To avoid such pitfalls, Sen. Hubert H. Humphrey, D-Minn., has directed his schedulers to land him in areas with many media outlets.

Sen. George S. McGovern, D-S.D., battling Humphrey for the Democratic nomination, has been scheduled into areas where there are both plenty of media *and* plenty of Democrats.

HUMPHREY

Humphrey's schedule is dictated by the location of media outlets and the existence of events, planned in advance, that often have nothing to do with him. At the same time, his handlers make efforts to keep him clear of early-morning appearances. They concede that he is not at his best then and they conserve his energy for campaigning well into the evening.

National Strategy

Ursula R. Culver, Humphrey's director of scheduling, said Humphrey's daily schedule is worked out by Jack L. Chestnut, the national campaign director; John M. Morrison, deputy director; Humphrey; and herself.

The principal aim of the schedule, she said, is to have "one good visual, every day, at 10 or 11 in the morning, then meet with party workers, have time to rest in the afternoon and pop in one more visual at 3 p.m."

A "visual," in political parlance, is an event with news value starring the candidate which the scheduler hopes will be filmed by television cameramen and broadcast later in the day. "The way the news goes, you have to have a platform every day and be able to discuss an issue question," said Mrs. Culver.

Decisions. Humphrey's appearances are the result of negotiations among his local supporters, a national advance man, the state organization and the national staff.

Generally, a draft schedule is developed by state organizations and national staff men, acting on suggestions from local Humphrey backers.

"They (national staff advance men) have to have enough judgment to call me and tell me if the schedule drafted is bad or great," said Mrs. Culver.

Her 27 advance men are instructed to look for variety in the events they select. They know that media outlets are the prime consideration. For example, they have been told that film crews will not bother to show the candidate barnstorming shopping centers all day long. "Even if he sees 1,000 people in those shopping centers, television will not show him walking through them, and thousands more won't see it either," said Mrs. Culver.

People. Nevertheless, Mrs. Culver is careful to schedule frequent stops which may not offer Humphrey good "visuals" but do keep the candidate in touch with the voters.

"If we put him in front of cameras all day, he wouldn't think he had campaigned. My candidate cannot work that way. He needs to be with flesh and blood. He's got to have people, he thrives on people," she said.

Problem. Mrs. Culver's biggest difficulty in scheduling Humphrey has to do with the nature of his job. As a Senator, he is on call for votes on the floor or important committee meetings.

At any time, he may be forced to leave the campaign trail for Washington.

"Sudden changes are our biggest trouble," she said. For this reason, she said, all the elaborate planning for a visit can collapse "like a set of dominoes. You don't have a firm schedule until he arrives."

Arbiter. Mrs. Culver's job runs the gamut—from giving the order to charter a jet to telling the local Humphrey organization that a visit has to be canceled. "I give the noes," she said.

By assuming this responsibility, she saves her advance men from counter-productive battles with local supporters when an event is rejected. "When it gets a little bit hairy between the local host and an advance man, I get involved. Let them say Washington did it," she said.

Advancing

Once the Humphrey schedule has been set, advance men are assigned to ensure that everything occurs according to plan and on time.

Assignment. An advance man usually is sent to a city three or four days before the candidate's arrival.

After checking with local Humphrey supporters and Democratic Party officials, whose names he has been given by national headquarters, the advance man goes to work.

If the candidate is to stay overnight in the city, he checks out the Senator's hotel suite and ensures that there is privacy.

He examines the route to and from a planned event, as well as the site picked for an appearance, to determine what facilities are needed and whether they are available. He will take the route to an event at the same time of day the event is to occur to get traveling time.

A day or two before the candidate's arrival, Secret Service advance men, who coordinate all security arrangements with local police and handle all motorcades, arrive in the city and review the planned visit with the Humphrey advancer.

Insurance. Mrs. Culver tells her advance men to have every detail under their control. This means advance men must take out insurance that nothing can go wrong. In the advance business, insurance means having "backup systems" all along the way—an extra car if one breaks down, a second public address system if the first one does not arrive or is inoperative, a band in reserve if the first one fails to show.

"If there are supposed to be 300 ministers at a meeting, the advance person must make certain the invitations went out," said Mrs. Culver. "He has to meet with all of the people doing the inviting; he contacts people responsible for each detail all the way down the schedule; he checks the speaker system and if it is not what is needed, he must get one that suits."

The advance man also must know enough to ensure that there is a supply of salted crackers, cheddar cheese and root beer available for Humphrey in his hotel suite.

Manual

A brand-new Humphrey advance man, on his first assignment in the field, does not arrive at his destination completely in the dark about what he must do. All Humphrey advancers, who draw $30 a day from which they must pay living expenses, carry a bible of sorts—Mrs. Culver's advance manual, a green plastic-covered handbook.

The manual stresses the importance of keeping clear of political debate; the advancing function is to set up the event properly—nothing more. "Do not participate in partisan political discussion; do not get involved in pro and con conversations about the other candidate," is the Culver warning.

A "visitation sheet" must be worked up by the advance man, the manual says. It must cover the background of the area, the local political situation, the identity of local political and civic leaders, Humphrey's friends, delegate-candidates pledged to him and information on Humphrey's last visit to the area.

Advance men are advised to negotiate for good prices at hotels. Ideal meal and room rates for groups are listed in the booklet.

Since Mrs. Culver believes advance men are often the best-informed national staff members when it comes to grass-roots opinion, she has delegated to them responsibility for offering the candidate advice. "One of the greatest sins in advancing is not to give advice," she said in an interview.

In her book, she wrote: "Try to obtain ideas on local color that can be used in the Senator's talk."

Since an advance man cannot possibly build a crowd, prepare all the signs, finance the event and do all the other necessary preparation all by himself, the manual offers a solution:

"You will need lots of help . . . establish committees for every job you can think of . . . press, advance, office manager, band, entertainment, transportation, arrangements, platform, sound, finance, candidate girls, songs, volunteers, phone."

The candidate's arrival at an airport often begins with a press conference. So that he can be heard, the candidate must have relative silence. Thus, the manual advises, "consider regular airport traffic, airplane noise," when picking a press-conference location.

As to the crowd itself, Mrs. Culver's rule is: "It's always better to fill a small hall than to half-fill a large hall." Her directive on motorcades is to stage them "when people are automatically on the streets," such as during the lunch hour.

Mrs. Culver's book also urges her charges to be skeptical of what local political leaders tell them. "Never fully rely on what a big local political power states that he might do in getting a crowd out. It is possible he might have another objective other than getting a crowd for the Senator."

In building a crowd, Mrs. Culver counsels her men to touch base with groups that in the past have served Humphrey, including labor, politicians from city organizations, "patronage holders and senior citizens."

Qualities

To Mrs. Culver, there is more to advancing than being a good detail man, ready with the comb, making sure that the candidate has speech in hand as he approaches the rostrum, and that there is a glass of water at the lectern.

"Obviously, an advance man must be able to work 24 hours a day, distributing handbills when he's free," she said.

"His behavior should be such that a candidate can be relaxed with him. He should be discreet, honest and loyal. At an event, he should be there, but don't hang on to the man," she said in an interview.

California Team

Humphrey's schedule-and-advance strategy was put to its most important test in California, where 271 delegates to the convention are the prize.

The man most acutely aware of how much California means to Humphrey is Harvey Englander, the Senator's 21-year-old scheduler in the state.

"My stomach hurts every time I turn on the radio and hear Humphrey say California is *the* state," Englander said during an interview in Los Angeles.

Unlike the arrangement in most other states, Humphrey's California campaign is being run from Los Angeles, not Washington. Schedule-and-advance decisions are made by Joseph R. Cerrell, the state campaign director, and Eugene L. Wyman, Humphrey's principal fund raiser.

"The schedule is very important to me, so I must have total control of it," said Cerrell.

Englander's California schedule is built around media events. Geographically, this means Humphrey spends a large part of his time in the Los Angeles area. "Anyone who does scheduling knows that 54 per cent of the media outlets are in the Los Angeles area," Englander said.

The first week of Humphrey's California campaign reflected this concern for media. In the seven days between May 18 and May 25, he spent at least part of six days in Los Angeles.

"He (Humphrey) calls me Harvey Ballbreaker," Englander said.

Events. Englander heeds the Culver dictum to seek a good location as backdrop for a message of importance.

"I want to give him a forum to say something about things of vital concern to Californians," he said. "My idea of a beautiful visual is to go to a plant that is closed, leaving 20,000 out of work, and have him stand at that plant gate and talk about the unemployment problem."

(Englander came close to that ideal when he booked Humphrey into the Lockheed Aircraft Corp. plant in Los Angeles, where the candidate made much of his vote in favor of the Lockheed loan, which McGovern opposed.)

Englander said that "rallies are tough to build." As a result, he directs Humphrey to pre-existing events, where a crowd is guaranteed for a purpose that has nothing to do with the Humphrey campaign. On May 24, for example, Englander sent Humphrey to a meeting of the California Parole and Probation Association. Englander asked association officials if Humphrey could address the group and they said yes.

Englander's fear of failing to build a crowd has moved him to avoid even using the word "rally." When Humphrey goes before a crowd gathered only to hear him, Englander usually calls such appearances "receptions."

He explained: "If the mass media writes that we call it a reception, and if 300 are there, it doesn't sound bad."

"Receptions," he added, "are more homey types of things."

Headquarters

One such "reception," which had all the trappings of a full-scale rally, was held May 18, when Humphrey opened his state headquarters on Wilshire Boulevard in Los Angeles. (The event was billed as "a happening" on leaflets promoting the event.)

Phinney. In charge of the event was Michael Phinney, who specializes in media advancing.

A former editorial writer for the Madison, Wis., *Capital Times,* Phinney, after consultation with Englander and Humphrey's Washington-based speechwriters, passed the word to Los Angeles media outlets that the candidate would open his headquarters and California campaign with a major speech.

In arranging this event, Phinney:

- supervised the mailing of 2,000 invitations to organization Democrats;
- arranged for volunteers to deliver sandwiches to the headquarters before the ceremonies, occurring during the lunch hour;
- arranged for a "holding room" and bathroom to which the Senator could go before making his appearance (The room was located at radio station KIIS, lodged above Humphrey headquarters. Humphrey could have reached it through a rear entry, going unseen by the crowd in front of headquarters.);
- arranged for the appearance of Hawaiian musicians, as well as a record player and loudspeaker system that could be heard more than a block from headquarters;
- arranged for installation of platforms for both the candidate and television crews;
- persuaded some local teachers to bring their classes on a field trip to the headquarters opening.

Delivering. Although Humphrey was half an hour late, the event went as programmed. The crowd seemed content to listen to the Hawaiians, and a recording of "The Hubert Humphrey March," as well as a country-western singer who had written a laudatory song about the candidate, using the tune from a soft-drink jingle.

The crowd inside the steamy headquarters was packed closely together. More people, unable to get in, craned for a look through the windows. Humphrey delivered on Phinney's promise of a major address, challenging McGovern to a series of television debates.

Coverage. Phinney's advance work paid off on the media that night and the next day. Television news broadcasts of the event showed films of the crowded headquarters, while *The Los Angeles Times* referred to "a crowd in his (Humphrey's) jammed headquarters."

While Humphrey's schedule of appearances is decided almost exclusively by media outlets, McGovern's national strategy is aimed at two targets: media *and* Democrats.

For this reason, McGovern rarely was seen at pre-existing events. Instead, he sought to broaden his support among Democrats by staging events built around his candidacy.

Base

The architect and administrator of the McGovern travel strategy is Stephen Robbins, the campaign's director of scheduling.

Robbins said he believes that if McGovern is to broaden his base, he must campaign among groups and in areas where he is not strong. Translating this theory into practice, Robbins generally avoids stops on college campuses, where McGovern already has support, preferring to send the candidate into minority and blue-collar areas, where he is less well-known.

The plan, said one McGovern aide who declined to be identified, is to bring McGovern in contact with potential supporters not generally thought to be part of his existing constituency. The aide said of blue-collar and minority groups: "McGovern thinks he can say things to these people that have validity to them."

In planning McGovern's appearances, Robbins said, he concentrates on "media and Democrats." This dual concern has governed schedule decisions from the earliest days of McGovern's campaign.

Robbins explained McGovern's movements focusing on media and Democrats by reciting the history of the candidate's appearances in several primary states:

"In Massachusetts, he started every day in Boston; in Ohio, he started every day in Cleveland; in Nebraska, every day began in Omaha; in Michigan, every day began in Detroit; in Oregon, each day started in Portland. From every one of these big media centers, after a morning event, he would go elsewhere."

Robbins plots McGovern's travels on a map of each state in which the candidate is to campaign. He marks symbols for media outlets and Democratic registration. He studies the voting history of the state, in particular the turnout for Humphrey when he ran for President in 1968 and for former President Johnson in 1964.

"What you're trying to look at is long-range shifts," said Robbins, during an interview in Detroit.

Appearances

Once the area that McGovern will visit is chosen, negotiation over the kind of events he will attend begins.

"We don't go to other people's events," said Robbins. "Hubert is constantly invading previously existing events. When you do that, you're at the mercy of the people who invited you."

A McGovern event is argued out at five different levels of the McGovern organization. Local McGovern supporters suggest options to McGovern advance staffers, who evaluate the proposals and discuss them with McGovern field schedulers, who are Robbins' state liaison men. Robbins established a team of field schedulers "to transmit whatever theory we have more effectively. It also reduces the hostility you usually have."

Robbins generally makes all final decisions on McGovern campaign stops, but McGovern is far from passive in the decision-making process. "George McGovern wants to know what he's doing and why," said a staff aide who asked not to be quoted by name.

In blocking out events, the McGovern field scheduler has been instructed "to play not so much to strength as to weakness."

The organizational arrangement gives McGovern advance staff members considerable leeway in their method of operation.

Frederick C. Boucher, who advanced McGovern's travels in southern Oregon, said he believes that his freedom allows a relaxed relationship to develop between the advance staff and local McGovern organizations.

"The key to advance work is to delegate all the responsibility to local people. It's their event. I'm just there to ensure the proper arrangements are made," he said.

Boucher said that while advancing is important—if only to avoid a catastrophic empty hall—"the key to the McGovern campaign is the canvass."

"The event is just superimposed on top of the canvass," Boucher said. After McGovern workers have gone house-to-house, seeking support for the candidate, "McGovern appears and the voters can see that he stands for what the canvassers said he stood for," Boucher said.

Boucher worked to set up events for McGovern built around working people. "He's very effective in showing the working people that he is concerned," he said.

Local Problems

Occasionally, the field scheduler—Robbins' first line of defense— has found himself in the midst of controversy that has threatened to engulf McGovern in divisive local political issues.

Schools. That happened in Portland, Ore., where the public schools, out of money, were forced to close for the year on May 12, a month ahead of schedule.

James Keller, McGovern's Oregon field scheduler, said he thought that it would be a "groovy event" if McGovern toured an empty school in Portland, pushing for federal funding of education. The idea had initial support from Washington.

Less excited about it were many McGovern supporters in Portland, including Julie Williamson, McGovern's Portland coordinator. Mrs. Williamson, with two of her own children idled by the school closing, said she doubted the wisdom of the McGovern appearance in an empty school.

Complicating the matter was the inclusion on the May 23 primary ballot of a referendum question that would raise the property-tax rate $2.27 per $1,000 to support the Portland schools.

Mrs. Williamson, who also was leader of a group of Portland citizens pushing for approval of the tax increase, said in an interview that she was afraid that McGovern, by stressing his own programs for more equitable taxation, "will kill the increase." The effect of its defeat would be to place in jeopardy the accreditation of the city school system, she said.

While she said that she agreed with McGovern on his tax program, in Portland "the property tax is all we have."

"Some people would be very glad to find an excuse to turn down the tax increase, and tell you George McGovern told them to," Mrs. Williamson said.

"A lot of people will be angry at McGovern. They'll be mad at me, too," she said.

Her arguments were persuasive. The empty-school event never was held.

While McGovern was winning 50 per cent of Oregon's vote, Portland citizens turned down the tax increase, 78,695 to 66,486, in the May 23 primary.

Kerry.   Although Robbins and others stress the importance of doing homework on a state before arrival, sometimes there are slip-ups.

John F. Kerry, the Vietnam veteran who gained prominence arguing against the war at antiwar rallies, toured Oregon, speaking for McGovern, but did little to help the candidate in Portland.

Kerry went before an audience and mispronounced the state's name. The next day, *The Oregon Journal* reported on the Kerry error, spelling out the way he had pronounced the word—"Ory-gone." Oregonians are quite sensitive about the state's name and want it said correctly.

Had Kerry read the McGovern staff briefing paper on Oregon, a six-page examination of its geography, society and politics, he would have avoided such a goof. At the very top of the memo, in parentheses, appears this advisory: "That's Ory-gun, not Ory-gone."

Coos Bay

Sometimes, McGovern advance staffers cause problems for themselves by inadvertently slighting local organizers, although they are advised to stay in touch with local supporters.

In Coos Bay, Ore., May 15, for instance, Boucher, who was there to advance a McGovern rally in neighboring North Bend, drew a hostile reception from a local McGovern press coordinator as he arrived at local headquarters.

Boucher, who had been in the area a few days earlier in connection with the event, had surveyed the proposed site and spoken to some local people. The word got back to Thomas Lasewell, the local press man.

The red-bearded Lasewell, wearing a T-shirt, boots and overalls, confronted the slightly built advance man, who was dressed in slacks and sport coat.

"The problem I have with you, Rick, is that you never made contact with us," said Lasewell.

Boucher told him he had tried to call, but was unable to reach him.

His temper rising, Lasewell began to walk away, then turned on Boucher again, complaining that the advance man was trying to limit the rally to union members only. "What kind of elitist campaign is this?" he demanded.

Boucher began to explain that McGovern was trying to build up his support among union members, then dropped the subject, appealing instead for unity. "There's no reason for this to get personal," he said. "Let's work together on this for McGovern."

Later in the day, the two resolved their differences.

Moreover, Lasewell won his point. The McGovern rally was opened to non-union as well as to union members of the lumbering and shipping community. The crowd filled the hall and overflowed outside, where loudspeakers had been set up.

Qualities

Robbins, who has dismissed advance staffers who failed to live up to his expectations, has placed only three of his 18 national advance people on salary. The rest receive only a rental car and money for gasoline, as a general rule.

An ideal advance person, he said, has "intelligence and bargaining ability. If you can't persuade, you're not a politician."

In addition, advancers must "pay attention to detail and hard work."

Working on a low budget, the McGovern advancer should be able to locate sleeping accommodations at the homes of local supporters. Robbins said. This means staff members must have a tolerance for sleeping on floors, and have "an ability to scrounge."

ASSESSMENT

Political scheduling and advancing provide those who practice the two sciences with ample frustration when an event they have worked hard on is called off. But it also offers some elation when an appearance turns out to be a success.

But essentially, advancers and schedulers agree, their work is more negative than positive: they must strive constantly to stave off disaster.

"When the candidate comes into a room with 350 chairs and 35 people in them, and the cameras pan over that, it can kill you," said Englander, Humphrey's California scheduler.

"Advancing is trying to avoid catastrophe and create the impression of big support," said Fairborz S. Fatemi, who has been an advance man for the late President Kennedy and his brother, the late Sen. (1965–68) Robert F. Kennedy, D-N.Y.

"Good advancing can mean the difference between victory and defeat in a close race."

If the job is so risky, fraught with opportunities for blunder, why are so many eager to try it?

Mrs. Culver thinks she knows, and Robbins agrees.

"When they actually see an event that they set up working well, they feel that applause is for them, too," she said. "They really feel part of it. The results are right there in front of them."

BUILDING CROWDS FOR WALLACE

Until he was wounded seriously May 15 during a rally in Laurel, Md., Gov. George C. Wallace, D-Ala., had made some of his rivals for the Democratic Presidential nomination envious of his crowd-pulling ability.

What is not generally known is that Wallace campaign rallies were carefully planned in advance, and the crowds built with systematic thoroughness by staff men taking orders from national headquarters in Montgomery, Ala.

The Wallace political style relied almost exclusively on rallies, plus press conferences along the way to build voter support.

John P. DeCarlo, Wallace's national coordinator, said Wallace did not need to make appearances at plant gates or at other spots where crowds already existed. He said the voters thought enough of Wallace to go where he was. "McGovern and Humphrey can't get big crowds," he said, referring to Sens. George S. McGovern, D-S.D., and Hubert H. Humphrey, D-Minn., his rivals for the nomination.

"Hell, why shouldn't we have them come to him?" DeCarlo asked.

Schedule

Wallace's daily campaign schedule was held flexible until the very last moment. This served to protect him against the possibility of an appearance before a small audience. He would not go to a rally until reports from staff men in the field indicated the turnout would be acceptably large.

Dorothy House, the Montgomery-based national scheduler, supervised eight salaried Wallace advance men.

Mrs. House assigned the staff representatives to major cities in states where primary elections were being held within two or three weeks.

Their assignment was to survey the chances for a successful rally operation. Their two basic tools were a telephone and a hotel meeting room.

Advance Operation

Typical of the preparation that went into organizing a Wallace appearance was the advance work in Oregon May 9-13.

Mrs. House detailed a team of five advance men to the five major metropolitan areas in Oregon—Medford, Corvallis, Eugene, Salem and Portland.

Each advance man was assigned to set up an evening organization meeting in his city, with the first commencing in the southernmost city May 9 and the last held in Portland, near the Washington state border, May 13.

Each advance man was given a list of names of residents in the area he would visit. The names had been drawn from computer tapes listing Wallace supporters from the 1968 campaign.

In each city, Wallace staff representatives called 50 to 75 persons and invited them to an organizational meeting. They also were asked to bring along other Wallace backers.

The advance men told the Wallace supporters that the meeting was for the purpose of building a local organization to further the Governor's candidacy, opening a headquarters and setting up a rally.

Wallace aides also placed advertisements in local newspapers announcing the session.

Meeting

At each meeting, the speaker was DeCarlo, the national coordinator.

A lawyer, he was on leave from his job as deputy district attorney of Birmingham, Ala. DeCarlo was the principal strategist in Wallace's successful effort to get on the ballot as the American Independent Party candidate for President in all 50 states in 1968.

At the Portland session, held in a crowded hotel room May 13, he spoke briefly about the Wallace campaign, stressing the Governor's opposition to busing and high taxes. Aware that a property-tax increase was on the Portland May 23 ballot, he asked:

"You folks having a problem here with taxes?"

DeCarlo fielded a number of questions, most of them friendly, and stood silently while several Wallace supporters rose to make statements against the Portland newspapers and the federal government.

He then asked an advance man, Tony Santoro, to distribute questionnaires to the audience of about 75 persons. The questionnaires asked the name, address and phone number of the supporter, as well as the time each could devote to running a headquarters or phoning people to invite them to a Wallace rally.

Nucleus

It was from a nucleus such as the Portland group that crowds were built for Wallace rallies.

After the session, DeCarlo left town but the advance man remained to coordinate the volunteer drive for rally-goers, locate a headquarters and organize the rally.

DeCarlo, impressed with the turnout at the organizational meeting, said he would recommend that the Governor come into the state; he was satisfied that sizable crowds could be raised.

Although Wallace was unable to travel to Oregon, DeCarlo's intuition that Wallace was popular there proved correct. With no personal campaigning, the Alabama Governor nevertheless placed second in the May 23 primary, with 20 per cent of the Democratic vote, behind McGovern, who picked up 50 per cent of the vote.

FOURTEEN HOURS OF UNCERTAINTY

Los Angeles

The day of May 17 began for Barbara H. Houston much as it would end 14 hours later—in uncertainty; it is a perpetual hazard of her profession.

Miss Houston, on the national advance staff for Sen. George S. McGovern, D-S.D., had been told by William Holzman, McGovern's southern California field scheduler, that she would be meeting a shopping center manager at about 11 a.m. The session would concern logistical arrangements for a McGovern rally at Lakewood Center, a large shopping mall in Long Beach.

As the time approached for her to leave the Los Angeles head-quarters for the drive south, the manager called and rescheduled the meeting for afternoon.

Miss Houston was not idle in the interim. She called McGovern's Long Beach headquarters, asking for progress reports on planning for the rally, tentatively scheduled for May 20.

Among those she spoke to on the telephone that morning was Stephen Robbins, McGovern's director of scheduling. It was Robbins who told her that Mrs. Coretta Scott King, widow of Martin Luther King, was going to endorse McGovern the following day, May 18, in Los Angeles. The endorsement would help to boost McGovern's image in the U.S. black community, where Sen. Hubert H. Humphrey, D-Minn., had been so strong. Robbins told Miss Houston that she was to advance the endorsement meeting and press conference. He said he expected it to be an event that ran smoothly from start to finish.

By 1 p.m., when it was time to leave for Long Beach, Holzman had not supplied any details about the King advance. He was her immediate supervisor and the only thing he had told her to do was work on the Long Beach shopping rally.

Long Beach

On her arrival at the Long Beach mall, she met Jack R. Newman, a Los Angeles lawyer who was doing some volunteer advance work. Together, they toured the mall, looking for a rally site.

After an hour of examining the area, she selected a spot in front of a department store. "I like the flat wall behind him so you can put a sign up," she told Newman. He nodded.

Miss Houston, writing notes to herself in a small tablet, turned to Newman and asked: "Do you have a holding room for him?"

"A holding room?" Newman asked.

She explained that the candidate needed a room in which to freshen up and confer with aides before a public appearance.

Newman said one of the stores nearby might cooperate, since the shopping center manager, Samuel G. Lampel, had expressed willingness to assist the McGovern staff on the rally.

Miss Houston excused herself while Newman and Lampel discussed the event in his office. She called her headquarters from another phone. Holzman had a new assignment for her:

Meet two Secret Service agents at the Second Baptist Church in Watts, where arrangements were being made for Mrs. King's meeting with McGovern the next morning.

Watts

The agents were awaiting her at the church, a huge stucco edifice in a low-income area.

They walked through the building, picking a holding room for the Senator.

They passed through a classroom and a small chapel. In front of the small sanctuary was a gold cross. The white walls of the room shimmered red, green and orange in the late afternoon sun, filtered by stained-glass windows. She told the agents the sanctuary would be ideal for the meeting and press conference.

In the main atrium, Miss Houston frowned. The pews made a 180-degree arc around the podium.

An agent said: "We'll need 15 men to secure this place. It'll hold 2,000 people."

"It's too big," said Miss Houston. "I don't know if we can fill it."

"It's what Mrs. King wants," said the agent.

Miss Houston and the two agents discussed the problem for some time, then decided to call an aide to Mrs. King and ask him to persuade Mrs. King to hold the event in the sanctuary. The call was made, and Mrs. King agreed on the smaller room.

As the agents left the church, Miss Houston said: "It's a good thing I got here, or we would have been in a 2,000-person room."

Airport

Miss Houston again called headquarters to report on her progress. This time, she was told to proceed to Los Angeles International Airport, where McGovern would arrive the next morning, to help arrange for a press conference there.

Miss Houston arrived at the airport as darkness fell and located Arthur T. Farley, a local advance man for McGovern.

By 10 p.m., an American Airlines official had told her and Farley that McGovern could use a public area above a waiting room for the press session, and said he would try to arrange for some chairs and a desk for the Democratic candidate.

Miss Houston, exhausted, headed back to the headquarters office to check on arrangements for the Long Beach rally—her one and only assignment when she had left early in the afternoon.

Epilogue

Of the three events Miss Houston advanced, only the King endorsement survived.

The morning press conference was canceled and the Long Beach rally was called off, replaced by a trip to Phoenix where McGovern obtained the support of Cesar Chavez, the Chicano farmworkers' leader.

—5—

THE ROLE OF POLITICAL PARTIES
IN THE NEW CAMPAIGNING

Robert Agranoff

The advent of new styles and techniques of campaigning has definitely diminished the role of the American political party organization in the campaign. As candidates have turned to new means
of mobilizing their electorates, the party organization, with its
tradition of getting out the partisan vote on a face-to-face basis,
has become less important. Constituencies are larger, electorates
are more fluid, candidates are more independent of the party organization, and the new technology appears to be beyond the reach
of party. As more and more candidates employ the new style of
campaigning, they accelerate the pace with which the role of party
in the campaign declines. As Frank Sorauf observes, the political
party has failed to preempt the campaign skills and services of
modern campaigning.[1] Yet, one might suspect that there is a party
role in the new campaigning, to replace the status lost to technology.

    If political party organizations do have a role to play in the
new era, they have been slow to develop it, and many party organizations seem to act as if the new campaigning does not even

The information for this paper was gathered while I was on leave of absence from
Northern Illinois University, directing the Minnesota Democratic-Farmer-Labor (Demo-
cratic) Party's 1968 legislative program. I wish to thank Professors Donald E. Fouts and
Robert E. Crew, Jr., for their many helpful comments.

A different version of this paper was presented at the Conference on Strategies in The
New Politics, College Park, Maryland, December 4-6, 1970. It was published in short-
ened form in Ray E. Hiebert et al., *The Political Image Merchants: Strategies in the New
Politics* (Washington, D.C.: Acropolis Books, 1971).

exist. Few of these political organizations offer much assistance to candidates who need modern management, reliable information and media assistance. And when they do, it is often difficult for the candidate to deal effectively with it. More importantly, political party organizations have been slow to offer the new campaigning to those candidates who need party assistance most—the non-incumbent, the financially disadvantaged, and those running in small constituencies.

Party organization still performs some of its traditional functions, especially where party remains strong and well organized. Activities such as registration, voter identification, and get-out-the-vote, where performed, can have an effect on the margin of victory. Indeed, studies of the campaign process seem to indicate that this is exactly where the party impact lies.[2] The fact remains, however, that the contemporary party's role in the campaign is being overshadowed by the new techniques and the experts who apply them.

Thus, the challenge of a new role is there for American party organizations. There are those who charge that the party structure is no longer capable of dealing with the major issues. They claim that the impact of party independents like Eugene McCarthy, John Lindsay, and Paul McCloskey is possible because political parties have ducked the major problems of society. These critics charge that parties will not survive if they remain oriented to patronage and service while important matters such as the Indo-China war, the problems of the cities, and the poor are swept under the rug. This question of issues is paralleled by a less visible challenge—one of technique. How can the political party deal with the central questions of the new campaigning and find a role for itself, be in tune with a new technology and help the disadvantaged?

The purpose of this chapter is to highlight some of the dimensions of contemporary party involvement in the new campaigning, and to suggest how parties might adopt a role in modern campaigning—with emphasis on the case of the Minnesota DFL's 1968 legislative campaign, in which a state party attempted to bring new campaign-related services to candidates in the small constituencies. Although party control has traditionally been local,[3] this analysis focuses on organizations above the constituency level, because parties at the local level are not now constituted to assume a meaningful role in the new campaigning.

PARTY SERVICES AND THE NEW POLITICS

Contemporary party involvement in the new campaigning can best be described as evolutionary and peripheral. In most cases, central organizations are involved only in fragments of management, information and media. The services they offer generally have very little to do with the day-to-day management of the campaign or with the making of key campaign decisions. Basically, parties have reacted to specific service requests made by candidates rather than assessing their role as an organization in a new era. In only a few cases has a central party organization undertaken a full-scale campaign service operation. As a result, one finds a mixed pattern of new politics involvement, ranging from obliviousness to the whole process to rather complete support.

The national committees of the two major parties have begun to move in the direction of back-up services. They both have developed computerized systems for the basic campaign housekeeping functions. They have the capability to store and handle address files, canvass information, and financial data (see Chartrand article). In addition, the committees provide backup media services for candidates. The Democratic National Committee has an in-house radio service, which offers the candidate taping facilities and foreign language translation services for ethnic constituencies. The Republican National Committee has developed an allocation system whereby candidates can develop their own radio and television plans. Both committees have television consultants, who are supposed to be available in Washington, D.C., to answer questions. The problem with these media and information services is that they are inaccessible to those who need them most. They operate primarily for Congressmen and Senators who are in Washington, D.C. and generally have the means to acquire these services on their own. Moreover, as incumbents, they have assistance on Capitol Hill. Increasing numbers of Congressional staff members are among the new experts of politics as they necessarily deal with the problems of reelection. Both Houses appear to provide much more elaborate and accessible multi-media services on a cost basis than either national party headquarters.

The two national committees have made moves to extend their reach beyond Washington. They have prepared campaign manuals in tune with the new politics which contain information on modern campaign management, polls, planning and writing for the media, and performing aggregate electoral data analysis.[4] The Republican National Committee, recognizing the differences in state election laws and campaign practices, has produced 37 different manuals for the 50 states, and it has developed a computerized precinct priority system in which the local campaigner can fill in the relevant variables.[5] The Democratic National Committee has held closed-circuit television seminars during recent campaigns on the techniques of campaigning. Both committees have embarked on a program of developing data banks, containing previous poll and election data, which are available to candidates. Finally, both committees serve as clearinghouses for political consultants by providing candidates with lists of managers, pollsters and media men who work exclusively for candidates of their party.

The problem with all of this assistance is that it is not very meaningful to the candidate who wants access to the new politics but has difficulty acquiring it. The parties make no attempt to evaluate the effectiveness of one consultant's methods vis-a-vis another's. With only a list of consultants' names the buyer cannot distinguish between the charlatan (of which there are many) and the true expert. Those best able to afford the consultant are in a better position to compare and judge quality because they are sought after by the consultants themselves. The data banks contain the most readily available and least useful information for planning a campaign. Old polls tell the candidate little about current issues and nothing about candidate images. The election data are on the county and congressional district level, which are so grossly overaggregated that they are subject to many limitations and pitfalls. Most important of all, the candidates who need the greatest assistance are seldom able to deal with technical manuals, priority systems, and media plans and do not enjoy the services of experts who can expedite campaign strategies. If they are to adopt the new techniques they need relatively frequent consultation with those who know how.

One state organization which has met this challenge is the Minnesota Republican State Central Committee. The state party organization regularly employs the services of political consultants to study its operations, test the effectiveness of campaign techniques, and train its staff in the modes of modern campaigning. All GOP candidates are given access to these management consultants. In addition, the party centrally contracts with a national polling firm, which conducts a series of polls for all state-wide and Congressional candidates. The state party has a research operation, which supplies issue, roll-call, and voting data for candidates at all levels. The organization retains an advertising agency, which handles the media section of the campaigns for all major candidates. Finally, the party is involved in central fund-raising and allocation—direct grants of funds to candidates from U.S. Senator to the state legislators.

The British model, in comparison, is much more party-centered than the American. Research and advertising services and the experts who develop them are a part of the party structure. The major party national organizations hire experts in advertising, market research and media production and make them part of the party bureaucracy. These new party bureaucrats provide both party and candidate consulting services.[6] The only exception to this rule appears to be private polling; a growing number of American and British pollsters are operating independently for specific candidates.

It is difficult to determine whether American parties will follow the British system of developing a bureaucracy that possesses the skills to wage a modern campaign, or follow a pattern similar to the Minnesota GOP and make the services of experts available. The role of parties will be worked out as more central party organizations embark on programs of management, information, and media. The study that follows represents a single case of a party's extensive role in providing the new campaigning to state legislative candidates who do not ordinarily enjoy it. The Minnesota state DFL had been in the legislative campaign management field for six elections, but 1968 represented the first attempt to offer the new technology. It is, of course, difficult to generalize from a single case, but the experiences of this campaign can suggest the type of role modern party organizations might play and underscore some trends for parties.

THE MINNESOTA CAMPAIGN

The Minnesota DFL campaign in 1968 offered its 117 House candidates professional management, assistance of specialists, and access to some of the newer campaign techniques. A professional staff employed by the party organization and a group of specialists in research and media—both volunteer and paid—assisted DFL legislative candidates in their campaigns. The entire operation was coordinated by a professional political scientist experienced in research and campaigning, and familiar with the new approach to campaigning. His staff consisted of five full-time fieldmen and two part-time research writers.

The DFL's media group consisted of eight working professionals from radio and television, advertising, public relations, printing and journalism. The campaign research group was comprised of seven persons with previous research experience, primarily in the areas of polling and data analysis, legislative issues, and legal research. In addition, other full-time party staff members assisted the campaign in fund-raising and technical services.

The DFL legislative campaign reflected the new style of campaigning in four basic ways. First, the technology of campaigning was made accessible to candidates. Such proven techniques as research, budgeting, systematic long-range planning, data analysis, polling, media, and advertising were utilized. Secondly, recognizing the trend toward candidate-centered campaigns, the DFL's professional legislative staff adopted a policy of supporting the development of candidate organizations and playing down the importance of candidate relationships with the formal party organization within the legislative district.[7]

Thirdly, in response to the increased cost of modern campaigns, the party organization allocated more funds to the legislative effort than it had in previous campaigns. A program of central fund-raising and direct grants of funds, primarily for media acquisition, was instituted. The State Chairman and the party's Executive Committee were committed to raise and spend amounts in excess of six figures for staff and for direct party contributions to campaigns. Fourthly, from the state party's standpoint it tried to adopt a more management-oriented approach to its own campaign operation. The state organization began its own form of long-range planning, budgeting, setting of priorities, central finance, and efficiency studies of campaigning. The leadership of the party decided that if it was to get into campaign consulting for a large number of candidates, the work had to be performed on a cost-effective basis.

In sum, the DFL's legislative campaign represented an attempt to use a management approach to apply new campaign techniques to candidate-centered campaigns through the expenditure of relatively large sums of money. The specific services offered were: research, planning and management, cost-effectiveness and polling, finance, and candidate services.

Research

The earliest stage of the 1968 DFL legislative campaign began with the opening of the 1967 session of the Minnesota Legislature and ran until the legislative candidates were identified. During this period the DFL legislative operation was primarily concerned with building cases against GOP incumbents, developing issues for the campaign, and performing election research to assist in campaign decision-making.

The research consultants decided that their most useful effort would be the building of a GOP incumbent file for use by DFL challengers. Legislative observers gathered unpublished information on the performance of GOP legislators in committee sessions and in the House's Committee of the Whole. Other volunteers kept complete records on GOP-sponsored bills, developed newspaper clipping files on each GOP legislator, and analyzed legislative roll calls in terms of indices such as party support, liberalism-conservatism, and missed roll calls.

The research program was also marked by the DFL's first serious attempt to perform computerized analysis on aggregate electoral data. The 1966 general election vote from every precinct in the state was recorded on data processing cards and analyzed extensively. The electoral study was designed to help the staff determine priority seats by offering a precinct-by-precinct profile of an incumbent's vote-gathering ability; to determine areas of GOP incumbent strength and weakness, thus suggesting areas from which a DFL candidate might profitably be recruited; to develop campaign strategy and tactics through examination of the data for each precinct in a legislative district; and to allow the party to perform research on its Sample Ballot, a direct mail technique used to identify DFL candidates in non-partisan ballot elections.

In the final and critical aspect of the research phase, the professional staff translated the research into a determination of priority seats for the election. The basic information used for setting priorities was a combination of "hard" data, including the number of terms an incumbent had served, the electoral strength of the incumbent, and party strength of the district; and "soft" or judgmental information on the electoral strength of the incumbent. The importance of candidate personality factors in Minnesota's nonpartisan ballot legislative elections meant that the potential strength of DFL challengers was assessed almost entirely on such "soft" information as past public service, community standing and apparent ability to wage a campaign.[8]

This information was translated into weighted quantitative ratings in three categories—incumbent strength, party strength and candidate potential—and an overall priority ranking of high (A), medium (B), or low (C) was assigned for each district.

Planning and Management

Many of the DFL candidates, both novice and experienced, were unfamiliar with the newer techniques of campaigning. While they were experienced in party politics, they were not accustomed to campaigns that utilized professional assistance, computers, and polls. The legislative campaign staff therefore established a candidate planning and management program which emphasized training in campaign organization and techniques, issue development, and advertising and promotion.

In a more conventional enterprise, the party staff cooperated with the media and research groups in producing legislative handbooks on campaigning, similar to those published by the national party Congressional Campaign Committees. The DFL Legislators' Campaign Handbook stressed the "how to" aspects of the new campaigning from organization to media. The House Issues Handbook was designed to educate the non-incumbent candidate on the key issues of statewide importance. It included research data on GOP incumbents.

The advertising campaign was developed by the media group and by the legislative staff members. It was decided to have common advertising, with an identical color scheme and design, in which only the candidate's name and legislative district number would be varied. The program included signs, posters, billboards, and newspaper and radio advertising. In addition, the media group decided to develop a general advertising campaign, bearing the name of no particular candidate, urging voters to find out who their DFL legislative candidate was and vote for him.

The entire advertising campaign was organized around a central campaign theme: opposition to the 3 percent sales tax enacted by GOP majorities during the previous legislative session. The GOP Governor, Harold LeVander, was to be linked with the GOP Caucus and attacked for his failure to keep his promise to oppose any sales tax. The physical symbol was a "Lavender Penny," a purple disc resembling a penny bearing a caricature of LeVander, the designation "Three cents," and the words "E Pluribus Tax 'Em."

The training period began with a series of candidate workshops. After the candidate filing deadline all candidates were brought to Minneapolis to discuss campaign techniques—door-to-door campaigning; radio, television and newspaper advertising; literature and sign preparation; and other special techniques. The candidates were given a chance to obtain personal advice from media and research experts and incumbent legislators.

This phase of the campaign also featured a series of issue training workshops, held in various parts of the state in order to sensitize candidates to regional concerns. The staff of incumbent State Senators and Representatives offered basic information about issues and attempted to train new candidates in methods for using or, alternatively, avoiding issues in a campaign. Upon completion of the regional workshops, a single state workshop was held at which more general issues were discussed.

The major emphasis of the planning program was on staff assistance to candidates and campaign organizations through numerous individual conferences between fieldmen and candidate groups. Each fieldman was responsible for approximately fifteen of the seventy-one high and medium priority races. Candidates from the low priority districts were largely ignored. The fieldman's instructions were to "camp on the doorstep" of each candidate until his campaign was organizationally and strategically planned. Major emphasis was placed on non-incumbents and the six DFL incumbents who were facing difficult reelection races.

The initial step in campaign development at the district level was the establishment of the major campaign committees. The fieldmen first asked each candidate to select members for his general campaign, finance, and publicity committees. The next step was to develop a campaign strategy. Data gathered by the research operation were explained to the candidate, and a written summary of each body of data was provided. The end of this summary suggested an overall strategy, which proposed a proper campaign "mix" of candidate, issue, and party appeals.[9] The information was then discussed in the light of the candidate's own perception of the incumbent, his district and his campaign. The end-product of the discussion was an overall campaign strategy.

After this initial session the candidates assembled their committee volunteers for subsequent meetings with the fieldman to decide on the tactics which would best serve their strategy. At these sessions specific decisions were made on fund-raising events, promotion and advertising, issue emphasis, and candidate image. The physical output of this aspect of the campaign comprised three important internal campaign documents: first, a weekly campaign calendar which stated the exact day of each campaign event; secondly, a campaign budget, which projected all conceivable revenue and expenditure; and thirdly, a block-work plan, which pinpointed on a weekly basis the exact area in which the candidate would be campaigning door-to-door. Each of these documents was projected through election day.

Upon the completion of campaign planning as evidenced by the three campaign documents, the field staff returned to their districts to offer technical assistance to candidates and volunteers on the practicalities of campaigning—how to secure a postal permit, buy envelopes, secure printing, write copy for a brochure, or plan a dinner for a candidate.

Cost Effectiveness and Polling

At the mid-point of the campaign important information was gathered as a basis for allocating scarce resources for the last stages of the campaign. Over the course of the campaign it had become clear that election priorities could not be determined by party strength and incumbent vulnerability alone; the performances of the DFL candidates had to be evaluated before reassessing the initial priority ratings assigned to the districts.

The most important aspect of this information-gathering phase was the determination by the legislative staff of whether the campaign plan was being successfully implemented.

The three documents—the overall plan, the budget, and the block-work plan—were "field tested" by staff members as a measure of candidate and campaign effort. The type of information gathered was largely based on the response of the candidate and his campaign workers to questions about implementation of the plan, direct observation of the campaign and a check with party leaders in the area. Candidates and their supporters were questioned as to the number of campaign workers recruited, the number and character of groups before which the candidate had appeared, the date of their initial literature distribution, and the extent of planning for events scheduled next on the campaign calendar. Special attention was paid to the actual timing of events in relation to the plan. In addition, the implementation of the candidates' block-work plan was given close attention because the amount of door-to-door work actually undertaken at this stage of the campaign was an excellent indicator of the individual effort which a candidate was willing to put forth. Other "collective" indicators, such as local monies raised, were considered evidence of the effectiveness of the campaign organization.

Unfortunately, information about the campaign and the candidates offers little insight into how a candidate is being received among the voters of his district. Thus, a polling program was established to measure the impact of various campaigns and to provide valuable campaign information. Scarce resources limited the conduct of surveys to thirty-one higher-priority districts with questionable status in the "A" or "B" category. A sample of registered voters was drawn, and trained interviewers asked questions designed to test voter identification of both legislative candidates; knowledge of party affiliation of both candidates; voting intentions in the upcoming Presidential, Congressional, and legislative races; reasons for voting intention in legislative races; and knowledge of distributed campaign literature. In addition, an open-ended question asked respondents to identify the major legislative issues.

In general, the candidate and his campaign group were able to use the survey to make assessments about the impact of the campaign and the candidate. The survey information helped local campaign groups measure the extent of voter cognizance of the candidate's party identification effort. In all surveyed districts a rough picture could be drawn of the "candidate image" of both candidates and explanations for projected voting behavior suggested. Finally, the open-ended questions could generate issues for the campaign which had not already been identified.[10]

The survey and field information was also used as a device to exert pressure on reluctant campaigners to accelerate the pace of their campaigns. Candidates were provided further stimulus by the prospect of additional money from the state party coffers in the last stages of the campaign.

Finance

Candidates for the state legislature have traditionally received very little money from the DFL party organization. In the 1960's Minnesota Democrats faced an additional financial burden with Hubert Humphrey and Eugene McCarthy taking DFL money outside the state while running for national office. In 1968, party leaders decided that the new campaigning would require substantial contributions from the DFL and, therefore, made a party commitment to raise and expend direct grants of funds to candidates.

Beginning in the fall of the off-election year, the party engaged in the traditional political fundraising practices of holding dinners, appealing to interest groups for funds, and directly soliciting money from its regular contributors.[11] In keeping with a "management-oriented" approach, an attempt was made to pool legislative funds from various party sources for redistribution to candidates on a priority basis. Thus the direct grant of funds and the pooling effort were the innovative aspects of the party's fundraising program.

From these various revenue sources, a total of over $200,000 was raised and spent in the DFL legislative campaign.[12] About one-third of these monies were used to defray operating expenses for the legislative program. The remaining sum was used for direct contributions to candidate campaigns. The total revenue and expenditure figure of over $200,000 was impressive by DFL standards.[13]

After all the campaign information was gathered from the cost-effectiveness studies and polls, party officers and staff met to reassess priority ratings and allocate funds. Very few adjustments were found necessary. In general, each "A" and "B" candidate was to receive some money from the party organization/legislative caucus pool, and some from the interest groups. The sums ranged up to $5000 for "A" priority districts. The "C" candidates received little or no money from the party. Thus in the all-important financial area, the priority system of campaign management was carefully followed.

Candidate Services

In the later stages of the campaign, the party provided direct services to campaign organizations to help them more effectively to implement the plans they adopted. Unlike the technical assistance programs that emphasized management and strategy, these services were designed to provide day-to-day campaign support in those skill areas most generally lacking at the local constituency level.

The legislative staff made itself available for service on special projects. The office staff assisted in the writing of press releases, speeches, and research reports. The field staff worked with the campaigns on special eleventh-hour problems, including block-working, literature distribution, media advertising, and election day "get-out-the-vote" plans. The fieldmen remained in their assigned districts until election day, overseeing the implementation of the campaign plan.

A final legislative activity was the joint publicity campaign. In the last ten days of the campaign, lawn signs, posters, newspaper and radio advertising, and literature stressed the DFL theme of opposition to the recently enacted sales tax. This candidate advertising program was supplemented by a party program of newspaper and radio advertising.

Another aspect of the joint publicity effort was the sample media material prepared by the party's research and writing staff. These news and advertising items, in which a candidate could insert his own name and local information, included a weekly "canned" press release for radio or newspaper use, bi-weekly radio "spot" scripts, and a series of sample newspaper ads.

These services offered to candidates were not considered a central part of the DFL's campaign. In fact, during this final stage of the legislative campaign the individual candidates were relatively free to implement the strategies and tactics agreed upon. The funds contributed to their campaigns, the research explanations, the issues developed, the services and advice provided were available for the candidates and their groups to incorporate into their campaigns. It was left up to the candidate-centered groups to implement strategy by employing the new techniques which were now made available to them.

The Record

If success is measured by victories, the DFL party was successful. After suffering losses in five consecutive campaigns, the new party management effort was able to reverse this trend and elect fifteen new House members. Six other DFL candidates were defeated by margins of 151 votes or less. One cannot prove that the new campaigning caused this reversal in party fortunes. Nor is victory the most important lesson to be learned. While not unprecedented, this comprehensive approach to the new campaigning suggests that there is still a place for party in the campaign.

This case illustrates that the use of the new approach offers impressive advantages in campaigns for lower-level offices, especially at the legislative level where dramatic constituency growth is reducing the effectiveness of more traditional campaigning. But a serious problem of implementation remains: few candidates for lower office possess or can afford to buy the high-priced skills and services necessary to mount a full-fledged modern campaign. A possible solution may lie with existing state party organizations and their proven ability to mobilize financial and skill group resources. If party organizations were to establish programs of professional campaign assistance, the new techniques might be available to candidates not otherwise able to afford them. Moreover, in the process of managing candidate access to the new techniques, state party organizations would have the opportunity to develop a significant new electoral role to compensate for the decline of the traditional constituency party function.

PARTIES AND THE NEW TECHNOLOGY

The Minnesota DFL experience clearly indicates that parties *can* play a central role in modern campaigning by making the new technology available to candidates. The Minnesota GOP has taken a different route, but its purpose is similar—to make polls, advertising, and professional management available to candidates for such offices as State Auditor, Attorney General, or state senator. Other state parties are beginning to adopt programs following one of these two patterns.[14] Indeed, many state party organizations appear to be in a transitional state between deemphasizing the traditional door-to-door "party vote" mobilization and taking steps in the direction of the new campaigning. The message is clear. If political parties are to remain a significant force in the electoral process, they will have to develop a role more in tune with the new candidate-centered campaigns.

What political party leaders must do is to examine the role of their groups as political organizations in the light of important changes in voting patterns and techniques. Party voting is on the decline, yet the old techniques are best suited for this type of vote mobilization. As candidates have grasped the phenomena of candidate and issue appeals, party leaders have let them develop their own means of appealing to electorates. These two trends reinforce each other, rendering campaigns and voting less party-centered. In the process of developing candidate-centered campaigns, a class of "have-not" candidates has been created. Their loss of control over electioneering, and the creation of a class of disadvantaged candidates, is as fundamental to the nature of the party structure as is the issue dimension, yet very little attention has been given to this problem.

If party organizations were to embrace the new approach to campaigning, they might well recapture some of the control they have lost over the electoral process. When party leaders are made aware of the political implications of change in technical and electoral behavior, they can respond to the challenges by forging a new electioneering role. The case of the DFL Campaign and experiences elsewhere point in this direction and suggest how this role might develop in the future:

1. Parties will play a greater role in the management of entire campaigns. As they begin to offer such wide-ranging and specialized services as budgeting, computerized analysis of aggregate electoral data, polling, advertising assistance, and even the development of comprehensive door-to-door plans, they will get into the critical areas of strategy, tactics and day-to-day management.

2. Parties will require the services of a variety of experts. In order to provide a comprehensive package for candidates who cannot readily gain access to these skills, parties will have to acquire the services of consultants in such diverse areas as campaign management, advertising and public relations, media production and allocation, polling, issues research, and electoral data analysis.

3. Regular party staff will have to be skilled in interpreting and applying the new technology of campaigning on a day-to-day basis. Owing to time and cost factors, many candidates will not ordinarily enjoy regular contact with campaign consultants, but they will have to have access to someone skilled in the preparation of advertising copy, the pre-testing of a poll, or the interpretation of computer printouts of election statistics in the field. Party employees can fulfill this role though it will inevitably mean that the important skills for professional party work will be less interpersonal and more technical in character.

4. Parties will have to make a substantial commitment to, and investment in, different kinds of research. The new campaigning is highly oriented to usage of the methods and findings of behavioral research in voting behavior, legislative behavior, polling, management science, advertising and public relations. In order to meet this challenge, party organizations will have to alter the direction of their research operations toward research for candidates, at the expense of the traditional "issues" research, which is so often based on the development of the public image of parties rather

than candidates. Under such programs, parties would be responsible for the creation and maintenance of data sets and data bases on precincts, census tracts, legislators, and voters for use at campaign time in planning candidates' strategies, appeals and image-building.

5. Campaigns will be more expensive and will require heavier financial commitments on the part of central parties—national, state, or metropolitan—for candidates who cannot afford the new techniques. The available evidence indicates that central parties have not given a great deal of financial assistance to these candidates.[15] If parties are to facilitate access to the new campaigning, they will have to provide the services of consultants, perform research, and make direct grants for media acquisition. All this is more expensive than the local party volunteer-oriented old-style campaigning. The money and services will have to come from the central party level because local constituency parties simply do not have the financial or managerial resources to do the job.

6. As party campaigns become more expensive, and as the scale of party campaigning increases, political parties will have to become more management-oriented and more cost-effective. The cost of using consultants, using media and advertising, and employing a staff will be so great, relative to what party leaders have previously experienced, that parties will have to initiate practices and make decisions unfamiliar in most campaigns. For example, the wise allocation of resources may require the writing off of many contests, even to the point of not fielding candidates. Campaign management devices such as tight scheduling, block-work plans, budgets, and cost-effective devices like polls and the DFL's field-testing procedures will have to be utilized as a matter of course in lower-level campaigns.

7. Lower-level campaigns will begin to require fewer persons and different skills. Mass media approaches and personal campaigning do not require the manpower required by the older style of campaigning. Traditionally, the chief recruiting ground for party workers was the local party organization—the largest single repository of persons likely to support a candidacy. As campaigns begin to use more radio, television, direct mail advertising, and other types of candidate contacts with voters, the need for party loyalists to mobilize party votes will diminish. What the lower-level candidate will need is a group of personal loyalists who are amenable to the new technology of campaigning and are willing to provide the organizational and financial underpinning for such an

endeavor. As far as the formal party committee at the local level is concerned, it will become less able to provide the electioneering services required by the new politics.

8. Efficient implementation of campaign plans, utilizing priority systems, will ignore the traditional area-neighborhood plan of party organization. In the DFL plan, the electoral data were used to determine the order of priority for block working and for direct mail advertising. In other campaigns similar studies have been used to determine the proper "media-mix" for an entire constituency. Once the priorities are set, implementation no longer depends on the availability of party workers in the neighborhood or the willingness of the local party to purchase advertising materials. Rather, workers are assigned to areas on a priority basis without regard to area availability, and the use of media is determined by priority factors such as "impact" and "reach." In this scheme of campaigning the important boundary lines are not counties, wards or precincts but newspaper, radio and television markets, address files, and ZIP codes.

9. All the preceding trends will reinforce the development of candidate-centered campaigns and accelerate the declining role of traditional local organizations in electioneering. The plan fact is that, under present circumstances, local parties are not offering needed campaign assistance because they simply are not geared up to perform such services. Nor is it conceivable that a great proportion of local constituency parties will acquire the wherewithal to meet this challenge.

10. The same trends in campaigning suggest a new role for political parties above the local constituency level. The experience of the DFL offers evidence that state party organizations can become significant and highly powerful agencies in candidate-centered campaigns. Other parties at the state level and the National Committees are beginning to recognize that modern campaigning requires a different type of service from the party organization and are beginning to take the necessary steps to provide it. If the trend continues, the state, national, or metropolitan parties could become managers of congressional, legislative, and other campaigns and thus play a vital role in the electoral process. In the long run, such events could conceivably contribute to a shift in party power from the local to the central level. As candidate-centered groups realize that the central party organization is the meaningful agency in winning elections for them, allegiance will shift toward that body and its resources.

The DFL effort to make some of the new techniques of campaigning available to its legislative candidates represented one of the first attempts at providing such a comprehensive package of research, technical assistance, and finances. During a time when political party organizations are losing their hold on electioneering, the DFL experience suggests that parties might continue to play a role in this vital aspect of politics if they recognize the value of providing sophisticated new services.

Future campaigns for the lower visibility offices will always be faced with the problem of marshaling sufficient resources to implement the new techniques. Nevertheless, in an era of declining importance of party—both as a symbol which motivates voters and as an organizational force in mobilizing votes—candidates will increasingly be called on to mobilize their own voters, using their own appeals. In the absence of a preexisting party sentiment, candidates will be forced to manufacture favorable sentiment toward themselves, using the new techniques, for they must get their messages across to a large number of people in a short period of time. The problems of mobilizing resources for the new techniques and of a party role in campaigning may both be alleviated by a new form of party participation in campaigns.

NOTES

1. Frank J. Sorauf, *Political Parties in the American System* (Boston: Little, Brown and Company, 1964) p. 109.
2. Phillips Cutright and Peter Rossi, "Grass Roots Politicians and the Vote," *American Sociological Review,* LXIII (April 1958), pp. 171-179; William J. Crotty, "Party Effort and its Impact on the Vote," *American Political Science Review,* LXV (June 1971), pp. 439-450; Daniel Katz and Samuel J. Eldersveld, "The Impact of Local Party Activity upon the Electorate," *Public Opinion Quarterly,* XXV (Spring 1961), pp. 1-24; Gerald H. Kramer, "The Effects of Precinct Level Canvassing on Voter Behavior," *Public Opinion Quarterly,* XXXIV (Winter 1970-71), pp. 560-572.
3. V. O. Key, Jr., *Politics, Parties, and Pressure Groups,* 5th ed. (New York: Thomas Y. Crowell Company, 1964), p. 316.
4. Eg., *Democratic Campaign Manual '70* (Washington D.C.: Democratic National Committee, 1970); *Electronic Data Processing Technical Manual* (Washington, D.C.: Republican National Committee, 1969); *Vote History and Demographic Analysis* (Washington, D.C.: Republican National Committee, 1969).

5. For an example of one precinct priority system, *see* Vincent P. Barabba, "Basic Information Systems—P.I.P.S.," below.

6. Richard Rose, *Influencing Voters: A Study of Campaign Rationality* (New York: St. Martin's Press, 1967), Chs. II and III.

7. Sorauf, *op. cit.*, p. 108.

8. Charles R. Adrian, "Some General Characteristics of Non-Partisan Elections," *American Political Science Review,* XLVI (September 1952) p. 776.

9. Lewis A. Froman, Jr., "A Realistic Approach to Campaign Strategies and Tactics," in M. Kent Jennings and L. Harmon Zeigler, (eds.), *The Electoral Process* (Englewood Cliffs, N.J.: Prentice Hall, 1966); John H. Kessel, "A Game Theory Analysis of Campaign Strategy," in Jennings and Zeigler.

10. The use of polls in campaigns is discussed below in Charles W. Roll, Jr. and Albert H. Cantril, "Meaningful Uses of Polls in Politics."

11. Herbert E. Alexander, *Responsibility in Party Finance* (Princeton: Citizens Research Foundation, 1963), pp. 10-31; Key, *op cit.*, pp. 498-499.

12. Candidate contributions from interest groups were disbursed directly from the contributing group, but the allocation of these funds was the responsibility of a combined DFL Legislative Committee consisting of representatives from the party organization, the DFL House Caucus, Labor and the Farmers Union.

13. Prior to 1968 only a few thousand dollars were directed to candidates for office at any level. Robert Agranoff, "The Minnesota Democratic Farmer Labor Party Organization: A Study of the 'Character' of a Programmatic Party Organization," (unpublished Ph.D. thesis, University of Pittsburgh, 1967), pp. 303-304.

14. *See* Chartrand, "Information Technology and the Political Campaigner."

15. Cf., Alexander, *Responsibility...*, *op. cit.*, pp. 31-37; Donald G. Balmer, *Financing State Senate Campaigns: Multnomah County Oregon, 1964* (Princeton, N.J: Citizens Research Foundation, 1966), pp. 33-39. Robert J. McNeill, *Democratic Campaign Financing in Indiana, 1964* (Princeton, N.J.: Citizens Research Foundation, 1966), p. 28.

PART THREE

INFORMATION SYSTEMS
AND THE CAMPAIGN

The traditional methods of gathering campaign information were remarkably unsystematic and limited in scope. The campaign manager received most of his intelligence from campaign workers who were largely party workers. These people gave the manager an assessment, based on discussions with voters, as to how the party and given candidates would fare in the upcoming election. The first attempts at systematically assessing public opinion were undertaken by Tammany Hall in the nineteenth century. Workers would fan out across New York City, positioning themselves at bridges and other key spots asking people their preferences. Workers at each location were changed daily so as to reduce bias and ensure as accurate a headcount as possible.[1] If election figures were used, they were more than likely to be a few party percentages for the counties, wards, and scattered precincts. Very little action ever resulted from the scant information collected. If an area here or there sounded weaker than normal, the party would put on an extra effort in that area. The party percentage figures were used as a crude ranking of where the party effort should be greatest, and then were stored until election night for purposes of comparing the old returns with the new.

The modern campaign organization acquires the necessary data to operate the enterprise efficiently much as any other large-scale organization uses information. Many different types of information are used and are handled systematically at every stage of the campaign for planning, organization housekeeping, decision making, and for the formulation of appeals. The types of information employed are as varied as the campaign activities they are used for: name files, finances, demographics, voting statistics, media markets, and opinion polling. Increasingly, such information systems are being stored and manipulated by computer, today's functional equivalent of the ward and precinct leaders' personal knowledge of their neighborhoods.

The new information systems have become a part of the campaign because of expansions in knowledge and technology. Technological developments in both knowledge and machinery have made it possible to deal with complex behavioral phenomena. Research on voting behavior, demography, and market characteristics has been developed to the point where reasonable explanations are possible. The electronic computer has made it feasible to deal rapidly with large amounts of data and to perform relatively sophisticated analytical tests. In addition, technological advances have made information systems more available. Voting statistics, census files, poll data files, media information, and canvass information are now kept in formats that can be readily called upon and even merged with each other, thus increasing accessibility. Also, these information systems have made it possible for candidates to supplement the information supplied by party and campaign workers, which was not the most complete and accurate information available. Candidates have come to rely on more scientific means of information gathering.

A very important reason for the advent of information systems is that the new technologists of campaigning are recruited from fields where key organizational plans and decisions are made with the use of the best information available. Consultants are used to operating on the premise that people tend to behave somewhat consistently and that the researcher can project the parameters of behavior. They are accustomed to defining a "market" and then trying to stake out a place in that market. Their new market is the electorate, and the buyer types are: (a) the committed, (b) the latent supporters, and (c) the undecideds.

The information technologist, especially the pollster, has become a key operative in the American political campaign. At one time cast as a straw-vote artist, a sort of amusing side show in the campaign spectacle, the private pollster has become one of the most highly valued members of the campaign team—an advisor, a chief strategist, and sometimes a *de facto* campaign manager. The pollster has become so central that he is often the new politician's confidant, performing some of the same advisory functions as Franklin Delano Roosevelt's James A. Farley. Candidates have been known to alter their position 180 degrees on the advice of a pollster. Candidates regularly take or duck stands indicated by pollsters. Senator Edward Brooke of Massachusetts tried to counteract the white backlash in his first campaign, not because he had experienced any, but because his pollster told him it was present.[2] After polls indicated that a majority of the country thought the "Negro has had too many hand-outs," Hubert Humphrey was advised to drop his talk of a Marshall plan for the cities and to switch to law and order.[3] A private poll taken for Humphrey by the late Oliver Quayle before the 1972 California primary revealed that a substantial number of voters who favored McGovern were unaware of their candidate's position on key issues. When voters were made aware of McGovern's stand, they disagreed with it. Hence, Humphrey had key direction from a poll to attack certain of McGovern's issue positions, which he did.[4] McGovern's pollster, Patrick Caddell, used polls to test viewer reaction to the Humphrey-McGovern "media debates" in the California primary and to test the voter impact of potential Vice-Presidential running mates. The latter revealed that, with the exception of Senator Edward Kennedy's strength, no other possibility had a significant effect on McGovern's chances.[5] Polls have a major impact on candidates' entry into and exit from contests for office. Congressmen John B. Anderson decided not to challenge Illinois Senator Adlai Stevenson III in 1974 when a private poll taken one year before the election revealed that he had an enormous identification gap compared with Stevenson, as well as strong indications that Watergate might hurt Republicans.[6] George Romney withdrew from his 1968 Presidential bid before a single primary vote was cast because his pollster, Fred Currier, reported to him on the eve of the New Hampshire primary that he could expect no more than 10 or 12 percent of the vote.[7] In addition, such key campaign decisions as which issues to emphasize, which media markets to concentrate on, and which groups to appeal to await the report and advice of the information technologists.

The reporting of polls, both public and private, has had some interesting effects on campaigns. The acquisition of key campaign resources appears to be related to electoral standing—as poll positions are reported money and workers often begin to flow in or shut off. The Humphrey people were able to use his surge in the polls in September 1968 to get financial backers to open their wallets and McCarthy-oriented volunteers to support him after both groups had displayed considerable postconvention skepticism. Publication of poll results in Presidential primaries, as Martin Mayer has observed, produces a crazy definition of victory—not whether in fact a candidate wins or loses, but whether he does better or worse than the published polls said he would.[8] Polls have an effect on setting the issue context of a campaign. That is, as they uncover and publicize issue domains, candidates are often forced to work within them. For example, some issues like abortion are revealed as so sensitive that all candidates will avoid them. Other issues, like foreign policy, often reveal that "confidence" in the candidate is more important than any specific direction, so specific positions are often avoided. Other issues are so obviously on people's minds, such as stimulation of employment during a recession or a war issue, that both candidates are forced to take some position on the issue. Campaign efforts are sometimes predicated on effecting poll results. The McGovern forces apparently had this in mind in starting their television spots in early September, as did the Nixon forces when they began a house-to-house canvass in the same week. They knew that Gallup would be in the field in the third week of the month and hoped to influence that survey.[9] As will be discussed in Section 4, the release of poll reports have also been used as devices in reinforcing, activating, and converting party convention delegates and voters.[10]

The most reliable estimates place the number of polling and information technology firms in the United States at over 200.[11] They range from about seventy-five of the biggest market research firms to one-man postcard operations. There are basically five types of information operations:

1. National public opinion firms, such as the Gallup organization, Daniel Yankelovich, and Louis Harris and Associates, which publish the results of their findings. Their major clients are the news media. They generally have no private political clients.
2. National firms having large numbers of private political clients, such as The Market Opinion Research Co., Oliver A. Quayle & Co., Opinion Research Corp., and John F. Kraft, Inc. They generally work for many clients and often work in as many as thirty-five to forty states in a given election.
3. Regional firms that specialize in a single state or a few surrounding states, such as Central Surveys, Inc. of Shenandoah, Iowa, and Belden Associates

of Dallas, Texas. These firms generally perform a wide range of research services for a small number of candidates.

4. Groups of specialists formed to conduct information research for a single campaign. One such group has worked for Governor Patrick Lucey's campaigns in Wisconsin and has included political scientists David Adamany, Aage Clausen, Jack Dennis, and Austin Ranney.

5. Local pollsters, one-man operators, and postcard-polltakers. One small local pollster is North Star Surveys of Minneapolis, Minnesota, which does research for Minnesota Republican legislative candidates.

A recent survey of poll usage by major office holders indicated that private polling is not only becoming widespread but is almost universal at the higher levels. More than half of the Congressmen, four-fifths of the Senators, and almost all Governors conduct polls. Party affiliation makes little difference in the extent of usage.[12] Presidential candidates often employ more than one pollster; a major candidate can employ as many as six simultaneously. Many other candidates are beginning to use more than one pollster.

Direct mail solicitation and its attendant information software have become an increasingly important part of 1970s campaigns. The 1972 and 1974 elections were waged under broadcast media spending limitations, but with no direct mail limitations. Thus, availability of technology and the stimulus of unlimited spending has made the recent development of direct mail applications the single largest campaign growth area, particularly in fund raising and in making appeals. The McGovern forces, under direct mail consultants Morris Dees and Thomas Collins, began building their contributor lists two years before the election. They used Mc-Carthy supporter lists, Kennedy supporter lists, anti-war group lists, liberal magazine subscription lists, and other contribution lists to amass over 350,000 names by the candidate's January 1971 announcement of candidacy and close to one million names by the primary season. Their candidacy announcement appeal for funds yielded $300,000 on an investment of $30,000, and this group formed a core of regular givers who gave the campaign a regular income.[13] By election time, over 600,000 givers were on the McGovern contributors' list and the campaign raised about $12 million through direct mail appeals to small donors.[14] In addition to their direct mail fund-raising efforts, the Nixon campaign used extensive mailings to appeal to voters. In New York State, they targeted election districts for specialized mailings based on: (1) past voting behavior, identified by a computer study; (2) polling on attitudes in general population segments; and (3) demographic, income, and ethnic stratifications. They were sent in the form of "neighborhood letters," with a signature from a New Yorker such as Senator Javits or Buckley when their signatures would presumably carry some weight. In some conservative Democratic areas, a Democrats for Nixon leader stated that "radicals have taken over the Democratic Party," whereas in high-crime areas, letters described Mr. Nixon as "a man of action and determination" who "is directing a strong fight against crime and drugs."[15] Many such techniques and practices long established in the direct-mail product advertising field are becoming a regular part of the campaign.[16]

Information technology is also becoming an important tool for candidate-centered organizational activities, particularly as a support device for direct voter-contact activities like voter registration, voter identification, and get-out-the-vote. As campaign workers gather valuable information about thousands and thousands of citizens, it is put into machineable form so that this information can be used for other, related purposes at a later stage in the campaign. A number of information firms have the capability to transform telephone books, the answers to canvasser questions, party registration lists, city directories, or similar information into "master tapes," which, by constituency or voter category, can print out address labels, personalized letters, a canvassers' walking list, an areawide list of undecided voters, an areawide fund appeal to high income voters, or a sample ballot to every home in the constituency. The McGovern campaign organized and carried on an extensive voter identification-voter registration effort for the Democratic National Committee. They targeted areas of low registration, checked phone books against registration lists, identified voters, and urged Democrats to vote. Interestingly, there was considerable dispute over whether to identify only McGovern supporters or all Democrats, but they settled on the latter to encourage party unity.[17] After registration closed, the new lists became the basis of election-day efforts. The Nixon re-election effort contained an even more extensive canvass, which was based on identifying degrees of Nixon support. This information was fed into one of eleven computers for use in addressing letters, sending get-out-the-vote telegrams, and developing telephone lists and walking lists.

Information technology can offer a candidate a variety of types of information. It tells the candidate that voter motivation is vastly different from what the classical democratic theorist assumed and that the process of campaigning is much more complex than turning out partisans and discussing the problems facing the constituency. The following is representative of the types of findings and trends that modern campaign information systems offer campaigners:

1. Persons with similar life styles (e.g., condition of housing, income level, occupation) tend to live in certain areas, and their political outlooks are similar.
2. Even when people have similar political outlooks, there is no simple alignment between these outlooks and candidate or party allegiance. The same is true of group affiliation: not all members of a group favor one candidate or party.
3. There are notable numbers of committed party and candidate supporters who must be reinforced and mobilized.
4. Supporters of both candidates and both parties often agree on many of the important issues facing the constituency.
5. The issues that are uppermost in the minds of voters are few in number and subject to change over relatively short periods of time.
6. The personal dimension of a candidate is critical in the minds of some voters. Aspects of this dimension include: the degree of warmth of the candidate's personality, skill and competence for the office, personal appearance, and issue domains.
7. Perceptions of party image have less to do with voting in high-visibility races than perceptions of candidate image.
8. Electorates can be stratified in a number of ways—by party affiliation, vote contribution of the electoral unit, voting habits of the electoral unit, socio-economic characteristics, liberalism-conservatism, political awareness, candidate preference, and media audience patterns.
9. Because electorates can be stratified in many ways, the "targets" of campaigning are necessarily diverse yet overlapping: e.g., homeowners, the elderly, parents of school children, middle income, Democrats, clerical workers, television viewers, multi-media followers, news followers, undecideds.
10. The impact of the candidate's campaign itself is an important information input by surveying, panel studies, and post-election polls.
11. Information levels can be merged into campaign system models. For example, census block-face files, precinct electoral data, and voter canvass information are being joined into direct-mail systems. Media-allocation models are being developed that integrate voting, audience, demographic, and financial data so that with the input of a given expenditure an output of maximum impact and reach can be established.
12. Campaign information can be used to test the outcome of certain campaign conditions and situations through simulation techniques.

The following selections are illustrative of the various information systems in campaigning. Robert Lee Chartrand, in "Information Technology and the Political Campaigner," explores the range of information systems and emphasizes their usage for many of the organizational aspects of the campaign. He illustrates how machines now perform many of the chores once performed by party workers and campaign volunteers. Robert Chartrand is the Information Science Specialist in the Science Policy Division of the Library of Congress. He has authored a number of books and articles on information and government and is one of this nation's foremost authorities on information technology and politics.

Rex Hardesty explains one very important application of information technology in "The Computer's Role in Getting-Out-The-Vote," which is an account of the AFL-CIO's political data processing project. There are a number of considerably involved steps that one must go through before the lists can be used during the campaign period. While perhaps more extensive than those of other groups, the AFL-CIO project also reveals the ascendency of interest group involvement in areas of campaigning once considered the province of parties. Rex Hardesty is Associate Editor of the *American Federationist.*

Backstrom and Agranoff explain that if the researcher understands the limitations and pitfalls involved in using aggregate electoral data and works within them, usage of these data can be valuable in planning a campaign. Election data are the most widely used and often the only kinds accessible in a campaign, but candidates rarely are aware of how and when they should be used. Charles H. Backstrom is Professor of Political Science at the University of Minnesota. He has served as a consultant to candidates at all levels, from the state legislature to President of the United States, and as a polling consultant to various news media, including CBS news.

Vincent P. Barabba, in "Basic Information Systems—P.I.P.S.," develops a campaign management system by combining basic secondary data sources (aggregate electoral statistics, census data), political data (canvass information, registration), and political judgment into a profile of the constituency. This profile is used to implement the campaign strategy in a number of ways by establishing hard priorities among the precincts of the constituency. Vincent Barabba was Chairman of the Board of Decision Making Information, Inc., a national firm that performs a wide variety of campaign information studies including polling, management systems, and media allocation modeling. DMI is also a business and governmental information consulting firm. Mr. Barabba is on leave from DMI to serve as Director of the U.S. Census Bureau.

Roll and Cantril provide an overview of campaign polling in "Meaningful Uses of Polls in Politics." In particular, they show how polls are used to measure the degree and locus of strength, candidate image, the impact of certain events, and the role of polls in determining and positioning issues. Charles W. Roll, Jr., is President of Political Surveys and Analysis, a national polling firm, and is a Study Director for the Gallup Organization. Albert H. Cantril is a political scientist who has served in government and presently is an independent consultant in political and social research.

NOTES

1. Charles W. Roll and Albert Cantril, *Polls: Their Use and Misuse in Politics* (New York: Basic Books, 1972), p. 9.

2. For an account of how polls were used in the Brooke campaign, see John F. Becker and Eugene E. Heaton, "The Election of Senator Edward W. Brooke," *Public Opinion Quarterly* 31 (Fall 1967):346–58.

3. Leo Bogart, *Silent Politics: Polls and the Awareness of Public Opinion* (New York: John Wiley & Sons, 1972), p. 31.

4. *National Journal* 4 (June 10, 1972):967.

5. Gordon L. Weil, *The Long Shot* (New York: Norton, 1973), pp. 113, 161.

6. *DeKalb Daily Chronicle,* November 14, 1973, p. 2.

7. Stephen C. Shaddeg, *Winning's A Lot More Fun* (New York: Macmillan, 1969), p. 132.

8. Martin Mayer, "What Did We Learn From the Polls this Time?" *New York Magazine* 5 (November 1972):55.

9. *Ibid.,* p. 59.

10. Bogart, *Silent Politics,* pp. 25–41.

11. "Political Pollsters Head for Record Activity in 1968," *Congressional Quarterly Weekly Report* 26 (May 3, 1968):992; Andrew J. Glass, "Pollsters Prowl Nation as Candidates Use Opinion Surveys to Plan '72 Campaign," *National Journal* 3 (August 14, 1971):1693–1705.

12. Robert King and Martin Schnitzer, "Contemporary Use of Private Political Polling," *Public Opinion Quarterly* 32 (Fall 1968):433–35.

13. Jonathin Cottin, "Democrats Tap Fresh Financial Sources but Encounter Money-Raising Problems," *National Journal* 4 (May 13, 1972); *New York Times,* July 24, 1972, p. 14.

14. Jonathin Cottin, "McGovern Reliance on Small Donors Aids His Chances of Party Control," *National Journal* 4 (November 4, 1972): 1703.

15. *National Journal* 4 (October 28, 1972):1677.

16. For more information on direct-mail fund raising, see "Conservative Fund-Raisers: New Hope for 1974," *Congressional Quarterly Weekly*

Report 32 (September 7, 1974):2436–40; "Liberal Fund-Raisers: A Tighter Squeeze in 1974," *Congressional Quarterly Weekly Report* 32 (June 15, 1974):1551–55.

17. *New York Times,* August 7, 1972, p. 20; *New York Times,* September 8, 1972, p. 20.

—6—

INFORMATION TECHNOLOGY AND
THE POLITICAL CAMPAIGNER

Robert L. Chartrand

The political environment is not what it used to be. Most candidates today are coping with a constituency of increasing sophistication, yet one that tends to be casual about its voting opportunities. Population mobility is high, thus posing problems for the candidate who attempts to maintain current files of potential or registered voters. Political personalities and issues—factors lending themselves to exposition and discussion on television—are often more significant than traditional party and group (vocational, civic, ethnic) affiliations, and straight-ticket voting is on the decline. According to Walter DeVries, there is a perceptible shift in certain quarters of "political power from party leaders, political brokers, and special interest group leaders to those who are information and communications experts"[1]—a shift attributable, at least in part, to the broadened use of mass media, increased accessibility of politically useful information (such as urban planning, census, and federal assistance program data), and the fading of traditional voter identifications.

In this environment of greater risk and competition, the campaigner must attempt to make the art of decision-making into a science by carefully organizing his efforts into three major phases:

> First, performance of a thorough post-mortem on the most recent election involving the office and constituency which are his objectives.

This article prepared for this volume. The views expressed in this paper are those of the author and are not necessarily those of the Congressional Research Service or the Library of Congress.

Secondly, establishment of a campaign strategy attuned to key personalities, issues, and conditions affecting the fulfillment of candidate and party goals. If properly assessed, these factors can be instrumental in systematically planning how to use man-machine techniques and scheduling methodology.

Thirdly, execution of campaign tactics based on the control of information—its collection, indexing, processing, and later recall—which allows taking defensible positions on prime issues, and reacting to opposition actions or statements within an acceptable time frame.

It is especially important that political decision-makers come to understand the value of the new technology, including computer and microform processes. They should consider its use in the context of society:

> The politician must compete with soap, cars and beer (as well as his opponent) for the attention of the voter. His appeal for votes, money and volunteers must pierce the "background noise" generated by a consumer-oriented economy. Electronic Data Processing is one of the tools which can get the Party's message through.[2]

Both benefits and limitations of the new technology ultimately must be weighted against the realistic requirements of party objectives, the idiosyncrasies of a particular campaign, and the limits of time and organization resources.

INFORMATION TECHNOLOGY: ITS MEANING TO THE CAMPAIGNER

In recent years the political professional has joined his counterparts in industry, commerce, government, and education in an intensified effort to understand "information technology." This term includes automatic, or electronic, data processing—ADP or EDP—equipment (computers and punched card devices); micromation devices; advanced dual systems which allow a transfer of data from microfilm to magnetic tape and vice versa; and an array of techniques which enable man to "talk" to a computer via a telephone, keyboard, or videoscreen console.

A classical definition of automatic data processing describes it as the process:

> Whereby a machine or computer can accept information or "input data," process the data according to a predetermined "program," and provide the results in a usable form. In an automatic data

processing system, the electronic computer is the heart or focal point of the system. An ADP system consists of a number of components including input, processing, storage, and output devices.[3]

It should be noted that punched card data processing, with its qualities of easy access, convenience in handling and data transfer, and relatively low cost, often can be justified for use by the political campaigner more readily than elaborate computer-supported systems. Many state and local organizations, after investigating the possibilities, have chosen to acquire punched card equipment, or contract for such support with commercial service bureaus.

Microform systems, although predating computers, have been eclipsed by electronic technology until quite recently. These systems feature mass-memory film storage of great volumes of words, numbers, and symbols. Through microminiaturization techniques, many times the amount of data may be "packed" on film than on, for example, magnetic tape. Attention has been focused on microform technology in recent years because (1) a high-quality, long-lasting product has been developed, (2) equipment and software have been produced which allow the rapid transfer of data to other media, and (3) the plethora of paper forms is crippling information handling systems everywhere, and substitute storage media must be found.

An example of microform technology used in processing political data is the MIRACODE system, which permits selective retrieval through electronic searching of machine-readable code numbers linked to textual passages.[4] Each 100-foot roll of film contains 2,400 one-half inch frames and costs about $6.00. The political campaigner, in using this type of system, could store and index selected significant statements by all partisan spokesmen, editorial comment and news features, and headquarters' press releases. Quick referral to these materials would be possible by a staff person entering selected "key words" germane to the immediate topic in focus. Relevant entries could be screened and a hard copy printout obtained at once.

Prognostications concerning machine and software evolution have been discouragingly unreliable. However, the "fourth generation"[5] of computers now in the offing, can be expected to bring the following innovations: multi-processor computer utility systems, allowing various types of units to exchange data; highly flexible computer terminals offering input-editing-retrieval-capabilities and operation by non-professionals; significant improvements in display technology, including rapid transfer of data within the hard copy-microform-ADP triad; and many magnitudes of improvement in memory (disc, drum, bulk core) storage. Cost-performance ratios should continue to improve, as the analyst-programmer cadre—which one political figure termed "a new kind of priesthood"[6]—extends its mastery over an expanding electronic domain. In *The Year 2000,* Kahn and Wiener offer this prediction:

> By the year 2000, computers are likely to match, simulate, or surpass some of man's most "human-like" intellectual abilities, including perhaps some of his aesthetic and creative capacities, in addition to having some new kinds of capabilities that human beings do not have.[7]

Nevertheless, the importance of the human being in managing, programming, and operating computer-oriented information systems cannot be overstated. Experienced technical personnel must be on hand to advise the political campaigner and his staff of the nature and utility of the equipment. The role of the information specialist becomes quite critical in blending professional and amateur efforts in the pre-election campaign.

APPLYING THE NEW TECHNOLOGY IN CAMPAIGNING

When the subject of computers in politics arises, there usually are as many biases and interpretations as discussants. But in one area all can usually agree: "If you can do the job cheaper or faster with a pencil and 3 X 5 cards, use them."[8]

Experience gained in national, state and local campaigns during the past decade indicates that ADP offers the greatest potential benefit in handling the following: information about constituents, voter registration data, correspondence records, survey results, listings of organization candidates and workers, key data on the opposition, indexed information on major issues, a master file on party resources (e.g., radio-TV-press coverage, campaign literature, speakers available), and analyses of recent election results. The flow of information through a typical campaign headquarters is shown in Figure 1.

There are several guidelines which should help the campaigner and his advisors decide whether or not to invest in ADP-supported information handling. Leadership time, money, and the impact on morale of the campaign organization must be considered. The can-

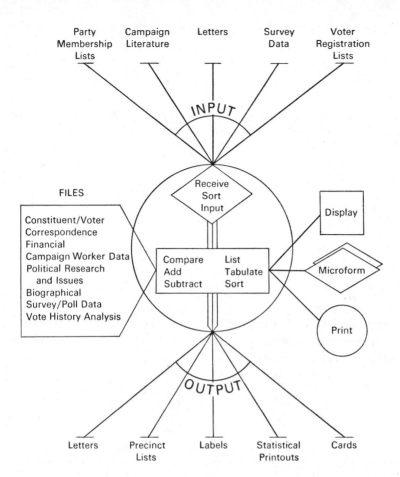

Party Membership Lists Campaign Literature Letters Survey Data Voter Registration Lists

INPUT

Receive Sort Input

FILES

Constituent/Voter
Correspondence
Financial
Campaign Worker Data
Political Research
and Issues
Biographical
Survey/Poll Data
Vote History Analysis

Compare   List
Add   Tabulate
Subtract   Sort

Display

Microform

Print

OUTPUT

Letters   Precinct Lists   Labels   Statistical Printouts   Cards

FIGURE 1

didate with a rural constituency is likely to view the ADP issue question differently from one running in a high density metropolitan area. Questions to be considered before actually establishing a computer facility for the exclusive use of the campaign organization include:

1. Can the application(s) be justified on the basis of a savings in cost or a measurable improvement in performance?
2. Will the facility provide long range as well as short term support to the organization? Will there be funds available to ensure maintenance of key machine-readable files?
3. Has the installation been scheduled far enough in advance to allow the collection and keypunching of requisite data? If special computer programs are required, has enough time been allowed for their preparation?

4. Have key personnel been recruited and trained if necessary? Has a consultant been hired to provide the necessary early planning support?
5. Will the facility be available for other party users? If so, can priorities be established to allow responsive ADP support for *all* users?

As the role of computerized processing has grown, some campaign management firms have added services that capitalize on ADP capacities. Merrill Research Associates, for instance, offers a full range of innovative applications of computer technology, including demographic studies, redistricting and reapportionment plans, and opinion survey analyses. With the aim of developing a complete file on every registered voter in a given congressional district, Scientific Political Services, Inc. provides coverage of populace opinion on significant contemporary issues and screens elected officials' casework requests, thereby making a client more sensitive to constituent needs. Campaign analyses are among the specialty services offered by Decision Making Information, Inc., which conducts a low visibility operation in order to better serve the interests of its customers.[9] Although a few organizations offer their services on a nonpartisan basis—Computer Campaign Services is an example—most of them cater exclusively either to Democrats (e.g., Joseph Napolitan, Matthew A. Reese and Associates) or Republicans (F. Clifton White, Campaign Consultants, Inc.).

In 1970, the new focus on ADP services resulted in a two-day seminar on "Information Systems, Computers, and Campaigns" sponsored by the American Association of Political Consultants. At that time Walter DeVries, stressing the need for enhanced candidate-voter communication, expresssed a concept of five basic information subsystems (Figure 2) which may provide the candidate and his manager with information for making key decisions: voting behavior, demographics, media markets, opinion polling, and organizational activities.[10]

Thus the opportunities for mechanized services to assist the candidate are numerous and very real. Every sign points to much wider dependence upon the new technology during the next decade.

THE CAMPAIGN MILIEU

The prime objective of any political campaign is, of course, to win, but there are important secondary considerations. A good show-

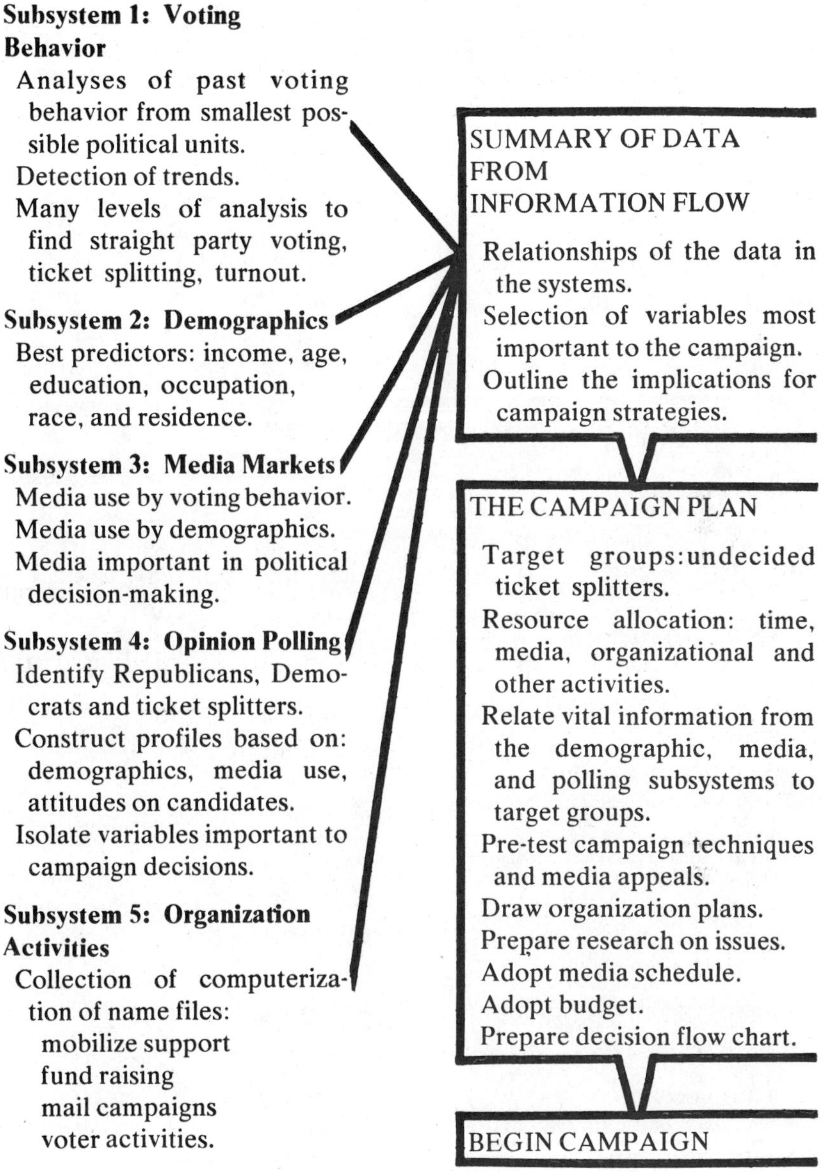

Subsystem 1: Voting Behavior

Analyses of past voting behavior from smallest possible political units.

Detection of trends.

Many levels of analysis to find straight party voting, ticket splitting, turnout.

Subsystem 2: Demographics

Best predictors: income, age, education, occupation, race, and residence.

Subsystem 3: Media Markets

Media use by voting behavior.

Media use by demographics.

Media important in political decision-making.

Subsystem 4: Opinion Polling

Identify Republicans, Democrats and ticket splitters.

Construct profiles based on: demographics, media use, attitudes on candidates.

Isolate variables important to campaign decisions.

Subsystem 5: Organization Activities

Collection of computerization of name files:
mobilize support
fund raising
mail campaigns
voter activities.

SUMMARY OF DATA FROM INFORMATION FLOW

Relationships of the data in the systems.

Selection of variables most important to the campaign.

Outline the implications for campaign strategies.

THE CAMPAIGN PLAN

Target groups:undecided ticket splitters.

Resource allocation: time, media, organizational and other activities.

Relate vital information from the demographic, media, and polling subsystems to target groups.

Pre-test campaign techniques and media appeals.

Draw organization plans.

Prepare research on issues.

Adopt media schedule.

Adopt budget.

Prepare decision flow chart.

BEGIN CAMPAIGN

FIGURE 2. Campaign Information Systems

ing, even in a losing cause, may strengthen the balance of political power; similarly, building for the future is important, as is the tactic of trying to force a schism in the ranks of the opposition. In order to achieve any of these ends, the campaigner and his staff must establish and maintain certain basic files of information.

In his *Handbook of Practical Politics,* Paul Van Riper identifies several files which are considered necessary and useful in the conduct of a campaign: basic memoranda, candidate's speeches, research (on selected topics), political literature (own party and opposition), clippings, candidate's correspondence, campaign manager's correspondence, and general correspondence.[11] Duplicate files, which may be microfilmed, often must be maintained in order to guard against fire, other damage, or carelessness in data handling. Several other files that may be desirable to maintain—for example, at the precinct level—are those containing constituent data, party financial records, mailing lists, schedules of local events, and party organization data.

The mere presence of these files, of course, affords no guarantee of success. An information system can aid the decisionmaking process but rarely supplants human judgment. The need for each file of information, the problem of keeping it current, the necessity for devising an index so simple and yet so useful that volunteer workers can participate in its creation and manipulation, the control of material going into and being taken from the file, and the ability to reproduce quickly and upon demand the contents of the file—these are important considerations for the managers of the campaign.

After a decision is made to utilize ADP or microfilm, a number of practical questions must be answered:

Which files are to be converted from handwritten or typed forms to computer or microfilm formats?

Do organization workers use a given file so often that it would impede their work to have the data placed on punched cards, microfilm, or magnetic tape?

Can the users of the file wait while inquiries are "batched" (i.e., several requests are collected and submitted to the ADP system for retrieval at the same time), or must immediate access—using a keyboard or video-screen terminal—be provided?

Does the placement of key data on punched cards in coded form drastically reduce the usefulness of the ADP printout to a system user who may be a semi-trained volunteer?

Can the functions identified by the campaign staff and its advisors as requiring ADP support be justified in terms of staff time, financial expenditure, response time, and flexibility under duress?

As the tempo of the campaign accelerates, the candidate and his staff often find that they cannot afford to wait for anyone or anything. Decisions must be made based on the information at hand. Experienced political campaigners are well aware of the role that intuitive judgment plays in "calling the shots" during the campaign, a fact which reemphasizes the subordinate role of information handling, with or without the benefit of automatic data processing. It should be remembered that:

> No amount of complex manipulation of simple, raw data with the aid of electronics can substitute for a carefully conceived system of reports to management.[12]

Thus, in determing *how* ADP should be used, there are five crucial imperatives for the campaign organization.

1. The type and degree of support which ADP alone can offer must be identified in specific terms.
2. The personnel resources, both in-house and consultant, required to design, test, and operate the system must be acquired.
3. If a service bureau is to furnish the requisite support, a staff competent to define needs, identify products, and measure results still must be provided.
4. The initial and operating costs of the machine-supported system must be projected. (Two non-recurring costs are data conversion and system development, but even these can exceed expectations if new files are added or new products required.)
5. The management and maintenance of the system is a serious responsibility even in the doldrums between campaigns, for that is the time when services and products are reevaluated and modifications introduced.

Although each campaign environment is somewhat different, it is fair to say that the ramifications of running for office in a complex society are forcing candidates to systematically define and evaluate their campaign alternatives. In commenting upon this emerging mode of operation, the National Commission on Technology, Automation, and Economic Progress pointed out that:

> The advantage of specifying objectives in systems terms is that it forces decisionmakers to so delineate the factors that a rational comparison of alternative solutions is possible.[13]

While both the Republican and Democratic National Committees have shown an appreciation of computer technology in the political arena, they have done so in different ways. Emphasis within the Republican National Committee (RNC) has been on providing state organizations with technical assistance, including the preparation of guidance manuals, technical staff for consulting support, limited developmental funding, and advice on state service bureau selection and monitoring. The Democratic National Committee (DNC), which originally concentrated upon providing centralized ADP support for Congressmen, now has initiated a series of services for candidates, as well as providing housekeeping backup for the DNC leadership and limited addressing and mailing services for about 25 members of Congress. It should be noted that the Committee on Political Education of the AFL-CIO also has been active in promoting the use of ADP.

In 1966, when the first appreciable interest in using ADP in campaigning was being manifested in numerous newspaper and magazine articles,[14] the RNC leadership—headed by Ray C. Bliss, national chairman—authorized a special study to see if a central ADP facility should be established. Responsibility for recommending how and where RNC resources should be allocated was given to Edward J. Nichols, who prepared a handbook entitled *Electronic Data Processing and Politics,* which explained in layman's terms the potentialities of the computer in politics. After undertaking a pilot study in Colorado, which featured the collection of income and family composition data from test precincts, the RNC sponsored two "electronic data processing training conferences" in 1967 (in Chicago and Washington, D.C.) which were designed "to update information and exchange views on political EDP for Republicans with limited or no experience."[15] These sessions proved to be of considerable benefit, as the participants learned of actual experiences in state-wide campaigns.

At this juncture, the RNC initiated its program to furnish state and local organizations with carefully developed working tools. In addition to the *Electronic Data Processing for the Political Executive* document which was designed to show "how computers can be used to communicate with small and large groups,"[16] technical manuals were issued on such subjects as "Vote History and Demographic Analysis," "Voter Name File, Data Element Definitions," and "Finance System, Program Documentation." A total of 16 manuals and 11 computer program "support packages" offering a standardized approach and techniques were prepared.[17] By the summer of 1968, more than 20 states were actively using ADP; Tennessee, for instance, was assigned a technical advisor by RNC headquarters to assist in establishing a personalized campaigning capability.

Next, the RNC moved to established a "data bank concept," including election statistics for the period of 1960-1968 on 3,000 counties. This allowed an analysis of regional voting patterns and gave state chairmen hard data for advance campaign planning. Five reports went out to each state chairman and all national committeemen showing, for example, plurality statistics and the impact of the Wallace vote. The RNC has concentrated on providing "non-scare," understandable material which is educational and quasi-technical in nature, backed up by the type of highly technical documentation which helps state organizations to get off the ground in using the new technology.

The pattern of development within the Democratic Committee has emerged quite differently. In the early years (1965–1967) the DNC placed heavy emphasis on providing computerized (IBM 1401) addressing and mailing support for Congressmen and for state and local organizations. The document describing the new services, "Data Processing Support at Democratic National Committee," stressed that DNC would do "systems work and programming tailored to fit your needs."[18] So great was the customer response and the demand for rapid delivery of lists and labels that serious priority problems arose in scheduling the use of equipment and preparation of the final products. As the system became saturated and response time lengthened, more powerful equipment (IBM 360 Model 30) was acquired, but it could not provide relief.

In 1969, a recasting of the ADP support role for DNC was effected. As a result a leased computer (IBM 360 Model 20) operated by Demographics, Inc. now turns out computerized letters and specialized mailings for DNC, and maintains records on party contributors and performs other routine bookkeeping chores for the DNC management. Most recently, the Democratic National Committee has developed a "Voter Identification System" that advises candidates on how data processing can be helpful in organizing and properly using voter lists, as well as closing the communication gap between the central campaign staff and the block workers. In describing the new service, DNC promises "guaranteed mailing lists of any combination of the following groups:"[19]

Humphrey voters	Young voters
Nixon voters	Older voters
Wallace voters	Low turnout voters
Democrats	Men
Republicans	Women
Independents	Union members
Negroes	Voters who prefer Democratic
Spanish-speaking	candidates
Non-registered adults	Voters who prefer the
Lower/Middle/Upper	opposition
socio-economic classes	Voters who are indecisive[19]

The costs of utilizing a Voter Identification System are estimated at $7,500 for a Congressional district of 100,000 households. The cost covers all activities from obtaining a list of people in the target area to designing a special data processing card (Figure 3) to conducting the canvass and sorting the returns.

In these ways, the two national committees have taken their place in the forefront of groups trying to educate political workers and candidates about the potential of ADP.

CAMPAIGN FILES: THEIR CONTENT AND USE

The extent to which the campaigner will prepare and use formal files varies with the individual, his organization, his financial resources, and his goals. Similarly, his willingness to rely upon the "mysteries" of automatic data processing will be influenced by his background and the words of his advisors. Few political figures have, for example, the first-hand experience of Rep. Donald W. Riegle of Michigan, who formerly worked for the IBM Corporation and used his personal expertise during the campaign in "analyzing voter trends, areas, problems and needs; studying his opponent's record; and sending out individualized letters to special groups of voters—farmers, union members, independent voters."[20] The files shown in Figure 1 accurately reflect the aspects of campaign activity that involve information handling, and each in turn poses its own set of problems of data collection, transfer to machineable form, restructuring, access to storage, manipulative potential, maintenance, and retrieval alternatives.

Constituent/Voter Files

Every campaigner would like to have complete information on each constituent, and he would like to have this file completely

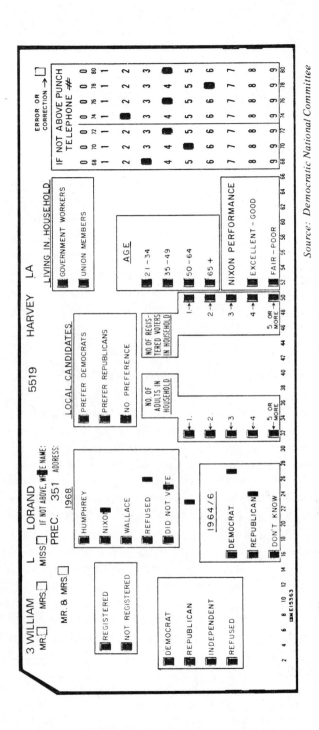

FIGURE 3. DNC Voter Information Card

Source: Democratic National Committee

up-to-date at all times. Unfortunately, this condition is never attained. Building a comprehensive name file and keeping it current takes careful planning and considerable organization effort. In many areas, however, names of registered voters are available to the campaigner, and in an increasing number of locations (particularly large counties or cities) the listings may be maintained by computer.

Congressmen of both parties have learned the value of assembling voter data in mechanized form. When still a freshman Representative, William E. Brock of Tennessee (now Senator) directed that a magnetic tape file be created, containing essential data on each adult in his district. The state of Ohio would seem to contain an unusually great amount of political computerization. Governor John J. Gilligan of Ohio began relying on ADP early in his political career, starting with a volunteer canvass which resulted in 40,000 signatures supporting his candidacy for the House of Representatives. In this way, he was able to "build up a list of sympathizers, firm supporters and active workers to be inscribed on the computer's magnetic tape reels."[21] Senator Robert Taft, Jr. relied upon an automated "voter census" in his 1966 contest for a House seat with the incumbent Gilligan. Representative Donald D. Clancy of the Second Congressional District in Ohio was able to put together an 80,000-card list containing the names, addresses, state legislative districts, ZIP codes, telephone numbers, and political preferences (if any) of qualified and non-qualified voters.

Creating a usable magnetic tape or punch card file has not been an easy task, and many candidates have discovered that "off the shelf" computer programs to help them with the chore are rare. A highly mobile population compounds the problem, as in King County, Washington. Here, with a significant percentage of the working population employed at aerospace corporations— which have experienced sharp vicissitudes in the past several years—a politician's contact with his constituent group is difficult at best. Representative Brock Adams, in explaining his view of the situation, had this to say:

> I represent approximately 700,000 people with roughly 400,000 voters being involved. These people move on an average of once every two years. This is going to become worse rather than better in terms of reaching them because as the younger people increase in proportion they tend to move more rapidly . . . . It is impossible for me to keep track of my constituency and give them any kind of decent service unless I can keep up with their addresses and be

certain that their inquiries to me have been answered. Now we have been trying to create a computerized service, and it is extremely difficult because the general patterns of computerized service throughout the business community do not fit a political constituency or a legislative problem.[22]

The shifting patterns in voter registration are receiving attention on many fronts, as reflected in such efforts as the Committee on Political Education pilot project in the seven counties of the San Francisco area or the 1967 Fort Wayne, Indiana special study. Industry has offered its assistance to the campaigner, as in the case of the Mail Advertising Corporation of America (MAC), which prepared an "Advanced Techniques for Republican Organization" release containing recommendations for the creation of various types of data files. One of these, called a "Political Data Bank System," places names and family data on registered voters in a computer-supported repository that can assist states, counties, or districts with a need for information on voters. Keeping the local list current involves the merging of update entries from local sources with the MAC National Data Bank.[23]

State organizations, often stirred to action by observing successes in ADP-serviced campaigning in other jurisdictions, have mounted large-scale efforts to acquire information on voters. The Republican party in Louisiana, in 1963-1964, obtained more than 500,000 household file entries by a person-to-person and telephone canvass and subsequently used ADP in preparing a statewide voting history by precinct and a demographic analysis.[24] Computerization of files costs money, but some state groups have planned to sell portions of the data files to retailers and other commercial customers. In Indiana, Gordon St. Angelo, chairman of the State Democratic Committee, projected an expenditure in the 1968 campaign of up to $150,000, but hoped to recoup some of this expense through resale of the name lists.[25]

Often cited as the outstanding example of a state-level candidate's use of ADP is the successful effort of Winthrop Rockefeller to become governor of Arkansas. Faced with an uphill battle, his campaign organization began to collect lists of names as early as 1961. In the words of Marion B. Burton, Mr. Rockefeller's executive secretary and manager of the ADP project:

It was a mound of information. We couldn't handle it. It would have taken hundreds of people just to sort things out and address envelopes.[26]

The decision was made in 1965 to place voter data on punched cards, and in April 1966 an ADP office was opened. The initial lists were obtained from telephone books, but additional information was acquired: size of household, number eligible or registered to vote, occupations, ages and—most difficult to obtain—political inclinations and willingness to work for Rockefeller. This information was processed by a 1401 computer, later replaced by an IBM 360 Model 30. In commenting on the methodical planning and execution of the Rockefeller campaign, observer James N. Perry judged that:

> The Rockefeller people have every reason to be pleased with their EDP accomplishments. They will probably be the first organization in the nation to establish an EDP file for every voter in as large a political unit as an entire state.[27]

So essential to the candidate is the voter data base that ingenious steps have sometimes been taken to garner names. In Nassau County, New York, more than 100,000 persons eligible to vote had not registered. The solution to reaching these persons, scattered through the three towns, 63 villages, and two cities of the county was to arrange for mobile units to visit each area.[28] Surprisingly, the actual registration time per person was 90 seconds, as compared to 10 minutes at the central board. This example of a non-traditional approach to a long-standing problem underscores the importance of flexibility in overcoming the problems of locating and officially listing all eligible voters.

Although the level and variety of support available at the national headquarters is limited by choice and resources, as noted earlier, the Democratic National Committee has made a serious effort to service party Congressmen desiring to have their mailing lists maintained and letters distributed by the ADP facility. For each constituent, the following information can be recorded:

Name	Age
Address	Religion
Constituent Code	Special Interest
District	Special Problem
County (numeric)	Key Union Leader & Member
Precinct	Party Worker Skill
Ward	Party Interest
Party	Veteran
Registered	Office Holder
Sex	Occupation

Corporate Officer	Home Owner
Firm Supporter	Number of Dependents
Nickname	Education
Organization Affiliation	Welfare Recipient
Nationality	Office Visitor (during year)
Alien	Dinner Attendee (invitation list)
Key Contributor	Legislative Interest
Contributions (year to date)	Government Worker
Income Group	Patronage[29]

Experience has shown that it is very difficult to obtain data for all the entries listed, but Congressmen have acquired enough information to justify the continuation of the service. File sorts may be run on the following patterns: control sequence (such as a unique number for a voter, sometimes called a "constituent code"), alphabetically by last name, street number within street name, street name, ZIP code, city district, ward, county within district, precinct within districts, and others.

A good maxim for any campaigner might read: "Comprehensive, current constituent files are one essential underpinning for any successful campaign." Add to this the benefits of ADP handling, and many of the functions which must be performed during *any* campaign are made easier. Furthermore, computerization of such key files allows manipulation of their contents and the use of data in a variety of ways previously impossible.

Correspondence Files

A vital part of every campaigner's resources is his knowledge of what his constituents want, are thinking about, will support with their votes and dollars, and distrust or oppose. Correspondence files can become the clearinghouse for such information. How effectively these are utilized varies widely with the campaigner, his manager, and those who direct the lower levels of activity. The incumbent, of course, has an advantage over his challenger in that he is able to send out newsletters or special "press releases," often as a congressionally authorized free mailing. In addition, the United States Senate uses its IBM 360 Model 40 installation, under the aegis of the Sergeant at Arms, for computerized addressing and mailing.[30] The House of Representatives, after a prolonged study of the correspondence needs of its members, has recently issued a "Special Report of the Special Subcommittee on Electrical and Mechanical Office Equipment on a Computerized Addressing and

Mailing System for the House of Representatives,"[31] and will decide whether to implement this service in the near future.

The value of being able to correspond with voters on the basis of their occupation, age, income level, or sex seldom is questioned by the experienced campaigner. Having these elements of information in a special, computer-supported file allows the candidate to mention specifically the subject of known interest and concern to a given constituent group. As he gains a better feel for the reactions to his communications, he then may decide that a selective mailing (e.g., to all dairy farmers) is warranted. On issues of sweeping concern, the newsletter may be sent to all postal patrons. Sometimes, rather than undertake the more expensive effort of compiling an exhaustive voter listing, the campaigner will prepare a carefully screened listing of the persons who read large and small newspapers and periodicals in his district.

The preparation of response letters or other constituent-oriented writings through the use of "robotyping" devices has become an established practice in many political quarters. A personalized letter is more likely to be opened and read than one sent to "Occupant" or "Postal Patron." Special typewriters such as the Friden "Flexowriter" or IBM "2741" unit allow insertion of the recipient's name at key points and modification of a paragraph or sentence to match the interests of particular voters. The computer letter may seem to be an unnecessary artifice, or designed to fool the constituent, but in many areas of the United States the traditional person-to-person missive no longer is practical for reaching large numbers of people.

In terms of cost per mailing, one rule of thumb for converting a list of names to machineable form is 5c to 9c per name. In *Machine Politics,* prepared by COPE, the initial cost for a 65,000 entry file is estimated at $6,000, which includes keypunching of the data, file establishment, programming, card cabinets, and the cost of cards or magnetic tape.[32] One study prepared for a Senatorial office presented costs for storing, indexing, and answering approximately 400 letters per day at $4,000 a month per user, when up to five offices shared an on-line system.

It should be understood that there are both initial (or "one-time") costs in establishing a computer-serviced system, and recurring costs for time and material involved in continuing operations. These costs must be projected with care, for the burden of monthly payments on a computer—as much as $10,000 per month—or regular payments for service bureau support can quickly put a political organization in debt.

Although an incumbent usually has a heavier volume of correspondence by virtue of his recognized position, some of the "outs," too, are dedicated to maintaining complete files of correspondence with their supporters. Careful analysis of these files often aids the campaign staff in perceiving trends in interest or bias, and the sampling provided allows the campaign staff to follow the course of "using the past as our guide to the future."[33]

Financial Files

In order to achieve sound financing of a campaign, the campaign manager must consider the best way to use ADP, for the computer has proven its worth in this area on many occasions. Automatic data processing has been used in helping the campaigner plan his fund-raising effort, taking various "cuts" at the data on potential givers, and tying the financial aspects of his campaign to critical issues affecting the voters. Representative Bob Wilson of California was among the first to use the computer heavily in determining his constituents' "contribution capacity" on the basis of their occupations.[34] Elwyn A. Bagley, Finance Director for the Republican Party of Wisconsin, says:

> The systematic processing of finance data has contributed greatly to the highly coordinated fund raising in Wisconsin. With multidimensional service potential the system augments fund raising efforts at all political fund raising levels. To put it another way—it produces *more* money![35]

Various types of reports can be computer-generated for use by the campaign finance committee: lists of contributors, history of giving of various groups and individuals, special listings (e.g., industrial complexes, minority groups), fund-raising progress reports, record keeping on expenditures, inventory counts on mailing labels, and other routine housekeeping functions.

At the state and county levels, as well as nationally, the electronic computer and its peripheral equipment are providing the support—quickly, accurately, reliably—that the campaigner demands. In Texas, Republicans "utilized EDP widely and effectively in Dallas and other areas as an aid to local organizations and audits of strength."[36] As far back as 1959, in the "Dollars for Democrats Drive" in the same state, it was recognized that fund raising, properly organized and technically supported, could serve as "an instrument for strengthening local party organization."[37] The Texas AFL-CIO also took steps in the mid-sixties to automate lists of 250,000 members, families, and sympathetic non-union voters.[38]

The United Republican Finance Committee in Los Angeles County has employed ADP to trace sources and frequency of contributions, using initial data consisting of "three punched cards for each contributor containing: identification number, name, home address, firm name, firm address, political district numbers, a history of amount given and method of giving—membership, dinners, special gifts, etc."[39] Several states have reported significant increases in the amount of money raised owing to the more thorough, timely handling of fund-raising efforts through ADP.

There also has been increasing ADP use in national financial operations; the public press reported that this technology was:

> . . . expected to be useful to record daily income and expenses of the (Democratic) National Committee to carry on voter registration campaigns and to help make arrangements for political conventions.[40]

The "EDP Finance System" created by the Republican National Committee emphasized a two-fold file organization: the Large Contributor System (for those giving $50 or more), and the Sustaining Membership System (for small contributors). As the contributor's cards are prepared, the computer can perform these functions automatically:

1. Print a "Thank You" receipt or membership card.
2. Add the amount of the contribution to the appropriate quota analysis. Even though a contribution may come from a company or city drive, the amount can be included in the quota of the contributor's home county.
3. Summarize the amount received from each different drive so that the financial director can place future emphasis on the most profitable sources.
4. Update the contributor's history record so that the current contribution will be shown in future history reports.
5. Enter the amount of the Collection Report for balancing with the bank account.[41]

In addition, the finance director can request such special reports as a list of unreturned contributor cards and the names of the solicitors to whom they were issued, and a list of previous contributors who did not give money during the current drive.

The cost of establishing a financial file, in terms of constituent or contributor name entries, depends on the sophistication expected in the output from the system. Professional keypunching costs should not exceed 9c per name record; mailing labels used in certain types of mass distributions cost about $15 per thousand, but could be only a fraction of this amount if a computer is available in off-hours at a reduced operating charge.

Professional fund raising is no longer unfamiliar in American society, but the successful utilization of computer technology in fund-raising and campaign fiscal management still requires a close analysis of the situation at hand in order to achieve more effective management control of limited resources.

Campaign Worker Data Files

The backbone of any campaign effort is the group of workers comprising the organization, those men and women who do everything from working the precincts to manning the telephones at headquarters. The critical importance of keeping this campaign team well informed cannot be over-emphasized. Each worker must know what to do, when to do it, and how to proceed. In the words of Samuel Alexander, architect of information systems:

> It is the binding together of the entire organization into an effective, integrated whole, through the flow of information, that permits the information channel to serve as a means of improving not only the day-to-day operations but the projected operations as well.[42]

The campaign manager seeks to utilize to the fullest the talents of each worker, and to this end the use of automatic data processing and systems methodology must be assessed carefully. The editors of *Machine Politics* draw an analogy regarding the effect of automation on industry and politics:

> Just as automation can, in modern industry, free men and women from more routine chores to perform more demanding and rewarding tasks, so automation in the political process can free volunteers for more creative effort.[43]

Automatic data processing can serve as a valuable aid to the campaign worker by organizing, storing, and making available a surprising variety of information. Hundreds of hours of laborious manual handling of registration data can be replaced—with the aid of a carefully devised system—by the processing capabilities of the electronic computer. Lists of workers, voters, funding sources, and special interest groups can be prepared in a variety of formats within a relatively brief time. This can mean that during special registration drives, or on election day, when time is of the essence, the worker can function at peak efficiency.

Various types of computer listings can be made available to help both the professional and volunteer campaign worker. In addition to basic registration data—generally considered the key in the "find 'em, vote 'em, count 'em" process[44]—which can be handled by the computer, "precinct walking lists" (Figure 4) can be prepared, listing street addresses in even and odd sequence. Such a report can be printed either on 3 X 5 cards (pocket-sized) or on regular sized paper. The worker should be able to write in useful supplementary information such as names and ages of unregistered household members and special interests. At a later stage, these data can be entered on punched cards and used for special or mass mailings.

In reflecting on the role of the computer during the 1966 election, Senator Robert Taft, Jr., who at that time was running for the Ohio's First Congressional District seat, felt that its use gave him a "significant advantage":

> We were able to provide our precinct people with a list of unregistered Republicans prior to election day and a list of Republican voters on election day. EDP provides the easiest method of giving a volunteer organization the full information for an effective campaign.
>
> In essence, EDP will do what the outstanding precinct executive has traditionally done, namely, provide a list in his precinct of the Republican voters. There are never enough of such precinct executives, but the use of EDP will duplicate his work and enable a new person in a precinct to do the same job.
>
> I don't know how anyone can run a truly effective campaign without Electronic Data Processing.[45]

In many metropolitan areas, "domicile inventories" in ADP form are being established. This requires, as in the Winthrop Rockefeller effort in Arkansas, painstaking checks by volunteers of telephone books, commercial lists of residents, voter registration lists, and city directories. In New York State, where the number of voters poses a major problem for both parties in the logistics of data handling, canvassing manpower, conversion of collected information to machine-readable form, and financing these time-consuming tasks, every possible technique or device known is under consideration for use by candidates at all levels. The Republican

FIGURE 4. Precinct Walking List

Source: *Appendix L in "Electronic Data Processing and Politics"*

EDP CODES PAGE 74 1428	DALLAS COUNTY PRECINCT #132 SHANNON LANE	DALLAS	PZ 5 TEXAS	PRECINCT MASTER LIST	PARTY	WILL HELP TIME CANVASS POLLS	1960 1961	1962
1430 -1	03900	MRS DOROTHY REED	F 57 W H W	LA8-7634	RC	X	X NA TX	X CA X
-2		BERTHA DENNIS	F W HSKPR	LA8-7634	IC			X
1431 -1	03904	JOHN O WHARTON	M 77 W EXECT	LA1-9359	IC	X	X NA O	XO
-2		MRS JOHN O WHARTON	F 68 W H W	LA1-9359	IC	X	X NA O	XO
1433 -1	03908	LOGAN FORD	M 56 W LAWYR	LA1-3977	RC	X	X NA TX	XO CA X
-2		MRS LOGAN FORD	F 54 W H W	LA1-3977	RC	X	X NA TX	X CA
1435 -1	03916	GEO P MACATEE	M 34 W ADV	LA1-5694	RC	X X	X NA TX	XX CA X M4
-2		MRS GEO P MACATEE	F 31 W H W	LA1-5694	RC	X	X NA TX	XX CA
1436 -1	03920	CHAPMAN ANDERSON JR	M 55 W MFG	LA1-3612	IC	X	X OA	XO CA X
-2		MRS CHAPMAN ANDERSON JR	F 53 W HW	LA1-3612	IC			
1438 -1	04000	MRS LANHAM CROLEY	F 62 W HW	LA1-9188	RC			
1439 -1	04006	CONRAD A LAU	M 41 W MKT MG	LA8-0889	DL			X
-2		MRS CONRAD A LAU	F W HW	LA8-0889				
1440 -1	04008	A P KIMBROUGH	M 38 W ENGE	LA8-5943	RC	XXXX	X NA TX	XX CA XG3
-2		MRS A P KIMBROUGH	F 37 W H W	LA8-5943	RC	XXX	X NA TX	XX CA
1442 -1	04011	JASON B SOWELL JR	M 30 W ATTNY	LA6-6257	RC			XO CA G3
-2		MRS JASON B SOWELL JR	F 26 W HW	LA6-6257	RC			
1443 -1	04016	JACOB H KRAVITZ	M 53 W SOCL W	LA8-5679	DL		X OO	XO
-2		MRS LOUIS E KRAVITZ	F 51 W H W	LA8-5679	DL		X OO	XO
1445 -1	04022	GEORGE E PARKER		LA8-3547				
-2		LAURA C PARKER		LA8-3547				
1447 -1	06401	MRS ALINE F MCCLURE	F 68 W H W	LA1-9873	DC	X	X NA	XOXCA X
1448 -1	06401	REV C V WESTAPHER		LA6-8034				

ROBERT L. CHARTRAND   175

State Finance Committee recently has sought to place all registered Republicans' names in a computerized file, while the Democratic leadership has urged its candidates to use ADP when it would be useful; Representatives John M. Murphy and Jonathan B. Bingham, for example, reportedly look to the Democratic National Committee facility for support.[46]

Computers also can be helpful in arranging the details of a campaign schedule, including speaking dates, funds required, travel accommodations, availability of key local figures, and opponents' schedules. The critical path method of scheduling, designed by William H. Wilcox and James J. O'Brien, allows a realistic appraisal of campaign objectives and the path to their attainment. Figure 5 presents a time-scale CPM for a Philadelphia referendum vote.[47]

In his discussion of "Campaign Guideposts," Ben A. Franklin sees the use of computers as "the pattern of the future" and cites the need for "critical path" campaign scheduling, in this way making sure that the candidate makes maximum use of his time among voter groups where he will have the greatest impact.[48] Although only a handful of candidates have used such sophisticated techniques, innumerable others have been observing and laying their own plans for the future.

The human complement in the overall picture is cogently summed up by one experienced political consultant:

> Only the naive and the poor depend solely on volunteers to keep the campaign machinery in gear. It's nice to think that unpaid zealots will man the headquarters, coordinate the mailings and handle the detail, but it seldom happens. People, being what they are, don't respond properly over a long period of time unless there's an economic ax hanging over their heads. Volunteers can rise to almost any occasion—but only for short periods of time.[49]

The trend today, within the campaign organization, is toward a strong man-machine combination. The computer now joins the telephone, typewriter, and duplicating machine as a vital tool.

Political Research and Issue Files

The increasing complexity of the political environment poses serious problems for any candidate who must prepare to take a stand on a number of key issues. Thus, meaningful research on issues of local, regional, or national importance has become a significant aspect of the contemporary political scene. The national committees of both major parties maintain permanent research divisions

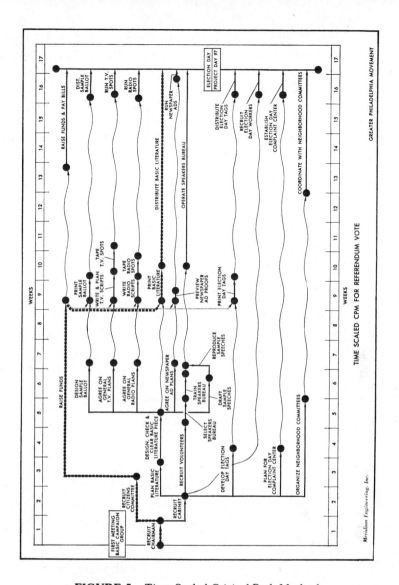

FIGURE 5. Time-Scaled Critical Path Method

that conduct studies-in-depth and prepare fact sheets on current issues. These researchers also prepare studies of voting records of the members of Congress and predictive statistical studies on the party's prospects and posture in various sections of the country. Political research capabilities also exist as the result of sponsorship by an individual candidate or a state committee.

The 1970 census, serving as a coercive impetus for reapportionment, and in many cases redistricting, has forced state and local officials to become more familiar with population characteristics, voter registration patterns, and various groups' voting performance. The *1970 Census Users' Guide* (Parts 1 and 2), published by the Bureau of Census, includes such valuable information as a comparison of printed reports and summary tapes, the variety of data delivery media (computer tapes, microfilm, printed materials) available, and detailed information on the physical characteristics, format, and languages associated with the Bureau tapes.[50]

Various commercial organizations now collect, store and process many types of data of value to the campaigner. Census data have been made available for commercial distribution, and with 1,739 reels of tape covering the five census counts, many users prefer to have the preliminary copying, extracting, and summarization handled by a professional staff. Specialty firms now offer a range of services on this material and indicate that they can provide needed data at a less-than-government cost. Also available now in summary form is information on federal assistance programs—their status, present allocation of funding, and qualifications for participating in them. Applied Urbanetics, Inc., for example, not only offers an on-line service to customers, but will prepare an ADP-generated, easy-to-read demographic map illustrating such situations as government spending related to human needs.[51]

Political researchers use information about the institutions, physical layout, and inhabitants to define those issues which mean something to the people in a given area. Decision Making Information, Inc., has developed a computer-centered "social-area analysis,"[52] which concentrates on three selected social variables: economic status, familization, and ethnic status. By indexing the first two elements by numbers (economic status) and figures (familization), the resultant coding—a "4A" district might have few people with less than an eighth grade education, few laborers, fairly large families, most families in owner-occupied (single family) dwelling units, few women in the labor force—allows the campaigner to decide which message to communicate, and in what fashion, to this tract. A color spectrum chart also is prepared as part of the social-area analysis. The use of such graphics makes understanding of the nature of a geographic district much easier for the strategist.

In recent years, local and state campaigners have become aware that activities on Capitol Hill—the bills introduced, the hearings, the investigations, the passage of new public laws—are having a far greater impact on them than before. Congressional hearings and reports are now summarized by the fledgling Congressional Information Service, offering a monthly ADP-produced master index to the contents of congressional publications; more than 400,000 pages of these documents are summarized and indexed each year, and the source publications placed on microfiche.

Professional assistance for the candidate who may want to be very sure of the laws related to a complex issue is available from such groups as the Aspen Systems Corporation, which has placed the full text of all fifty states' statutes and the United States Code in computer storage, and will perform an automated search on a word-by-word basis. Also available are such voluminous materials as the Comptroller General's decisions (published since 1940) and decisions of the United States Supreme Court (since 1950).

In certain instances the campaign staff may have to delve into records of past legislatures or individuals; in many cases the reduction of the essential information to a machineable form may be of great benefit in the future. As early as 1938, Mona Fletcher, writing on "The Use of Mechanical Equipment in Legislative Research,"[53] urged that old methods of "laying off a chart and tallying the desired information" be replaced by mechanical means "to provide accurate and permanent records, available at any future time for additional analyses." Modern retrieval languages may allow the system user to "browse" through files of probable interest where "precise information is non-indexed or poorly indexed," or when he is not sure of what he wants.[54]

Yet another resource for the political campaigner is the Inter-University Consortium for Political Research established in 1962 and comprised of approximately 100 universities and research organizations, with direction from the Institute for Social Research at the University of Michigan. Data includes collections of survey data, aggregative statistics and public records including cross-national survey studies, which reflect ethnic origins, religious affiliations, status, location and mobility, political partisanship, political socialization, occupational and income distributions, and attitudes toward the political system and major institutions, actors and events.[55]

As issues multiply and the demands on a candidate and staff mount during the course of a campaign, the importance of employing the computer-microform arsenal becomes more apparent. The decision to use them must be based on a calculated weighing of cost and performance factors and then finessed with common sense. And finally, reluctance to perform old tasks in new ways must be overcome. Ithiel de Sola Pool of the now famous Simulmatics team argues:

> All that machines do is provide more data to more people more quickly than otherwise. Questions have been raised about the morality of using advanced computer programs in political research. It seems ironical that people should view decisions made on the basis of confused guesses about what the public wants as more democratic than decisions made on the basis of careful compilations of information.[56]

Biographical Files

A candidate can often benefit from inviting a "name" personality to visit a community and boost his local campaign, but he should first make a careful check of the visitor's public utterances and record. The campaigner who maintains files of biographical information on his party's candidates is in a strong position to call the shots on who should appear at rallies, whose quotations should be used in press releases, and which key figures should be paired in photographs.

In collecting biographical information on key figures, the campaign staff can turn to government and private publications which relate salient personal facts and career achievements and convert these data to machineable form. Basic information on a candidate at the county or large-city level might include:

Name	Family Status
Address	Occupation
Present party affiliation	Religion
Tenure in party	Age
Offices held	Special Interests
Prior candidates for local office	Special Problems
Contributions made by the candidate	Nationality
	Home ownership
Known positions on key issues	Special personal or political assets

When a campaign headquarters is charged with building biographical files on more than a few candidates, the use of punched cards or other mechanized media should be considered.[57] During the 1960 Democratic convention, card files were assembled and rapidly updated by the Kennedy staff on each delegate and delegation—name, residence, religion, occupation, etc.[58]

Since an incumbent may be judged by the bills he has introduced, supported, or opposed, the challenger may seek to attack him on the basis of that record as well as on other grounds. Perhaps the incumbent abandoned the party position on a critical issue, or he may have reversed himself on a stand previously taken. In some instances ADP manipulation of data about the man, his record, and his views has been instrumental in turning up damaging inconsistencies and falsehoods.

It should be noted that the cost of establishing a comprehensive biographical file, with related press material and candidates' public statements, in computerized form—with the attendant retrieval programming and file maintenance costs—is not insignificant. However, the expenditure can be distributed among a slate of candidates and its impact minimized for any one campaigner.

File Data Commonality

In the several kinds of files discussed (and others a candidate may have, such as files on survey results and vote history analysis) there may be duplicated elements of information, such as constituent name, address, sex, age, and occupation. Automatic data processing lends itself well to the sorting, matching, and tabulating of such repeated data. This allows a saving in human effort through the reduction of staff effort, storage of large quantities of information in a non-paper (ADP or microform) medium, the introduction of multiple file utilization, and inter-file data element sharing. A graphic depiction of instances where key data elements may appear in more than one file—thereby having an effect on file maintenance, data transfer, and information utilization—is shown in Figure 6.

Candidates and office holders at all levels would like to have instantaneous access to all possible data categories that would help them to campaign effectively and successfully. To achieve this the technologist on the staff must have a voice that can be heard amid the vetoes which abound when it comes to parceling out scarce resources. The ability to utilize several files concurrently demands considerable management effort (e.g., identifying which files are critical), and a willingness on the part of all workers to participate in a trial-and-error interlude.

Once the desired data are captured in ADP form and the proper programs written, the system can give the campaigner new flexibility—within a time frame previously unattainable—for struc-

Information Element	Constituent File	Correspondence File	Financial File	Worker File	Survey File
Constituent Code	P	P	P	P	P
Name	P	P	P	P	P
Address	P	P	P	P	P
District	P	X	P	P	P
County	X	X	X	P	X
Precinct	P	X	P	P	X
Ward	P	X	X	P	X
Party	P	P	P	P	P
Registered	P	P	P	P	X
Sex	P	P	P	P	P
Age	P	P	X	P	X
Religion	X	X	X	P	X
Special Interest	X	X	X	P	X
Special Problem	X	X	X	P	X
Key Union Leader and Member	X	X	X	P	X
Party Worker Skill	P	X	P	P	X
Occupation	P	P	P	P	P
Corporate Officer	X	X	P	X	X
Firm Supporter	P	P	P	P	X
Nickname	X	P	X	P	X
Organization Affiliation	X	X	P	P	X
Nationality	X	X	X	P	X
Alien	X	X	X	X	X
Key Contributor	P	X	P	X	X
Contributions (year to date)	X	X	P	X	X
Income Group	X	X	P	P	X
Home Owner	X	X	P	P	X
Number of Dependents	X	P	P	P	X
Education	X	P	P	P	X
Welfare Recipient	X	X	P	P	X
Office Visitor — during year	X	P	X	X	X
Dinner Attendee (invitation list)	X	X	P	X	X
Party Interests	P	P	P	P	X
Veteran	X	X	X	P	X
Officer Holder	P	P	X	P	X
Legislative Interests	X	P	X	X	X
Government Worker	X	X	X	P	X
Patronage	X	X	X	P	X

FIGURE 6. Selected Campaign Files: Information Elements

Legend: "P" denotes a priority information element
"X" denotes an optional information element (useful but not critical)

Note: The decision to assign a "P" or an "X" to an information element necessarily is subjective and contingent upon the nature of the campaign effort involved.

turing, processing, and retrieving information tailored to his personal needs. When the organization is geared to collect the specified information and collectors and transcribers have been well trained for their work, the mechanism is set in motion to receive, store, and process the captured data elements.

GREAT EXPECTATIONS FOR THE FUTURE

American politics is being challenged by change as never before. The continued development of information technology presages a new age to come, an age which will allow the communication of words and images on a scale never before imagined; "talking to computers" will become commonplace, and the videophone will personalize the remote spoken conversation. One analyst, in taking the long view of ADP usage, urges his colleagues to remember that "the machine or computer does not replace people. It does not think, create ideas, or win elections. . . . It does force you to organize."[59]

Simulation is a sophisticated computer technique that may be used more widely in the future. When the Kennedy organization, overcoming the derogatory comments of many of its venerable advisors, risked turning to Ithiel de Sola Pool and his colleagues, it became clear that simulation, as a political technique, could parallel conventional polling and analysis and the political "hunch." Many have been deterred from trying simulation because of its costliness; it is estimated that $250,000 is required merely to prepare the data and program the computer.[60] Even now, there is no consensus as to the value of the simulator reports; indeed, Theodore C. Sorenson declared that they:

> . . . were no more valuable than the "issue polls" that were fed into their computers. They contained all the same faults; they restated the obvious, reflected the bias of the original pollsters, and were incapable of direct application.[61]

Since there is a dash of the opportunist in any successful politician, it is highly likely that the computer, microfilm technology, simulation, and all the accompanying systems analysis and planning techniques and devices will continue to be thoroughly explored, and used wherever possible in order to help candidates understand their environment, reach out to their constituents, and address the issues of the times. The role of the new technology has yet to be fully defined, but thoughtful persons in high places are showing a willingness to learn about and evaluate the innovations. The need for information specialists has been accepted and understood, and perhaps the concept of a "West Point for politics"[62] which can train the political professionals of the 1970's, is not too farfetched.

NOTES

1. Walter DeVries, "Information Systems in Political Consulting," Remarks before the Seminar on "Information Systems, Computers, and Campaigns," sponsored by the American Association of Political Consultants, New York City, March 1971, p. 3.

2. "Electronic Data Processing for the Political Executive" (Washington, D.C.: Research Division, Republican National Committee, 1968), p. 1.

3. Senate Committee on Government Operations, *Report to the Committee, Senate Report*, No. 938, 89th Cong. 1st sess. (Washington, D.C.: U.S. Government Printing Office, 1965), p. 6.

4. Kenneth Janda, *Information Retrieval, Applications to Political Science* (New York: The Bobbs-Merrill Company, Inc., 1968), p. 39.

5. Robert L. Chartrand, "The Fourth Generation: Intimations of Reality," *Data Management*, VIII (September 1970), pp. 99-102.

6. Charles McC. Mathias, Jr., quoted in "Polls," *Time*, LXXXIII (December 16, 1966), p. 28.

7. Herman Kahn and Anthony J. Wiener, *The Year 2000* (New York: The MacMillan Company, 1967), p. 89.

8. Edward J. Nichols, "Electronic Data Processing and Politics" (Washington, D.C.: Republican National Committee, 1966), p. 30.

9. Warren Weaver, Jr., "Computers Counseling the Candidates," *The New York Times*, October 29, 1970, p. 4.

10. DeVries, *op. cit.*, following p. 5.

11. Paul P. Van Riper, *Handbook of Practical Politics* (Evanston Illinois: Row, Peterson and Company, 1960), pp. 104-105.

12. James D. Gallagher, *Management Information Systems and the Computer* (New York: American Management Association, Inc., 1961), p. 13.

13. National Commission on Technology, Automation, and Economic Progress, *Technology and the American Economy*, I (February 1966), p. 100.

14. An example of this interest is an article by Alan L. Otten, "Punch Card Politics: Parties and Unions Use Data Processing Gear," *The Wall Street Journal*, May 24, 1965, pp. 1, 20.

15. Letter from Ray C. Bliss, chairman of the Republican National Committee, to Republican Senators, May 8, 1967. p. 1. (Talks at the April 21,

1967 session included Lance Tarrance, Jr. speaking on "EDP research for a major candidate," and Edward J. Nichols talking about "Planning through the use of critical path method," noted in RNC press release, April 19, 1967).

16. "Electronic Data Processing for the Political Executive," *op. cit.*, p. 1.

17. Information provided the author by Lance Tarrance, Jr., in letter dated April 14, 1970.

18. Data Processing Support at Democratic National Committee" (Washington, D.C.: Democratic National Committee, 1965), foreword.

19. "DNC Voter Identification System," unpublished paper, Washington, D.C. 1970, p. 2.

20. William H. Harrison, "Former IBMer in Congress; Young Man with a Computer," *National Edition* (June 12, 1967), p. 3.

21. David S. Broder, "48 Freshmen Build Their Fences," *The New York Times Magazine* (December 12, 1965), p. 104.

22. Brock Adams, Comments made for the videofilm presentation at the Fall Joint Computer Conference, Las Vegas, Nevada (November 18, 1969), p. 4.

23. "Some Plans and Recommendations for a 'Republican Data Bank' for Your Area," ATRO release no. 1. (Chicago: Mail Advertising Corporation of America, 1967), p. 5.

24. "Electronic Data Processing for the Political Executive," *op. cit.*, p. 1.

25. "Computers Try the Campaign Trail, *Business Week* (January 20, 1968), p. 88.

26. James M. Perry, "Wooing Voters with a Computer," *The National Observer,* VI (September 11, 1967), p. 1.

27. James N. Perry, *The New Politics: The Expanding Technology of Political Manipulation* (New York: Clarkson N. Potter, Inc., 1968), p. 148.

28. "The Story of Mobile Registration in Nassau County, N.Y." Brochure distributed by the Nassau County Board of Elections.

29. "Data Processing Support at Democratic National Committee," *op. cit.*, foreword.

30. For a discussion of congressional development, *see* Robert L. Chartrand, "Redimensioning Congressional Information Support," *Jurimetrics Journal,* I (June 1971), pp. 165-178.

31. House Committee on House Administration, *Special Report of the Special Subcommittee on Electrical and Mechanical Office Equipment on a Computerized Addressing and Mailing System for the House of Representatives,* 91st Cong., 2nd sess. (Washington, D.C.: U.S. Government Printing Office, December 1970).

32. AFL-CIO Committee on Political Education, *Machine Politics.* COPE Publication No. 158C (Washington, D.C.: AFL-CIO, 1966), pp. 20-21.

33. Jack Moshman, "Computers in Elections: How Business Benefits," Remarks before the Business Equipment Manufacturers Exposition, Los Angeles, California, October 22, 1964, p. 2.

34. Betty Foster, "Computers in Politics," unpublished paper, Washington, D.C., 1966, p. 21.

35. "Electronic Data Processing for the Political Executive," *op. cit.*, p. 2.

36. Jon Ford, "Labor Puts Automation Into Politics," *The San Antonio Express,* July 11, 1965, p. 2-H.

37. Bernard Hennessy, *Dollars for Democrats,* 1959 (New York: McGraw-Hill Book Company, 1960), p. 2.

38. Ford, *op. cit.,* p. 2-H.

39. Nichols, *op. cit.,* p. 50.

40. "Computer Purrs Out Demo Data," *The Austin American,* December 27, 1965, p. 7.

41. "Electronic Data Processing for the Political Executive," *op. cit.,* p. 4.

42. Samuel N. Alexander, quoted in Gallagher, *op. cit.,* p. 20.

43. *Machine politics, op. cit.,* p. 20.

44. "Campaign Management—Remarks of Some of America's Foremost Political Experts" (Washington, D.C.: Republican National Committee, 1966), p. 136.

45. "Electronic Data Processing for the Political Executive," *op. cit.,* p. 24.

46. "Democrats Face Elections with Staff, Money Problems," *Congressional Quarterly Weekly Report,* XXIV (May 27, 1966), p. 1076.

47. Perry, *op. cit., The New Politics . . .,* p. 163.

48. Ben A. Franklin, "Campaign Guideposts," in Harold Faber, (ed.), *The New York Times Election Handbook, 1968* (New York: New American Library, 1968), p. 147.

49. Hank Parkinson, *Winning Your Campaign: A Nuts-and-Bolts Guide to Political Victory* (Englewood Cliffs, New Jersey: Prentice-Hall, Inc., 1970), p. 66.

50. U.S. Department of Commerce, Bureau of the Census, *1970 Census Users Guide* (Washington, D.C.: U.S. Government Printing Office, April 1969).

51. Alan Paller and Samuel Berger, "A Map Is Worth a Thousand Printouts," *Computer Decisions* (November 1970), p. 39.

52. Perry, *op. cit., The New Politics . . . ,* pp. 152–159.

53. Mona Fletcher, "The Use of Mechanical Equipment in Legislative Research," *The Annals of the American Academy of Political and Social Science, CVC* (January 1938), p. 168.

54. Malcolm Rigby, "Browsability in Modern Information Retrieval Systems: The Quest for Information," *Proceedings of the Symposium on Education for Information Science* (Washington, D.C.: Spartan Books, 1965), p. 51.

55. For a description of the Consortium activities, *see Social Science Data Archives in the United States,* 1967, pp. 11–13.

56. Ithiel de Sola Pool, quoted in Thomas B. Morgan, "The People Machine," *Harpers Magazine* (January 1961), p. 5.

57. Kenneth Janda, *Data Processing, Applications to Political Research* (Evanston, Illinois: Northwestern University Press, 1965), p. 28.

58. Fred G. Burke, "Senator Kennedy's Convention Organization," in Paul Tillet (ed.), *Inside Politics: The National Conventions, 1960* (Dobbs Ferry, New York: Oceana Publications, Inc., 1961), p. 29.

59. William Amos, "Electronic Paths to Success," in "Campaign Management", *op. cit.*, p. 137.

60. Franklin, *op. cit.*, p. 148.

61. Quoted in Perry, *op. cit., The New Politics . . .* , p. 169.

62. Richard Harwood, "Television Shaping the New Politics," *The Washington Post* (March 29, 1970), p. A19.

—7—

THE COMPUTER'S ROLE IN GETTING OUT THE VOTE

Rex Hardesty

The accurate, up-to-date "precinct walking list" has for years been the political Lost Dutchman gold mine, searched after by organizations engaged in the American electoral process. By use of a newly expanded, increasingly sophisticated computer program, the AFL-CIO Committee on Political Education is attempting to break through the thickets barring the way to this long-sought goal.

The goal is a "walking list" of union members that can most effectively bring labor's political program directly to union members in their homes across the country and help dramatically to increase member participation in the democratic process.

This is, after all, the reason for labor's presence in political action—to involve union members and members of their families, to reach them so they can be registered, to get materials to them in their homes to help inform them on issues and candidates' records, to get them out to vote on election day.

The "walking list" opens the door to this kind of direct contact and the AFL-CIO computer program is the tool that can make it possible. Such lists are far from new. They have long been a staple of labor's political operations—the bread and butter of politics. What is new is the method of compiling them, their scope and—most importantly—the accuracy and the speed of delivery the computer permits.

While the "walking lists" constitute the single most valuable potential computer output, its benefits and impact spread importantly into other facets of labor's political programs. The computer becomes, in effect, the ultimate mailing list, making possible fast, accurate mailings, as the need arises, to union members in almost any selected political subdivision in the nation. As well, it provides 3 X 5 index cards for precinct work.

And inside the computer is a two-way street, pouring traffic not only out of the computer to the state and local COPE groups, but routing new traffic, new data and new names into the main computer from those same state and local bodies. Continually the computer requires considerable specific information, and it will keep sending printouts back to the field until a satisfactory amount of information is returned.

The project, which involves the participation of 88 of the 116 international unions affiliated with the AFL-CIO, also requires constant updating for accuracy. In its formative stages, it has also required an education process for local COPE activists, union officials and volunteers on the use of the potential.

A major milestone was passed in January 1973 when the operation was moved into the AFL-CIO Data Processing Department for the first time. Previously, COPE had used the computer facilities of the Machinists and rented time on other computers in the Washington area.

At mid-summer 1973, the COPE project had about 8.9 million names committed to the computer memory bank, putting the program ahead of schedule on its goal of 10 million before the 1974 elections.

Periodic updatings and processing to compile more information—or more detailed information—are going on constantly.

It has taken almost eight years for the COPE computer program to develop to its present level and probably forever the "potential" of the program will lie just ahead of its reality. A few unions are forbidden by their constitution to provide their membership lists to the program—or at least the international union is forbidden to provide them. In many of these unions, locals are under no such restraint, so a list can be provided by the locals within a given state. Overall, it is turning out that about 80 percent of the union members' names can be compiled in a given state.

Some states have a union membership so small or so widely scattered that computer work isn't worth the time and expense— the whole job can be done by hand more practically. And for some very rare states, it isn't needed: New Mexico has 20,000 union members, for instance, and 94 percent of them are now registered to vote as they have been for a long time. Since registering union members and getting them out to vote is the object of the whole process, New Mexico simply doesn't need that much help.

Lists—or at least partial lists—have been compiled on about 34 states, mostly from among the heavily populated corridors of the northeast, the upper midwest and the west coast. That total is expected to reach 37 states by the end of 1973.

Eight years ago, the program was born from an experience in New Jersey in the 1964 elections—the election in which the most liberal of recent Congresses, the 89th, was elected along with Lyndon Johnson. As part of the labor effort in 1964, the response to an appeal to unions with sizable memberships in New Jersey produced a list of 400,000 names of union members.

After the election, that list, compiled and maintained totally by hand, was still around. In 1965, COPE spotted the potential of computerizing such lists and COPE Director Al Barkan launched the project on its first halting steps. As a pilot project for the future, work was begun on a similar list for Pennsylvania. As befits its status of a highly unionized state, Pennsylvania has remained a mainstay throughout the program.

For the 1966 elections, experimentation was extended to a few more states and by the time that election was over, the computers borrowed at the Machinists building had membership lists from at least parts of seven more states—Maryland, Virginia, Ohio, Colorado, California and Texas. Even then, Pennsylvania was carrying a sizable total of between 800,000 and 900,000 names. Work in Texas produced a list of 300,000, with a high degree of sophistication in how the Texas state federation broke down the list.

In April 1968, there were about 3.2 million names in the computer for use in labor's all-out campaign drive of that fall. But if mailing lists aren't updated they deteriorate rapidly and the problem was complicated further in those years by the U.S. Post Office Department's continued experimentation with zip codes. Scott Davis, then working in the Machinists computer department, recalls watching as many as three new zip codes be assigned to one area.

While almost anything that could be done with the computers was a bonus for the political work in those states, the problem of those years was keeping lists current during the political off-years. Since corrections are needed as often as every three months, catching up just ahead of each election was an overwhelming job.

It was in the wake of the 1968 elections that COPE director Barkan turned the data processing effort into a year-around project. An additional assistant director, John Perkins, came from the COPE field staff at that time, with the data processing project among his responsibilities. To coordinate distribution and field work, Perkins has incorporated the computer project into an overall pre-election preparation known as the "critical path" method, designed to assist state AFL-CIOs and central bodies in planning, scheduling and controlling data processing activities.

"Critical path" isn't much different from the way a construction superintendent might organize work crews to make sure the forms are finished before the cement arrives, or the system an airline ground crew might employ to get the gasoline and meals aboard the right flights. This method is important to the data processing because it spells out deadlines well in advance and incorporates the concept of activities which are simultaneous but with separate deadlines.

The program has to be keyed from the start to the election laws and habits of a given state—the words county, ward and precinct aren't used everywhere and registration isn't required in small towns and rural areas of some states. The data processing also depends on who keeps the voter registration planning information—county, city or township; how that information is organized; what kind of access to it is allowed by law; and full details on the voter registration, for instance, if the state allows registration only at the court house and forbids deputy registrars.

For example, when a computer file is "passed" to be printed out and sent to the field for the processing of political data, the cards are put in a sequential sort by county for areas with county government. But in New England and other parts of the country where the registration lists are kept by town, an assignment is made either by the name of the post office or the political subdivision and the sorting is done accordingly.

Consequently, a registration survey has to be conducted in the field to determine which sort is necessary for the computer to print a format that can be easily processed against the local, county or city registration lists.

The combination of critical path and data processing has enabled COPE representatives in the field to determine the location of union members, the work loads that are involved in determining their registration status and costs in capturing telephone numbers and other critical political data. It provides those in charge with an overview, helping them allocate their resources for the maximum impact on election day.

Ironically, Perkins has found that the political workers who are the most accomplished in working with precinct lists are sometimes the most reluctant to utilize the computer's full potential on the next step. That's because they know how valuable the lists are and are reluctant to part with them for further revision.

That's why he urges the wider use of 3 X 5 cards. They can be bursted into sections, passed out to volunteers, marked on and generally folded, spindled or mutilated. A fresh supply, incorporating new information marked on them, can be sent quickly—and often at far less cost than the new information can be manually updated in the field. But the naked feeling of being without the lists for even a limited amount of time is hard to overcome for some.

Another part of that feeling is born of the necessary concern for security. The absolute necessity that even fractions of a state printout don't fall into the wrong hands—such as commercial mail order houses—prompts COPE to build in security measures all along the way.

First, all printout material may be ordered by and will be delivered only to the state AFL-CIO. This guards against improper use of the list and protects the integrity of COPE endorsements. It also builds a clear checkpoint and responsibility into the system, as well as expediting the distribution of a massive printout for various metropolitan regions.

Secondly, all material printed out in the AFL-CIO building, and not sent for whatever reason, is shredded, even when only a handful of items are duplicated.

Finally, the fictitious Ruth Cope is ubiquitous. If AFL-CIO headquarters or the state federation office ever gets a solicitation addressed to Ruth Cope, the alert goes out, with the printing codes on the mailing list quickly checked. It has never happened, but vigilance is permanently built in.

While no mail order outfit has ever gotten hold of the lists, slipups do occur—and correcting them is part of the constant improvement of the system.

For instance, it used to be a problem when union members gave a shop or downtown office address far removed from the residence where they vote. As the card winds its way through the system, the downtown precinct would be checked for the member's voter registration, to no avail. When neighboring precincts also fail to show the registration, the person may get a "dear union member" form letter urging him to register to vote—and it's the president of the international union who gets the letter.

Consequently, the bottom of the 3 X 5 card carries a code by which retired member, full-time union official or non-residential address can be quickly and easily identified.

One discrepancy is a sad embarrassment which occurs constantly and as yet no one can provide an answer. Many times, survivors will ask to keep a deceased spouse's name on the publication list for the union's journal because they are accustomed to reading and enjoying it. But when that publication list becomes the starting point for the COPE computer project, the name on the mailing list shows up as unregistered and the "dear union member" letter will go out. Sometimes the carefully handwritten reply reflects a great pride of "indeed he was registered and interested in the activities of his union" but it is still an occurrence which everyone would like to avoid.

Lists from the unions arrive at COPE in a wide variety of ways, from lists already committed to computer (magnetic) tape, to addressograph, scriptograph or other semi-automated lists which, while containing most of the needed information, still have to go through the keypunch process before being committed to magnetic tape. And of course the same is true of typewritten lists.

Of the 88 unions which have members enrolled in the program, 61 of them provided membership lists from the union's international headquarters.

Since the majority of the lists do originate with the union publication, they are organized by zip code, then alphabetized within that area. Since the goal of the precinct work is political information—registered or unregistered, party affiliation, ward and precinct—along with accurate names, address and telephone numbers, a far different kind of breakdown will be wanted. But the zip code remains there, invaluable both for massive national mailings, such as a presidential election year, and for the redistricting of congressional districts. Counties, cities, wards and precincts may jump all over the map during reapportionment—but zip codes can be used to pinpoint the new district very quickly.

Once the starting list has been received at the AFL-CIO in any form, it is keypunched to be added within the proper state and coded with an 18-character top line for future computer reference.

The next step is verification, a mailing of the new names to find unworkable or changed addresses. Sometimes an address can change such as when annexation assigns a street number to a rural route. Early verification will save a lot of trouble down the road for the volunteer who is trying to locate a member at an address that doesn't exist anymore.

Once the list is verified, the hard work begins. A printout is made, most likely on 3 X 5 cards, and is sent to the state AFL-CIO for the first compilation of "below-the-line," or political information. There's no substitute for the local voting list, a map, a phone book and precinct locator in compiling the next information: ward, precinct, party affiliation, registration status and phone number. If a voter is registered, a lot of that information comes quickly off election rolls in jurisdictions that make them public. But if all you have to go on is an address, identifying the unregistered by precinct requires a map and a lot of work.

Since quarterly updatings are made on all state mailing lists, the gathering of information missed the first time, such as phone numbers, goes on constantly—as does the potential of learning that the member has subsequently registered to vote.

Once the political information is filled in as accurately as possible, the new information is re-coded to fit in with all other union members in the state. At this point, it is available for a printout in any form the state or local COPE may call for—mail labels, lists, 3 X 5 cards—and organized under various identifying characteristics—by county, unregistered voters only, by union and so on.

At this stage, the computer is also capable of giving COPE officials, locally or nationally, a quick overview. This can show the number of union members in each county in the state, the number unregistered or the ones on whom phone numbers are still not available. This keeps them ahead of their "critical paths" and provides a constant check on overall COPE activities.

Figuring the fastest, cheapest and most usable form is complex and COPE has issued several manuals advising political workers on what is available and how to order it. The program is still new enough that prepping everyone on the various alternatives remains difficult.

The potential of the program is considerable, but political observers know it's risky to start counting potential voters and predicting victory margins. When you look back at a close race, you can find the group that provided the margin almost anywhere you want—even attributing it to the left-handed Lithuanians, as election analyst Richard M. Scammon often says.

But since labor's strategy has always been the simplest of formulas—get workers registered and out to vote—the numbers game is a little more germane, if no more accurate, in predicting an outcome.

The examples are legion:

In two congressional districts of Connecticut, for example, COPE-endorsed candidates won one and lost one in 1972 by margins on which the unregistered union members could have had a distinctive impact. In the fifth district, the COPE-endorsed candidate lost narrowly in a district which has 29,364 union members on the data processing list. Of that total, only 18,828 were registered and 10,536 were not—almost twice the 5,436 margin by which the COPE candidate lost.

In Connecticut's third district, the COPE candidate won with 53.3 percent of the vote. That was a margin of 14,904 votes, but another 9,511 union members in the district were not registered. Had they been, and had they voted in the usual 7-3 range in favor of COPE-endorsed candidates, the 53.3 percent margin could have been much wider.

Similar examples abound, but of course the industrialized states—and working class districts—are the most important. With one-man, one-vote setting fairly tight population limits of 500,000 for a congressional district, the rule of thumb is that two-thirds of that population will be eligible to vote. That's an electorate of nearly 350,000 for any congressman, but only 164,000 turned out in 1972, for instance, when COPE-endorsed Rep. James O'Hara squeaked to reelection with 50.8 percent of the vote in his Michigan district, a margin of 2,684. One Massachusetts district was even closer, with the COPE-endorsed candidate winning by only 1,206 votes out of 234,300 cast.

The potential of unregistered union voters may be even greater in election units smaller than congressional districts and the COPE data processing program has the potential of going into the level of alderman—or whatever.

Getting union members to register and vote is of course a long haul—and the computer isn't wired to people who respond like marionettes to COPE's appeal. But if the manpower is available, it can provide the information for very sophisticated undertakings which go beyond the time-honored telephoning, car pooling and baby sitting services of election day.

In sheer speed the computer is awesome. In sorting information, the computer can read 350,000 numbers per second off a disc. When information is going out, the computer performs equally prodigious feats: in one hour, it can turn out 30,000 of the 3 X 5 cards, 66,000 lines on a listing or 75,000 mail labels. A lot of volunteers have to do a lot of typing to match that.

What the computer means to improved political work is equally impressive:

- In the past, when a state COPE made endorsements for such races as state representative, it would have to combine several districts, perhaps all from one county, in the mailing to union members informing them of the endorsement. Or it would be necessary to send a cumbersome list covering endorsements in the whole state—in either case leaving the union member to dig out his own district. Now, by calling for a printout by ward or precinct, a very specialized mailing can be made on each district.
- In voter registration drives, the multiple available listings make it possible to reach some members at their home through street or telephone lists; others on the job by calling for a printout by union, then publicizing a date when deputy registrars will be at the plant—or some combination of both methods.
- In metropolitan areas where both the election board's registration lists and the telephone company's subscriber lists are available on magnetic tape, Perkins expects that within a few years, the AFL-CIO will be able to pass the COPE file of union members against those lists (in the same computer) and electronically capture the information on union members and their telephone numbers without a human hand being lifted. When COPE volunteers can throw away all the phone books, precinct locators and the like, the time and cost savings will be tremendous.
- On election day, it is possible for a precinct worker to draw up a list of the voters in triplicate, then tour the polling places periodically during the day. Union members who have already voted are scratched off, with the remain-

ing names turned in to the COPE telephone bank for calls. The same can be done on the carbon copies later that day, so by dusk every union member in the precinct may have been reminded, or provided transportation to vote.

Of course, attaining that optimum is also a little like seeking the Lost Dutchman gold mine.

The kind of lists and response COPE is trying to achieve are nothing that haven't been done before, in precincts across the country—it's again a matter of the computer expediting the process and helping get maximum use from available manpower.

—8—

AGGREGATE ELECTION DATA IN THE CAMPAIGN: LIMITATIONS, PITFALLS, AND USES

Charles H. Backstrom
Robert Agranoff

There are many approaches to the planning of election campaigns, but one of the most frequently used by candidates and their strategists is aggregate data analysis. Election data is the most readily available information for the campaigner. In most cases, the entire data gathering effort amounts to securing a photocopy of the official abstract of votes from the public official who keeps such records. From this raw data, a great deal of insight can be gathered from relatively simple calculations and statistical routines that are easy to explain and discuss with candidates and campaign workers. Moreover, research has indicated that election statistics are the most widely used means of campaign data, even in small constituency campaigns.[1] Indicators of the most important information required in a campaign can be derived from voting results: partisan strength, swing voting, turnout, and candidate strength.

Actually vote returns are the "hardest" data that a campaign manager is likely to have available. They represent an imperishable record of actual behavior by people in a real situation. Election figures are not as suspect among practitioners as the results of a public opinion survey, which is an estimate of a much larger universe from a small sample, and thus subject to sampling error. Also a poll contains only *reported* data about voting (which after all

Prepared for this volume. The authors wish to thank Eric L. Stowe for his assistance in preparation of the manuscript.

elections is always inflated by people who do not admit, or do not remember, not having voted).

A further advantage of aggregate election data analysis is its favorable impression on campaign managers. Somehow, columns of figures, yards of adding machine tape, or stacks of computer output give the presentation by an analyst an aura of expertise that he may need to convince old-time campaigners not yet enamoured of the new politics. Hopefully—surely after reading this chapter—the analyst will have content as impressive as the form of his data.

Some political scientists have viewed aggregate data analysis with skepticism because, although it relies heavily on mathematical computation, it is so unsophisticated a statistical device that it would seem to produce few more meaningful political insights than the average ward leader's common knowledge. Indeed, many political scientists are afraid that aggregate data analysis would compare quite unfavorably with the old politico, whose vast experience enabled him to know his people so well that he knew intuitively how they would vote in any given election. Here, we must stop and examine how this reluctance to use aggregate data analysis arose.

First, much has been written about the omniscient "ward boss." In truth, there probably never were more than a handful of such sage old ward leaders. Their reputation for infallibly predicting election results probably arose because few people had sufficient electoral data to challenge them and, most importantly, because, in the days of the political machine, prediction and control of election results were never quite distinguishable. Now with the demise of the machine in all but a very few urban centers, the old politico is a rapidly vanishing species.

Secondly, the reluctance to use aggregate data analysis is partially the fault of the political scientists who have misused it. That is to say, aggregate data analysis, like any other mathematical technique which is applied to the study of practical politics, is subject to some extremely critical limitations.

ECOLOGICAL FALLACY

The most critical limitation is what W. S. Robinson has termed "the ecological fallacy"—the common practice of making inferences about the behavior of individuals on the basis of correlations between the same variables based on groups of people as units.[2] As applied to aggregate electoral data analysis, it means that the analyst cannot necessarily infer that individual voters exhibit both characteristics that show up together in the area they are in.

If in a precinct of 150 voters, 100 (67%) voted for Candidate A in one race, and 100 (67%) voted for Candidate X in a second race, we can't be sure that they are the same 100 people (although the mathematics here indicates that at least 50 of them must be the same). Likewise if the Republican candidate in a black ghetto precinct gets 10% of the vote, we do not know if 10% of the blacks are voting Republican; it may be their remaining few white neighbors.

A number of writers have pointed out, in response to Robinson, that not all correlations between variables measured at the grouped level are intended to infer the behavior of individuals.[3] As Austin Ranney maintains, aggregate data studies can be useful if they bypass questions about individuals and types of individuals. In terms of election data studies, he argues that the sole object of inquiry should be the behavior of electorates.[4]

In utilizing election data for campaign purposes, the analyst must be aware of the ecological problem, but he can perform certain types of analysis that treat individuals as electorates. As will be demonstrated, electoral data is used in campaigns to get an area political map of the district, to plan area based strategy, and to manage a campaign (tactics). Campaigning is essentially a matter of mobilizing electorates,[5] often calculating the aggregate effect of an aggregate effort. Very little contemporary campaigning is face-to-face in nature; it is planned and executed on a group basis. Thus, with the limitations of its usage in mind, election data can provide valuable tools in planning and managing campaigns, if some commonalities can be identified.

CORRELATION CAUTIONS

In any association of characteristics, even on an individual voter level, caution must be exercised in concluding that voting behavior is the result of the interaction of those characteristics. For example, we may find that in Dakota County, Minnesota, the correlation between the percent Catholic vote and the percent Democratic vote is .77, a rather high correlation, but we have no way of knowing whether specific Democratic voters who are Catholic vote for the party because of Catholicism, or for any other stated reason. When the precinct by precinct correlation between the Republican candidates for the state senate and state house is .89, the researcher can surmise that being on the Republican ticket was an important factor in candidate vote totals, but he cannot necessarily infer that most voters cast their ballots in this way because they identified with the Republican party. They might have had a dozen different reasons for voting for a given candidate, from his party label to his position on the ballot, to the ethnic ring of his name, to issue positions or his personal appeal in door-to-door campaigning.

LEVEL OF ANALYSIS PROBLEM

The task of identifying commonalities and distinguishing one area from another is more difficult the larger the area under study. Given American residential patterns, people who live near each other will tend to be more alike than those people who live farther apart. Thus it is preferable to use the smallest unit available for the analysis. Because the precinct is the smallest vote reporting area, it usually is relatively homogeneous. Using precincts instead of larger units vastly increases the workload for the analyst. In Minnesota, for example, there are 87 counties, but almost 4000 precincts.

MANIPULATION OF DATA LIMITATION

With the advent of the electronic computer, the level of analysis problem is not as severe. Computers make it possible to enter, store, and calculate large amounts of data from a large number of units.[6] It allows the aggregate data researcher to go down to the lowest available unit, the precinct, and thus bridge the level of analysis gap. The ease of data handling by the computer does not, however, reduce the considerable management burden involved in acquiring, entering, verifying, and storing large amounts of data.

Where precinct data is overwhelming, such as in nationwide analysis of some 170,000 precincts, samples of precincts can be drawn to represent whole states. The same method is commonly used by the major broadcast networks to project results early and to describe voting patterns.

In several states, however, no central collection of precinct data is made at all; thus someone will have to contact every single county election chief (auditor, clerk) and obtain the precinct data.

In some states, voting records are not required to be preserved, and in others only for a very short period of time.

County election figures from all over the nation have been published in the *America Votes* series since 1956, and the Inter-University Consortium for Political Research is moving toward accumulating past county figures. It has been found impractical, because of undocumented boundary changes, to try to resurrect a historical precinct data file that would contain strictly comparable data. The major television networks, in their effort to provide election night projections and analysis of presidential, senatorial, and gubernatorial elections, have gathered enormous data banks of election data and accompanying precinct maps for their own use.

Most states publish a canvassing board report, a "blue book" or legislative manual that contains at least some voting figures. These may consist of only state totals, or they may include county totals, or even precinct data, although the latter is usually only on the major statewide races. This information may have to be supplemented with other unpublished figures to study all the races an analyst wishes to consider for a particular campaign.

PRECINCT BOUNDARY LIMITATION

Another major difficulty in using aggregate voting analysis is the change in *precinct boundaries.* One of the attractions of using county data is the relative stability of county lines once a state has been fully settled. Municipal lines are more fluid. Boundary changes often go unnoticed or unrecorded in state public records, in spite of the fact that they can result in rural areas being annexed (from a township) by a village, thereby effecting changes in reported vote turnout and composition between two elections. Since precincts exist only for election administration, the boundaries are set by such criteria as convenience of the voters, existence of a public building in the area to avoid having to pay rent to a private facility and, most often, the number of voters that can be accommodated by the officials at one polling place. The change from paper ballots to voting machines usually is accompanied by enlarging precincts, in order to maximize the number of people voting on a single machine.

Any attempt at comparison of voting data across the years must cope with the problem of fluctuating precinct boundaries. If a precinct has been split, and parts of it added to other precincts, some estimate of numbers of voters in each part must be made, and a division of the vote apportioned to each part. On-the-spot observation, or testimony of knowledgeable people in the area may give some suggestion of a realistic way to apportion the precinct, but sometimes the analyst will have to be content with eye-balling the precinct and deciding, say, that about one-third of it went one way and two-thirds the other.

This allocation of vote is necessary to explain superficially drastic distortions of size of vote and percentage of turnout. The precinct should carry a tag throughout the analysis so that the data concerning it is not considered a "real" as for unaltered precincts. Besides boundary changes, name changes might occur, making it necessary to verify which name this year represents an equivalent area in some past year.

One cue as to whether precincts, boundaries, or names have been changed is often a change in the number of precincts per municipality or per county. But this is not always reliable, since a municipality can adjust the boundaries of its 10 precincts without changing the total number. The only foolproof way to make sure of what happened is to get a copy of the current election map or municipal ordinance setting boundaries, and compare it with the old map to see if the boundaries are the same. Lacking this, a phone call or letter to the municipal clerk may elicit information as to whether any changes have occurred.

Even when precinct lines do not change, comparisons across years must be made with care. The precinct is, after all, only a geographical box whose contents may change over time. The mobility of the American public is well-known.[7] The 1960 census data showed that an average of 20 percent of the people move every year. Destruction prior to urban renewal can decimate an area between elections, or the change from slum area to luxury apartment area can occur over a span of two or three election periods. The building of a subdivision in a farming township can increase the population by 1000 percent between elections, and may drastically change the partisan composition of the area. On-the-spot observation and the testimony of informed observers again are the only safeguard against mistaken conclusions about apparent changes in voter behavior.

Even where no population movement has occurred, we must beware of a "temporal fallacy"—like the ecological fallacy, but where the measurement is made at two different times. Likewise over time, if 50% of the people in a precinct voted for Candidate

A in one election, and 40% in the next, we cannot say that 10% of the people changed their minds and turned against the man, because there is no proof that the same people were voting in the first and second elections.

SELECTION OF DATA

There are several approaches for selecting electoral data for analysis.

Base Race

One form of comparative analysis depends upon the use of a "base race" in which an elective office of "low visibility" is purposefully selected. Because the office being examined is not a volatile point of controversy, it gives an excellent indication of the percentage of bedrock party support for that constituency. The most straightforward way is to calculate the two-party percentage for a given election for the base race office. It is also useful to display the absolute vote for the office, which will give the strategist an estimate of the minimum number of votes he can expect in that precinct.

In Minnesota, political analysts have long used the office of Railroad and Warehouse Commissioner, one of the many row offices which tend to be relatively invisible to the public eye, in which, therefore, the candidate is assumed to be selected mostly by partisan affiliation rather than by personality of issues.

Representative Race

Another form of comparative analysis is the selection of a "representative race," in other words, a previous campaign is chosen which has as many situational similarities to the present race as possible. The presumed areas of the present candidate's strength can then be tested against the data of the representative race. For example, in a Democratic primary campaign for mayor in Minneapolis in which a good-government type was challenged by a labor leader, a political science professor suggested as a "representative race" a previous school board race in which labor had selected a troika who were beaten by some specially recruited citizens with a broader based community support. The precinct results of this race were analyzed and made to constitute part of an index of where to campaign most intensively. The same good government Democrat also wanted to attract support from Republican voters. Previous campaign observers came up with a race for a state office in which a challenger to the Republican endorsed candidate for a state office had won. These figures constituted an index of where normal Republicans were less likely to follow party endorsement.

It is important to note, however, that the selection of a representative race does not guarantee that the past and present elections are exactly comparable. Naturally, if the candidate is an incumbent, his previous race would usually be an ideal choice. But, every election is unique to some extent; it has different candidates, or at least the same candidates with two more years of experience, the candidates are spending more or less (probably more) on media and polls, the issues have changed, voters have come of age or died or been enfranchised or stimulated to register. Yet we know enough about the relative stability of voting[8] and the importance of name identification to believe that substantial comparisons can be made. It would be ideal to avoid selecting any race that diverged markedly from "normality," of course, in choosing the representative race.

Swing Vote

Most strategists feel the necessity to develop a relative measure of voter deviation from normal partisan voting. The practice of ticket splitting is becoming increasingly common and thus, the campaign strategist ordinarily develops a measure of "swing" away from the normal partisanship of a given district. The measurement of swing voting is too often assumed to be very complicated. In actuality, after some political judgments are made, it is one of the easiest determinations. The most basic means of calculating swing is to obtain the percentage difference between the base race and the representative race. Another commonly used technique is the calculation of the percentage difference between the highest and lowest vote getters on a party ticket.

The measurement of swing need not be restricted to a single election year, but the comparison of different years is subject to the effects of all of the concomitant situational differences. On occasion, campaign strategists may wish to determine areas of swing for a single office over a long period of time. For example, in planning a congressional campaign in Minnesota, the five previous congressional campaigns were used.

Researchers should also be aware of two adjustments to the rate of swing. First, one must account for voter fall-off from one race to another; many voters will mark their ballots for some offices but not for others. Secondly, the variance in the number of voters per unit should be accounted for. The absolute number of swing votes per district is often more critical than the percentage.[9]

It is also useful to measure the percentage and number of straight and split tickets cast. Unfortunately, few states keep such records on the precinct level.

Partisan Index

While swing, base race, and representative race can be tested statistically by analyzing a single office, some analysts prefer to rely on an index incorporating several races. An index of party vote, constructed by a simple average of the two-party percentage for each of several races at a previous election, may be an acceptable figure around which to measure the variation of each candidate, with some attempt to try to explain the deviations by personality, campaign, incumbency, candidates' home county or other factors.

Related Data

To assist in explaining vote changes, as much related information should be gathered as possible. Ideally each campaign should be seen as one that would be a precursor for future activities and complete records of all campaign techniques utilized—such as the nature, thrust, and quality of mass media broadcasts and advertisements. A map of the billboard campaigns, a list of the precincts that were block-worked, phonoramaed, literature dropped, sound-trucked, and supermarket-blitzed—should be kept. Any campaign technique with geographic distinctions should be carefully logged for later comparison with aggregate data. Unfortunately, few campaigns are this well organized. And no candidate thinks beyond the immediate campaign. He would never think of delegating scarce staff personnel to keep such records. In lieu of this, managers can be interviewed immediately after the campaign. While this entails the danger of 20/20 hindsight and self-serving explanations, a campaign manager's account of activities can be useful.

MANIPULATING THE DATA

Arithmetic Computation and Display

Once the basic data has been chosen, gathered, and checked, it needs to be processed to facilitate analysis. Elemental analysis does not require complicated statistical procedures.

Among measures commonly calculated precinct by precinct are the following:

1. Percentage of total two-party (or multi-party) vote for each office received by each candidate.
2. Percentage point differences among the vote received by candidates from several different races in the same year, or by candidates for a single office over a period of years.
3. Pluralities of vote of a candidate for each office over his opponent.
4. Percentage of eligible voters registered.
5. Percentage of registered voters turning out to vote.
6. Percentage of voters who turned out who actually voted for one or the other of the candidates for each office (the fallout or "voter fatigue") down the ticket.
7. Percentages of the actual raw votes received by a candidate of the vote for other candidates of the party (the "party falloff," including both ticket splitting and voter fatigue). Once all measures are computed for each precinct in a larger unit (ward, county), additional measures are useful.
8. Proportion of total area wide registration and vote accounted for by each precinct.

Obviously, such extensive computations when performed for, say five races in every precinct in a major city, or in all precincts in a state, can become quite compendious. The computer is the obvious tool for repeated computations on a large number of similar units. Simple programs can be devised to do this work.

After the elemental computations and displays have been made, more complex statistical analyses could be helpful. Extremely handy, for example, are simple and multiple correlations among vote percentages for different offices. Scattergram plots of the two-party percentage of two offices will instantly reveal deviant cases that require further explanation, as well as the general relationship, or lack of it, between the two races.

Pitfalls in Aggregate Data Analysis

Conclusions from aggregate data demand care to avoid some rather elementary mathematical traps.

Overaggregation results from the use of units of analysis so large that significant differences within the unit are masked. Thus, if a study lumps together all the people in one city and measures them on some characteristic, such as percent voting Democratic, it will indicate a figure somewhere between the percentage of the most Democratic and the least Democratic sub-areas. This masking pitfall is illustrated in Table I and II from a 1969 city election in Minneapolis.

Tables I and II illustrate how very great differences among areas of the Minneapolis city are masked. If this citywide vote of 61.4% for a mayoral candidate is disaggregated, first to wards, the result can be seen from column 3 of Table I. Wards (there are 13 in Minneapolis) are arranged by decreasing percent of vote for the independent candidate. This ward vote runs from a high of 79.3 in Ward 3 to a low of 39.4 in Ward 7, a difference of 2 to 1. If wards are used as the units of analysis instead of the city as a whole, quite different conclusions can be drawn about the support for this particular candidate. But even the ward data masks real differences within the city. If ward totals are disaggregated further to precinct totals, column 4 of Table I shows that the mayor's percentage actually runs from 13.7 to 88.2, a difference of more than 6 to 1. Even within individual wards there is still a substantial difference. Taking the strongest ward for the mayor as an example, Table II shows in column 3 a spread among precincts between 88.2 and 66.1 percent. This is the lowest level possible to disaggregate election data. It can easily be seen how in trying to understand the source of the victorious mayor's support (or in planning his defeat), close examination of the disaggregated data is a necessity.

Percentage Myopia results from the use of percentages exclusively and ignoring actual vote totals. Percentages are probably the most useful device in analyzing election figures. They make possible the direct comparison of areas of different size in order to group precincts with similar proportions of support for a candidate. This is important because it tells us the ratio of support to opposition, and gives us a quick and accurate idea how close we came to victory, assuming that all people in the precinct react in the same proportions to some difference in candidate or campaign.

This kind of comparison is useful, because precincts often differ widely in size, yet may be similar in other regards. But it is this very setting aside of size considerations that creates the percentage

TABLE I. Minneapolis Mayor Vote Analysis, 1969

Rank of 2-Party Percent	Ward	Percent for Independent Mayor*	Precinct % Range	Rank of Wards by Plurality	Ward Plurality	Rank by Mayor's Proportion of Vote	Proportion of Mayor's Vote
1	3	79.3	66.1 - 88.2	5	3688	8	6.6
2	4	77.8	72.8 - 84.9	1	6391	1	11.8
3	1	74.3	61.9 - 81.0	3	5041	3	10.2
4	12	73.1	65.3 - 81.6	2	5453	2	11.4
5	9	72.7	63.3 - 83.2	4	3800	6	8.0
6	8	62.3	34.4 - 78.8	6	1911	9	6.4
7	5	61.9	25.8 - 81.3	7	1685	11	5.8
8	6	59.4	26.9 - 70.9	10	938	13	3.9
9	10	58.0	47.5 - 74.6	9	1423	7	6.8
10	11	55.6	37.4 - 67.0	8	1497	4	9.9
11	2	52.0	22.7 - 73.1	11	358	10	6.1
12	13	46.3	24.1 - 64.3	12	-989	5	8.2
13	7	39.4	13.7 - 68.2	13	-2118	12	5.2

*Mayoral vote is that of an independent candidate, Charles Stenvig, who was running against a candidate endorsed by the Republican Party after the Democratic-Farmer-Labor (Democratic) endorsed candidate had been eliminated in the non-partisan primary.

TABLE II. Ward 3, Minneapolis Mayor Vote Analysis, 1969

Rank by 2-Party Percent	Precinct	Percent Ind. for Mayor	Rank of Plurality	Plurality
1	14	88.2	14	13
2	10	84.1	13	43
3	2	83.4	3	434
4	9	82.9	6	296
5	11	82.3	7	293
6	8	81.5	9	266
7	1	80.4	1	494
8	5	79.7	10	231
9	7	79.5	5	328
10	4	79.2	4	358
11	3	78.2	2	470
12	12	74.6	11	91
13	6	74.5	8	290
14	13	66.1	12	81

pitfall. It is not a percentage that wins votes, it is a plurality of votes. Therefore, if percentages only were to make up the analysis and priority system for a campaign, a manager could easily be trapped into setting a high priority on a precinct that had very little to offer in terms of total votes.

The data on Minneapolis will illustrate this point. Ward 3 (the top line of Table I), which exhibits the highest percentage of two-candidate vote for mayor, actually is fifth out of thirteen wards in plurality of votes (columns 5 and 6); Ward 12, in contrast, is fourth in percentage and second in plurality.

The same type of differentials are shown within a single ward, though even more extremely. Using Ward 3 as an example again (Table II), Precinct 14, the strongest in the city for the mayor, actually was last within the ward in plurality, with only 13. This is obviously a function of its tiny size—it has only 17 voters, only 2 of whom voted for the defeated candidate.

Any rating of precincts as to their potential contribution to a winning margin must take into account the potential registration, the actual registration (which is the potential turnout), the percentage split between the candidates, and the plurality that contributes to a candidate's victory.

The manager faces the same percentage pitfall at the other end of the scale. He may tend to write off areas where his candidate is not likely to receive a high percentage. Ward 11, for example, is tenth of thirteen in terms of percentage for the candidate, at 55.6; yet this same ward is eighth in plurality with 1497. This results from the fact, shown in Table III, that Ward 11 is first among all wards in the proportion of the total city's registered voters who reside in it, nearly 10 percent (compared to the expected one thirteenth or 7.69 percent). Ward 11 realizes its potential by being first also in the city in total turnout, with almost 11 percent of the total turnout for this election coming from this ward (column 5). Note the considerable difference in some wards on this characteristic. Ward 6, the transient and lower class downtown area, for example, is last in proportion of the city's registration, and last in proportion of city's turnout, with less than half that of Ward 11.

Ward 13 is the second to last in the city on the percentage vote for the mayoral candidate (he got only 46 percent of the vote—Table I). The candidate fell almost 1000 behind his opposition in this ward. Yet so large is this ward, being second in the city in proportion of registrants and voters residing therein, that it is fifth in proportion of the candidate's total vote received (columns 7

TABLE III.

Registration and Turnout in Minneapolis, 1969

Ranking of Proportion of Ward Registration	Proportion of City Registration	Rank on Total Voter Turnout	Proportion of City Turnout
1 W 11	9.92	1	10.92
2 W 13	9.91	2	10.83
3 W 12	8.87	3	9.60
4 W 7	8.66	6	8.20
5 W 10	8.43	8	7.18
6 W 4	8.27	4	9.29
7 W 2	8.14	7	7.31
8 W 1	8.10	5	8.44
9 W 8	6.96	10	6.30
10 W 9	6.89	9	6.83
11 W 5	6.10	11	5.83
12 W 3	5.24	12	5.13
13 W 6	4.51	13	4.13

and 8). To put this more bluntly, even in losing Ward 13, the candidate received a hefty proportion of his votes there. Many votes will come from a minority percentage of the vote in a large ward. The campaign manager must decide how to elicit the votes of his supporters wherever they may be found, and cannot write them off just because they live among the enemy.

County Unit Pitfall results from treating all government or party organizational units as though they were equal. This pitfall is another function of differing size. Traditionally in the United States, the principal and strongest unit of party organization has been the county. Counties differ vastly in numbers of voters they contain, but all county chairmen, having the same title, seem to expect and demand equal treatment from the state organization. The same could be true of wards and precincts, as we have seen, but wards and precincts lend themselves to redistricting more than do counties, with their historic governmental and psychological real boundaries. The differential in total vote among counties in a state is likely to be far greater than the difference between city wards. A manager needs to study aggregate data proportions of total vote with percentages and pluralities as described in order to get a realistic picture of where the potential voters for his candidate actually reside. He must not unwittingly be dragged into treating unequal units equally. In Illinois, for example, the 10 counties in the Chicago metropolitan area account for approximately 65% of the vote—the other 91 counties for only 35%. If one examines the 44 counties in the major urban centers of the entire state, one discovers that they account for 83% of the vote.

MANAGEMENT TECHNIQUES

Using Aggregated Data Analysis in Campaign Strategy: A Case Study

Once the indicators are selected and calculations are made, large amounts of data must be organized into a form which can be used to design a strategy and make management decisions. Columns containing hundreds of figures of split-voting, party strength, turnout and pluralities can be arranged in readable form by putting them into some categories.

The most basic approach is simply to rank each factor from the highest to the lowest precinct. Ranking quickly displays the range of values and enables rapid plotting by hand or by computer. If one wishes to know the best party percentage areas, he can consult the ranking of the party index or any other indicator of party strength.

In most cases ranking indicators individually will not be sufficient to integrate a campaign plan. Rarely will a great number of favorable indicators occur in the same precincts. Democratic candidates are often faced with low turnout and low split ticket vote in high ranking partisan percentage precincts. Republican candidates often face Democratic split ticket precincts, but the proportion of the vote is low. Such contingencies make it necessary to find some means of organizing the data into a single priority system so that a number of strategies can be implemented simultaneously. Thus, a single overall ranking using a mean or weighted average of a number of factors is often in order. More complicated but useful ranking indices can include census data, cumulative vote totals or even contrived ratings.[10]

The completed basic rankings provide a political map of the district, containing measures of turnout, partisan strength, candidate swing and proportions of the vote, which can be combined with knowledge of the district to suggest to the candidate how and where to campaign.

In our model state legislative campaign, in a rural-smalltown district at the fringe of the Minneapolis-St. Paul metropolitan area, a young Democratic challenger is from Hastings, the largest town in the district, and is the son (Jr.) of a well-known local Democrat, a former state administrator of the Small Business Administration, and presently a local attorney. The district is close in terms of party strength, but the 1966 House Democratic candidate hardly campaigned, and he was defeated by 3166 votes out of a total of 10,888 (35%).[11]

Even though this candidate was soundly defeated for the house, the data indicated that the U.S. Senate candidate, Walter Mondale, carried it rather handily and the state senate candidate, George Conzemius, carried this half of his district by a larger margin. The Democratic candidate for Governor ran close to the party index. Thus, it is not impossible for a Democrat to win in this district.

The Democratic Party organization is built around the house district but in actuality it is only a paper organization, with the exception of the city of Hastings. During campaign time a reasonable number of Democratic workers are willing and able to work in Hastings. More recently, the closest thing to a district-wide organization was the dormant (four-year-old) Conzemius for State Senate organization.

An examination of the data in the following tables provides several suggestions for campaign strategy. It is obvious that over half of the votes in the entire district are from nine of the thirty-three precincts, the towns, and one suburban township, Lakeville.* Regardless of percentages, a large plurality of votes will have to come from these precincts. Senator Mondale received the overwhelming share of his plurality from the four precincts of Hastings and from one of the Lakeville precincts. The rest of his margin was spread among the small rural precincts. The state senator candidate, Conzemius, was able to add his present residence, Cannon Falls, to these large precincts to construct a winning total. Note that while he carried almost every precinct, it was the large precincts that contributed the most to his margin, even though some of the small precincts gave him much larger percentages. The first conclusion, then, is to concentrate in the largest precincts, especially those which tend to be friendliest to the Democratic candidates.

Now that we have some measure of size, we can turn to areas of party strength. The ranking of the percentages tells us that some large and some small precincts are Democratic. If we take the governor's race as a base race, we see that of the top four precincts, each went Democratic by over 60 percent, but contributed only 96 votes to the plurality. The precinct of Hastings 1 contributed 596 votes to Rolvaag's total even though this percentage was 39.2. Thus, size and partisan percentage must be considered together. If one examines the poorest precincts for the governor's race (mostly Republican), and compares these back to size, one will find that these precincts all contribute less than 100 votes to the plurality. They are obviously very low priority precincts. The second conclusion to be drawn is to concentrate on large vote areas that are also Democratic, then move to smaller Democratic rural areas, and then give Republican rural areas the lowest priority.

Another conclusion the percentage tables suggest is that overwhelming Democratic precincts are so few in number that a canvass of voters to identify the partisan disposition of individual

*Lakeville Township and Village consolidated into single precinct between 1966 and 1968.

TABLE IV.

Goodhue County Begins at Precinct 1
Dakota County Begins at Precinct 7

Data Input

Precinct		Reg	Vote	Ussen		Gov		M.Sen		M.Rep	
				Rep	Dfl	Rep	Dfl	Rep	Dfl	Rep1	Dfl1
1CANF		-0	279	139	131	161	113	104	171	186	73
2CANF	1	-0	516	293	214	336	174	206	300	337	149
3CANF	2	-0	378	181	186	221	151	139	233	280	79
4STAN		-0	212	127	83	152	60	108	103	175	34
5VASA		-0	317	127	186	156	159	145	170	255	50
6WELCH		-0	191	92	97	105	85	109	77	150	33
7CASK		-0	324	174	143	202	120	152	154	237	84
8CATS	V	-0	69	16	50	23	44	17	50	44	25
9EMPIR		-0	428	222	199	265	157	178	235	327	100
10EARECKA		-0	274	161	106	195	76	153	108	189	82
11FARM	V1	-0	323	143	172	171	147	155	154	235	87
12FARM	V2	-0	690	343	327	417	269	342	322	494	188
13GRENV		-0	184	64	114	84	100	66	105	111	69
14DOUG		-0	183	55	121	86	97	41	140	102	77
15VERM		-0	238	96	129	124	111	79	151	168	63
16HAMP		-0	175	96	73	123	50	67	103	150	24
17HAMP	V	-0	142	50	86	70	70	41	91	109	26
18HASTG	1	1117	1005	294	681	393	596	248	730	544	420
19HASTG	2	1083	1072	404	644	522	528	365	668	639	398
20HASTG	3	833	777	243	526	341	426	241	522	408	355
21HASTG	4	765	701	259	435	331	359	230	463	425	260
22LAKVIL		-0	1023	408	609	489	508	466	467	444	543
23LAKVIL	V	-0	405	177	212	215	187	140	231	129	274
24MARSHAN		-0	269	91	166	131	134	77	183	168	96
25MESV		-0	72	13	55	23	47	15	52	31	38
26NWTR		-0	49	4	44	18	31	10	37	26	21
27NINO		-0	164	78	79	96	64	88	72	120	41
28RAND		-0	92	46	43	63	29	27	62	66	21
29RAND	V	-0	154	48	96	53	91	57	86	110	33
30RAVN		-0	89	31	55	43	45	39	49	73	16
31SCIO		-0	85	47	36	61	24	35	47	69	16
32FERM	V	-0	119	37	78	50	66	28	87	69	48
33WATFOD		-0	204	129	71	145	58	88	97	157	38
34DIST TL		3798	11203	4688	6247	5865	5176	4256	6520	7027	3861

TABLE V.

District 6A   1966 GE

Precinct		Reg	Vote	Percent of Total Vote Ussen	Gov	M.Sen	M.Rep	Ussen	Plurality Gov	M.Sen	M.Rep
1CANF		0.00	2.49	2.10	2.18	2.62	1.89	-8	-48	67	-113
2CANF	1	0.00	4.61	3.43	3.36	4.60	3.86	-79	-162	94	-188
3CANF	2	0.00	3.37	2.98	2.92	3.57	2.05	5	-70	94	-201
4STAN		0.00	1.89	1.33	1.16	1.58	.88	-44	-92	-5	-141
5VASA		0.00	2.83	2.98	3.07	2.61	1.30	59	3	25	-205
6WELCH		0.00	1.70	1.55	1.64	1.18	.85	5	-20	-32	-117
7CASK		0.00	2.89	2.29	2.32	2.36	2.18	-31	-82	2	-153
8CATS	V	0.00	.62	.80	.85	.77	.65	34	21	33	-19
9EMPIR		0.00	3.82	3.19	3.03	3.60	2.59	-23	-108	57	-227
10EARECKA		0.00	2.45	1.70	1.47	1.66	2.12	-55	-119	-45	-107
11FARM	VI	0.00	2.88	2.75	2.84	2.36	2.25	29	-24	-1	-148
12FARM	V2	0.00	6.16	5.23	5.20	4.94	4.87	-16	-148	-20	-306
13GRENV		0.00	1.64	1.82	1.93	1.61	1.79	50	16	39	-42
14DOUG		0.00	1.63	1.94	1.87	2.15	1.99	66	11	99	-25
15VERM		0.00	2.12	2.06	2.14	2.32	1.63	33	-13	72	-105
16HAMP		0.00	1.56	1.17	.97	1.58	.62	-23	-73	36	-126
17HAMP	V	0.00	1.27	1.38	1.35	1.40	.67	36	0	50	-83
18HASTG	1	29.41	8.97	10.90	11.51	11.20	10.88	387	203	482	-124
19HASTG	2	28.52	9.57	10.31	10.20	10.25	10.31	240	6	303	-241
20HASTG	3	21.93	6.94	8.42	8.23	8.01	9.19	283	85	281	-53
21HASTG	4	20.14	6.26	6.96	6.94	7.10	6.73	176	28	233	-165
22LAKVIL		0.00	9.13	9.75	9.81	7.16	14.06	201	19	1	99
23LAKVIL	V	0.00	3.62	3.39	3.61	3.54	7.10	35	-28	91	145
24MARSHAN		0.00	2.40	2.66	2.59	2.81	2.49	75	3	106	-72
25MESV		0.00	.64	.88	.91	.80	.98	42	24	37	7
26NWTR		0.00	.44	.70	.60	.57	.54	40	13	27	-5
27NINO		0.00	1.46	1.26	1.24	1.10	1.06	1	-32	-16	-79
28RAND		0.00	.82	.69	.56	.95	.54	-3	-34	35	-45
29RAND	V	0.00	1.37	1.54	1.76	1.32	.85	48	38	29	-77
30RAVN		0.00	.79	.88	.87	.75	.41	24	2	10	-57
31SCIO		0.00	.76	.58	.46	.72	.41	-11	-37	12	-53
32FERM	V	0.00	1.06	1.25	1.28	1.33	1.24	41	16	59	-21
33WATFOD		0.00	1.82	1.14	1.12	1.49	.98	-58	-87	9	-119
34DIST TL		100.00	100.00	100.00	100.00	100.00	100.00	1559	-689	2264	-3166
						Dem	Plurality	1910	488	2383	251
						Repub	Plurality	351	1177	119	3417

TABLE VI.

Dist. 6A   1966 GE

Ranking of 2-Party Percentage		Ranking of Plurality	
Gov	M. Sen	Gov	M. Sen
MESV 67.14	NWTR 78.72	HASTG 1 203.00	HASTG 1 482.00
CATS V 65.67	MESV 77.61	HASTG 3 85.00	HASTG 2 303.00
NWTR 63.27	DOUG 77.35	RAND V 38.00	HASTG 3 281.00
RAND V 63.19	FERM V 75.65	HASTG 4 28.00	HASTG 4 233.00
HASTG 1 60.26	HASTG 1 74.64	MESV 24.00	MARSHAN 106.00
FERM V 56.90	CATS V 74.63	CATS V 21.00	DOUG 99.00
HASTG 3 55.54	MARSHAN 70.38	LAKVIL 19.00	CANF 2 94.00
GRENV 54.35	RAND 69.66	FERM V 16.00	CANF 1 94.00
DOUG 53.01	HAMP V 68.94	GRENV 16.00	LAKVIL V 91.00
HASTG 4 52.03	HASTG 3 68.41	NWTR 13.00	VERM 72.00
RAVN 51.14	HASTG 4 66.81	DOUG 11.00	CANF 67.00
LAKVIL 50.95	VERM 65.65	HASTG 2 6.00	FERM V 59.00
MARSHAN 50.57	HASTG 2 64.67	VASA 3.00	EMPIR 57.00
VASA 50.48	CANF 2 62.63	MARSHAN 3.00	HAMP V 50.00
HASTG 2 50.29	LAKVL V 62.26	RAVN 2.00	GRENV 39.00
HAMP V 50.00	CANF 62.18	HAMP V 0.00	MESV 37.00
VERM 47.23	GRENV 61.40	VERM -13.00	HAMP 36.00
LAKVL V 46.52	HAMP 60.59	WELCH -20.00	RAND 35.00
FARM V1 46.23	RAND V 60.14	FARM V1 -24.00	CATS V 33.00
WELCH 44.74	CANF 1 59.29	LAKVIL V -28.00	RAND V 29.00
CANF 41.24	SCIO 57.32	NINO -32.00	NWTR 27.00
CANF 2 40.59	EMPIR 56.90	RAND -34.00	VASA 25.00
NINO 40.00	RAVN 55.68	SCIO -37.00	SCIO 12.00
FARM V2 39.21	VASA 53.97	CANF -48.00	RAVN 10.00
CASK 37.27	WATFOD 52.43	CANF 2 -70.00	WATFOD 9.00
EMPIR 37.20	CASK 50.33	HAMP -73.00	CASK 2.00
CANF 1 34.12	LAKVL 50.05	CASK -82.00	LAKVIL 1.00
RAND 31.52	FARM V1 49.84	WATFOD -87.00	FARM V1 -1.00
HAMP 28.90	STAN 48.82	STAN -92.00	STAN -5.00
WATFOD 28.57	FARM V2 48.49	EMPIR -108.00	NINO -16.00
STAN 28.30	NINO 45.00	EARECKA -119.00	FARM V2 -20.00
SCIO 28.24	WELCH 41.40	FARM V2 -148.00	WELCH -32.00
EARECKA 28.04	EARECKA 41.38	CANF 1 -162.00	EARECKA -45.00

voters should be conducted. Campaigning as a Democrat in a 60% Democratic district means that 40% of the voters are unlikely to be motivated by Democratic party appeals. As stated earlier, it is impossible to tell which voters identify with which party without some method of identification. A very early and high priority should be the updating of an existing canvass or conducting a new survey.

To what extent can a candidate rely on the votes of candidates higher on the ticket to "pull" him in on his coattails? There usually is a correlation between votes of candidates on the same party ticket, but it varies from race to race and district to district.[12] In this district the relationship found is very common; at the top of the ticket, the congressional candidate runs very close to the ticket leader, Senator Mondale, but as one goes down the ticket, and the races become more local, there is more deviation between various partisans.

As Table VII indicates, legislative candidates who were more local in orientation and appeal (and in this case not identified by party on the ballot) did not run as close to the top of the ticket. It also must be remembered that the candidates for Congress and Governor failed to carry the district. The two-party percentage of the State House candidate is less than one third ($r^2 = .305$) related to that of the U.S. Senate candidate. The State Senate candidate campaigned more as a partisan Democrat, and his vote was more closely associated with the U.S. Senate candidate's, but is still only

TABLE VII
Correlation Between Democratic Candidates
District 6A Minnesota, 1966 General Election

	Congress	Governor	S. Senate	S. House
U.S. Senator	.963	.945	.725	.552
Congress		.936	.734	.578
Governor			.662	.555
State Senator				.471

about half related ($r^2 = .526$). Other explanations must be sought, therefore, such as personality appeal, personal campaigning and partisan swing.

The task at hand for the model district candidate is to win enough votes on the basis of candidate appeal to overcome slight minority party status in the district. The key is to find an equivalent race in a recent election. Fortunately the 1966 state Senate race of Conzemius is a fairly equivalent race. Both races are nonpartisan ballot races, both candidates are young, university educated natives of the largest city, Hastings. They both have some name identification. Both candidates take similar stands on state issues. More importantly, both candidates plan to run together as a team in this half of the Senate district. Therefore, the 1966 senate race appears to be a suitable comparative race.

Where was Senator Conzemius able to do better than the other candidates for office? Both Table VII and Plot I point to the same conclusion. Senator Conzemius did better than the base race (Governor) in three distinct areas: in small Democratic precincts (MESU, NTRR, CATS, DOUG) by holding close to Senator Mondale's percentage, in his hometown of Hastings by running well

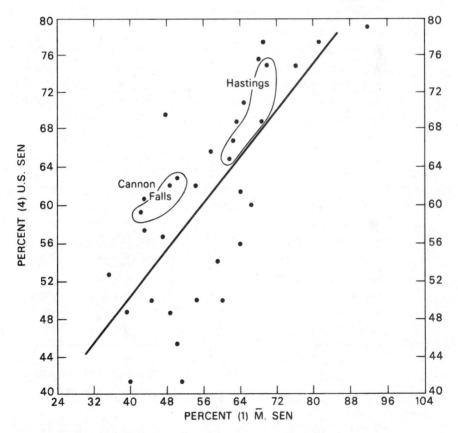

PLOT I.   District 6A, 2-Party Percentage, 1966 GE

ahead of the base race and slightly ahead of Senator Mondale, and, in Cannon Falls village and township, his present residence, by running well ahead of Mondale.

The house candidate should follow these findings and assume he can have similar appeal in all but the Senator's home area. But going door-to-door in Hastings reminding voters that he is a "hometown boy," he can run from 7 to 14 percent, or from 100–160 votes over the base race per precinct. The candidate now knows from which small rural precincts he can get the most votes, and his travels to the rural areas should begin here. If he cannot get a reliable township coordinator for every small precinct, the aforementioned four precincts should be highest on the list. When campaigning in the Cannon Falls area, he should be sure to go with Senator Conzemius, a local who can carry this solid Republican area by around a 60% margin.

Other information which might be valuable for planning strategy in this district deals with registration and turnout. Only Hastings has permanent registration. Since it is a higher priority area, an effort should be made to determine the percentage of eligible voters registered, and to register all voters who are likely to be supporters. As the turnout figures indicate, over 90 percent voted in Hastings in 1966. This unusually high turnout for an off-year election was probably the result of both an intensive effort by the Conzemius organization and a hotly contested race for the county board. In the absence of this local contest in the upcoming year, a superhuman effort will have to be made to match that turnout record. Turnout will also be important in other areas of the district, especially the suburban Lakeville area which contains so many new residents.[13]

A final consideration is voter falloff, or the percentage of the actual raw votes received by the candidate of the vote for other candidates of the same party. First, the house candidate will have to be careful to locate voter "fatigue" falloff, or failure to vote at all in the legislative race. In 1966, 2.3% of all voters failed to vote in the state house race and 3.3% in the state senate race. Many of these occurred in good precincts for the Senate candidate, such as Hastings 2, where 3.6% failed to vote. Even worse was Lakeville Township and Village, where the non-voting rate was over 8%. Campaign appeals must be based on urging persons to vote for every office.

A more serious problem can be partisan fall-off, the percent difference between one race and a race higher on the party ticket.

In this district, we will compare our equivalent race, Conzemius for state Senator, with the base race, Rolvaag for Governor. Conzemius ran well ahead of the base race, making his vote a good indication of swing. The Senate candidate did better, so there actually was a positive partisan fall-off between our representative race and base race. This again demonstrates that in precincts where great discrepancies are found (such as in the House race, where there was a negative partisan fall-off from governor for all but three precincts) an effort should be made to get partisans to continue voting for candidates of their party.

In summary form, the following strategy-tactics can be derived from the information already in hand:

1. At the outset, a voter canvass should be conducted, probably by telephone because of the rural nature of the district and the weakness of the organization. Efforts should be made to ascertain the names of unregistered voters in Hastings and they should be registered.
2. Campaign efforts should be concentrated in Hastings, Lakeville, Cannon Falls, and then Farmington. Do not ignore Farmington village, the opponent's home town, which is Republican. It has over 1000 votes, almost half of which a Democratic candidate could get if he worked for them. The next order of procedure should be tackling the rural Democratic precincts, which are capable of swinging even higher than the base race for a local candidate. The small Republican precincts from which even Conzemius was unable to swing more than a few votes, should be ignored. The candidate's time schedule should follow those precinct priorities exactly. Ideally, he should start in Hastings and end in Hastings.
3. The candidate should run with Senator Conzemius wherever possible, especially in the Cannon Falls area, where another Democratic candidate cannot expect to do as well. He should go door-to-door with him in Cannon Falls and in Hastings. He should not be afraid to run with the head of the ticket in 1970, Hubert Humphrey, who is the U.S. Senate candidate from Minnesota. Humphrey may have lost to Nixon in the U.S., but he ran 8 points better than the party index and he carried this district by 1684 votes, and nine key precincts by 1512 votes. The literature which is sent into heavily Democratic precincts and to partisan identifiers should link the candidates with proven vote-getters, Conzemius and Humphrey.
4. In less Democratic precincts, or to voters who are identified as Republicans or independents, the candidate should stress his experience, his interest in serving government, his name (which is better known in his stronger precincts) and issues. In other words, he should not stress partisan appeals. This seemingly conventional bit of campaign wisdom is violated by as many candidates as follow it.
5. A convenient organizational breakdown for the candidate might be as follows: use the party organization in the city of Hastings, cooperate with the Conzemius organization where he is strong in the district and use

personal organization in areas in which you can help him. A high priority area should be Lakeville, where there is considerable spill-over from the metropolitan area. Do not try to build the party while conducting a three-month campaign.

6. Begin to organize a telephone campaign for the last few days (this effort often takes months) which will (a) maximize the get-out-the-vote efforts (b) once again identify the candidate (c) urge the voter to vote for the legislative candidate.

This strategy, developed entirely from aggregate data analysis, would lead to other decisions, such as the scheduling of the candidate, the targeting of direct mail appeals, the placement of newspaper and radio advertising, the targeting of the party's sample ballot, the placement of volunteers for literature distribution, and the development of specific campaign appeals.

This example of the Minnesota race indicates that the data do not speak for themselves. One must incorporate knowledge about voting behavior and political judgments with the aggregate electoral data. But as this case study illustrates, although aggregate data analysis is subject to certain limitations, it can provide the basis from which to make political judgments, and it should be an integral component in the practice and study of electoral politics.

NOTES

1. John W. Kingdon, *Candidates for Office: Beliefs and Strategies* (New York: Random House, 1968), pp. 95–96s,

2. W. S. Robinson, "Ecological Correlations and the Behavior of Individuals," *American Sociological Review*, XV (June 1950), pp. 351–357.

3. E.g., Herbert Menzel, "Comment on Robinson's 'Ecological Correlations and the Behavior of Individuals,' " *American Sociological Review*, XV (October 1950); Austin Ranney, "The Utility and Limitations of Aggregate Data in the Study of Electoral Behavior," in Austin Ranney (ed.), *Essays on the Behaviorial Study of Politics* (Urbana: University of Illinois Press, 1962), pp. 91–102; W. Phillips Shivley, "Ecological Inference: The Use of Aggregate Data to Study Individuals," *American Political Science Review*, LXIII (December 1969), pp. 1183–1196.

4. Ranney, *op. cit.*, p. 99.

5. Frank J. Sorauf, *Political Parties in the American System* (Boston: Little, Brown and Company, 1964), pp. 108–109.

6. The most useful beginning to this field is provided by Kenneth Janda, *Data Processing.* 2nd ed. (Evanston: Northwestern University Press, 1969).

7. U.S. Department of Commerce, Bureau of Census, *Characteristics of the Population,* 1971.

8. CBS 1970 Vote Precinct Analysis correlation of partisan percentages of 66 U.S. Senate and Governor races with an earlier race, showed 11 to have coefficients of .90 or higher, 35 between .80 and .90, 11 between .70 and .80, and 9 lower than .70. Source: CBS News Election Unit.

9. For an extensive discussion of adjustments to swing voting *see Vote History and Demographic Analysis* (Washington, D.C.: Republican National Committee, 1969), pp. 28-31.

10. *See* in this volume, Vincent P. Barabba, "Basic Information Systems— P.I.P.S."

11. The Republican endorsed incumbent ran without opposition in 1968.

12. E.g., Milton C. Cummings, Jr., *Congressmen and the Electorate* (New York: The Free Press, 1966), p. 25.

13. Voter registration is required by Minnesota law only in cities over 10,000.

—9—

BASIC INFORMATION SYSTEMS — P.I.P.S.

Vincent P. Barabba

The phrase "deal from strength" is probably the best capsule statement of winning campaign strategy devised. For a campaign strategist, dealing from strength means finding citizens most likely to vote for his candidate and campaigning to them. If the number of citizens likely to vote for the candidate exceeds 50 percent of the total vote, then, naturally, the campaign strategy will focus almost entirely on pinning down that support and getting it to the polls on election day.

However, not all candidates are in the enviable position of holding a probable majority at the outset of the campaign. In these instances, the strategist who wishes to deal from strength must find and campaign to voters not only in his candidate's strongholds, but in the stronger of his weak areas as well.

The problem of finding favorable votes requires both factual data and political judgment. This blend of information and judgment will result in a campaign strategy that, if it is sound, can lead to victory. However, if either facts or political judgment is inadequate, the resultant strategy can spell disaster for the campaign.

The goal of Precinct Index Priority System (P.I.P.S.) is to help campaign strategists find areas containing citizens most likely to vote for their candidate. P.I.P.S. highlights the relative priority (or strength) of the areas in question on the basis of the facts and information which political judgment indicates will be important. P.I.P.S. can help to organize political judgment, to place evidence behind political judgment, and to develop a factual check of politi-

This article was prepared for this volume.

cal judgment. But P.I.P.S. will not substitute for good political judgment, the single most important ingredient in the system.

The result of using P.I.P.S. is a list of every precinct (or any other reporting unit one may choose) in a district, ranked according to its likelihood of supporting a given candidate. In other words, P.I.P.S. pinpoints the precincts likely to yield the most vote for effort expended (as well as those precincts which will yield the least vote for effort expended).

Precincts are evaluated as more or less important to the campaign on the basis of factors (chosen by the strategist) that meet two criteria:

1. The factors are regarded as significant in the strategists' political judgment.
2. It is possible to obtain systematic information about the factors.

The same criteria are being used when a campaign manager requests a listing of precincts on the basis of party registration. He has determined that party registration is an important factor, and he can systematically obtain registration data for each precinct.

It is worth noting that a computer is not mandatory in obtaining a rank ordering of precincts on the basis of party registration. Likewise, a computer is not mandatory in the development of P.I.P.S., though it often lends speed, efficiency and flexibility to the process.

Obviously, the factor of party registration is not the only clue to the importance of a precinct. A campaign strategist may consider a precinct important on the basis of:

a. Social factors (e.g., number of school age children).
b. Economic factors (e.g., prevailing types of occupations).
c. Voting behavior patterns (which candidates have voters supported in the past?).
d. Party preferences (party registration, if the district registers by party).
e. Survey information factors (e.g., how do people feel about the candidate?).
f. Canvass information factors (any items of important information that volunteers obtain).
g. Other factors that may be deemed important.

P.I.P.S. is able to absorb all these factors and any others that meet the two criteria of judgment and availability of information.

Imagine how difficult it would be for a campaign strategist to rank order every precinct in his district on the basis of the factors listed above. How could he combine all of this information?

Moreover, suppose he considered one factor to be more important than another. He might decide that party preference was twice as important as economic factors, but only 25 percent more important than voting behavior and 10 percent *less* important than survey information. How does a campaign strategist handle a problem like this and still come up with an accurate ranking of every precinct in his district—a list on which he is willing to base his campaign planning?

P.I.P.S. is designed to help campaigners solve this problem by allowing relative weights to be assigned to factors, thereby yielding an accurate list of every precinct's importance, on the basis of the conditions described in the preceding paragraph.

It is worthwhile to study one example of an actual campaign situation in which P.I.P.S. was employed. In 1963, the citizens of South Bend, Indiana, elected Republican Lloyd Allen mayor by a truly overwhelming margin. South Bend usually elects Democrats; this rare exception came about because of a split in the Democratic ranks. Eugene Padjakowsky had lost the Democratic primary to Democrat Paul Krueper, to the intense disappointment and anger of South Bend's sizable Polish and Eastern European community. Padjakowsky, disenchanted with his party, gave his endorsement to Republican Allen; Allen carried the city, including the traditionally Democratic Polish and Eastern European bloc.

In 1967, matters did not look as bright for Mayor Allen. Although it was generally recognized that he had done an outstanding job, the Democrats, having learned an important lesson in 1963, nominated Eugene Padjakowsky to oppose him. Furthermore, not once in the history of South Bend had a Republican mayor been re-elected. Even the fact that Allen's campaign chairman was Sheriff Elmer Sokol (a Hungarian with great influence in the Polish and Eastern European community) provided no guarantee that Allen would repeat his 1963 success.

The Allen strategy in South Bend was based on the assumption that the mayor would not do as well in 1967 as he had in 1963. The goal of the Allen campaign consultants was to minimize the "drop-off" as much as possible. Accordingly, they decided to predict which areas of the city were least likely to drop off and place their high-priority campaign efforts there. In short, they were to find the areas of relative strength and concentrate most heavily on voters there.

One of several P.I.P.S. employed in this campaign was designed to tell the strategists where to place the most effort on election day. In what areas of South Bend should Allen's organization concentrate on getting out the vote—because it was most likely to be an Allen vote?

Careful planning indicated that the following factors (Chart I) met the two conditions necessary for developing an election day P.I.P.S.: political judgment said they were important, and systematic information was available. It will be noted that all these factors represented the political judgment of the campaign consultants and campaign managers. If that judgment had been wrong, the planning would have been wrong.

It should also be noted that weights were attached to each factor. In other words, the strategists believed that Allen's 1963 percentage (weighted 6) was twice as important as Krueper's 1963 primary percentage (weighted 3), but only 33 1/3 percent more important than the "For Allen" vote in the 1967 poll (weighted 4). The resultant P.I.P.S. quickly listed every precinct in the city on the basis of the priority it should be assigned on election day (given the factors selected as important).

Immediately prior to election day, however, the results of a survey had an effect on P.I.P.S. The survey was able to indicate the kinds of "undecided" voters who were going over to the Allen side. Using the flexibility of computers, this information was quickly incorporated into the "For Allen in 1967" factor of P.I.P.S. Thus, areas containing a high percentage of previously undecided voters, whom the survey identified as "For Allen," became more important on election day. This is one example of how a computerized P.I.P.S. allows a campaign the flexibility necessary to quickly adapt strategy on the basis of last-minute information.

The entire get-out-the-vote drive in South Bend was run on the basis of the election day P.I.P.S. Headquarters were organized and volunteers were assigned according to the priorities P.I.P.S. had established for the precincts. When the election results were tallied, Lloyd Allen was the first Republican mayor ever to be re-elected in South Bend.

It is gratifying to report that P.I.P.S. was extremely accurate in its instructions. The goal of the election day P.I.P.S. was achieved: to pinpoint precincts where effort would provide maximum vote return.

Chart II represents a correlation analysis made after the 1967 election. A computer was asked to compare the P.I.P.S. score of each precinct (from 0 to 100) with the actual percentage of the Allen vote in each precinct (from 0 to 100 percent).

CHART I.

South Bend
Election Day P.I.P.S.
Legend of P.I.P.S. Headers

Code	Description	Weights
Allen	Mayor Allen's percent of the vote in 1963. (The greater Allen's percentage, the more important the precinct.)	6
Krueper	Krueper's percent in the 1963 primary. (Since Krueper opposed Padjakowsky in the 1963 Democratic primary, the greater Krueper's percentage, the more important the precinct to Allen.)	3
Al-Pol	"For Allen" in 1967 precinct poll. (Volunteers canvassed precincts. The greater percentage for Allen in 1967, the more important the precinct.)	4
Sokol	Sheriff Sokol's percent in 1966. (Since Sokol was Allen's campaign chairman, the greater the Sokol percentage in the 1966 election for sheriff, the more important the precinct for Allen.)	5
Polish	Percentage Polish. (Since Padjakowsky was Polish and had great influence with the Polish community, the greater the percentage Polish, the *less* important the precinct for Allen.)	3
Educat	Educational ranking of census tract in which precinct is located; rank order based on number of people over 25 having an eight-grade education or less. (It was the strategists' opinion that less educated voters would tend to vote against Allen. Therefore, the more people with or below an eighth-grade education, the *less* important the precinct to Allen.)	3
Locind	Percentage of laborers, operatives and craftsmen in relation to total labor force. (It was the strategists opinion that laborers, operatives and crafts-	

men would tend to vote against Allen.
Therefore, the greater the percentage
of these occupations, the *less* important the precinct to Allen.)

A perfect correlation (or 1.00) would indicate that in every
case, the precinct's P.I.P.S. score and the precinct's percentage of
vote for Allen were exactly the same. This would result in a line
running at a 45 degree angle midway between the P.I.P.S. score
(vertical line) and the Allen percentage (horizontal line).

Each dot in Chart II represents a precinct. Its location is determined by the percentage of Allen vote and its P.I.P.S. score; its
proximity to the 45 degree-angle line is determined by how close
the Allen percentage is to the P.I.P.S. score.

The heavy black line represents the extent to which the
P.I.P.S. was identical to the Allen percentage in every precinct in
the city. The correlation was .95, very close to the ideal of 1.00.
In other words, P.I.P.S. was extremely accurate in saying: "con-

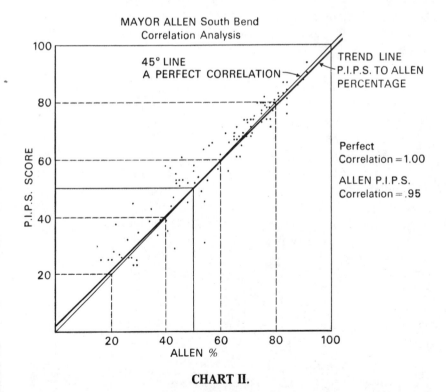

CHART II.

centrating on each precinct as it is listed promises maximum vote return for effort expended."

A second example of P.I.P.S. includes portions of an actual P.I.P.S. computer print-out. Chart III represents the campaign strategists' opinion as to the factors that should be used in determining the political importance of precincts to the Republican candidate in a Congressional district. (Although this district actually exists, the names have been changed.) By studying Chart III, Chart IV and Chart V (the P.I.P.S. computer printouts) can be easily understood. Charts IV and V represent the results of running P.I.P.S. information through the computer. The final P.I.P.S. score is affected not only by the scores for the individual factors but also by the weight that the strategists' political judgment has attached to each factor.

In Chart III, for example, the REGOV factor, assigned a weight of 6, is twice as important as MODDEM, assigned a weight of 3, and 33 1/3 percent more important than REPCAN, assigned a weight of 4. In other words, REGOV has twice as much effect on the final P.I.P.S. score as MODDEM and a third more than REPCAN.

The most important difference between the two charts is that Chart IV provides information in what is called precinct order, whereas Chart V provides information in priority order. That is, Chart V lists precincts (column 3) in their usual numerical order regardless of how important they are (in terms of their P.I.P.S. score) to the campaign. This listing enables planners to find specific precincts easily.

On the other hand, Chart V lists precincts (column 3) on the basis of how important they are to the campaign, as determined by their P.I.P.S. score. Thus, Precinct 82 and Precinct 83, both having the highest P.I.P.S. scores of 89, appear first and second, respectively. Next comes Precinct 80 with a P.I.P.S. score of 88, and so on down the column. It should be noted that only Chart V contains data on CUMTRV and CUMTVC, as these factors have more relevance to the importance of precincts than they do to the simple numerical listing of precincts in Chart IV.

One of the many ways in which P.I.P.S. can benefit a campaign organization is to assist in planning a direct mail promotion. Suppose a campaign strategist has decided that a special kind of letter should be mailed on a selective basis, depending on the needs, interests, and importance of a precinct. Keeping in mind his total budget for the mailer, he simply lists:

CHART III

District X
Center City P.I.P.S.
Legend of P.I.P.S. Headers

Code	Description	Weights
City or Twp	Name of city or township.	
Pre	Precinct number	
Gl	Grid location. (A grid drawn on the map of Center City enabled strategists to locate any precinct very quickly.)	
Ct	Census tract. (In what census tract is the precinct located?)	
Regov	Percent vote for the Republican governor in 1964. (The greater the percentage, the more important the precinct.)	6
Moddem	Percent vote for moderate Democrat candidate in the 1968 gubernatorial primary, which was between a liberal and a moderate candidate; the liberal, with union endorsement, won the primary election. (The greater the percentage for the moderate, the more important the precinct.)	3
Repcan	The results of a volunteer Republican canvass to determine the percentage of Republicans in each precinct. Voters do not register by party in this district. (The greater the percentage Republican, the more important the precinct.)	4
Remay	Percent vote for the Center City Republican mayoralty candidate in 1967. In the rest of this one-county district, the percentage voting for the Republican candidate for County Supervisor was substituted; both men won. (The greater the percentage, the more important the precinct.)	5

(Chart III. continued)

Code	Description	Weights
Educat	Educational ranking of census tract in which precinct is located; rank order based on number of people over 25 having an eighth-grade education or less. (It was the strategists' opinion that less educated voters would tend not to vote for the Republican candidate. Therefore, the more people with, or below an eighth grade education, the *less* important the precinct.)	3
Scouts	Number of girls registered in Brownies, Girl Scouts, or Senior Scouts in proportion to women between the ages of 14 and 44. (It was the strategists' opinion that families placing their daughters in such organizations would be more likely to have ambitions and hopes that would tend to make them vote Republican. Therefore, the greater the percentage, the more important the precinct. This factor is not a special device for finding Republican-thinking people but it does illustrate the range of political hunches that can be incorporated into P.I.P.S.)	3
Recwel	Number of welfare recipients in proportion to the number of heads of households. (It was the strategists' opinion that welfare recipients would tend not to vote Republican. Therefore, the greater the percentage, the less important the precinct.)	3
Locind	Percentage of laborers, operatives and craftsmen in proportion to the total working force. (It was the strategists' opinion that laborers, operatives and craftsmen would tend not to vote Republican. Therefore, the greater the percentage of these occupations, the less important the precinct.)	4

(Chart III. continued)

Code	Description	Weights
Trv	Total registered voters in the precinct.	
Tvc	Total votes cast in the precinct in 1966.	
Cumtrv [Only on Chart V]	This column keeps a running count of how many registered voters P.I.P.S. has described. (For example, the first precinct on the list contains 720 registered voters, and 720 appears in the CUMTRV column. The second precinct on the list contains 544 registered voters; then 544 is added to 720, and 1264 appears in the CUMTR-V column.)	
	The cumulative total enables the campaign planner to find the spot at which he has accounted for 50 percent of the total registered vote in his district, or 60 percent, etc.	
Cumtvc [Only on Chart V]	This column keeps a running count of how many of the total votes cast in the district (in 1966) P.I.P.S. has described. (The CUMTVC column can be used in much the same way as the CUMTRV column described above.)	
Pips	Precinct Index Priority System score. (When all the information is combined, the P.I.P.S. score indicates the importance of each precinct in relation to all other precincts in the district. The higher the P.I.P.S. score, the more important the precinct.)	

CHART IV

CITY OR TWP	PRE	GL	CT	REGOV P¹ SDS²		MODDEM P SDS		REPCAN P SDS		REMAY P SDS		EDUCAT P SDS		SCOUTS P SDS		RECWEL P SDS		LOCIND P SDS		TRV	TVC	PIPS
CENTER CITY	1	K7	1	49	50	42	45	31	44	40	42	434	29	12	18	66	5	57	40	769.	549.	42
CENTER CITY	2	K7	1	38	37	36	37	16	23	27	26	434	29	12	18	66	5	57	40	604.	423.	34
CENTER CITY	3	K7	1	15	13	21	13	5	5	14	9	434	29	12	18	66	5	57	40	665.	505.	20
CENTER CITY	4	K7	1	11	9	18	16	5	5	8		354	47	18	27	73	4	58	38	568.	435.	21
CENTER CITY	5	K7	2	11	4	20	26	2	2	8		354	47	18	27	73	4	58	38	608.	445.	22
CENTER CITY	6	K7	2	34	33	34	35	17	24	33	34	354	47	18	27	73	4	58	38	520.	399.	36
CENTER CITY	7	K7	2	35	34	34	35	20	29	32	32	354	47	18	27	73	4	72	16	592.	432.	38
CENTER CITY	8	J7	3	14	7	15	10	2	3	13	8	495	16	7	9	15	12	66	26	525.	420.	9
CENTER CITY	9	J7	3	14	8	10	17	2	5	12	7	495	16	5	9	15	10	72	16	580.	415.	10
CENTER CITY	10	J7	3	15	10	21	9	2	5	12	6	495	16	5	6	26	20	66	26	331.	249.	10
CENTER CITY	11	J7	4	8	7	22	19	0	0	7	1	537	9	4	4	14	14	62	32	638.	495.	12
CENTER CITY	12	J7	4	16	10	26	20	11	10	15	6	498	15	5	4	9	9	62	32	226.	165.	7
CENTER CITY	13	J7	6	21	16	23	23	10	10	19	10	498	15	4	4	14	14	62	32	303.	404.	13
CENTER CITY	14	J7	6	19	16	41	45	14	20	24	16	498	14	12	18	9	9	55	43	590.	206.	13
CENTER CITY	15	J6	26	19	13	32	32	8	12	18	14	500	21	4	4	39	39	60	35	489.	402.	28
CENTER CITY	16	J6	9	19	14	23	20	4	6	14	8	469	20	18	9	2	2	57	35	744.	289.	18
CENTER CITY	17	J6	9	18	13	16	11	2	4	13	9	477	1	27	27	58	58	57	40	530.	577.	20
CENTER CITY	18	J6	9	19	14	15	10	2	5	14	8	477	1	18	0	6	6	57	40	442.	406.	20
CENTER CITY	19	K6	5	28	12	20	16	4	7	13	10	562	1	1	0	14	14	40	66	519.	337.	10
CENTER CITY	20	K6	5	21	8	8	19	2	8	14	16	562	1	1	0	14	14	40	66	822.	381.	12
CENTER CITY	21	K6	15	28	26	22	19	7	10	19	19	562	1	19	29	71	71	40	66	892.	586.	10
CENTER CITY	22	K6	15	74	82	60	69	50	72	68	79	310	57	19	29	71	71	54	54	602.	714.	34
CENTER CITY	23	K6	15	67	74	65	77	46	67	68	79	310	57	29	29	71	71	40	66	598.	473.	68
CENTER CITY	24	K6	10	67	73	71	84	43	62	47	78	310	57	43	68	54	54	48	54	896.	487.	66
CENTER CITY	25	K6	10	67	61	49	55	30	44	60	72	291	61	43	68	92	92	48	54	887.	679.	71
CENTER CITY	26	K6	10	71	71	50	57	42	60	61	69	291	61	43	68	92	92	48	54	970.	668.	59
CENTER CITY	27	K6	10	65	76	65	55	36	61	61	63	291	61	43	68	92	92	48	54	692.	767.	66
CENTER CITY	28	K6	10	53	55	49	77	5	50	56	63	291	61	43	68	92	92	48	54	715.	531.	68
CENTER CITY	29	J6	10	40	39	41	44	21	35	17	43	291	61	43	68	92	92	48	54	545.	571.	60
CENTER CITY	30	J6	10	58	63	48	47	35	51	40	43	291	61	43	68	76	76	48	54	681.	416.	37
CENTER CITY	31	J6	31	44	44	50	56	30	44	51	57	456	24	10	14	54	54	55	42	381.	480.	50
CENTER CITY	32	J6	31	55	59	53	35	32	47	56	57	456	24	14	14	97	97	46	57	712.	290.	62
CENTER CITY	33	J5	30	60	65	53	54	32	51	64	63	374	43	10	45	89	89	38	70	751.	561.	45
CENTER CITY	34	J5	27	57	65	54	57	37	60	60	68	302	59	29	22	89	89	38	70	773.	599.	47
CENTER CITY	35	J5	27	42	61	57	52	36	54	53	59	302	59	15	22	92	92	43	61	352.	613.	60
CENTER CITY	36	J5	32	51	54	47	33	24	40	40	43	302	32	27	42	92	92	43	61	826.	267.	61
CENTER CITY	37	J5	32	52	54	45	34	32	47	51	56	421	32	27	42	64	64	39	61	403.	633.	58
CENTER CITY	38	J6	28	47	51	50	33	30	43	51	57	421	21	13	26	47	47	36	72	880.	321.	46
CENTER CITY	39	J6	8	46	47	44	21	21	35	34	61	419	45	15	9	58	58	45	58	812.	414.	54
CENTER CITY	40	J6	25	35	33	33	34	21	34	31	31	370	33	10	14	47	47	47	55	611.	609.	48
CENTER CITY	41	J6	23	35	33	34	34	15	35	24	31	351	48	37	59	34	34	34	75	732.	483.	49
CENTER CITY	42	H7	23	62	67	57	66	39	56	58	66	351	44	37	59	97	97	34	75	517.	527.	46
CENTER CITY	43	H6	36	65	71	60	69	41	60	64	74	269	66	37	59	97	97	34	75	659.	357.	38
CENTER CITY	44	H6	36	69	76	57	51	49	70	65	71	269	66	35	55	97	97	28	85	643.	502.	37
CENTER CITY	45	H6	36	67	74	46	60	45	65	62	74	269	63	35	55	81	81	28	85	492.	552.	32
CENTER CITY	46	H6	24	50	52	31	44	31	45	48	53	284	63	35	55	2	2	28	85	619.	416.	68
CENTER CITY	47	H6	24									284								387.	516.	70
CENTER CITY	48	H6																				274.	71
CENTER CITY	49	H6																					71
CENTER CITY	50	J6																					58

¹ Percent

² Standard Score: The highest precinct is given a score of 100 and the lowest a score of 0. Other precincts are then given a score relative to 0 and 100.

Standard score provides an indication of the relative differences in value.

CHART V

CITY OR TWP	PRE	GL	CT	REGOV P	REGOV SDS	MODDEM P	MODDEM SDS	REPCAN P	REPCAN SDS	REMAY P	REMAY SDS	EDUCAT P	EDUCAT SDS	SCOUTS P	SCOUTS SDS	RECWEL P	RECWEL SDS	LOCIND P	LOCIND SDS	TRV	TVC	CUMTRV	CUMTVC	PIPS
CENTER CITY	82	H5	16	87	98	69	82	63	90	78	92	116	100	29	45	0	98	18	99	720.	610.	720.	610.	89
CENTER CITY	83	H6	37	88	92	99	99	65	89	79	92	226	76	44	70	0	98	33	76	435.	544.	1264.	1045.	89
CENTER CITY	80	H5	16	82	92	85	85	60	86	78	92	116	100	29	45	0	98	18	99	689.	547.	1953.	1592.	88
CENTER CITY	59	H5	38	82	86	82	87	77	77	75	88	199	69	45	72	0	96	30	81	474.	356.	2389.	1948.	83
SATURN TWP	3	G8	12	83	94	87	87	65	94	84	99	257	69	57	91	0	92	59	37	436.	453.	2863.	2401.	83
CENTER CITY	81	H5	16	76	84	59	72	55	72	69	88	116	100	29	45	0	98	18	99	923.	752.	3786.	3153.	81
CENTER CITY	58	H5	38	78	87	72	89	50	92	69	79	199	82	45	72	0	96	30	81	528.	464.	4314.	3617.	81
SATURN TWP	15	H8	12	78	91	69	75	63	92	75	78	257	49	57	91	0	92	18	37	386.	323.	4700.	3940.	81
CENTER CITY	84	H6	27	74	81	64	78	62	84	66	76	226	71	44	70	0	98	33	76	977.	783.	5677.	4723.	80
THOR CITY	5	A2	37	78	87	67	81	67	79	72	87	246	76	62	99	0	86	40	63	583.	448.	6260.	5171.	79
CENTER CITY	96	G7	41	78	87	69	81	55	75	74	86	298	60	49	78	0	95	30	66	903.	762.	7163.	5933.	79
CENTER CITY	56	H5	38	77	81	56	81	56	79	74	86	199	80	45	72	0	96	30	81	577.	481.	7740.	6414.	78
CENTER CITY	69	H6	17	72	80	64	74	52	73	70	81	226	76	44	70	0	98	33	76	727.	610.	8467.	7024.	78
SATURN TWP	8	G7	12	80	84	66	66	53	65	72	84	257	91	57	91	0	92	47	37	479.	441.	8946.	7465.	77
CENTER CITY	63	H6	35	80	90	63	74	61	89	80	94	273	65	23	36	0	92	47	55	945.	809.	9891.	8274.	77
THOR CITY	1	A2	32	76	76	68	72	58	81	67	83	246	66	50	80	0	86	25	63	595.	595.	10636.	8869.	76
TUONELA TWP	5	J5	6	76	85	80	89	58	84	72	84	271	61	50	80	0	93	60	35	556.	490.	11192.	9359.	76
VULCAN TWP	2	J5	15	73	79	89	88	58	84	72	84	292	61	31	49	0	64	28	88	722.	616.	11914.	9975.	76
ODIN CITY	4	J2	22	81	81	74	78	50	72	66	73	271	66	50	80	0	93	25	35	522.	409.	12436.	10384.	76
CENTER CITY	55	B2	34	87	98	66	82	61	88	79	93	326	53	22	34	0	86	53	47	625.	520.	13148.	10953.	75
THOR CITY	4	J5	32	67	74	63	78	46	76	66	73	246	71	44	99	0	93	42	63	664.	524.	13773.	11473.	74
CENTER CITY	68	H5	32	65	75	58	74	42	66	64	73	246	76	45	70	0	86	43	76	652.	538.	14437.	11997.	74
ODIN CITY	3	J2	6	63	71	67	82	35	61	64	84	199	82	44	72	0	93	30	81	524.	425.	15089.	12535.	74
CENTER CITY	70	H6	37	67	76	56	76	44	64	67	81	226	66	44	80	0	93	60	35	735.	558.	15613.	12960.	73
ODIN CITY	3	G8	12	73	80	61	71	63	82	58	66	271	69	44	70	0	98	33	35	340.	611.	16337.	13518.	73
SATURN TWP	67	H6	37	64	70	71	68	45	59	66	76	257	76	39	81	0	92	59	76	675.	413.	17072.	14129.	73
CENTER CITY	10	G3	64	81	90	79	95	69	99	62	71	377	42	44	70	1	98	59	29	435.	307.	17616.	14542.	72
PLUTO TWP	12	G8	37	74	82	50	57	57	82	71	83	302	69	39	62	0	93	64	76	1400.	538.	17916.	14849.	72
SATURN TWP	5	F1	28	74	73	67	79	55	79	64	73	291	61	33	52	0	96	46	56	595.	429.	18631.	15387.	71
KRONUS TWP	25	K6	10	69	71	84	51	62	62	65	63	269	66	68	68	0	97	34	59	598.	1157.	19066.	15874.	71
CENTER CITY	48	H6	36	69	76	46	70	49	70	63	56	224	76	59	59	0	98	28	50	565.	158.	20466.	16974.	71
CENTER CITY	61	H6	22	67	73	32	42	35	61	56	79	212	71	38	60	0	99	37	84	582.	487.	21161.	17531.	71
ADONIS TWP	7	B2	33	67	61	46	64	54	78	72	84	246	61	27	42	2	98	42	84	524.	416.	21759.	18018.	71
THOR CITY	10	A2	31	57	74	60	73	43	62	65	78	287	71	41	99	0	99	49	70	613.	463.	22251.	18434.	71
ADONIS TWP	49	B1	24	67	74	64	64	61	65	67	78	284	62	35	65	2	96	52	63	524.	462.	22816.	18897.	71
CENTER CITY	3	H6	17	69	76	60	50	45	72	66	74	263	63	55	55	0	86	49	52	619.	411.	23398.	19359.	70
PHAETON TWP	3	G4	17	69	76	62	72	50	67	63	76	264	65	39	62	0	81	28	85	965.	500.	23922.	19770.	70
PHAETON TWP	47	H6	40	65	71	57	72	46	72	64	63	264	67	39	62	0	90	48	53	591.	516.	24535.	20786.	70
CENTER CITY	74	H5	17	65	72	57	66	41	67	63	71	269	66	37	59	0	97	48	53	643.	804.	25154.	21590.	70
CENTER CITY	4	G4	22	74	82	52	60	38	54	64	61	197	82	37	59	0	96	34	75	986.	514.	26119.	22104.	70
PHAETON TWP	87	G6	41	64	70	53	74	50	55	65	74	264	67	39	62	0	90	43	52	911.	552.	26710.	22656.	69
CENTER CITY	94	G7	60	66	63	63	40	39	56	63	73	247	71	34	54	0	93	40	55	725.	755.	27353.	23411.	69
CENTER CITY	75	G5	12	64	72	61	69	39	65	63	74	298	60	49	78	0	95	43	66	385.	725.	28339.	24136.	69
SATURN TWP	14	H8	12	55	59	62	71	45	50	58	58	197	69	57	91	1	92	61	61	407.	250.	29250.	24521.	69
ADONIS TWP	8	B1	33	61	66	55	63	49	71	64	74	212	79	27	42	0	99	39	67	362.	385.	29696.	24928.	69

VINCENT P. BARABBA   235

1. Fixed printing costs for a minimum printing run.
2. Additional costs per thousand units.
3. Addressing and handling costs per thousand units.
4. Postage costs per thousand units.

P.I.P.S. can now suggest the precincts to which the letter should be mailed, and at what costs, with a considerable saving of time and error.

Further, suppose that a donor has just appeared with an extra $1,000 which he will make available for this special mailing. But the strategist has only 48 hours for production, printing and mailing in order to have the letters reach their destinations with the greatest impact in terms of timing.

Again, P.I.P.S. can quickly suggest where the $1,000 gift can best be utilized. It must be emphasized that P.I.P.S. does not dictate, but operates on instructions previously supplied.

With or without the aid of a computer, P.I.P.S. can be used for a wide variety of campaign purposes. The system is especially well suited to:

a. Develop and implement campaign strategies.
b. Help pinpoint specific areas for direct mail, and help develop messages appropriate to those areas.
c. Plan and implement get-out-the-vote drives.
d. Help schedule the candidate.
e. Help pinpoint areas containing potential volunteers.
f. Help plan neighbor-to-neighbor fund-raising programs.

P.I.P.S. can be an extremely versatile campaign tool within the limits of political creativity and budget.

—10—

MEANINGFUL USES OF POLLS
IN POLITICS

Charles W. Roll, Jr.
Albert H. Cantril

> *In no other peacetime pursuits is the need for*
> *reconnaissance so great as in love and in politics.*
>
> Dr. Henry Durant,
> British poll-taker

When an individual contests for public office at the higher levels he is more than likely engaged in a once-in-a-lifetime opportunity. He is either standing for election to an office that has long been esteemed and sought, or he is running for a lesser office as the stepping-stone to greater political opportunity. At this point, why fail to take advantage of every fair means of presenting the strongest candidacy? In contrast to the misuses of polls, imaginatively conceived and skillfully executed opinion polls can provide the cutting edge—especially when the opponent probably also has the advantage of polling information coming in to him.

Polls are now an essential. The candidate who usually prevails is the one who most effectively responds to the concerns of the people, and there is no better way to learn of these concerns than through opinion research. Polls can also help the candidate learn what segments of the population need to be reached out for.

Candidates are inundated with information and advice. Political lieutenants, confidants, club-house politicians, and political

Chapter 3, "Meaningful Uses of Polls in Politics," from *Polls: Their Use and Misuse in Politics*, by Charles W. Roll, Jr., and Albert H. Cantril. © 1972 by Basic Books, Inc., Publishers, New York.

commentators all have their own judgments of what the mood of the people is, what the issues are, etc. But often the candidate can be seriously misled by well-intentioned supporters who whisper erroneous hints: campaigning too closely to a given individual could be dangerous; the candidate's record on an issue will hurt and, thus, should be avoided; particular segments of the electorate can be counted on only if a coalition can be created; endorsements of other public figures or advocates for special points of view are essential; etc. Without the benefit of a scientifically conducted poll, the candidate is equally often at a loss where to turn. Thus, one of the most important practical uses of the political poll is to put these kinds of counsel into perspective and to provide an "objective" check on the hunches of even the most loyal supporters.

This use of the polls is a matter quite different from the characterization by George McGovern. The night of the Ohio Presidential primary, he was seen on nationwide TV defining the difference between the old politics and the new politics as the same as the differences between "telling people what the public opinion polls say is safe and actually doing what is right for the country."

THE CONCERNS OF THE PEOPLE

"Senator Taft had never believed in polls prior to his celebrated 1950 reelection campaign for the Senate from Ohio," recalls L. Richard Guylay, who handled public relations for the late Senator's campaign. "One day at a strategy meeting of his advisers at his home in Cincinnati, he went around the table asking each in turn to give what he thought would be the principal issue of the campaign. Everyone there had a different answer. Obviously, all couldn't be right and maybe none of them was right. I said that much when it came my turn and then I added, why don't we take a poll and find out what the voters think. He told me to go ahead."[1]

Seven decades earlier, a fellow Buckeye had faced the same issue. In 1878, two years before his election as President, James Garfield remarked: "Real political issues cannot be manufactured by the leaders of political parties. The real political issues of the day declare themselves, and come out of the depths of that deep— which we call public opinion."[2]

In the days of the razzle-dazzle that makes up much of "the new politics," there is cause for concern that politicians may cynically assume that the public is impressionable enough to be whipped into a lather about almost any issue by the new political communications technologies. This, in our view, is a relatively naive assumption, for the well-spring of a political issue is to be found in the basic concerns of the people.

In recent years, the telling political issues have come *up* from the people, not *down* from the politician—Vietnam, law and order, the cost of living, etc. Thus, it was that in 1970 candidates quickly jumped aboard the law and order issue—not only the Vice President but also good "liberals" like Adlai Stevenson, III.

Probably no other kind of data are more important to a candidate than those that portray the concerns of the people. The candidate that effectively addresses these concerns is the most likely winner. All the secondary types of poll data, such as trial heats and candidate recognition, will follow an upward trend if a candidate has managed to tie in effectively to the public's view of what the issues of real salience are. Clearly, the candidate must articulate the issues, bringing to bear information and perspectives not found among the public at large. But his posture must basically be one that comes to grips with what is on the people's minds.

Illustrative of a response to public concern was Governor Rockefeller's treatment of the issue of crime and narcotics in the 1966 political season. A survey conducted in New York State showed that two of the most salient concerns of voters throughout the state were crime and narcotics. Table 1 shows the priority of concerns among a list of problems respondents were presented on a card. The twin problems cropped up particularly in the minds of people living in New York City.

When respondents were asked whether they would be "more likely" or "less likely" to vote for a candidate advocating various positions on state issues, the crime issue emerged as the most telling one. (See Table 2.) A candidate urging the "development of an all-out program to combat crime and juvenile delinquency" would be more likely to garner support than a candidate advocating any other position tested—including issues many political advisers would probably put forth as key in the voter's minds: equal rights in housing, support for Medicaid, aid to education. As Table 2 shows, closely allied to the crime issue in the public's mind was the strong appeal that could be made, particularly in New York City, for "a proposal that narcotic addicts be hospital-

TABLE I

Public's View of Problems
Facing New York State, 1966

| | | Percent Mentioning in: | |
	Statewide	New York City	Suburbs & Upstate
Providing for state and local needs to education	23	25	21
Combating crime and juvenile delinquency	22	26	19
Dealing with the problem of narcotic addicts who take dope	9	11	7
Providing adequate state care for the mentally ill and retarded	9	8	10
Attracting industry and promoting economic growth	8	9	7
Cleaning up our rivers to reduce water pollution	6	2	10
Providing a sound program of State Medicaid for lower income families to pay their medical bills	6	3	9
Handling the problem of minimum wage level in New York State	6	5	6
Protecting consumers and the buying public	5	5	5
Keeping corruption out of the state government	4	3	5
Reducing the influence of the political bosses	3	2	3
Providing a better system of roads and expressways	1	*	2

Less than one percent.

ized for treatment even against their will." Thus, the Governor's narcotics program demonstrated to the voters his concern and action about a problem foremost on their minds. In the November election, after campaigning vigorously on this issue, the Governor carried three of New York City's five boroughs.

The success of Governor Rockefeller in heavily Democratic boroughs of the city is to be contrasted to the poor response of

TABLE 2

Appeal of Various Stands
a Candidate Could Take, 1966

	Percentage Saying They Would Be "More Likely" to Support a Candidate Making Each Proposal Exceed the Percentage Saying They Would Be "Less Likely" to Support Him by:		
	State Statewide	New York City	Suburbs & Upstate
Development of all-out programs to combat crime and juvenile delinquency	+84 pts.	+89 pts.	+82 pts.
Spending more state money to expand and improve the care of the mentally ill and retarded	+77	+82	+71
An extensive program to clean up the state's rivers and reduce water pollution	+69	+61	+78
A proposal that narcotic addicts be hospitalized for treatment even against their will	+66	+71	+62
Spending state money to help more students in New York State attend the public or private college of their choice	+61	+72	+51
Spending over one billion dollars a year on state aid to local communities for schools	+49	+64	+34
Strong support for the Medicaid program under which New York State helps pay the medical bills of lower income families	+40	+53	+28
Spending state money to provide a better system of roads and expressways	+35	+36	+34
Stong support of equal rights and opportunities in jobs and housing for Negroes and Puerto Ricans	+34	+45	+23
Strong opposition to off-track betting	−3	−13	+5

the nation to Vice President Agnew's pronouncements during the 1970 Congressional elections. Agnew spoke out again and again about protests and the general feeling of unrest across the country. His failure to capture the public imagination—as evidenced by disappointing Republican showings nationwide—is due primarily to the fact that he offered nothing affirmative. He was surely touching a sensitive nerve ending of the public with his rhetoric, but he pointed to nothing on the positive side that might help solve the problem.

MAXIMIZING POTENTIAL STRENGTH

Resources and time in a campaign are limited—and usually scarce. Thus, decisions about how and where a candidate spends his time can tip the balance to victory or defeat. Beyond that are a host of decisions with respect to media and promotional activities, research on campaign issues, and the like.

The polls are looked to for answers to many of these questions. Two aspects of the problem arise repeatedly in political research. The first has to do with the extent to which a candidate is known to the voters; the second has to do with attending to those areas in which there is the greatest chance of picking up electoral strength.

Much is made in political circles of the so-called "candidate recognition" scores. These follow from responses to questions asked whether people have heard or read about particular candidates. For example, as late as November 1971—just four months prior to the New Hampshire and Florida Democratic primaries— the name of Senator Henry Jackson was known by only 52 percent of the American public. This represented a marked improvement over the 29 percent who knew about him the previous April, but it remained a weak showing in contrast to Senators Kennedy, Humphrey and Muskie, who were known to the public with percentages of 95, 94 and 89, respectively.

The Gallup Poll which reported the 52 percent recognition figure for Senator Jackson pointed up the fact that the Senator was significantly less known among the less educated and the non-white population. This, however, was to be anticipated and told the Senator's campaign relatively little about what to do to increase his recognition other than to simply get more exposure.

Politicians tend to take these recognition scores very seriously, apparently feeling they represent an important barometer, and urge their inclusion in most political surveys. While recognition is often a real problem for the newcomer or nonincumbent, we question the utility of repeated measures of the degree to which a candidate is becoming better known to the voters. Knowledge that a candidate is not widely recognized does not help solve the problem, though areas where greater efforts need to be made may be pinpointed. As a campaign progresses, a previously little-known candidate will become more familiar to the public, particularly if he can tie into the basic concerns of the voters in a meaningful way.

In other words, candidate recognition is not important in its own right. As with trial heat figures, recognition scores have more meaning for measurement of progress already made than for insight about future strategy in a campaign.

A superb illustration of the point is the 1969 gubernatorial election in New Jersey, in which former Governor Robert Meyner started the campaign extremely well-known and well liked in contrast to his challenger William Cahill, a Congressman virtually unknown in the state outside of his district. Throughout the campaign, Meyner had the advantage of being better known. In spite of this awareness advantage for Meyner, Cahill gained strength with the voters and by September—although still less known—held a nine percentage point lead over the former Governor. (See Table 3.)

The second aspect of maximizing potential strength is targeting a campaign on those areas where there is the greatest chance of picking up votes. For this a campaign needs to know three things. First, it must be determined which subgroups in the population

---

TABLE 3
Awareness of Gubernatorial Candidates in New Jersey, 1969

	Percent Able to Name Candidates		Percent Supporting Each Candidate	
	July	September	July	September
Meyner	59	79	43	37
Cahill	44	66	42	46
Meyner margin	+15 pts.	+13 pts.	+1 pt.	−9 pts.

are particularly favorable or opposed to the candidate or what he stands for. Second, a campaign will want to learn which voters presently favorable to the opposition are the most likely to switch to its own candidates; some political research firms have elaborate techniques to pinpoint these "switchers." Third, it is necessary to learn what the attitudinal make-up is of both present supporters and potential switchers from the opposition; involved here are both the priority of problems as viewed by voters and the division of opinion on specific issues.

Armed with this kind of information, a campaign can target its efforts. There then follows the decision of striking a balance between taking off from one's strength and galvanizing it or attacking areas of one's weakness in hopes of minimizing it. While this is seldom an either-or kind of decision, a campaign will ultimately have to lean one way or the other.

In our judgment, the more effective course is the former. For by working in those areas where a candidate is particularly strong, a campaign can accomplish a number of objectives. It can solidify that strength, thereby ensuring the turnout of supporters on election day. Also, it can mobilize supporters into working for the candidate, ringing doorbells and the rest. We have already reported how effective the house-to-house blitz was in Goldwater's California campaign in which the last ditch effort was concentrated in the southern part of the state where he was strong.

Another example of the success of this approach is found in the Republican primary in 1962 when Ogden Reid challenged the incumbent Congressman in New York's 26th District. Polls showed Reid ahead of the incumbent in the northern portions of the district. They showed also that an inordinately large percentage of voters there were unable to choose between the two men. Despite the fact that this portion of the district was less populated than others, the Reid campaign was advised that it was more advantageous to concentrate on this region, working to get Reid better known and taking advantage of the favorable margin that existed in the hope of gaining the support of the undecideds. Thus, while this northern area represented only about 15 percent of the Republicans voting in the primary, 30 percent of Reid's victory margin came from there.

An historic example of going where the votes are not occurred in the last hours of the 1960 Presidential campaign. Richard Nixon, choosing to fulfill his pledge to carry his campaign into all fifty states, flew to Alaska to nail down its three electoral votes.

While he did carry the state, one wonders whether the time would not have been better spent on a whirlwind tour in St. Louis, Chicago and Minneapolis-St. Paul—all areas in states falling into the Kennedy column election day by less than one percentage point. Precise last-minute polls in such key areas could have warned (and probably did) against the folly of flying off to Anchorage just before the closest election in the nation's history.

INFORMATION ON IMAGE

There is still another use of polling which can immeasurably aid the politician in formulating an effective campaign strategy. This use has to do with gathering intelligence on the public's view of officeholders or the competing candidates in a campaign.

"A political leader's successfully projected appearance of competence, concern, sincerity, his image in a word, can carry a far greater impact than his utterances," Professor Elmer Cornwell of Brown University perceptively points out. "The skillful executive," he adds, "will, thus, do all that he can to create and project a favorable image for himself, to build up and conserve what might be termed his 'image capital' " because "wise investment of this capital will pay better dividends than mere exhortation."[3]

And why is this so? Despite Oscar Wilde's injunction that "it is only the shallow people who do not judge by appearances,"[4] Cornwell finds that "the citizenry's capacity for information and argumentation is less than its capacity to absorb and respond to images projected by public figures. . . ."[5]

Midway in his term as Governor of Pennsylvania, Raymond Shafer had a survey conducted on his stewardship. The favorable aspects of his image in connection with the way he was handling his job were somewhat less in number and more vague than were the unfavorable aspects. (See Table 4.)

Rightly or wrongly, the people of Pennsylvania obviously were concerned about Shafer's spending policies in terms of what they felt they were getting back for their tax money. They also sensed that Shafer, in levying more taxes in a limited way on several minor items, had gone back on an impression of promises he had given before his election that he would not raise taxes as governor. Opposition Democrats lost no time in capitalizing on this.

Even with these poll results in hand, the governor sought a state income tax at the next meeting of the legislature. The mark

TABLE 4
Things Liked and Disliked about Governor Shafer

Favorable		Unfavorable	
Just like him, he's doing a good job, doing his best (general)	13%	Taxing too high, a wasteful spender	20%
He's bringing in industry, reducing unemployment	2	He breaks promises, doesn't fulfill pledges	6
He's for improving education	2	Has done little or nothing	4
Miscellaneous favorable	7	Not for little people, the working man	3
		Just don't like him (general)	3
		He's too political	2
		Miscellaneous unfavorable	7

of the man was that, overriding this information on these unfavorable aspects of his image, he followed his conscience and pursued the income tax so the dire educational and institutional needs of the Commonwealth would be met. The fact that he did not slavishly avoid the financial issue rendered the survey findings no less useful to him. With this information he could have better understanding as to why it eventually required two years of exhortation and a Democratic successor Milton Shapp to get the Shafer income tax idea enacted.

Data on candidate image can also explain suddenly appearing weaknesses (or strengths) in a candidate's standing. We referred earlier to the 1969 gubernatorial race in New Jersey. In these two months between the July and September surveys, Robert Meyner's strength dropped six percentage points, while that of his challenger, William Cahill, gained four points.

Between these surveys, the Cahill campaign centered around charges that the former Governor's freedom to act in certain areas would be limited because of certain business relationships he had established since leaving office. Whatever may be said about charging someone holding no political office with conflicts of interest—or even potential conflicts of interest—the Cahill game plan worked. The impossibility of making favorable aspects of Cahill's image equal to or surpass the originally high level of Meyner's popularity in the short period of a campaign necessitated an alternative approach—attack. Evidence of the success of this approach is that the only significant difference in either the Meyner or Cahill image data between July and September occurred in the

Meyner side where the category "has integrity, sincerity, dedication" fell from 12 to 6 percent. (See Table 5.) This occurred too late in the campaign for Meyner to overcome it and, combined with several other skillful campaign steps, the Cahill team went on to win a 6—4 victory.

ASSESSING THE TRENDS

We have already noted the fluidity of election situations—particularly in primary contests where party loyalties do not come into play. Thus, keeping tabs on trends in opinion movement is an essential.

Overall trial heat figures are important in indicating fluctuation in voter loyalties, but far more important is learning about

TABLE 5
Things Liked about Meyner and Cahill

	July 1969	September 1969	Net Change
Meyner			
A good governor, good record, good job	18%	18%	—
Has integrity, sincerity, dedication	12	6	−6 pts.
Personable, popular, friendly, nice looking	8	11	+3
Qualified, capable, experienced	7	10	+3
Leans liberal, a Democrat	3	3	—
Kept taxes down, not a spender	2	1	−1
Leans conservative, like a Republican	2	1	−1
Strong, dynamic, a leader	2	1	−1
Just like him (in general)	2	1	−1
Miscellaneous on favorable side	1	1	—
Cahill			
Has done a good job, a good man	9	10	+1
Personable, pleasant, nice, patient	8	10	+2
Would make a good governor	7	9	+2
A family man	5	4	−1
Not like other Republicans	4	1	−3
Honest, fair	3	3	—
F.B.I. alumnus, ex-cop	2	1	−1
Young, dynamic	2	2	—
He's a Republican (favorable)	—	4	+4

gains and losses that are occurring within segments of the population. When some major event has an impact on overall trial heat figures, it is only a look at what has happened internally that gives insight about what a campaign should do.

Referring back to the 1966 gubernatorial race in New York in which Governor Rockefeller targeted his efforts on the problems of crime and drugs in New York City, it will be recalled that he was making impressive gains in this traditional Democratic stronghold. However, in mid-October President Lyndon Johnson—then exceedingly popular—made a campaign appearance in the city on behalf of Frank O'Connor. Thereupon, Rockefeller suffered a setback with the margin separating him from O'Connor growing from four percentage points to thirteen points. (See Table 6.)

While these overall trial heat figures showed that the President's visit had slowed Rockefeller's drive, it was only by examination of where the Governor had suffered that a recovery effort could be mounted. Table 7 shows that the President's visit had its greatest impact among the less educated, those living in households with an income of under $4,000, and nonwhites.

ASSESSING THE IMPACT OF A THIRD CANDIDATE

The survey technique can also be put to use to assess the interdependencies existing between races in a given state or between

TABLE 6
New York City Gubernatorial Preferences, 1966

	Rockefeller	O'Connor	Rockefeller Deficit
September	19%	38%	−19 pts.
Early October	30	34	−4
	Johnson Appearance		
Mid-October	29	42	−13
Late October	31	38	−7
Election	39	42	−3

Note: The "undecided" percentages were not allocated in this table and, therefore, percentages for both candidates are lower than the election results in which there are, of course, no undecideds.

TABLE 7
New York State Gubernatorial Preferences, 1966
(among special groups)

	Rockefeller	O'Connor	Rockefeller Deficit
Grade-School Educated			
September	17%	41%	−24 pts.
Early October	24	38	−14
Mid-October	25	49	−24
Late October	29	42	−13
Household Income			
under $4000			
September	21	41	−20
Early October	27	39	−12
Mid-October	25	48	−23
Late October	34	39	−5
Nonwhites			
September	17	46	−29
Early October	29	38	−9
Mid-October	21	48	−27
Late October	30	43	−13

the sources of strength of candidates in the same race. Research can stave off the common error of political strategists in assuming that the support for candidates of like political complexion is almost interchangeable. Thus, it might be concluded that "liberals" in the same contest detract from each other.

Much has been made of the "spoiler" role Franklin D. Roosevelt, Jr. is supposed to have played in the reelection of Nelson Rockefeller as Governor of New York in 1966. It is held by some commentators that Roosevelt's defection from the Democratic fold to stand as the Liberal Party's candidate cost O'Connor, the Democratic candidate, a sufficient number of votes to ensure Rockefeller's victory. It is pointed out that the number of votes Roosevelt won (507,234) exceeded the margin dividing Rockefeller and O'Connor (392,263). Thus, had Roosevelt not run, it is contended, his support would have been enough to put O'Connor over the top.

Surveys just prior to the November election, however, showed that for every three votes Roosevelt drew from O'Connor, he also drew one vote from Rockefeller. Thus, while Roosevelt's candidacy obviously hurt O'Connor considerably more than it did Rockefeller, it is doubtful that it kept Frank O'Connor from the governorship.

As Democratic Presidential aspirants were sorting themselves out prior to the 1972 convention, it was commonly assumed that if Senator Edward Kennedy were not a candidate, Senator Muskie would be the prime beneficiary. Not only are both men Roman Catholics and from the same section of the country, but they are regarded as having much the same kind of "liberal" appeal in contrast to Senator Humphrey, for example, who it was alleged had the legacy of Vietnam and the 1968 Chicago Convention to overcome. Yet, pundits were surprised in December 1971, when the Gallup Poll reported that if Kennedy did not run the bulk of his support among Democrats would go to Humphrey. In fact, Humphrey would gain more than twice as much as Muskie. Thus, other factors were at work in the public's mind. (See Table 8.)

This kind of polling information can help alert a candidate to the impact on his campaign of his party's candidate for another office in the same election. Looking to New York again, the strength of James Buckley, the Conservative Party's candidate for the Senate in 1970, presented serious problems for Nelson Rockefeller, who was up for reelection. A poll just prior to the election showed Buckley to be a very strong candidate—drawing 34 percent of the total vote and 47 percent of the vote among Republicans—against the Republican Party's candidate Charles Goodell and the Democratic candidate Richard Ottinger. The poll also showed that only 31 percent of Rockefeller's backers intended to vote for Goodell, whereas 51 percent of his supporters intended to vote for Buckley. (See Table 9.)

TABLE 8
Impact of Kennedy Candidacy on Preferences of Democrats

	With Kennedy in	With Kennedy out	Net Gain
Kennedy	32%	—	—
Muskie	25	31%	+6 pts.
Humphrey	19	34	+15
All others	18	27	+9
Undecided	6	8	+2

TABLE 9
Senate vs. Gubernatorial Voter Preferences in New York, 1970

	Senate Preference			
	Goodell	Ottinger	Buckley	
Rockefeller supporters	31%	18%	51%	100%
Goldberg supporters	24	64	12	100
Adams supporters	7	24	69	100

Rockefeller's opponent Arthur Goldberg had a somewhat similar problem because the Liberal Party had endorsed both him and Goodell. Of Goldberg's supporters, about one-in-four (24 percent) intended to vote for Goodell. However, Goldberg's problem was not comparable to that faced by the Governor. Thus, when the press charged that Rockefeller was not going all out for his fellow Republican, Goodell publicly recognized that the Governor's constituency of support was considerably different from his own.

POSITIONING THE ISSUE

A continuing dilemma for the candidate is finding the most appropriate context within which to address an issue—or to use Lloyd Free's phrase, "positioning the issue."[6] This assumes the candidate has made up his mind as to his own stand on an issue and is looking for the best way to present his case.

Survey research can make important contributions by trying out arguments and appeals on the public to find out which are the most effective in convincing people of the soundness of one's position.

In early 1968, for example, both sides of the Vietnam debate could have learned how best to argue their case from a survey conducted by the Institute for International Social Research. This study showed that both the Johnson Administration and the peace movement were using some of the least effective arguments in behalf of their causes.

Specifically, respondents in a national sample were shown a card on which were listed "arguments that have been given for continuing our military efforts in Vietnam." They were asked "which two or three of these do you, yourself, feel are the very strongest arguments?" As Table 10 portrays, two of the least effective arguments at the time were those advanced by proponents of a continued U.S. presence in Vietnam: "we are committed to South Vietnam" and "if we pull out and the communists take over, they will kill many of the Vietnamese who have opposed them."

On the other side of the coin, respondents were shown another list of "arguments that have been given for our discontinuing the struggle to win the war and beginning to pull out gradually in the near future." They were again asked which two or three arguments were the strongest. Table 11 shows that three of the arguments used by the peace movement were, at the time, among the least effective: "our participation in the war in Vietnam is basically illegal and immoral . . . ," "our national interest and security do not require us to fight in Vietnam," and "we are doing too much damage to the Vietnamese people, their way of life and their economy."

The same technique was employed in New Jersey during the gubernatorial race of 1965. At the same time, there was much debate over the kind of tax program that should be instituted and people were divided over the relative merits of an income tax as

---

TABLE 10
Strongest Arguments Selected for
Continuing Our Military Effort in Vietnam, 1968

If we do not continue, the Communists will take over Vietnam and then move on to other parts of the world	49%
We must support our fighting men	48
If we quit now, it would weaken the will of other countries to defend their freedom	33
If we give up, the whole expenditure of American lives and money will have been in vain	33
The U.S. should never accept defeat	24
If we do not continue, we will lose prestige and the confidence of our friends and allies abroad	23
We are committed to South Vietnam	19
If we pull out and the Communists take over, they will kill many of the Vietnamese who have opposed them	14
If we persevere, we are sure to gain our objectives	8

TABLE 11
Strongest Arguments Selected for
Discontinuing the Struggle to Win the War, 1968

Too many Americans are being killed or wounded	39%
The war is dividing the American people and affecting our national unity	31
The South Vietnamese are not doing their share in the war effort	30
The people in South Vietnam are so divided and there is so little national unity that there is no foundation for a strong independent country	29
We may end up having to fight China, Russia, or both—even a nuclear war	29
Expending so much of our military strength on the war in Vietnam has weakened our ability to respond to danger in other parts of the world	22
We are wasting too much money that could be better used for other purposes	21
The chance of succeeding either by military force or through negotiations is remote	14
Most people abroad are highly critical of our actions in Vietnam	11
Our participation in the war in Vietnam is basically illegal and immoral; we have no business being there at all	9
Our national interest and security do not require us to fight in Vietnam	9
We are doing too much damage to the Vietnamese people, their way of life and their economy	9

opposed to a sales tax. A survey in June 1965 showed that advocates of the unpopular income tax proposal could make their strongest case by pointing out to the public two things: that "a sales tax would make everything cost more" and that "an income tax would allow deductions for dependents, medical expenses, etc." They would be ill-advised to argue that "a sales tax would hurt business conditions" or that "if the state had an income tax, the people least able to pay could expect to pay nothing or almost nothing (in taxes)." (See Table 12.)

Conversely, proponents of a sales tax over an income tax would likely gain more supporters by arguing that a sales tax is fairest "because everyone would pay the same rate." They would likely persuade fewer by arguing that a state income tax on top of the federal income tax would be too much of a burden, that an

TABLE 12
Strongest Arguments Selected for an Income Tax
Rather Than a Sales Tax in New Jersey, 1965

A sales tax would make everything cost more (except food and drugs)	34%
A state income tax would allow deductions for dependents, medical expenses, etc.	26
A state income tax is fair to me and my family because people with more income would pay a higher tax	21
A state income tax would in the end cost me and my family less than a sales tax	18
Paying the two or three cents sales tax on each dollar spent would be a nuisance	18
The state income tax would not hurt too much because it would be paid through payroll deductions	18
A sales tax would hurt business conditions by affecting the sales volume of our merchants	14
If the state had an income tax, my family and I would expect to have to pay nothing or almost nothing	11

income tax would keep industry from coming into the state, and that the amount of a sales tax paid could be controlled by a family through the device of buying less.[7] (See Table 13.)

TARGETING THE OPPOSITION'S WEAKNESS

In a manner related to positioning the issue, it is possible to target the opposing candidate's areas of weakness—particularly with respect to issues that will most adversely affect his candidacy. When an opposing candidate is clearly identified in the public's mind with a given stance on a salient issue, the task of targeting is simplified considerably. However, even when the opposition is not so clearly perceived as holding a controversial or unpopular position, the survey technique can provide useful insights as to where vulnerabilities may begin to appear.

Referring again to the New Jersey gubernatorial election of 1965, Wayne Dumont, the Republican candidate, had long been an advocate of a sales tax and had opposed any move toward a state income tax. He had also spoken out against bond issues to raise money for state projects. His opponent, the incumbent

TABLE 13
Strongest Arguments Selected for a Sales Tax
Rather Than an Income Tax in New Jersey, 1965

The sales tax is fair to me and my family because everyone else would pay the same rate	39%
A sales tax is being paid partly by people from other states who buy things in this state	30
The sales tax would not hurt too much because it is paid in small amounts at a time	26
Filling out still another income tax form each year—this one for the state—would be a great nuisance to me	26
A sales tax would in the end cost me and my family less than an income tax	24
A state income tax would keep industry from locating in the state and affect jobs	22
A state income tax, on top of the federal income tax, would be too great a burden from this kind of tax	22
If the state had a sales tax, my family and I would be able to keep the total amount down by buying less	15

Richard Hughes, was not closely identified with any tax alternative in the view of New Jersey voters.

In the June 1965 survey respondents were asked whether the advocacy of various positions with respect to state revenues would make them "more likely to support a candidate, less likely, or wouldn't make much difference one way or the other." As Table 14 vividly shows, the greatest opposition among voters would be toward the candidate who advocated a state income tax. A sales tax and bond issues were not popular but were less troublesome than the income tax. What people did favor was a state lottery.

As the campaign went forth, Dumont had to overcome his past identification with the sales tax, while Governor Hughes was not burdened by any tax image at all. Hughes's relative advantage over Dumont probably contributed largely to his victory. After the election, when it became clear some revenue measure was necessary, Hughes advocated a state income tax. But failing this, he advocated and put through the less unpopular sales tax. The strong showing for the lottery pinpoints why New Jersey has one today.

The same issue appeared in the 1964 gubernatorial race in Indiana. A survey conducted in the state in March reported that "Marshall Kizer and Thomas Lemon (two contenders for the

TABLE 14
Impact of a Candidate's Advocacy of
Alternative Revenue Plans in New Jersey, 1965

| | How Proposal Would Affect Vote | | | |
	More Likely	Less Likely	More Likely Minus Less Likely	Wouldn't Make Much Difference
A Candidate Who—				
Favored a state lottery or sweepstakes	59%	20%	+39 pts.	10%
Favored a state sales tax	34	45	−11	9
Consistently opposed state bond issues	25	41	−16	8
Favored a state income tax	21	60	−39	7

Democratic nomination) have spoken out against the sales tax and in favor of a graduated income tax along federal tax lines. Only 17 percent of likely November voters who favored these candidates over Lieutenant Governor Richard Ristine (the Republican candidate) agreed with them in this position: over two-thirds of those who supported Kizer or Lemon over Ristine preferred one of the other tax alternatives."[8]

Whether the Democrats had information of this kind is not known. However, their decision to overlook Kizer and Lemon in favor of Roger Branigin, who was not identified by the voters with any particular tax position, was a shrewd one, for Branigin went on to defeat the conscientious Ristine, who was remembered by the public as breaking a tie vote in the State Senate to bring about a tax program combining a moderate sales and income tax.

No candidate in recent years has been so clearly pegged by voters with his stand on substantive issues as Barry Goldwater. The unpopularity of his stand on many issues was ultimately to be his undoing nationally in 1964. A foretaste of this came in the New Hampshire primary in 1964 when Governor Rockefeller outlined in detail to voters the Senator's stand on issues. A survey of Republicans in the Granite State three months prior to the primary reported that those voters supporting Goldwater over Rockefeller overwhelmingly opposed the Senator's stand (or at least his written position) on a host of issues:

66% opposed withdrawal from the United Nations if Communist China was admitted;

88% opposed breaking diplomatic relations with Russia;

68% approved of the Nuclear Test Ban Treaty;

80% opposed putting Social Security on a voluntary basis;

76% favored the graduated income tax;

70% favored Federal grants to the states to help those needing welfare aid;

62% favored Federal aid to education for school and college construction and loans to college students;

57% favored the inclusion of a public accommodations provision in a civil rights bill;

83% favored the fixing of minimum wages by the Federal Government.

While Rockefeller did not win in New Hampshire, he certainly did soften up the support that eventually went to Henry Cabot Lodge.

These instances are those in which candidates were especially identified with particular postures on central issues. What of the case in which a politician is not so identified? Surveys can indicate the weak links in the opposition's argument which may, at a later date, prove to be salient enough with the public to target efforts toward.

Illustrative of this use of a political survey was the interest of the Democratic National Committee in learning how best to respond to the economic policies President Nixon announced in the Fall of 1971. A study was commissioned in which people were given a card listing seven arguments against the wage and price control policies just announced by the President. They were asked which one or two of the arguments they felt were most compelling.

It was learned that of all the attacks that could be mounted on the President's economic program, none evidenced greater public support than the issue of the equity of the controls. As Table 15 indicates, there was little concern among the people over the international ramifications of controls. There was also little response to the argument that the President had not listened closely enough to representative of business, labor, and the public.[9]

These, then, are some of the practical uses to which polls are put in politics.

TABLE 15
Strongest Arguments against
Economic Policies of Nixon Administration

The freeze on wages and prices is not fair to the working man because business profits and dividends are not also included	34%
President Nixon is proposing too large a tax reduction for business and not enough for the working man, and this is not fair	34
The freeze on wages and prices is not likely to hold down the rising cost of living	25
President Nixon is more concerned about controlling the rising cost of living than he is about the rising rate of unemployment	20
By raising duties on products imported from other countries, the U.S. is risking an international trade war and is raising the cost of imported products for Americans	18
President Nixon has not listened closely enough to representatives of business, labor, and the public in formulating this new economic program	12
The program has undermined worldwide confidence in the American dollar	11

NOTES

1. Letter to Charles W. Roll, Jr., January 20, 1972.

2. Speech in Boston, Mass., September 10, 1878, as quoted in *A New Dictionary of Quotations*, ed. H. L. Mencken (New York: A. A. Knopf, 1942), p. 874.

3. Elmer E. Cornwell, Jr., "Role of the Press in Presidential Politics" in *Politics and the Press*, ed. Richard W. Lee (Washington: Acropolis Books, 1970), p. 19.

4. Quoted in *The Wit and Humor of Oscar Wilde*, ed. Alvin Redman (New York: Dover Publications, 1959), p. 137.

5. Cornwell, "Role of the Press in Presidential Politics," p. 19.

6. In conversations with the authors.

7. These reasons were designed by Archibald M. Crossley.

8. Unpublished survey report, April, 1964.

9. Center for Political Research, *National Journal* 3, no. 52 (December 25, 1971): 2,548.

PART FOUR

CAMPAIGN MEDIA IN THE AGE OF TELEVISION

Campaign communication has traditionally been conducted through a variety of general and specialized media. Specialized media are those that transmit only political campaign messages, such as buttons, literature and the party organization. General media are those in which both political and nonpolitical messages are transmitted, such as talks with family, friends, and coworkers and the media of mass communication. The hallmark of the contemporary campaign is its emphasis on general media—television, radio, newspapers, direct mail, billboards. Voters motivated by their desire to seek entertainment, general information, and communication join the vast media audience, and candidates have turned to mass-media campaigning because of the enormous attention the public pays to these media.

The use of mass media in campaigning has increased at a time when the role of the exclusively political and specialized medium, party organization, has diminished. Harold Gosnell's *Machine Politics: Chicago Model* indicates the extensiveness of precinct activity in the late 1920s and early 1930s in an urban area where precinct activity was unusually well organized. Of the precinct committeemen he interviewed, almost all regularly performed such campaign activities as canvassing, registration, and get-out-the-vote.[1] More recently, Samuel Eldersveld conducted a study of party organization in the Detroit area, a metropolitan region characterized by inactive party organization where the new style of campaigning has become the rule. He found that only 17 percent of the Democratic precinct leaders and 25 percent of the Republican leaders performed all three campaign tasks of registration, canvassing, and get-out-the-vote.[2] As a result, Eldersveld's study of Detroit voters indicated a low degree of party contact and awareness. Although three-fourths of all voters reported receiving party literature in their homes, only 8 percent said they had been personally contacted at home, 7 percent reported being contacted by party workers, and 7 percent remembered that they were contacted by the party on election day.[3] The study also indicated that only 29 percent of those sampled were aware of the fact that party precinct leaders existed in their neighborhood.[4]

As party has become less significant, the more generalized media have prevailed as vehicles for campaign communication. Candidates for office cannot ignore media as pervasive as the electronic media. Almost 98 percent of all households wired for electricity have one or more television sets; they use them an average of more than five hours a day.[5] The number of radios in use in the United States far exceeds the number of inhabitants—between 300 and 350 million. With so extensive an audience, it is hardly surprising that campaigners have turned to radio and television and that millions of voters follow the campaign through these media. A total of 115 million persons followed, on radio and television, at least some part of at least one of the four 1960 Kennedy-Nixon debates. The average television audience for all four debates was 71 million.[6] Any given television time slot for a campaign spot announcement can reach from 50 thousand to 1.5 million viewers in the Chicago media market. Paid political broadcasts attract about 70 percent of the audience of the program they replace, but national audiences for such political broadcasts average about 20 million. By contrast, an estimated 10 million people saw Richard Nixon in person during his energetic fifty-state campaign tour in 1960.

Survey studies indicate the vast reach of mass media in the campaign. In 1972, as had been the case in the three previous Presidential elections, nearly 90 percent of the persons interviewed by the Survey Research Center reported that they followed the campaign on television. As in the previous three elections, just under 50 percent listened to speeches or discussions on the radio and around one-third read about the election in magazines. The number of citizens following the 1972 campaign by reading newspaper articles dropped from three-fourths of the electorate in the three previous elections to just over 57 percent, making the electronic media even more pervasive.[7] Moreover, surveys have revealed that television is the single most important source of media campaign information in Presidential elections, with from 50 to 60 percent of citizens choosing that medium in various elections, whereas newspapers place second in importance, with around one-fifth of the population.[8] Media are also important sources of information in state and local contests: 43 percent of citizens claimed television, 42 percent claimed newspapers, and 10 percent talks with people as the most important state-campaign information source; and 43 percent claimed newspapers, 28 percent claimed television, and 22 percent claimed talks with people as the most important local-campaign information source.[9]

Today, practically all candidates for major office are using television, radio, and newspapers as a means of campaigning. The major resources in presidential, senatorial, and gubernatorial campaigns now go into media costs. Three-fourths of all congressional candidates use electronic media, and almost all use newspaper advertising. While data on state candidates below the level of governor are difficult to obtain, all indications point to increasing use of media campaigning.[10]

As campaigns have become more electronic media oriented, some significant changes have occurred in the campaign process. Generally, the new media require different electioneering approaches to reach a larger and less politically interested electorate; consequently, the campaign has lost some of its partisan flavor. The following are some of the key changes brought about by use of the electronic media:

1. Campaigns are attended by larger numbers of people. Radio and television can be attended passively, without the effort required by reading or going to a rally. These new media have brought the campaign to those least likely to attend a campaign—the uninterested, the old, the antisocial.[11]

2. Voters are now exposed to opposition candidates to a much greater degree. Selective attention is much more difficult when a candidate's messages are placed in the favorite program slot of viewers of any persuasion. Today, sponsored programs, newscasts, and debates are more likely to expose voters to both

candidates than in the old days, when a voter had physically to attend a political rally or select out newspaper coverage of a candidate.

3. Media have changed some of the long-standing conventions and traditions of American campaigning. The campaign train speech has given way to hopping by plane from media market to media market creating media events. The campaign rally is pitched to viewers at home as well as those in the hall. The candidate's personal campaigning is timed and located for the convenience of media newsgatherers. Senator Henry Jackson broke with the standing tradition of senators announcing their Presidential candidacies from the Senate Caucus Room by announcing his 1976 candidacy through purchased television time, with a five-minute montage introducing the candidate, shown between the late-night news and late-evening programing. The McGovern forces gave some thought to the selection of primaries according to media coverage. They reasoned that good coverage would progress across the country from east to west if they did not do too much hopping or force excessive moving of TV equipment. Hence, their major efforts went from New Hampshire to Wisconsin to Nebraska to Oregon and to California.

4. Electronic media have added tremendous impact and drama to the campaign. Well-conceived and well-produced broadcasting is designed to make the campaign as dramatic as the rest of the material conceived for the medium, not so much in the style of the drama of politics, but rather, in the style, the drama of sports, games, and military action—"infighting," "counterattack," "next move," and "home stretch" are part of the language of the campaign.[12]

5. The electronic media, and especially television, give the voter a chance to examine both the sight and sound of the candidate. President Kennedy once said, "Television gives people a chance to look at their candidate close up and close to the bone."[13] Ithiel de Sola Pool explains that "Television humanized Eisenhower by revealing him to be somewhat more sensitive and withdrawn than the iron soldier the public had previously imagined."[14] This human dimension, often referred to as candidate image, has become an important dimension of the modern campaign.

6. Electronic media put a greater emphasis on the production and merchandising of talent, something not generally considered to be intrinsically related to political issues and candidate stands. The 1972 Republican Convention was so completely planned and

staged that it was complete with backdrops and podium designed by a New York set designer, a written script detailing events minute by minute, and scheduling to conform to prime-time—i.e., no controversy or long speeches at night.[15] Whether the vehicle is a short spot announcement or a half-hour documentary, the modern media-oriented appeal tends to emphasize selling the candidate at the expense of conveying political knowledge.[16]

7. The media are said to have an agenda-setting function in campaigning.[17] That is, by their coverage of various facets of the campaign, the media call attention to certain events and issues. Media serves not only to build up public images but also to present objects and thereby suggest what individuals should think about. As Bernard Cohen once said in regard to the press, it "may not be successful in telling its readers what to think, but it is stunningly successful in telling its readers what to think *about*."[18]

8. The electronic media can help to thrust unknown candidates into prominence. Adali Stevenson, II, John F. Kennedy, Barry Goldwater, and George McGovern were Presidential candidates who were not well-known nationally; television assisted in their appearance on the national stage after they were nominated and facilitated their becoming well known in a short period of time. When Howard Metzenbaum and John Glenn squared off for the first time in an Ohio Democratic primary, Metzenbaum had a 6 percent recognition factor. By primary election time, Metzenbaum's massive media effort had raised that factor to 75 percent, and he won that time.[19] While he was a leader in the polls, McGovern broke with tradition and agreed to debate with Humphrey on national television, because he was in the curious situation of being unknown in certain long-standing Democratic coalition constituencies where he should have been well known. [20]

9. The campaign-following habits of voters mean that, for the offices well covered by the media, the candidate increasingly must be an adept media campaigner. No matter how good an organization is or how successful a candidate is at the person-to-person approach, the major-office candidate must "perform" for viewers, listeners, and readers. McGovern's former Press Secretary, Gordon Weil, observed that, despite the good organization the campaign had built up through the primaries and despite McGovern's extensive effort at meeting voters personally, the voters made a direct, personal judgment of the candidates through media.[21]

10. Television coverage gives the voter an opportunity to be a spectator at the entire campaign. The viewer sees the candidate from all available vantage points—in the primaries, on the hustings,

at conventions, in front of groups, perhaps even in debate with an opponent. According to Kurt and Gladys Lang, television gives people the notion "that they 'see for themselves,' that they are directly involved in history, that television takes them to the scene of the crime, that they have a clearer picture of what is going on than people right 'there'." Viewers seem less dependent on interpretation from reporters of what they can experience themselves.[22]

Despite these trends in media campaigning, the candidate must still face the test of time faced by his earlier counterpart. For some voters, the candidate must go beyond the projection of an image. Issues must at some point be discussed, and they must be presented in a way that some people find compelling. The candidate must face the probing of some politically knowledgeable individuals. He will have to pass the test of competence for the office sought. A careful examination of the record indicates that attractive and successful candidates also possess, as a rule, a certain governmental know-how and the intelligence to discuss issues. The record will show that some successful politicians aren't even attractive.

These changes in campaigning might lead one to expect that electronic media have become a powerful weapon in the shaping and changing of voter behavior, when in fact their effect is not as persuasive as often assumed. Joseph Klapper concludes in *The Effects of Mass Communication* that there are barriers between communication and the political attitudes and opinions of the electorate.[23] These barriers, such as ego-involved attitudes, group-held attitudes, and the views of key opinion leaders, serve as facilitators of opinion formation on occasion, but serve as impediments most of the time.[24] Klapper drew heavily on Lazarsfeld's landmark study, *The People's Choice,* which indicates that mass communications in a campaign are far more likely to reinforce convictions than to change them.[25] Other studies of the effects of media campaigning have indicated that the proportion of persons who are converted by the campaign is generally lower than that of those whose latent feelings are activated and those whose convictions are confirmed.[26] Thus, the prevalent media process appears to be facilitation of previously held opinions, a process usually called reinforcement.

The dimensions of the impact of mass media in the electoral process are well stated by Stanley Kelley, Jr. He explains that the effect of media on attitudes depends on certain conditions:

1. How a person votes seems most closely related to his party affiliation, his perceptions of the interests of the groups with which he identifies, his feelings toward the candidate, his opinions about issues, and his view of party performance in the management of governmental affairs. These views are relatively stable, and are difficult for campaign communication to alter. They are more likely to be reinforced.

2. Campaign communications always finds the voter in a certain context. He is tied to others in an intricate set of relationships that serve to anchor his opinions and convictions and thus will have a mediating effect on any communication received. The voter has to fit new messages into a pattern of thought that his associates have come to expect of him. Group norms, group expectations, and persons with highly valued views set limits on the ability of campaigning to induce opinion changes in the short run.

3. Media can serve to create opinion more easily than they can change opinion because, to the extent that an issue or personality is really "new," the communication about it is unlikely to be affected by unsympathetic predispositions, group norms, or opinion leaders. In other words, Kelley argues that all of the factors that usually operate to filter and bend mass media communications to reinforce opinion cease to do so if there is no existing opinion to reinforce.[27]

What, then, is the significance of the mass media for campaigners? First, the sheer size of the media audience is important. No other means of communication can offer the same potential for reaching large numbers of voters in a short period of time, and the larger the audience, the more likely it is to include those segments of the electorate amenable to persuasion. Secondly, media can influence and convert some people in a campaign. As Bernard Berelson maintains, "Some kinds of communication, on some kinds of issues, brought to the attention of some kinds of people, under some kinds of conditions, have some kinds of effects."[28] It is this small but growing margin of opinion conversion that is attractive to the candidate and his media specialist. Thirdly, it is believed that media exert a considerable influence on the voters' perceptions of the personal qualities of the candidates. Candidate-oriented stimuli in a campaign are, for most people, new communication, and thus are not subject to the forces that make it difficult to alter opinions. The candidate's personal appearances and advertising through the media are important for creating his image. As party voting diminishes in favor of candidate-oriented factors, the mass media become more attractive to those who wish to promote candidate images. Finally, media serve as important agencies of campaign reinforcement. Democratic candidates still must reach Democrats, and Republicans, Republicans. Mass-media advertisements and televised rallies can serve the same purpose as torch-light parades, rallies, buttons, and bumper stickers: they may not convert, but they inspire the faithful and reinforce their feelings toward the cause.

Within these fairly well defined limits and dimensions of media in campaigning, the campaign media specialist sets out to develop his client-candidate into a media personage. In addition to hired pollsters and any speech writers and press aides a candidate may have on staff, many large scale campaigns also employ a media entourage which can include a media consultant, time buyers, an ad agency or production company, technicians, and marketing specialists. The role of the media specialist in campaigning can be demonstrated by explaining the campaign activities of a media consultant. An illustrative case is Robert Squier, a well-known media specialist who has engaged in:

1. Coaching candidates for the purpose of improving their television performance on uncontrolled media formats—news shows, press conferences, interviews, and talk shows.
2. Long-range stimulation of the news media; assisting candidates and campaign staffs to understand how best to create and use news—for example, knowing the best time to release announcements, finding the best type of audience, making media-covered personal appearances appear warm, genuine.
3. Communications planning of all media selected for use in the campaign. Includes acting as a liaison with the pollster to learn information useful to the media design, analysis of the market situation, development of strategies, and development of a communications plan for both controlled and uncontrolled media.
4. Production of radio and television bits called for in the media plan. Includes production of film spots, videotape spots, radio spots, five-minute programs, half-hour documentaries, and telethons.
5. Communications consulting, i.e., coordinating the production activities of other producers or serving as a second reviewer of the work of others.[29]

Do these television consultants, or image makers, as they are popularly called, possess a specific technology with which they develop a candidate as a media personage? Do they, as is often charged, possess the magic formula with which to transform and ordinary politician into a television star? Except for a general knowledge of campaign processes and media audiences, the answer seems to be no. Each media consultant appears to operate with his own set of preconceived notions of selling candidates. Five examples well illustrate this diversity.

Media consultant Tony Schwartz has created close to 2,000 radio and television spots, has won dozens of awards, and has worked for many Democratic candidates—thirteen in 1974. He believes that the best political commercials are similar to Rorschach patterns: they do not tell the viewer anything—they surface his feeling and provide a context in which he can express those feelings. "The task of a media specialist is not to reveal a candidate's stand on the issues so much as to help communicate those personal qualities of a candidate that are likely to win votes."[30] Schwartz is a follower of McLuhan's "nonlinear" approach to "getting inside people", and he once used ink-blot associations to link mothers, Medicare, and Hubert Humphrey.[31] Schwartz believes in surrounding the voter with auditory and visual stimuli that evoke reactions and feelings that move him to pull a certain lever in the voting booth. "We really package the voter and deliver him to the candidate." Schwartz insists he doesn't sell candidates like soap, because "I don't sell soap like soap."[32]

Charles Guggenheim is a film maker who has worked in a number of campaigns, including managing overall media direction of the McGovern campaign. Guggenheim, who believes that, essentially, one must take a positive or a negative approach, handled the McGovern campaign by trying to build McGovern into a viable positive alternative to the perceptions many voters had of Nixon's competence as President. He believed that the only chance they had was to convince voters who disliked Nixon personally that McGovern was a realistic alternative.[33] Thus, the McGovern campaign was first built on long program formats and rather complex issue messages in the spots. Guggenheim used spots called "crawls" (on a black screen, white copy crawls up from the bottom to the top as the voice over reads it). These ads were severely criticized by other communications specialists as being newspaper ads on TV or "Western Union vehicles." Guggenheim's approach was overruled in the later stages of the campaign and Schwartz was brought in to the campaign to institute negative, anti-Nixon ads.[34]

Joe Azbell has been director of communications for Governor George Wallace's efforts in national campaigning. Azbell says what most people are concerned about is losing their individuality, and Wallace's media is produced around this theme. He believes in presenting the facts in Wallace's own words and hopes that if voters accept the case they will vote for him. The production is laced with the Nashville sound of country music, twangy guitars, and hand-clapping melodies. Most of the media productions leave the Governor himself out until the end, when he is likely to say

"Hear me out"; the only time they say "Vote for Wallace" is as an overline on a documentary or as a voice over.[35]

David Garth, who has handled many candidates, including former New York Mayor John Lindsay, believes that people want to see the man as he is. "We put John Lindsay on television with his coat off and his sleeves rolled up. We won. Last fall we spent money on TV showing John saying, 'I made mistakes.' It worked. You have to show the man." Garth believes that there is no way a media consultant can create an image for a candidate; one can only project what he already has.[36]

Roger Ailes, a well-known Republican consultant, disagrees with the Garth approach to spots. He emphasizes longer, issue-oriented presentations. "People just don't 'buy' the spots," says Ailes. "They're becoming more sophisticated, and they want to see more of the candidate talking, not just walking around with his sleeves rolled up, with his beautiful wife at this side, and a voice coming on saying what a good guy he is."[37]

Thus, there is considerable diversity, and, often, seeming contradictions, in the styles with which media consultants handle candidates. This is perhaps necessarily so, given the diversity of the audience-electorates to which appeals are made, the different types of approaches and motivational appeals used in advertising, and the different philosophies of production in media entertainment. Within the craft of television, the operatives have diverse backgrounds and outlooks.

Another very important reason why there is no technology of media campaigning is that there is no established body of knowledge from which these engineers can draw. Very little is known about how effective the candidate-with-the-sleeves-rolled-up approach is vis-a-vis the straightforward-issue-development approach. Advertising executive and sometime-political-media consultant Allan Gardner claims that "the political market place has done nothing more than borrow the imprecise research techniques developed in the packaged goods world."[38] No one is sure whether people are better motivated by well created and staged themes or by more natural productions. To be sure, effectiveness depends on the situation, but the situational variables have yet to be established. Moreover, there has been a considerable amount of "fadishness" and camp following among media consultants because of this uncertainty. In 1972, after a study revealed that ticket-splitters claimed they made up their minds by following the news, many consultants started to make their commercials look like news. In 1974, sincerity and honesty was a pervasive theme, because of the influence of Watergate. Too often, victories are simply credited to effective campaign techniques, and no attempt is made to assess the persuasive effects of specific techniques or to account for the fact that the losers may have used some of the same techniques.

There is, however, increasing attention paid to the study of the media in campaigns and their impact. The 1968 Robert Kennedy campaign was complete with studies of relative spot weights by market, polls asking people whether or not they has seen or heard television advertising, their reactions to the advertising, and tests of campaign-appeal credibility. Since that time, a number of other campaign studies have followed along a similar vein. Also, scholars are beginning to examine the impact of media use on the vote, as a part of studies of campaign finance.[39] Others are beginning to weigh the overall impact of various campaign media, as well as its relative position as a vote motivator.[40] And a more systemic examination of campaign spots has now been undertaken by a number of scholars, with some very significant and sometimes unexpected findings.[41]

As consultants and political scientists begin to pay more attention to the impact of media-oriented campaigning, answers to many questions will emerge. At present there are only a few conventions of media campaigning, which are based on studies of audience-electorates. These conventions indicate the trends of media campaigning in the 1970s:

1. The campaign must be planned and organized around the media schedule. The event to be covered must meet the news deadline of the radio and TV station. Different appeals can be made in different media markets through advance planning and the airplane. Some even argue that the media planners should think and operate like newspersons rather than campaigners. Careful attention must be paid to the production schedule. Local party officials and local supporters must share the candidate's time in their area with the television and radio studios and newspaper offices.

2. The telephone is an electronic medium that is becoming a more integral part of the person-to-person campaign than the party precinct worker. Considerations of speed, efficiency, and the personal security of campaign workers have made it more popular to install telephone banks at headquarters where volunteers or paid workers canvass voters for information. The data is put into a

computerized information bank and is used for later telephoning for such electioneering activities as voter appeals and voter turn-out.

3. Media should be mixed for selective appeals. Direct mail appeals are best suited for lower social and economic groups. Radio is used to extend the reach of television and to reach voter types difficult to reach by other means. Television spots are best for voters who are low in political interest, knowledge, and efficacy. Television newscasts and talk shows are best for knowledgeable voters.

4. Controlled media are purchased in varying patterns. The most familiar pattern is the accelerated finish, which begins a few weeks before the election and increases in frequency with a highly saturated finish. In some cases a flat buy, or constant purchases throughout the campaign, is employed. In campaigns where there is a desire to appear over a long period of time, a spurt schedule is often employed, where advertising is purchased for a week or two, only to disappear for a time and then to reappear. This pattern is repeated over a six- to nine-month period. Sometimes an event schedule is employed, which is a spurt schedule tied to an event, such as a television documentary, a candidacy announcement, or a telethon. With the renewed popularity of longer controlled formats, they have been purchased in recent elections through the Treyz plan of purchasing "local" time through the networks, buying more than one network, and/or spot buying in key markets to create a "road-block" effect in those markets. (Oliver Treyz is a former broadcast executive who devised the plan.)

5. The general format for controlled media depends on the visibility of the candidate. If the candidate lacks identity, then candidate exposure is developed first and followed by candidate-issue appeals. If the candidate is well known, then issues are discussed in the earliest wave of spots; then those issues are linked with the candidate in the second wave; and, in the third wave, candidate factors, particularly job competence and ability to deal with those issues discussed earlier, are stressed.

6. A movement is underway to re-institute the longer formats of purchased time. Nixon purchased seventy-four five-minute spots and two half-hour programs, and McGovern purchased forty-nine five-minute spots and nine half-hour programs. By contrast, Nixon and McGovern purchased only forty and thirty-six one-minute network spots respectively. Among the reasons for this shift are: some feel that an audience can be held if the longer

program is well produced or markets are blocked out, and others believe that more-sophisticated voters seek more informative programs; the candidates need these longer formats to develop certain positions; the candidates receive uncontrolled media coverage from these long formats, particularly when major policy announcements are made on longer programs; and the longer programs can be used to answer the critics who say short formats represent irresponsible campaigning.

7. Cable television (CATV) is becoming an increasingly popular medium. In the increasing number of cable systems capable of putting on their own programs (many are purely transmission facilities) there are large blocs of time available on public service channels, and, where time is sold, it can be purchased for a tiny fraction of commercial station rates. Moreover, its purchase is feasible for many candidates running in small constituencies, since many systems are small enough so that most subscribers fall within one constituency and media purchases are not wasted on viewers who cannot vote in that contest.

8. Campaign media must be prepared to capitalize on "instant information" by showing voters that the candidate is concerned, involved, and "there." For example, if a protest demonstration of great visibility and coverage occurs, the candidate must be prepared to travel to the scene, talk to the principals, and suggest that something be done about it.

9. Since many undecided voters seem to take their campaign cues from the uncontrolled media, media messages directed to them should appear less controlled. The premise is that the campaign should appear newsworthy. Major policy statements should be handled through press conferences. Coverage of the candidate at newsworthy events should be arranged. The candidate should be scheduled on as many talk shows as possible.

10. Controlled media can also follow a news-format pattern. Newspaper editorial support can be taped for radio play. Television spots can be produced to look like news formats by having the candidate stress problem identification and problem solution. Spots can be placed around the news shows and news events to attract a maximum number of ticket-splitters and undecideds.[42]

Stanley Kelley, Jr., traces the early history of campaign television in "The Emerging Conventions of Campaign Television" and describes how the contemporary practice of candidate exposure in short time periods developed. He also demonstrates how campaign television emerged into an entertainment format. Stanley Kelley,

Jr. is Professor of Politics at Princeton University. He is the author of many books and articles on campaigns and political public relations.

In "Political Advertising: Making it Look Like News," the staff of the *Congressional Quarterly* demonstrates how media approaches reflect the fadishness of an art. In 1972, following the publication of a book that claimed ticket-splitters and late switchers were more interested in following uncontrolled media, media consultants rushed to make their paid media appear like news programs.

In "Radio Use in the Television Era," Jules Witcover explains how President Nixon shifted emphasis from television to radio in the 1972 campaign and discusses some structural and political advantages to campaign radio. Mr. Witcover is a national political reporter for the *Washington Post* and has authored a number of books on American politics.

Yet another fad emerged after Watergate in the 1974 elections, as revealed in "Campaign Consultants: Pushing Sincerity in 1974," also by the staff of *Congressional Quarterly*. As Sanford Weiner revealed earlier, consultants reacted to Watergate by urging candidates to displace issues for pleas of personal honesty, integrity, and other human qualities.

In "Candidate Exposure in Uncontrolled Media," Robert MacNeil explores the ways in which candidates stimulate coverage of their campaign by the news media and gain access to free time formats. He explains how coverage by the news media becomes a campaign event. Robert MacNeil is a political editor for the Public Broadcasting Service and has been a television news correspondent in England and the U.S.

"On the Bus: Covering Presidential Campaigns," by Timothy Crouse, provides insight into how the travelling news corps gathers news as they follow Presidential aspirants. Timothy Crouse is a contributing editor of *Rolling Stone* and has worked for various newspapers.

L. Patrick Devlin's "Contrasts in Presidential Campaign Commercials of 1972" examines the contrasting philosophies of media directors and campaigns that were reflected in the television commercials of the Nixon-McGovern campaign. L. Patrick Devlin is a professor of speech at the University of Rhode Island.

Tony Schwartz's "The Inside of the Outside" outlines the opportunities available to campaigners through electronic media and offers insight into how one media consultant views the media and approaches it in a campaign. Tony Schwartz is a political- and commercial-media production specialist based in New York, and he has taught auditory perception at Fordham University.

NOTES

1. Harold F. Gosnell, *Machine Politics: Chicago Model,* 2nd ed. (Chicago: Univ. of Chicago Press, 1968), p. 81.

2. Samuel J. Eldersveld, *Political Parties: A Behavioral Analysis* (Chicago: Rand McNally, 1964), p. 350.

3. *Ibid.,* p. 536.

4. *Ibid.,* p. 451.

5. Richard S. Salant, "The Television Debates: A Revolution that Deserves a Future," *Public Opinion Quarterly* 26 (Fall 1962):337; Richard L. Worsnop, "Television and Politics," *Editorial Research Reports* 44 (May 15, 1968):353.

6. Salant, "Television Debates," p. 338.

7. The Survey Research Center, Univ. of Michigan, 1960–1972 Election Studies. Made available through the Inter-University Consortium for Political Research.

8. *Ibid.*

9. Burns W. Roper, *What People Think of Television and Other Mass Media, 1959–1972* (New York: Television Information Office, 1973), pp. 6–7.

10. For information on the extent of usage, see: "How Congressmen Use Radio-TV," *Broadcasting* 71 (March 16, 1964); "How the Candidates See Radio-TV," *Broadcasting* 75 (April 29, 1968); Edward C. Dreyer, "Political Party Use of Radio and Television in the 1960 Campaign," *Journal of Broadcasting* 8 (Summer 1964):211–17; Lawrence W. Lichty, Joseph M. Ripley, and Harrison B. Summers, "Political Programs on National Networks: 1960 and 1964," *Journal of Broadcasting* 9 (Summer 1965):217–29; James J. Mullen, "How Candidates for the Senate Use Newspaper Advertising," *Journalism Quarterly* 40 (Autumn 1963): 532–38.

11. Angus Campbell, "Has Television Reshaped Politics?" *Columbia Journalism Review* 1 (Fall 1962):13.

12. Stanley Kelley, Jr., "Elections and the Mass Media," *Law and Contemporary Problems* 28 (Spring 1962):313.

13. Quoted in Rowland Evans, "TV in the Political Campaign," *Television Quarterly* 5 (Winter 1966):25.

14. Ithiel de Sola Pool, "TV: A New Dimension in Politics," in Eugene Burdick and Arthur J. Brodbeck, *American Voting Behavior* (Glencoe, Ill.: Free Press, 1959), p. 242.

15. *National Journal* 4 (September 2, 1972):1384–85.

16. Tom Wicker, "TV in the Political Campaign," *Television Quarterly* 5 (Winter 1966):14–15.

17. Maxwell E. McCombs and Donald L. Shaw, "The Agenda-Setting Function of Mass Media," *Public Opinion Quarterly* 36 (Summer 1972): 176–87; Leonard Tipton, Roger D. Haney and John R. Baseheart, "Media Agenda-Setting in City and State Election Campaigns," *Journalism Quarterly* 52 (Spring 1975):15–22.

18. Bernard C. Cohen, *The Press and Foreign Policy* (Princeton, N.J.: Princeton Univ. Press, 1963), p. 120.

19. Source: private campaign polls.

20. Reported in *National Journal* 4 (June 10, 1972):968.

21. Gordon L. Weil, *The Long Shot* (New York: Norton, 1973), p. 225.

22. Kurt Lang and Gladys Engel Lang, *Politics and Television* (Chicago: Quadrangle Books, 1968), pp. 301–2.

23. Joseph T. Klapper, *The Effects of Mass Communication* (New York: Free Press, Glencoe, 1960), p. 45.

24. Elihu Katz and Paul F. Lazarsfeld, *Personal Influence: The Part Played by People in the Flow of Mass Communications* (New York: Free Press, 1955).

25. Paul F. Lazarsfeld, Bernard Berelson, and Hazel Gaudet, *The People's Choice: How the Voter Makes up his Mind in a Presidential Campaign* (New York: Duell, Sloan and Pearce, 1944), p. 103.

26. E.g., "Television and the Political Candidate" (New York: Cunningham and Walsh Advertising, 1959).

27. Kelley, "Elections and the Mass Media," pp. 309–11.

28. Bernard Berelson, "Communications and Public Opinion," in Wilbur Schramm, ed., *Communications in Modern Society* (Urbana: Univ. of Illinois Press, 1948), p. 184.

29. Based on discussions and correspondence with Robert Squier; see also *National Journal* 4 (February 19, 1972):327–28 for a feature on Squiers' role in the Muskie campaign.

30. Christopher Lydon, "Packaging Voters for Candidates, TV-Style," *New York Times,* October 29, 1974, p. 28.

31. Thomas J. Fleming, "Selling the Product Named Hubert Humphrey," *New York Times Magazine,* October 13, 1968, p. 46.

32. Lydon, "Packaging Voters."

33. Ernest R. May and Janet Fraser, *Campaign '72: The Managers Speak* (Cambridge, Mass.: Harvard Univ. Press, 1973), pp. 203–4.

34. *Broadcasting* (November 13, 1972):18–19.

35. Dom Bonafede, "New Hampshire, Florida Primaries Highlight Powers and Limitations of Media," *National Journal* 4 (March 18, 1972): 464–65.

36. Fred Ferretti, "Political TV 'Packager' Counts Ratings in Votes," *New York Times,* August 18, 1970, p. 27.

37. Morton Knodracke, "Television and the Elections—A Double Image," *Chicago Sun-Times,* November 8, 1970, sec. 2, p. 4.

38. Allan D. Gardner, "Political Ads: Do They Work?" *Wall Street Journal,* February 1, 1972, p. 10.

39. Gary C. Jacobson, "The Impact of Broadcast Campaigning on Electoral Outcomes" (Paper presented at the Annual Meeting of the American Political Science Association, August 1974); John Wanat, "Political Broadcast Advertising and Primary Election Voting," *Journal of Broadcasting* 18 (Fall 1974):413–22.

40. E.g., Walter DeVries and V. Lance Tarrance, *The Ticket Splitter* (Grand Rapids, Mich.: Eerdmans, 1972); F. Gerald Kline, "Mass Media and the General Election Process," *Maxwell Review* 9 (Spring 1973):35–55.

41. Three reports on studies of commercials in the 1972 campaign conducted by Thomas E. Patterson and Robert D. McClure are: "Political Advertising on Television: Spot Commercials in the 1972 Presidential Election," *Maxwell Review* 9 (Spring 1973):57–69; *Political Advertising: Voter Reaction to Televised Political Commercials* (Princeton, N.J.: Citizens Research Foundation, 1973); "Television News and Televised Political Advertising: Their Impact on the Voter" (Paper presented at the National Conference on Money and Politics, Washington, D.C., February 1974).

42. For further information, see: Robert Agranoff, *The Management of Election Campaigns* (Boston: Holbrook, 1976), chs. 11–14; *Broadcasting* (November 13, 1972); "Cable Television Offers Boon to Financially Pressed Candidates," *New York Times*, November 5, 1972, p. 68; Sig Mikelson, *The Electric Mirror* (New York: Dodd, Mead, 1972), ch. 11.

—II—

THE EMERGING CONVENTIONS
OF CAMPAIGN TELEVISION

Stanley Kelley, Jr.

NETWORK-CONTROLLED TIME

In 1960 the three television networks allocated a substantial
amount of network-controlled time to reporting the presidential
campaign and to appearances by the candidates. The campaign was
given regular and extensive attention in newscasts, which often
carried taped presentations of the candidates addressing rallies.
The candidates and their wives were interviewed on "Person to
Person," "Tonight," "Presidential Countdown," and "The Campaign and the Candidates." Kennedy, Henry Cabot Lodge, and
Lyndon Johnson were all subjected to the rigors of "Meet the
Press" and "Face the Nation," and Nixon, too, appeared on the
former. "Eyewitness to History," "Election Countdown," and
"The Campaign and the Candidates" featured reports on the progress of the campaign and speculation about the election's outcome. On two programs noncandidate representatives of the two
campaign organizations gave their views on how things were going
and on the virtues of their respective tickets. Exclusive of newscasts, the networks devoted some forty-one hours to campaign
programs, more than half of them commercially sponsored.[1]

This kind of programming of network-controlled time is probably a fair indication of things to come. If one disregards the
debates, what the networks did in 1960 differs from what they

From Stanley Kelley, Jr., "Campaign Debates: Some Facts and Issues," *Public Opinion
Quarterly* 26 (Fall 1962):352–359. Copyright © 1962 by Princeton University. Reprinted by permission.

had done in previous campaigns chiefly in that so many programs had appearances by the candidates as their main attraction. More than half did. The program formats used, however—the interview, the documentary, and the panel inquisition—were those long familiar in television public affairs programs. Because this was true, almost all the campaign telecasts of 1960 could have been offered even if section 315 had not been suspended: a 1959 amendment to 315 had already exempted from the application of the equal-time provision appearances by candidates on bona fide newscasts, bona fide news interviews, bona fide news documentaries, and on-the-spot coverage of bona fide news events.[2] If section 315 is not suspended or revised by 1964, the long-standing aversion of broadcasters to equal-time claims by minor parties—at least valid ones—will further reinforce their already demonstrated preference for the tried and true formulas of public affairs broadcasting.

PAID TIME

By 1960 the use that politicians were making of paid time on television had begun to crystallize into relatively well-defined patterns. These can be expected to persist. This statement is not made on the basis of any simple faith that what has happened in the past is the best guide to what will happen in the future, but because the current use of television by campaigners reflects a developing consensus among them as to how the medium can best be made to serve their purposes.

In retrospect the approach that the rival campaign strategists took to television in the 1952 presidential race—the first in which television played a role of any significance—seems unimaginative, notwithstanding a statement at the time by the Democrats that they planned to use it "in a more exciting, more dramatic way than any political party ever dreamed of. . . ."[3] By far the greater number of programs sponsored by both parties were simply half-hour telecasts of speeches delivered at political rallies. Among the exceptions were the filmed documentaries that each side presented. In addition, Adlai Stevenson delivered a few fireside chats; Republican Governors appeared on an hour-long program; and the Republicans ended with a final night show that was a fast-paced, hour-long, three-network "report on the campaign" involving eighty-one switches from city to city and from live telecasting to film. In the campaign's closing days the Republicans saturated the air waves with spot announcements, reputedly spending somewhere between $800,000 and $1,500,000 in the effort.[4] The Democrats roundly denounced this use of spots in 1952, but were in no position to do so in later years. The spot announcement has since won the secure respect of Democratic and Republican campaigners alike.

Some other trends in the use of television in United States presidential campaigns can be indicated quite briefly.

First, the parties have increasingly reserved their longer telecasts (those over five minutes in length) for appearances by their presidential and vice presidential candidates and by the incumbent President. In 1952 the candidates and the President were the principal speakers in 73 percent of such telecasts. In 1956 and 1960 the comparable figures were 90 percent and 88 percent, respectively.[5]

Secondly, the mean length of party telecasts has declined radically. In 1952 it was 29 minutes; in 1956, 13 minutes; and in 1960, 14 minutes.[6] This decline was due mainly to the heavy use of the 5-minute "trailer" in the campaigns of 1956 and 1960: the modal length of party programs was 30 minutes in 1952; in 1956 and 1960, it was 5.

Thirdly, the producers of party television programs have been engaged in an effort to make them visually interesting and to introduce audience participation, conflict, and other entertainment features into them. With a few notable exceptions most American politicians in television's early days used television as they had radio—they "gazed at their tables, script bound,"[7] as French politicians still did in 1958. By 1956 cue cards and the teleprompter had largely freed American politicians from scripts. They began to use visual aids and film clips. They tried panel discussions and interviews. They appeared with stars of the entertainment world: the most notable instance of this, perhaps, occurred during the 1956 campaign, when President Eisenhower was given a "surprise" party on his birthday, and entertainers rendered his favorite songs. They organized telethons: Vice President Nixon used this device on the last day of the 1960 campaign. They experimented with press conferences and programs modeled on press conferences: Nixon submitted to questioning from reporters in one show during the 1956 campaign; in another President Eisenhower held a "Citizens' Press Conference," where carefully selected citizens praised him and posed friendly questions.

What is to be made of this record? The most general explanation of the trends just outlined would seem to be this: They reflect the rational reaction of campaign strategists to what they have learned about the factors that affect the size and responses of audiences for political television. Most of their information about audience size and response has come to them from ratings, surveys, letters, and telephone calls. The inferences they have drawn from such data may not be entirely convincing to students of public opinion, but they have seemed sound enough to politicians to have influenced their behavior.

Audience survey data convinced politicians that voters are far more interested in hearing what candidates have to say for themselves than in hearing what other party leaders have to say for and about candidates—unless the "other party leader" is the President of the United States. In 1952 both the Republicans and the Democrats had numerous speakers who appeared on television on behalf of their respective party tickets: Robert A. Taft, Phillip Murray, Clare Boothe Luce, Walter Reuther, Herbert Hoover, and Wayne Morse, to name only a few of them. Now, the average audience for a Stevenson speech that year was approximately 3,620,000 television homes, and for an Eisenhower speech, over 4,120,000 television homes.[8] Of speakers who were neither President nor candidates for the Presidency or Vice Presidency, only Senator Joseph R. McCarthy attracted an audience that equaled either of these averages. Most drew audiences that fell far below them. The Republicans took explicit notice of the lesson implicit in these facts.[9] The later programming of both parties indicates that both had taken the lesson to heart.

Two additional conclusions that politicians have reached account for other features of television's use in recent campaigns, including the trend toward shorter programs and the innovations in program format. The first such conclusion is that undecided voters are the voters least likely to watch political television shows. This proposition, although it owes a good deal to intuition, squares with findings about the 1952 audiences reported by Janowitz and Marvick.[10] It also conforms with more general findings about attention to campaign propaganda: Lazarsfeld and his associates reported in their Erie County study that "the people who already knew how they were going to vote read and listened to more campaign material than the people who still did not know how they would vote."[11] R. S. Milne and H. C. Mackenzie made a similar observation in their study of voting in Bristol, England.[12]

The other conclusion is that political television in its usual forms cannot effectively compete for audiences with commercial entertainment. Evidence to substantiate it accumulated rapidly.

The 1952 conventions received considerably lower Nielsen ratings than the show, "I Love Lucy."[13] In the 1952 campaign the two parties adopted different strategies in the purchase of television time, with a result that gave campaigners further food for thought. The Republicans, in an effort to minimize the competition of commercial entertainment, pre-empted the time periods of leading commercial programs. The Democrats hoped to build an audience for *political* television; they attempted to do so by presenting Adlai Stevenson in a series of programs regularly scheduled for 10:30 to 11:00 P.M. on Tuesdays and Thursdays. The Republicans were vindicated in the more pessimistic assumptions of their strategy when the rating services showed that both Stevenson and Eisenhower drew larger audiences when they appeared in pre-empted time periods.

They had not discovered any final solution to the politicians's television problems, however, for party strategists soon learned that viewers were often highly annoyed when they tuned to one of their favorite programs to find a political speech instead. Carroll Newton, the Republicans' chief time buyer, has reported, "I think the most phone calls we had during our campaign (the 1956 campaign) we got after displacing a very popular program and, while we were highly flattered at the number of calls, we found out that 98 percent of them were disgruntled at us. . . ."[14] He has reported also that half-hour political shows in 1956 drew audiences from 25 to 40 percent smaller than those normal for the programs they replaced.[15]

If one puts oneself in the campaigner's place, it is not difficult to see the significance of what has just been said. The campaigner wants to arouse the enthusiasm of his least enthusiastic partisans and to gain the support of the undecided voter. To do either of these things he must reach voters and he must please them. If it is true that voters, and undecided voters more than others, prefer entertainment to politics, two general strategies are open to him. The first is to attempt to locate and reach captive audiences. The second is to make politics entertaining.

Carroll Newton has forcefully advocated the first of these strategies and cogently stated its rationale and consequences:

> People are not as interested in politics and in candidates as they are in entertainment. Therefore, the audiences you enjoy will be largely determined by three factors: Firstly, the size of the audience looking at the program immediately ahead of you; Secondly, the audience which normally every week, tunes in for entertainment to the time

period and the station you're buying for your political purpose; and Thirdly, of course, the attraction value of the programs on other stations at the same time ... it is further significant that the ability of a political program to hold its audience varies in inverse proportion to its length. ... I think you can conclude ... that the people who are really interested will follow campaigns from every source there is. You don't have to worry about reaching them, but the people who aren't interested—you have got to slip up on them through the broadcasting media. You have to catch them when they are looking or listening to something else, if you want to reach them at all.

Several prescriptions for action logically follow from these premises: (1) "Buy television at times when the largest number of people habitually use their receivers"; (2) "smaller units of time will reach more voters for your dollar," and, therefore, a large proportion of the television budget should be earmarked for spot announcements and 5-minute trailers, which are effective because voters "have to listen before they can get up and switch them off"; and (3) "Devote all the time you buy to issues of real significance (as determined by surveys) and present your point of view so simply that even the viewers who don't give a damn will understand what you're talking about."[16]

Newton's views are peculiar neither to himself nor to Republicans. The Democrats have been making essentially the same recommendations to their candidates as those just quoted. They, too, have noted that the candidate's principal competition on television is the entertainment program. They have advised against half-hour shows. They value the spot announcement that presents a simple and memorable slogan.[17] They have advised against giving advance notice of trailers on the grounds that such notice is more likely to repel than to attract voters.

The attempt to attract audiences by making politics entertaining has been pursued with considerably less determination than has been brought to the search for captive audiences. This is undoubtedly true in part because many politicians have been unable to see clearly how they might exploit the entertainment values inherent in political discourse. Many have been aware that a speech growing out of a dramatic situation—Nixon's 1952 speech defending his use of a specially subscribed fund is the best and almost the only example—could compete effectively for audiences with commercial shows. It is not apparent, however, how such situations might be contrived as a part of a conscious strategy.

But there is another reason for the politician's hesitation to adopt this strategy. Conflict is the most obvious entertainment appeal of political campaigns. The panel discussions, the interviews, and the "press conferences" have been very tentative and very timid steps toward tapping this appeal. Genuine conflict cannot be injected into political programs, however, without incurring one very heavy cost—that of exposing one's audience to an opposing point of view, forcefully presented. When this is not done but only simulated, the program is very likely to elicit a feeling similar to that expressed about a show in which Conservative Ministers were questioned by British editors—"it resembled a board meeting with the directors being questioned by a group of keen but generally sympathetic shareholders."[18]

The import of all this for campaign television can be summarized as follows: both the networks and campaigners will devote the lion's share of the time they control to presenting the candidates, and for basically the same reasons. The candidates are the headliners of the electoral drama. The networks will devote another large block of time to shows that explore the question, "Who is winning?" Television news departments have discovered, as newspapers did before them, that a sizable section of the mass media audience is interested in the game aspects of elections. The networks will rely primarily on the newscast, the interview, the documentary, and the panel program as formats within which to present campaign discussion. Paid political programs on the average, will be much shorter than those presented in network-controlled time. They will use a variety of formats, but the spot announcement, the trailer, the short speech, and the friendly interview are almost certain to be among those used most heavily.

NOTES

1. Federal Communications Commission, *Report to the Congress of the United States, March 1, 1961, Submitted Pursuant to Senate Joint Resolution 207, 86th Congress* in *Hearings on Review of Section 315 of the Communications Act,* Senate Committee on Interstate and Foreign Commerce, 87th Cong., 1st sess., p. 115.

2. 73 Stat. 557, 1959. Perhaps this statement should be qualified. It is certainly true as far as the formats of programs were concerned, al-

though a strict interpretation of "bona fide" by the Federal Communications Commission might affect the scheduling and reduce the number of such programs in the future.

3. Editorial, *The Democrat,* June 2, 1952.

4. See Charles A. H. Thomson, *Television and Presidential Politics,* (Washington: The Brookings Institution, 1956), p. 59.

5. These figures and those regarding program length to follow are necessarily approximate. No completely satisfactory record of paid party broadcasts in presidential campaigns exists. The figures used here were derived from an examination of newspaper announcements, data supplied by the Republican National Committee, and data presented in the report of the Federal Communications Commission cited in footnote 1 above.

6. These figures are averages for all paid programs 5 or more minutes in length presented on the national networks.

7. D. E. Butler, *Elections Abroad* (London: Macmillan, 1959), p. 27.

8. Stanley Kelley, Jr., *Professional Public Relations and Political Power* (Baltimore: Johns Hopkins Press, 1956), p. 197.

9. See *Ibid.,* p. 170.

10. Morris Janowitz and Dwaine Marvick, *Competitive Pressure and Democratic Consent* (Ann Arbor: University of Michigan Press, 1956), p. 64.

11. Paul F. Lazarsfeld, Bernard Berelson, and Hazel Gaudet, *The People's Choice* (New York: Columbia University Press, 1944), p. 124.

12. R. S. Milne and H. C. Mackenzie, *Marginal Seat, 1955* (London: Hansard Society, 1958).

13. Paul Seabury, "Television—A New Campaign Weapon," *The New Republic,* Dec. 1, 1952, p. 13.

14. In an address to Republican State Chairmen, June 1958.

15. *Ibid.*

16. All statements directly quoted in the foregoing paragraph are from Carroll Newton, *Ibid.*

17. See particularly *A Campaign Guide to Political Publicity,* Washington, Democratic National Committee, 1956.

18. William Salter, "The TV Election—Round Two," *New Statesman and Nation* May 21, 1955, p. 708.

—12—

POLITICAL ADVERTISING: MAKING IT LOOK LIKE NEWS

Congressional Quarterly

"The preceding was a paid political announcement." That surprised no one who watched a hard-sell campaign commercial during the 1950s and 60s. But it might in 1972, as low-key news-style political ads focus on President Nixon's travels to China and record George McGovern's chats with voters about taxes and defense spending.

Departing from political advertising's traditional look—a reflection of ads for pain killers, soap products and cosmetics—candidates this year are promoting themselves in commercials that resemble network documentaries and news programs. And for good reason. Media consultants have learned that voters are influenced to a far greater extent by TV news than by political advertising.

Besides the presidential contenders, candidates in state elections have jumped on the news-style bandwagon, according to a Congressional Quarterly survey of selected Senate and gubernatorial races.

The news technique, whether it takes the form of a mini-documentary, panel discussion or "man on the street" interview, is particularly suited for portraying a candidate's values and leadership ability, says Charles Guggenheim, the documentary film maker who is producing McGovern's commercials. Although his agency's ads feature the senator talking about issues such as Viet-

From "Political Advertising: Making it Look Like News," *Congressional Quarterly* 30 (November 4, 1972):2900–03. Copyright © 1972 by Congressional Quarterly, Inc. Reprinted by permission.

nam and tax reform, the real aim, Guggenheim has said, is to reveal the kind of man the candidate is.

For example, in a typical five-minute spot, McGovern tells a group of men filmed in a restaurant: ". . . I really think that the people in this room are probably paying a heavier tax burden because we have too many loopholes in the law at the top. . . ." One of the men: "Senator, is that what's called 'fuzzy on economics'?" McGovern: "It may be. But it's what I believe."

In similar fashion, the November Group—President Nixon's in-house advertising agency created especially for the 1972 election—aims to project the President's leadership in foreign affairs by reminding viewers of a recent diplomatic breakthrough: "China is the largest country in the world, yet no American President had ever been there," a narrator states in one five-minute ad. "China is one of the most populous countries in the world, yet no American leader had ever talked with them . . . until Richard Nixon."

The Nixon campaign, however, recently reverted to some old-style advertising when it telecast a spot symbolizing McGovern's proposed cuts in defense spending by a hand sweeping away toy soldiers, miniature ships and planes.

Although the McGovern campaign claimed that it would not use similar "produced" spots with cartoons or symbols, the Democratic nominee launched some strong media volleys at the President over the Oct. 21-22 weekend. One spot listed Nixon's "policy failures"; another flipped through scandal headlines.

Another difference between campaign advertising this year and previous elections involves the blitz—a tactic by which little-known but wealthy candidates flooded the airwaves with commercials and won elections.

The CQ survey of media advertising in state elections indicates that candidates are adhering to the Federal Election Campaign Act of 1971, aimed at ending the television blitz. (Candidates for Congress and the presidency are now allowed to spend no more than 10 cents per eligible voter in their constituency for advertising on television, radio, newspapers, magazines and billboards.)

"McGOVERN IN '72"

By piggybacking appeals for campaign funds onto weekly, issue-oriented telecasts, the McGovern organization filled out its campaign chest in addition to drawing impressive network ratings.

On Oct. 10, McGovern outlined his plan for ending the Vietnam war over 1,996 television stations; following the speech came a plea for campaign donations. According to CBS, the McGovern appearance received the highest rating of any political program in recent history, receiving 25 rating points in Los Angeles and 16 in New York. (Political candidates generally score a 7- to 8-point rating.)

Results of the plea for campaign funds proved equally impressive. "On Thursday (Oct. 12) and Friday alone, we received more than 15,000 individual contributions," McGovern told an audience in San Diego. As a result of the one telecast, which cost about $160,000 to produce, McGovern aides estimated that about 40,000 donations would be received for a total of about $800,000. The funds enabled McGovern to buy additional blocs of media time before Nov. 7. (An estimated $8.55 million, the federal limit, will be spent on advertising by McGovern.)

The Vietnam telecast was the second in a series of half-hour programs designed to reach large numbers of voters with the hope of overcoming Nixon's lead in the polls.

The first, a biography of the senator, was produced by Guggenheim. On Oct. 20, McGovern outlined his economic proposals to a national audience, and additional programs, including one on "morality in government" were telecast and concluded with appeals for contributions.

Spot Ads

Besides the half-hour speeches, the McGovern campaign is airing radio and television spot commercials. Most feature the senator talking to small informal groups, patiently explaining his stands on various issues. They were also produced by Guggenheim, a pioneer of the documentary approach in campaign advertising, who followed McGovern on the campaign trail with a small camera crew that shot reels of footage of the candidate engaged in conversation with voters.

An example of the Guggenheim low-key approach is a five-minute spot ("Small Businessmen") in which McGovern speaks to a group of men who provide a forum for the candidate's views: "Well, I certainly think we ought to repeal all those accelerated depreciation increases that were added last year. You really can't justify that. . . . Also, on the oil-depletion and mineral-depletion allowances, I think we've carried that too far. . . ."

Anti-Nixon

The McGovern commercials have gotten tougher in the final weeks of the campaign, often attacking President Nixon by name. Liz Stevens, media coordinator for the McGovern campaign, told *Broadcasting Magazine:* "The early stage of our campaign had to be acquainting the viewers with the candidate. We will get into some issues."

In a recent radio spot, which contrasts sharply with softer McGovern commercials, a narrator intones: "During the Nixon administration, $64-billion has been spent on the war in Vietnam. ... In 1968, President Nixon said, 'If after all of this time and all of this sacrifice ... there is no end in sight, then I say the time has come for the American people to turn to new leadership. ...' "

In a new five-minute television commercial, McGovern tells workers in a Milwaukee plant: "Richard Nixon goes around talking as though I'm some kind of radical because I believe in guaranteed jobs for people he's thrown out of work. He said he's going to cut welfare rolls, but he put four million people on welfare."

Some media observers felt that even the newer ads that were intended to challenge the President were still too vague with lines such as: "We've got to have a program that's better than the one we have now to deal with drugs if we're going to get on top of the crime problem." Ironically, a similar observation was made about Sen. Edmund S. Muskie's (D Maine) ads after the New Hampshire and Florida primaries. Before the Wisconsin primary, Muskie's commercials were sharpened up, but the *Wall Street Journal* later noted: "... The new ads were probably counterproductive. Wisconsin residents had heard and read about the new strategy and thus received it cynically."

"RE-ELECT THE PRESIDENT"

"While Senator McGovern's broadcast campaign is designed to build steady TV awareness over an extended period of time, President Nixon's organization appears to be using TV in a hypodermic fashion, helping to inject the audience with swift doses of advertising as the pitch of the presidential campaign rises." (*Broadcasting Magazine*)

Although the Nixon campaign held back heavy doses of advertising in September in favor of a "get out the vote drive," by mid-October the President's November Group commercials were frequently broadcast—and widely discussed.

The Republican ads come in two strains: those sponsored by the Committee for the Re-Election of the President that follow a "positive" approach, stressing the President's leadership and experience; and others, presented by Democrats for Nixon, which attack McGovern's proposals. Both varieties are produced by the November Group and, according to finance records, mainly paid for by the re-election committee.

"Russia," "China" and "Older Americans" are three documentary-style commercials designed to plug the President's accomplishments at home and abroad. In "Russia," a narrator sums up: "President Nixon offers a lasting message to the people of Russia. A pledge to continue the quest for peace among all nations." Then follows an appeal to U.S. voters: "This is why we need President Nixon now . . . more than ever."

The commercials give the "feeling of a man in obvious control of the situation who can handle the affairs of this country with great dignity," Peter Dailey, head of the November Group, has said.

Democrats for Nixon

In contrast to those commercials identified as the President's, advertisements presented by Democrats for Nixon take a "negative" approach. Reminiscent of the 1964 commercials which implied that Republican nominee Sen. Barry Goldwater would end Social Security and precipitate a nuclear holocaust if elected, the ads attack McGovern's welfare and defense proposals as well as his credibility by using symbolic devices and McGovern's own words against himself.

One ad, first telecast Oct. 3, depicts a formation of toy soldiers, ships and planes. A voice announces: "The McGovern defense plan: He would cut the Marines by one-half. He would cut Air Force personnel by one-third and intercepter planes by one-fourth. . . ." With each statement, a hand sweeps away portions of the toy models. The announcer concludes: "President Nixon doesn't believe we should play games with our national security. . . ."

A second spot focuses on the issue of McGovern's credibility. An image of the candidate rotates 180 degrees while a narrator quotes McGovern's "contradictory" statements on various issues.

The substantial difference between the positive and negative ads, according to Dailey, is that John Connally determines the basic thrust of the Democrats for Nixon ads. Dailey told *The Washington Post:* "Their films tend to be 'more comparative to traditional Democratic values,' as Governor Connally puts it, while ours depend on the President."

RACES FOR SENATE AND GOVERNOR

Following are descriptions of media techniques employed by candidates for the Senate and governor in contests selected and researched by CQ:

Rhode Island

Republican John Chafee's bid for the Senate seat held by Claiborne Pell has spurred an intensive campaign with both candidates spending near the limit for media advertising allowed by the Federal Election Campaign Act of 1971.

Pell. According to Tom Hughes, Pell's media director, "we're spending our limit" for television and radio advertising with about 60 cents of every media dollar going for TV commercials. Both staged and news-type ads are being aired, including two five-minute documentary films produced by Charles Guggenheim, a variety of television spots, and 30- to 60-second radio ads produced by Tony Schwartz of New Sounds Inc., New York.

The spots concentrate on issues, Pell's record and what he has accomplished for the state, Hughes said. In one, Pell teams up with the state's other Democratic senator, John O. Pastore, in a discussion of inflation.

Pell, a former foreign service officer, who speaks French, Italian and Portuguese is using 60-second foreign language spots to appeal to the state's blocs of ethnic voters. One television commercial shows Pell talking to a group of Italian-Americans, with one section recorded in Italian; a radio spot features Pell and his wife speaking in French and will be broadcast in the northern part of the state where there's a large French-Canadian community.

Although television and radio advertising is being increased, "no blitz is planned for the last weeks" of the campaign, Hughes told CQ. Instead, the campaign will concentrate on increasing rating points by placing more ads in prime time.

By Oct. 18, when the CQ survey was completed, the Pell campaign had run no newspaper ads. Several one-page ads were planned, however, and an 8-page political supplement was scheduled to be run in the state's largest Sunday paper, *The Providence Journal*.

Chafee. Direct mail is "about near the top" in the list of former Secretary of Navy John Chafee's campaign expenditures. "It's a great way to reach all the people and, of course, it's not counted in the campaign spending limit," said Chafee's press secretary, Dave Sweet. Campaign flyers are being mailed to all families in the state.

Spending near the limit allowed for media advertising, the Chafee campaign is placing most of its ads on television, although a "mild radio blitz" is running in the final three weeks. Emphasis is being placed on television, Sweet said, because "we have an extremely visual, attractive and active candidate."

Chafee narrates one five-minute, news-type commercial that focuses on his family background, record as secretary of the navy and governor; a half dozen 60-second spots that Chafee also narrates follow an abbreviated scenario of the longer ad.

The campaign has run an 8-page Sunday supplement and plans to place one-page and smaller ads in newspapers during the last campaign week.

Illinois

The television screen has become a major battleground for the governorship of Illinois. Both incumbent Richard B. Ogilvie and Democratic challenger Daniel Walker are relying almost entirely on the medium for their non-personal campaigning.

Ogilvie. Chuch Loebbak, the governor's press secretary, reported that a series of half-hour programs shown throughout the state in prime time during June and July featured a panel of community leaders questioning the governor on specific issues.

Since August, spot advertisements—30 to 60 seconds—have been telecast. A narrator reviews Ogilvie's record on a specific issue while film, representing the subject, is shown. Additional issue commercials with the governor on-camera began in October.

Although newspaper ads are given a low priority in the Ogilvie campaign, a series of 10-second TV spots—black and white stills of the governor greeting constituents—end with a voice quoting newspaper editorials and endorsements: *"The Chicago Tribune said. . . ."*

"Direct mail" is limited to storefront distribution of campaign materials.

Walker. No radio, direct mail, billboards or newspaper advertising will be used in the campaign, according to Norton Kay, Walker's press secretary. And because of financial problems, television advertising has been limited to six spot commercials. Three are shown a day. Reporting that between $250,000 and $300,000 had been spent on television advertising, which began in mid-October, Kay said, "Hopefully, the frequency of ads will be increased if we get the money."

Walker's campaign theme—"Taking the candidate to the people," "Getting politics out of government" and "Bringing government to the people"—is woven into three of the television ads that show the candidate traveling the state by jeep during the primary. The three other spots feature Walker discussing campaign issues.

New Hampshire

Radio, rather than television, is the major campaign advertising medium in the New Hampshire gubernatorial contest. Roger Crowley, the Democratic candidate, had spent nothing on television through October because the state has only two commercial television stations and because he considers the cost of advertising through a Boston station prohibitive. However, Meldrim Thomson Jr., the Republican candidate, has split radio-TV advertising "about down the middle."

Crowley. Three-fifths of all Crowley's media advertising budget is directed to radio time. Some ads on stations in high unemployment areas concentrate on the job issue, while messages in affluent regions focus on consumer and environmental problems, said Joe Zellner, Crowley's public relations director. In addition, "drive time," has been purchased to advertise on radio when people are driving to and from work.

Newspaper advertising has focused on the 20 weeklies in the state, but Crowley will concentrate on the nine dailies in the last week of the campaign.

Zellner said the campaign was planning an environmental radio message to point out the number of billboards (300) Thomson had erected in the state.

Thomson. During the primary, a half-hour "get to know the candidate" documentary was aired on television. By mid-October, however, Thomson had not resumed TV-radio advertising, although issue-oriented radio spots were scheduled for late in the campaign.

The owner of a publishing company, Thomson prepared an 8-page campaign tabloid that had been hand-distributed, inserted in newspapers or mailed directly to voters.

West Virginia

A heavy barrage of television, radio, newspaper and billboard advertising marks the media campaign of Arch A. Moore, West Virginia's Republican governor. Jay Rockefeller, the Democratic challenger, is relying primarily on television.

Moore. Using the theme "Re-elect a good governor" and the Robert Goodman agency in Baltimore, Md., to handle media details, Moore is advertising his record on the following: a half-hour documentary television show, 30- to 60-second TV spots, 5-minute TV programs; a series of 14, 60-second radio spots; 4-page color newspaper inserts in all the state's weeklies, and 200 billboards.

The half-hour documentary, to run three times between the first of October and election day in prime time, concentrates on Moore's staff (state commissioners) who explain what the administration has accomplished for the state. The 5-minute programs ("The governor reports") feature Moore discussing four subjects—jobs, education, social services and road building, the latter an important program in the state.

The 30- and 60-second TV spots are narrated and backed by catchy music and lyrics: "Hear what they're saying about West Virginia."

Rockefeller. About 80 percent of broadcast spending is directed to television in the Rockefeller campaign. On Oct. 1, 30- to 60-second spots began with the candidate discussing West Virginia issues. "There's not too much family in these," said Don Smith, a Rockefeller aide. Radio ads, such as one on coal mining problems, have been targeted to specific regions. Some direct mail has been used to reach specific interest groups, including one mailing to retired teachers. Billboards ("very few") have been used in conjunction with other Democratic candidates.

North Carolina

Both Rep. Nick Galifianakis (D) and Jesse Helms (R), a television editorialist, are allotting the major share of their media budgets for television advertising in their Senate race.

Galifianakis. Besides using two campaign buttons to spell his name, (Galifi) (anakis) is spending about $60,000 for all media advertising, which is "not near the limit," according to Margaret Sugg, his administrative assistant. Since the first of October, several 30-second spots have been telecast showing the candidate in "man on the street" interviews; in other spots, the candidate faces the camera and tells viewers that North Carolina needs someone with experience who can stand on his own record. The latter ads, according to Sugg, are to counteract Helms, who ran a heavy newspaper campaign with full-page ads attacking Galifianakis' record but then "offered nothing positive." On radio, the candidate has used six different 30-second spots; some direct mail has been sent to special interest groups, and no billboards have been used in the general campaign.

Helms. According to campaign director Tom Ellis, media advertising consists of: "A few" prime time television spots a week that feature Helms discussing campaign issues; radio spots which are similar to the TV commercials, and a limited amount of direct mail aimed at specialized groups. The candidate is not spending "anywhere near the media limit," Ellis said, adding the advertising theme is "to show the candidate to the people" and where he stands on the issues.

Oregon

Republican Sen. Mark O. Hatfield is using television spots that feature talks with constituents. His opponent, Wayne Morse, a former member of the Senate, has aired some TV spots but is relying mainly on radio which he has "found very effective" for speaking out on an issue, according to a campaign manager.

Morse had also sent out mail to special groups, such as the League of Environmental Voters, advertised exclusively in local papers (he had a dispute with the two major Oregon papers over a labor issue) and ruled out billboard advertising because it is an environmental issue in the state.

—13—

RADIO USE IN THE TELEVISION ERA

Jules Witcover

President Nixon, perhaps the most innovative user of the mass media in American political history, has found a novel way in the television era to get his message to the public.

It is called radio.

In the mass-audience epoch of TV, in which pre-emption of popular prime-time shows has become among the deadliest of politicians' sins, Mr. Nixon has turned increasingly to the old and neglected mainstay of Fred Allen, Jack Benny and Lamont Cranston. (If you don't know, ask your father.)

In both his presidential campaigns of 1968 and 1972, and occasionally in his first White House term, Mr. Nixon used radio for some of his more thoughtful and philosophical conversations with the voters. But TV remained the prime medium.

Now, however, the word from White House speechwriters is that the President plans to make radio talks an integral part of his communications arsenal. In a series of supplemental State of the Union messages he is to send to Congress in the weeks ahead, the plan is for him to explain them to the public on radio.

Why radio?

The question is one that opposition politicians, and newsmen covering the Nixon White House, have been asking each other for a long time. If the President can get free prime TV time just about anytime he asks for it, why bother with radio?

According to White House speechwriters who have discussed the matter with the President, have written radio speeches for him and have encouraged him to do more of them, the reasons are these:

- Mr. Nixon likes to make radio talks better than he likes going on television. They require less preparation on his part, less time, less electronic paraphernalia, no makeup.
- They are easier for him. One advance read-through sometimes is enough; he doesn't have to worry about facial expressions or gestures with his hands, or the heaviness of his celebrated beard, or his tendency to perspire, especially under heavy lights. And he can wear his reading glasses, which he never does on TV. He can concentrate on the text and not have to look up repeatedly.
- He does better on radio, or so he and those around him believe. He has a good radio voice and he can adopt a low-key style. Those around him recall surveys taken after Mr. Nixon's 1960 TV-radio debates with then Sen. John F. Kennedy that those who heard but didn't see him thought he had won.
- The audience is more selective, and hence likely to be more attentive. To those who argue that TV audiences are larger, the President reminds them that radio listeners "are the people who tuned in," rather than nightly TV watchers who suddenly were confronted by a speech pre-empting their favorite program.
- Radio for that very reason is less an intrusion on the desires and habits of the public, and less likely to be an irritant that could create a negative reaction to what the President has to say. "It takes something urgent to knock off 'I Love Lucy,' " says Raymond Price, until recently the chief Nixon speechwriter.
- By its nature, radio demands less of the audience and hence reaches an audience that TV often misses—the commuter driving to or from work, or the housewife busy preparing lunch for her children. Nixon radio speeches occasionally have been aired at noon on weekdays.
- Radio is more conducive to the thoughtful discussion of issues. "It doesn't grab you by the lapels and say, 'This is a national emergency,' the way TV does," says William Safire, another of the Nixon speechwriters, "and that's a good thing for the President to have. He can say to the people, 'If you are interested, tune in and we'll talk'."
- There is less risk of over-exposure on radio. "You don't want to wear out your welcome," says Price, "and with TV you can get the public 'up' too often. Television is such a dominating medium in people's lives."
- The audience is not insignificant—in fact, much larger than even the Nixon people believe, if network research is accurate. Nixon speechwriters say "up to ten million" listen to radio; the radio networks' RADAR (Radios All Dimension Audience Research) survey for the spring, 1972, said 85.4 per cent of all Americans age 18 and over listen an average of four hours,

10 minutes each weekday. An average of 30,643,000 listen around noon-time, 15,587,000 on a Sunday night about 6 o'clock.

- Radio for a politician really is not so much an alternative to television as it is an alternative to giving a rally or dinner speech, where the audience is several thousand at most. And on radio he doesn't have to worry about applause lines, nor does a President have to risk crowds or go great distances. "Don't sneeze at several million people," the President has told his speechwriters. "Have you ever seen that many in an audience?"

- Radio is a proven way to get featured play from the writing press—really a prime objective, the speechwriters say. A presidential position paper handed to the press gets short shrift, says Safire, "but by the action of a President passing a paper through his lips, it gives it a wholly different character."

- Radio is vastly cheaper than TV. According to Norman Ginzberg of CBS Radio in New York, the President's Jan. 28 budget speech on radio would have cost him as a candidate $3900 for 10 minutes. Half an hour on a TV network, Safire says, would cost about $90,000.

Ever since the days of Franklin D. Roosevelt's "fireside chats" on radio, Mr. Nixon has been partial to that medium, his speechwriters say. In the Diplomatic Reception Room of the White House, the President has pointed to the fireside at which FDR spoke and told some of them: "We'll have to do one here some day."

In the 1968 campaign, Mr. Nixon turned to radio heavily in the closing two weeks, delivering radio talks on 14 straight nights. The main reason, the speechwriters who were with him then admit, was the press' complaint that he was not dealing with issues in any depth, but was simply trying to hold onto his narrowing lead over then Vice President Hubert H. Humphrey.

Though the radio talks were Mr. Nixon's most thoughtful efforts of the campaign, they drew little attention at the time, primarily because Mr. Nixon was campaigning actively at the same time. The writing press focused on him personally, and on the drama of Humphrey closing the gap, and they dismissed the taped radio talks with a few paragraphs.

What particularly irritated Nixonites later on, Price says, was the charge by some that Mr. Nixon intentionally sought to slip serious discussion of the issues past the public, and hence turned to radio. If that had been the objective, he says, Mr. Nixon would not have given the talks at all.

Earlier in the 1968 campaign, when candidate Nixon planned to make what was expected at the time to be his most important public statement of that campaign—his speech on what to do in Vietnam in late March—he bought radio time, not TV.

But fate intervened; President Lyndon B. Johnson chose the same night to go on TV to talk about Vietnam—and to withdraw from the 1968 race—and Mr. Nixon canceled his radio talk. After that, he decided he didn't have to spell out his Vietnam position.

Throughout the first term, new Nixon speechwriters were always hearing about the "radio series" the President was going to do—easy conversations with the American people. But he never did it. Issues warranting the use of TV kept cropping up.

In the 1972 campaign, though, with the President choosing to stay off the campaign trail until the very last days, the press was looking for anything from the Nixon camp to provide balance to the frenetic McGovern campaign.

To the experienced Nixon campaign team and the speechwriters, radio was the answer. When he spoke on radio, and did not compete with himself on the hustings, the press treated the radio talks as major news—which they were, coming from an otherwise insulated President.

As always with the Nixon media operation, refinements have been added. Now when the President goes on radio, the network TV cameras are permitted to tape Mr. Nixon reading a selected portion of his talk—at most a minute or 90 seconds—for use on TV news shows later.

Significantly, they don't get to cover the whole speech—just the portion the White House thinks is most advantageous to the President. The White House retains what one speechwriter calls "the element of control"—the ingredient more than any other that has come to be the trademark of Mr. Nixon's media relations.

-14-

CAMPAIGN CONSULTANTS: PUSHING SINCERITY IN 1974

Congressional Quarterly

If the nation's top political consultants are right, voters will be given a massive dose of sincerity in this year's congressional campaigns—and not too much discussion of specific issues.

The consultants' view is more than idle speculation, because their ideas about what the campaign will be like translate eventually into recommendations about what their client candidates should be doing. The consensus within the profession seems to be that voters will be judging candidates as people in 1974, rather than as legislators.

"In some ways, this won't be an issues year," said Johnny W. Allem, a Washington-based consultant who works with Democrats. "People will want to know what the candidate believes in before they want to know what he's going to do about Interstate 75 . . . I'm recommending to candidates that they first demonstrate to voters that they're honest people, make some value statements and hammer out the issues in print."

John Deardourff, a Washington consultant who works mostly with moderate Republicans, is thinking along the same lines. He is working with William G. Milliken, the Republican governor of Michigan, who is seeking a second full term.

When Milliken ran in 1970, his campaign stressed the specific issues and accomplishments of the two years Milliken then had spent in office. This year, Deardourff is advising Milliken to talk about his personal background—his legislative experience, his education, even his war record. Deardourff wants the human side of his candidate to come through first.

"I'm not sure it's at all unhealthy," said Deardourff. "During one term, a governor or senator will have to confront issues that nobody can predict at the moment. There ought to be more attention paid to the guy's background, rather than to how he will vote on abortion."

I. Robert Goodman, a Baltimore consultant who also works with Republicans, believes the de-emphasis on issues simply reflects the profession's growing awareness of the things that have been influencing voters for a long time. "I think people have always voted for people," Goodman said. "According to surveys, they have always voted on honesty, competence and charisma, in that order. Many times issues are only used as a foil to express personal virtue. Our candidates have been expressing personal qualities since we've been in business."

Biden's Influence

One campaign that has been a major influence on consultants was the 1972 Senate race in Delaware. Democrat Joe Biden, a 29-year-old county councilman who was almost unknown in the state when the campaign began, won a stunning victory over two-term incumbent Republican J. Caleb Boggs. Biden came out of that campaign saying that people voted for him because they trusted him, not because they agreed with him on specific issues.

"I don't think issues mean a great deal about whether you win or lose," Biden said in a 1974 speech. "I think issues give you a chance to articulate your intellectual capacity. Issues are a vehicle by which voters determine your honesty and candor. I don't think a right or wrong answer on an issue makes up anyone's mind but the ideologues', and I distrust ideologues."

The consultant who worked with Biden in 1972 was John Marttila of Boston. The Biden victory and an upset earlier this year by Democrat Richard F. Vander Veen in a Michigan House race have given Marttila a reputation as the country's latest political magician.

It is not clear how much of a role Marttila actually played in developing the "sincerity first" strategy for Biden in 1972. "Nobody ran my campaign but me," Biden insisted, "and ask John Marttila, who came in to run my campaign. . . . I said, 'John, let me pay you $30,000, and don't interfere. The money will come back fourfold.' " Biden explained that he found it hard to raise funds unless he could invoke the name of a nationally known consultant.

Whatever the origins of "sincerity first" in 1972, it is clear that Marttila and other consultants are convinced of its value for 1974.

"It showed everybody," said Allem, "that if you get off your ass and recognize a voting audience that is frustrated because it doesn't have any access to the incumbent, you can overcome some very big odds."

Former Rep. Nick Galifianakis (D 1967-73), running for the Senate in North Carolina, is sticking closely to the theme that issues are not what really counts. "I think what you really have to demonstrate this time is that you care," Galifianakis said in a speech. "I don't think it's vital that you know all the answers to all the issues. I think it is vital in order to restore confidence that you show you can handle the job and that you do care."

Some Skepticism

Some political consultants are skeptical of a campaign year in which issues are secondary. "I can't separate issues from personality," said Charles Guggenheim, a Washington film-maker for Democratic candidates. "Candidates are in the business of issues. It's like trying to judge a lawyer who won't address himself to the law."

Sanford Weiner, a California consultant who works for moderates and liberals of both parties, is even more blunt. "Everyone is trying to put out the facade of honesty, purity and holiness," he said. "The public is not going to buy that any more than they buy the other crap they put out. What they're looking for is a candidate who's credible on any issue he talks about. They know the great white knight isn't going to ride down the trail."

CONTACT, PERSONAL AND SIMULATED

If honesty is the desired effect of 1974, personal contact is the method. The surprises of 1972 involved a lot of give-and-take between candidates and voters. Biden traveled through Delaware almost non-stop in his contest against Boggs, who was well-liked in general but rarely showed up in person. Sen. Dick Clark (D Iowa), another upset winner in 1972, walked the length of his state. Gov. Daniel Walker (D Ill.) used the same tactic, with the same result.

"People want to see more of their candidates," said Joseph Napolitan, who has been advising Democratic candidates longer than most of his colleagues have been in business. "They want to see who the hell they're voting for."

But it is easier to preach personal contact than to establish it. Biden blanketed Delaware in person, but Delaware is barely larger than most House districts. Candidates running for governor or senator in most states in 1974 are confronted by the impossibility of meeting every voter they seek to convert.

Long-distance walks have worked because they have drawn television coverage, not because the candidates have met every voter in person. And most consultants agree that the tactic is too familiar now to generate the kind of news interest Sen. Lawton Chiles (D Fla.) received in 1970 when he popularized the tactic.

Some consultants are skeptical of the trend toward personal contact. "I think it's a little idealistic," said John Deardourff. "The hard reality of most elections," said Deardourff, "is that the constituency is too large for it. Almost every other form of campaign activity is a substitute for personal contact."

But if it is impossible for most candidates for statewide office to achieve full personal contact, it is still possible for them to simulate it. And that is what many of them are doing in 1974.

Phone Calls and Letters

In Georgia, Democrat Bert Lance is seeking the governorship with the argument that he is less interested in telling people his views than in hearing theirs. "Anybody anywhere in Georgia," a Lance brochure says, "can pick up the telephone anywhere and dial toll-free with a message for Bert 24 hours a day, seven days a week. You will get a personal response from Bert himself, not just some campaign aide. . . . At the same time, Bert is receiving thousands of letters at P.O. Box 1974. Every one of them is read by Bert himself, who takes time out from his busy travel schedule just for that purpose."

Volunteers working for Lance receive a sample letter to send to their friends. "Have you told Bert Lance yet what you would do if you were governor of Georgia?" the letter asks. "I'm also sending you a 'Tell Bert' card which you can fill out to give Bert suggestions for making our state government more responsive."

This fits the theory sketched out by the consultant who has been working with Lance, who asked not to be identified. "I want a candidate who has spent three months out hustling among the voters," the consultant said, "one who is soaked in their value system, who communicates well one-on-one in the field. That's the kind of candidate who will do a direct message the best."

Galifianakis has used a similar approach to that of Lance in his North Carolina campaign. "It's really helpful when you open up and express your feelings," he has told voters. "Because I am a fellow who may end up representing you in the United States Senate, it's important to me what you think and how you arrived at your feelings. Because I share the feeling that right now there is a despair. People feel despair, don't quite know what to do."

Volunteer Surrogates

The simplest substitute for personal contact with candidates is personal contact with their volunteer workers. The "sincerity first" doctrine already has affected the technique of political canvassing. One consultant used to have volunteers go door-to-door with typewritten notes in behalf of their candidate. This year, he is asking volunteers to write those notes in longhand, to make them seem more genuine.

But volunteers are only a limited answer, too, because most consultants believe that in a year of post-Watergate disgust, they will be harder to find than ever. Matt Reese, the veteran Democratic consultant, has kept statistics on the rate of political volunteering since he went into business more than a decade ago. He noted a significant drop-off in the volunteer rate in 1972, and he is prepared for an even leaner 1974.

Computerized Campaigning

Much was said in 1972 about the potential of computerized telephone banks for personalizing a campaign. Each voter can receive an individual call, with the candidate explaining in a recorded message why he deserves to win. This is an extension of personalized direct mail, which, thanks to improved computer technology, can send any voters in any particular bloc a special letter the candidate thinks will appeal to them.

"Finally," one consulting firm said in 1972, "we have a campaign device which gives the candidate almost unlimited opportunity to direct the message to precisely that segment of the electorate he believes is important to his success."

All that led some writers to predict in 1972 that the era of the computerized campaign was at hand. "What the Republican mind-benders are thinking about," wrote Richard Reeves in *Harpers* magazine, "is individualized communication—computerized mail and telephones on a scale new to politics. . . ."

If computerized politics was fashionable in 1972, it is un-fashionable in 1974. "When these things were at their high point," said Weiner, "voters would get computerized letters and feel that it was a personal communication. Now it's been used so much that it isn't much different from bulk mail to many people. So we've stopped using it very much."

"Computerized phone calls are almost worthless in most cam-paigns," Napolitan agreed. He said he sees some value in phone messages from prominent third parties, such as calls from Sen. Barry Goldwater (R Ariz.) asking conservatives to support a local candidate. Other than that, he sees the method as not only fraudu-lent but expensive, at 10 cents a call.

This does not mean computers are losing their role in cam-paigns. Most consultants predicted computers would be used more than ever in 1974 to identify voting blocs within a constituency and target the ones needing special attention. But it was generally conceded that computers are not the way to simulate personal contact.

"The telephone was made to listen with and talk into," said Reese. "The gimmicks that don't recognize that fall into dis-repute."

TELEVISION: LESS COMMERCIALISM

The problems inherent in conducting a personal campaign by can-vassing or computer just about guarantee that television will be the main vehicle for whatever techniques of persuasion are dominant in 1974. And changes are already beginning to turn up.

Nothing illustrates that better than the thinking of Napolitan, who has always gone in heavily for television and is sometimes credited with inventing the pre-election media blitz.

In 1968, Napolitan helped win the Democratic Senate primary in Alaska for Mike Gravel by blanketing the state with a 30-minute film on Gravel the week before the election. Gravel leaped from obscurity to defeat Sen. Ernest Gruening (D 1959-69) and won the election in November.

Two years later, Napolitan was working for Maryland Gov. Marvin Mandel (D). Rumors persisted that R. Sargent Shriver, the former Peace Corps director, planned to return to Maryland and challenge Mandel in a Democratic primary. Napolitan used a barrage of early television commercials to create the impression that Mandel was invincible. Shriver stayed out.

Napolitan will be using television again in 1974 for Mandel and Gravel, among others, but he insists there will be few blitzes and little commercialism. "I think you will see a lot more of candidates speaking directly to the people on television," Napolitan said. He was working with Jerome Cavanagh, a Democratic gubernatorial candidate in Michigan, before Cavanagh's sudden withdrawal because of illness in April.

What they were planning was a series of five-minute television essays in which Cavanagh would address the voters in his own voice, while seated at a desk. It did not differ much from what candidates did on television in the early 1950s, before the medium became more sophisticated.

"It's very low-key, eyeball-to-eyeball stuff," said Napolitan. "It takes it back to the beginning. Voters are more sophisticated. We used to do very sophisticated things on television, but now they're no longer new. How long can you get away with things? Something is only new once."

In 1966, Napolitan advertised Milton Shapp's campaign for governor of Pennsylvania with the slogan, "Shapp makes sense for Pennsylvania." One reason he cannot employ that approach for anyone in 1974 is that General Motors is using it to sell Chevrolets.

No More Slick Cartoons

Deardourff, working on the Republican side with Gov. Milliken in the same race Cavanagh dropped out of, agrees that obvious commercialism is unlikely to work well in 1974. Working with New York Gov. Nelson A. Rockefeller in 1966, Deardourff helped with a television campaign of slick cartoons designed to sell Rockefeller's re-election. "I don't think we could ever go back to those Rockefeller '66 commercials," said Deardourff. "We had animation, fish talking to each other, a road unwinding to Hawaii to show how many highways he had built."

"It's now up to the candidate to prove himself," Goodman

commented. "The so-called imaging that is done is now only in terms of flattering camera angles and technical things."

Allem is also experimenting with a more direct approach to television. "The filming I've done so far," he said, "has accentuated direct eye contact with the voter. I still do it outdoors, because I like light. But very direct, simple rationale. . . . With most candidates I even try to have the candidate write the first draft of the essay, because he's almost like a newsman, trying to communicate his feelings to the people."

Weiner said almost exactly the same thing. "We're doing a lot of straight head-shot talking film, without people around, or the background stuff we used to use quite heavily. It's focusing on the face of the candidate, the eyes in particular."

If the idea of direct contact sounds elementary, it is useful to remember that as late as 1970, most political television was not done this way. Consultants borrowed heavily from commercial advertising, often making 30- or 60-second spots in which a narrator, not the candidate himself, made the sales pitch. In some cases, the candidate did not appear at all.

Lessons from Ottinger

Former Rep. Richard L. Ottinger (D N.Y. 1965-71) became a landmark figure in political television in 1970 when he won New York's Democratic Senate primary with a blitz of commercials that cost about $1 million. Produced by film-maker David Garth, Ottinger's commercials hammered at one simple phrase, "Ottinger Delivers." At least one such commercial appeared in prime time on New York City stations every night during the last three weeks of that campaign.

But Ottinger faded badly in the general election campaign, and after he lost, observers noted that he suffered from the discrepancy between the fighting image Garth had built for him in the primary and the mild manner he later displayed in person.

The "Ottinger syndrome" quickly joined the vocabulary of political consultants. As Guggenheim put it, "If a guy come off differently in paid advertising than he does in the news, you're in trouble."

Cinema Verité

If Ottinger's problems were one reason for consultants to turn away from outright commercialism, another was a study done after the 1970 election by Walter De Vries, a political scientist and a consultant in his own right. Questioning Michigan voters about the things that influenced their vote, DeVries found that television ads ranked 24th. Television news ranked first.

The solution, consultants reasoned in 1972, was to make their commercials look more like news and less like soap advertisements. That meant a move toward the kind of work Guggenheim had been doing for years—films of candidates moving and talking among the voters, with little script and no hard sell. It was the application of *cinema verité* to politics.

In 1974, some consultants are saying that even *cinema verité* must yield to the direct approach of the 1950s. Some argue that few voters make the distinction between *cinema verité* advertising and "Ottinger Delivers" advertising.

"We came to the conclusion at the end of last year," said Weiner, "that the public wasn't believing the *cinema verité* kind of spot any more. The public was considering that as phony as the other kind."

Guggenheim, who said he is disturbed by what he considers the faddish quality of the consulting profession, said he makes films based on what his clients are trying to express, rather than on what other consultants have decided is fashionable. "I'm always very suspicious," he says, "of people who say, 'Now we'll do this, and now we'll do that, and now we'll sit someone behind a desk.' "

Guggenheim said he does not know what themes will dominate his work in 1974 and that they will depend on what the candidates want to say. He had harsh words for consultants who seem to have a new technique every two years. "The only good political advisers are those who have gut feelings and value systems," Guggenheim said. "The ones who deal in formulas or styles or trends are fraudulent. Any candidate who takes that kind of advice is a fool."

Post Mortems

Consultants concede that many of them tend to sound alike at a given time. One reason may be the frequent meetings consultants hold to assess the state of their art and suggest new possibilities. After each major election there is a post mortem at which consultants offer theories about what worked and what did not. These sessions may determine the cliches of the next campaign.

After the 1970 election, consultants discussed the limited effect of media blitzes and the need to tone down the commercialism of their television advertising. One result was the "news look" of 1972. At the end of the 1972 campaign, consultants met to discuss the Biden upset and the year's other surprises. The consensus was that candidates who make a personal impression on the voters have an important advantage. That may be why sincerity and personal contact are familiar words in 1974.

—15—

CANDIDATE EXPOSURE
IN UNCONTROLLED MEDIA

Robert MacNeil

In 1959, the FCC removed regular news and news-interview programs from the Equal Time restriction. The only condition remaining is that broadcasters are still required to be "fair" in their treatment of candidates. For instance, in 1964, if President Johnson spent a day campaigning in New York and a five-minute report appeared that evening on *Walter Cronkite,* the Republican candidate was not entitled to mathematically equal time on the same program. CBS was required, under the Fairness Doctrine, to ensure that, on balance, during the campaign, the Republican views were presented as thoroughly in news programs as Johnson's. The Fairness Doctrine makes broadcasters even unhappier than the Equal Time provision, for reasons we shall see later.

Now, with hours of television news and panel programs open to them every week, the new campaign managers have made it part of their art to get their candidates on those programs. Their skill is considerable, although television often makes it very easy for them.

By appearing on a television news program, the candidate is guaranteed an audience that has some interest in public affairs and is predisposed to consider them at that time of day. He is not competing with entertainment programs and runs no risk of antagonizing the audience by preempting its regular fare. The audience, as we have seen, is an almost perfect demographic cross section of

From pp. 184–193 in *The People Machine* by Robert MacNeil. Copyright © 1968 by Robert MacNeil. By permission of Harper & Row, Publishers, Inc.

the electorate. For this audience largely dependent upon television for its information about current events, news programs form the windows to their minds: if a candidate is to reach them, those windows are the openings where there may be least resistance.

Perhaps the most important benefit is the intuition of authority in the audience. Vitally important things are happening in the cities, the country and the world, they are told, and it is on news programs that they learn about those happenings. A man whose activities are part of the news is credible, his doings have the authority of a news event. He is a bona fide news happening, not a commercial. And he is, if we believe the surveys quoted earlier, a more believable event on television than he is in a newspaper or magazine report.

The major disadvantage to a candidate is that he cannot control all the aspects of an appearance on a news program. He cannot edit the film and write the commentary. But if he is alert to the possibilities, he can control a great deal.

His campaign manager must first have a real understanding of the value of the "pseudo event." To make television and the other news media cover his activities, he must invent happenings which are likely to interest them. They are not real events because they are manufactured simply to attract the media, especially television. In the old days of campaigning, a candidate tried to meet and speak to as many people as he could. Today, if he understands his business, he still goes about meeting people and speaking, but he does not do it with those voters principally in mind. His attention is directed to the hundreds of times greater number of voters who will see him that evening on the television news.

If the events of his campaign are too repetitive, the coverage will dwindle, so there must be constant variety. The speeches he delivers must make different points and the type of setting should vary. But, principally, he should be placed in circumstances where something news-like will happen. If the first sentence that comes to the mind of a reporter summing up the day is: "Republican senatorial candidate Charles Percy today continued his campaigning through southern Illinois. . . ." Percy has not succeeded. If the day can be constructed so as to provide a lead sentence like: "Senatorial candidate Charles Percy today held a vigorous curbside debate with angry Negro demonstrators in Chicago," the incident has the appearance of an event. While it has always been an elementary rule not to run a dull campaign, television's hunger for visual incident has made that precept imperative.

Television hunger has also made it easier. As we have seen, in recent years the network evening news reports have expanded from fifteen minutes to thirty, and there is pressure to make them an hour long. The local news programs which precede the network shows have been lengthened to one hour by many stations. They can be very profitable for the stations but they consume what is for television a staggering amount of material. With so insatiable an appetite to feed, a candidate who runs a creative campaign has an excellent situation to exploit.

This is less true for Presidential campaigns—which will attract constant TV coverage in any case—than for congressional, gubernatorial or municipal races, where the coverage on local stations might be sporadic.

Election coverage for television is an arduous business in which technical and logistical problems are so important, just to get a piece of properly exposed film on the air, that the editorial considerations often come last. The campaign manager who enters most sympathetically into the problems of television journalism will be rewarded by the coverage his candidate gets. Television covers an election by sending reporters and film crews to record the doings of the candidates. There is always an early deadline to meet. They must return with the film to their own station (or, if a network crew, to an affiliate station), where the film can be processed and edited and the commentary added. That may mean breaking off from the campaign as much as five hours before air time. The alert campaign manager, therefore, will try not only to devise an event interesting enough to bring the TV people out, but schedule it before the early afternoon, when they must leave.

If a TV crew wants to travel with the candidate's plane, the manager should do his utmost to permit it and to let them film whatever they want. Holding things up a moment to let a film crew be first off an aircraft or a bus in order to get a shot they want; providing an extra car in a motorcade for TV equipment; or getting the candidate to exchange a few words with a TV reporter who has to leave to make a program deadline is a small price to pay for the exposure that results.

Some politicians have gone so far as to do some of the broadcaster's work. In Michigan, in 1966, Governor Romney's campaign apparatus regularly produced tapes of his remarks, already edited for use, which were made available to radio stations. The Romney people estimated that they received half a million dollars in free radio coverage with that device. If broadcasting pieces preselected by a political candidate seems an abdication of journalistic responsibility, such a lapse is certainly not going to worry the candidate.

Bob Price, campaign manager and later Deputy Mayor for John Lindsay, thinks it is easy to use the television stations in New York. "You have to make the stations give you free time," he says. "If you are imaginative you can get them to use thirty seconds on any news program. In New York City, it's duck soup. You just have to think of the personality of the individual TV newsman and think in terms of what he is likely to use."[1]

Although Governor Nelson Rockefeller spent over $5 million to be reelected in 1966, his staff were very alert to the opportunities news programs provided. Leslie Slote, the Governor's press secretary, says it is easier to get the cameras out during a campaign than in day-to-day affairs. "It needs inventiveness," he says. "The challenge is when they get there to make it good."[2]

He referred to the efforts of Rockefeller's chief opponent in 1966, Democrat Frank O'Connor. For a variety of reasons—late nomination, too little money and too many advisers—the O'Connor campaign had an amateurish air. Frequently, reporters would turn up at a place designated on the campaign schedule to find that no advance man had been there to produce a crowd. O'Connor would be seen pacing on an empty street corner or talking to people who were hostile. One night in late fall, the campaign motorcade with O'Connor, his aides and the press was streaming along a road outside New York City. The lead car made a confident turn off the highway, all the other cars followed and the press found themselves sitting with the candidate in a deserted drive-in movie theater—which had been closed for the winter.

It was not the same in Rockefeller's campaign, where the effect of every campaign stop was calculated. Slote went on: "It's not difficult getting the cameras out. It's showing up the Governor in a setting of enthusiasm and response. One of the keys is young people. We had lots of rallies at schools and universities. Most people are working during the days but there are always people at the schools. He goes to a school and there are six hundred kids. The Governor shakes hands and the TV cameras are cranking away. It is an enthusiastic, warm occasion. The locals will see it that night on the local station. In the middle of that sort of day we would stick a Kiwanis luncheon in as a way of getting the media."

All three Kennedys showed great ability to attract the attention of the media to their activities, both between campaigns and during. It did not happen accidentally. When Senator Robert Kennedy appeared in a full front-page photograph in the New York *Daily News,* leaning in the door of a squalid Puerto Rican tenement in Spanish Harlem, it was not a coincidence that the photographer was there. Nor was he pulled there by a high-pressure public relations man calling to say, "Hey, we've got a great picture for you today." It was all managed more subtly, but it *was* managed.

It is much easier for an incumbent than a challenger. In the opinion of his critics, President Johnson's sudden flight to Honolulu for a conference on Vietnam during the 1966 Senate hearings on the war was the pseudo event of the year. The press cannot ignore a President, so the newspapers and television shows were full of the Honolulu conference. However much the White House denied it at the time, the conference was very suddenly arranged and did divert public attention from the hearings, which were heavy with criticism of the Administration.

The need for visual incident to give variety and action to a television news program can have political effects that worry serious journalists in the medium. The practice is less true in the news departments of the major networks, which are peopled by trained journalists, than in the news operations of local stations around the country. There are more than six hundred of these and many of them still do not have extensive news resources, either in facilities or in personnel. Whenever a political candidate turns up, there is a competitive anxiety to put him on the local news. In the rush and excitement of getting to the politician and recording an interview, the last thing that may be considered is the content of the interview. The interviewer may be so preoccupied by other factors that his questions are sycophantic, or so uninformed as to let the politician simply walk away with the occasion. Such interviewing results in little more than a public relations exercise for the politician. Television viewers, seeing the interview on a news program in the context of other, real events, may give it the benefit of the same trust they bring to that station's other news items. Nor are such lapses unknown at the network news level. For economic reasons, however, the local station may be particularly vulnerable. To send out a cameraman and have him expose a roll of sound film (four hundred feet, or ten minutes, is the standard length) is an investment which stations operating on small news budgets cannot afford to sacrifice. Even if the politician's speech, news conference or private interview results in nothing significant or newsworthy, it is difficult not to run it once the film has been exposed and processed. For that reason, politicians both during campaigns and in normal times get uncritical television exposure that is of great benefit to them.

News programs provide particularly valuable exposure because they are scheduled most often on the fringes of prime time, just before 7:30 P.M., when the large audience for the evening's entertainment programming is beginning to build up, or just after 11:00 P.M., before the big audience goes to bed. Other opportunities for free television exposure, the regular panel or interview programs, usually occur on the weekends, when the audience is smaller, but their effect is still important.

Almost every television station runs at least one half-hour public affairs program a week as a comparatively inexpensive way of demonstrating public service. The most influential of such programs are these on the three networks on Sunday afternoons: *Meet the Press* (NBC), *Face the Nation* (CBS) and *Issues and Answers* (ABC). Appearance on such programs is by invitation, and to a relatively unknown figure an invitation from a network can be an important event (for example, the appearance of Edward Kennedy in 1962 on *Meet the Press*). Prominent politicians are invited often. At election time, these programs become "events" and can have an influence on the momentum of a campaign. Robert Kennedy agreed to appear on *Meet the Press* during his 1964 New York senatorial campaign only after careful thought and preparation. He followed closely the standards set by the late President in schooling himself for such an appearance. The day before the program, Kennedy spent several hours on the lawn of Gracie Mansion, the official residence of New York's then Democratic Mayor, Robert Wagner, with a group of advisers. Arthur Schlesinger, Jr., flew in from Washington to join the others in throwing at the candidate every hostile and tricky question they could think of.

Programs of this nature have an important built-in advantage for politicians in that the panels of questioners tend to protect them as much as they expose them. Competition among members of the panel each to shine with his own favorite questions may prevent any searching pursuit of a subject. *Meet the Press,* in particular, often conveys the impression that it is being much tougher with its interviewees than is the case. Any skilled politician knows how to exploit this appearance of being under attack and gain audience sympathy. In March, 1968, two days after his announcement that he was entering the Presidential race, Robert Kennedy again appeared on *Meet the Press.* His motives at the time were being severely questioned. By repeatedly diverting the discussion away from the harm he might do to Eugene McCarthy and by advertising his wider concern for the fate of the country, Kennedy probably helped to make his candidacy more acceptable.

These interview programs may not be good exposure for a candidate who is too exhausted from campaigning to bring a fresh mind to the studio. One of the incidents most harmful to Senator Goldwater occurred in May, 1964, shortly before before the California primary, where victory was thought to be crucial to his nomination. Appearing on *Issues and Answers,* he seemed to suggest that atomic weapons could be used to defoliate the jungle trails used by the Communists in Vietnam. At least, that was the way the Associated Press interpreted Goldwater in a bulletin flashed to every radio, television and newspaper office around the country a few minutes after his appearance. That was the last thing Goldwater should have been saying, from a point of view of campaign tactics. His opponent in California, Governor Rockefeller, had kept Goldwater on the defensive on "the bomb" issue all year. A major effort of Goldwater's California campaign was to escape from that issue while reassuring people that he did not have an itchy trigger finger for nuclear weapons. As soon as they heard of the Associated Press version, Goldwater's press people quickly produced the full text, but the operative sentences were ambiguous enough to keep reporters seeking clarification for the next two weeks.

"There have been several suggestions made," Goldwater had told Howard K. Smith on the program. "I don't think that we would use any of them. But defoliation of the forests by low-yield atomic weapons might well be done."

However valuable such nationwide exposure may be, it is quite possible to turn it to disadvantage if the candidate does not and his managers do not approach it with care and preparation.

In 1960, forty-four editions of these three network interview programs were devoted to politics, thirteen of them in the final two weeks. In 1964, there were twenty-eight during the campaign. At thirty minutes a program, that adds up to a great deal of free television time for the candidates, or supporters, who can use them well.

In addition, the networks mount a number of political news specials and documentaries in election years, in which politicians in prominent races are covered. Like regular news programs, they have the advantage of giving the politician wide exposure in a context not manufactured by his own publicity apparatus. For the most part, a candidate is treated gently on such programs because television does not usually consider itself as free as newspapers to put politicians under too searching or unfavorable a spotlight. Even when television has decided, because of the personality of the reporter or producer, to attempt a deeper analysis of a man, time limitations work against it. Campaign specials tend to be compendia, surveys of a group of candidates, with five or seven minutes devoted to each race in a series. Often that is simply not enough time to be thorough.

Herbert Mitgang, a journalist who returned to the *New York Times* in 1967 after several years with CBS News, has said: "I can't think of one profile either of a general nature or of a national political figure that really stripped away the sham and allowed the correspondent to be as outspoken as Reston and Wicker (two *Times* columnists) are in the press."[3] Mitgang further said that at CBS "the attitude on political documentaries was always not to jab the guy—it was never to go as far as any of the writers like Kraft or Lippmann would go."

In an effort to acquire even more sympathetic free exposure, national political figures have frequently accepted invitations to appear on completely nonpolitical programs. Richard Nixon was interviewed on *Open End* by David Susskind for nearly four continuous hours in May, 1960. Susskind asked the friendliest of questions to stimulate his subject to reveal himself. For a seasoned politician willing to relax, it is an opportunity to present himself in the most favorable light. Some entertainment programs, such as NBC's *Tonight,* with Johnny Carson, the *Merv Griffin Show* and others, use big political names to give prestige to their operations and for that reason go out of their way not to embarrass the illustrious guest. If veterans like Hubert Humphrey *are* embarrassed by being so cloyingly interviewed on these occasions, they have the good sense not to show it. Such shows do not fall within the category of programs exempt from the Equal Time ruling, however, so politicians are invited only before they have actually declared themselves candidates for office. Still, their supporters can continue to appear right up to election day. In 1952, the Eisenhower-Nixon forces estimated that appearances on such programs as *Junior Press Conference of the Air* and the *Kate Smith Show* by speakers favorable to their candidates were worth a million dollars in television time.

Such attention from the media, expecially television, does not happen accidently. A politician determined to exploit it can do so by cultivating the right people and by making news. Robert Kennedy was able to hook all the national media simply by shooting rapids in a rubber dinghy or climbing a mountain. If you are a lesser liminary, the effort is greater but the technique is the same. It consists of being active, making provocative suggestions, challenging the White House, going on foreign trips, investigating and criticizing. Whatever it is you do, you must unashamedly cause it to be publicized beforehand (to create suspense), while you are doing it (to report the event that all the suspense led up to), and afterward (to feed curiosity about the event everyone is discussing).

In New York, any candidate could get several television crews out at the crack of dawn because it was traditional to open campaigns with an early morning exchange of pleasantries at the now removed Fulton Fish Market. President Johnson, who is very adept at stimulating the mass media, merely has to embark on marathon walking press conferences. Senator Everett Dirksen tweaks his gray curls into a pompadour and growls mellifluously, but never begins the performance until every network camera is in position. Other senators ask interminable questions of hearings witnesses who have already answered them in their opening statements. Lady Bird Johnson formally inaugurates a dam that has survived, uninaugurated, for a generation.

The only politician I ever saw balk at an opportunity to gladden the national heart by an appearance on the television screens was President Kennedy. Shortly before the President was killed, representatives of the nation's turkey raisers had turned up in the White House Rose Garden for the traditional presentation of the Thanksgiving turkey at the White House. The President was so acutely embarrassed by the tawdry commercialism of the occasion that he delivered only the minimum courtesies and refused to be photographed with the turkey.

It is a matter of style and sophistication whether you willingly make small talk with turkey growers of don't. But an ability to attract publicity, always a prerequisite for political success, is the key to much free exposure on television.

NOTES

1. Interview with author, May 23, 1967.
2. Interview with author, June 1, 1967.
3. Interview previously cited, July 21, 1967.

—16—

ON THE BUS: COVERING PRESIDENTIAL CAMPAIGNS

Timothy Crouse

June 1—five days before the California primary. A grey dawn was fighting its way through the orange curtains in the Wilshire Hyatt House Hotel in Los Angeles, where George McGovern was encamped with his wife, his staff, and the press assigned to cover his snowballing campaign.

While reporters still snored like Hessians in a hundred beds throughout the hotel, the McGovern munchkins were at work, plying the halls, slipping the long legal sized handouts through the cracks under the door of each room. According to one of these handouts, the Baptist Ministers' Union of Oakland had decided after "prayerful and careful deliberation" to endorse Senator McGovern. And there was a detailed profile of Alameda County ("... agricultural products include sween corn, cucumbers, and lettuce"), across which the press would be dragged today—or was it tomorrow? Finally, there was the mimeographed schedule, the orders of the day.

At 6:45 the phone on the bed table rang, and a sweet, chipper voice announced: "Good Morning, Mr. Crouse. It's six forty-five. The press bus leaves in forty-five minutes from the front of the hotel." She was up there in Room 819, the Press Suite, calling up the dozens of names on the press manifest, awaking the agents of every great newspaper, wire service and network not only of

America but of the world. In response to her calls, she was getting a shocking series of startled grunts, snarls and obscenities.

The media heavies were rolling over, stumbling to the bathroom, and tripping over the handouts. Stooping to pick up the schedule, they read: *"8:00–8:15, Arrive Roger Young Center, Breakfast with Ministers."* Suddenly, desperately, they thought: "Maybe I can pick McGovern up in Burbank at nine fifty-five and sleep for another hour." Then, probably at almost the same instant, several score minds flashed the same guilty thought: "But maybe he will get shot at the ministers' breakfast," and then each mind branched off into its own private nightmare recollections of the correspondent who was taking a piss at Laurel when they shot Wallace, of the ABC cameraman who couldn't get his Bolex to start as Bremer empied his revolver. A hundred hands groped for the toothbrush.

It was lonely on these early mornings and often excruciatingly painful to tear oneself away from a brief, sodden spell of sleep. More painful for some than others. The press was consuming two hundred dollars a night worth of free cheap booze up there in the Press Suite, and some were consuming the lion's share. Last night it had taken six reporters to subdue a prominent radio correspondent who kept upsetting the portable bar, knocking bottles and ice on the floor. The radioman had the resiliency of a Rasputin—each time he was put to bed, he would reappear to cause yet more bedlam.

And yet, at 7:15 Rasputin was there for the baggage call, milling in the hall outside the Press Suite with fifty-odd reporters. The first glance at all these fellow sufferers was deeply reassuring—they all felt the same pressures you felt, their problems were your problems. Together, they seemed to have the cohesiveness of an ant colony, but when you examined the scene more closely, each reporter appeared to be jitterbugging around in quest of the answer that would quell some private anxiety.

They were three deep at the main table in the Press Suite, badgering the McGovern people for a variety of assurances. "Will I have a room in San Francisco tonight?" "Are you sure I'm booked on the whistle-stop train?" "Have you seen my partner?"

The feverish atmosphere was halfway between a high school bus trip to Washington and a gambler's jet junket to Las Vegas, where small-time Mafiosi were lured into betting away their restaurants. There was giddy camaraderie mixed with fear and low-grade hysteria. To file a story late, or to make one glaring factual error, was to chance losing everything—one's job, one's expense account, one's drinking buddies, one's mad-dash existence, and the methedrine buzz that comes from knowing stories that the public would not know for hours and secrets that the public would never know. Therefore reporters channeled their gambling instincts into late-night poker games and private bets on the outcome of the elections. When it came to writing a story, they were as cautious as diamond-cutters.

It being Thursday, many reporters were knotting their stomachs over their Sunday pieces, which had to be filed that afternoon at the latest. They were inhaling their cigarettes with more of a vengeance, and patting themselves more distractedly to make sure they had their pens and notebooks. In the hall, a Secret Service agent was dispensing press tags for the baggage, along with string and scissors to attach them. From time to time, in the best Baden-Powell tradition, he courteously stepped forward to assist a drink-palsied journalist in the process of threading a tag.

The reporters often consulted their watches or asked for the time of departure. Among this crew, there was one great phobia— the fear of getting left behind. Fresh troops had arrived today from the Humphrey Bus, which was the Russian Front of the California primary, and they had come bearing tales of horror. The Humphrey Bus had left half the press corps at the Biltmore Hotel on Tuesday night; in Santa Barbara, the bus had deserted Richard Bergholz of the Los Angeles *Times,* and it had twice stranded George Shelton, the UPI man.

"Jesus, am I glad I'm off the Humphrey Bus," said one reporter, as he siphoned some coffee out of the McGovern samovar and helped himself to a McGovern sweet roll. "Shelton asked Humphrey's press officer, Hackel, if there was time to file. Hackel said, 'Sure, the candidate's gonna mingle and shake some hands.' Well, old Hubie couldn't find but six hands to shake, so they got in the bus and took off and left the poor bastard in a phone booth right in the middle of Watts."

To the men whom duty had called to slog along at the side of the Hump, the switch to the McGovern Bus brought miraculous relief. "You gotta go see the Hump's pressroom, just to see what disaster looks like," a reporter urged me. The Humphrey pressroom, a bunker-like affair in the bowels of the Beverly Hilton contained three tables covered with white tablecloths, no typewriters, no chairs, no bar, no food, one phone (with outside lines available only to registered guests), and no reporters. The

McGovern press suite, on the other hand, contained twelve typewriters, eight phones, a Xerox Telecopier, a free bar, free cigarettes, free munchies, and a skeleton crew of three staffers. It was not only Rumor Central, but also a miniature road version of Thomas Cook and Son. As the new arrivals to the McGovern Bus quickly found out, the McGovern staff ran the kind of guided tour that people pay great sums of money to get carted around on. They booked reservations on planes, trains and hotels; gave and received messages; and handled Secret Service accreditation with a fierce, Tuetonic efficiency. And handed out reams of free information. On any given day, the table in the middle of the Press Suite was laden with at least a dozen fat piles of handouts, and the door was papered with pool reports.*

It was just these womblike conditions that gave rise to the notorious phenomenon called "pack journalism" (also known as "herd journalism" and "fuselage journalism"). A group of reporters were assigned to follow a single candidate for weeks or months at a time, like a pack of hounds sicked on a fox. Trapped on the same bus or plane, they ate, drank, gambled, and compared notes with the same bunch of colleagues week after week.

Actually, this group was as hierarchical as a chess set. The pack was divided into cliques—the national political reporters, who were constantly coming and going; the campaign reporters from the big, prestige papers and the ones from the small papers; the wire-service men; the network correspondents; and other configurations that formed according to age and old Washington friendships. The most experienced national political reporters, wire men, and big-paper reporters, who were at the top of the pecking order, often did not know the names of the men from the smaller papers, who were at the bottom. But they all fed off the same pool report, the same daily handout, the same speech by the candidate; the whole

---

*Every day, a "pool" of one or two reporters was delegated to stay close to the candidate at those times (i.e., during motorcades, small dinners, fund-raising parties) when the entire press corps could not follow him. The regular reporters on the bus took turns filling the pool assignments. After each event, the pool wrote a report which was posted in the pressroom, and was usually also Xeroxed by the candidate's press staff and distributed on the bus. According to the rules, the pool reporters were not supposed to include in their own articles any information which they had not put in the pool report. The reports usually dealt in trivia—what the candidate ate, what he said, whose hands he had shaken. Pool reports varied in length. Jim Naughton of the *Times,* the most meticulous pooler on the bus, once turned in a report that went on for eight double-spaced pages. Dick Stout of *Newsweek* wrote the year's shortest report: "Oct. 30, 1972. 5 P.M. to bed. Nothing happened untoward. Details on request."

pack was isolated in the same mobile village. After a while, they began to believe the same rumors, subscribe to the same theories, and write the same stories.

Everybody denounces pack journalism, including the men who form the pack. Any self-respecting journalist would sooner endorse incest than come out in favor of pack journalism. It is the classic villain of every campaign year. Many reporters and journalism professors blame it for everything that is shallow, obvious, meretricious, misleading, or dull in American campaign coverage. . . .

Around 8:15 A.M. on June 1 the buses rolled past the stucco housefronts of lower-middle-class Los Angeles and pulled up in front of a plain brick building that looked like a school. The press trooped down a little alley and into the back of the Grand Ballroom of the Roger Young Center. The scene resembled Bingo Night in a South Dakota parish hall—hundreds of middle-aged people sitting at long rectangular tables. They were watching George McGovern, who was speaking from the stage. The press, at the back of the room, started filling up on free Danish pastry, orange juice and coffee. Automatically, they pulled out their notebooks and wrote something down, even though McGovern was saying nothing new. They leaned sloppily against the wall or slumped in folding chairs.

McGovern ended his speech and the Secret Service men began to wedge him through the crush of ministers and old ladies who wanted to shake his hand. By the time he had made it to the little alley which was the only route of escape from the building, three cameras had set up an ambush. This was the only "photo opportunity," as it is called, that the TV people would have all morning. Except in dire emergencies, all TV film has to be taken before noon, so that it can be processed and transmitted to New York. Consequently, the TV people are the only reporters who are not asleep on their feet in the morning. Few TV correspondents ever join the wee-hour poker games or drinking. Connie Chung, the pretty Chinese CBS correspondent, occupied the room next to mine at the Hyatt House and she was always back by midnight, reciting a final sixty-second radio spot into her Sony or absorbing one last press release before getting a good night's sleep. So here she was this morning, bright and alert, sticking a mike into McGovern's face and asking him something about black ministers. The print reporters stood around and watched, just in case

McGovern should say something interesting. Finally McGovern excused himself and everybody ran for the bus.

8:20–8:50 a.m.	En Route/Motorcade
8:50–9:30 a.m.	Taping–"Newsmakers"
	CBS-TV 6121 Sunset Boulevard,
	Hollywood
9:30–9:55 a.m.	En Route/Motorcade
9:55–10:30 a.m.	Taping–"News Conference"
	NBC-TV 3000 West Alameda Ave.,
	Burbank
10:30–10:50 a.m.	Press filing
10:50–Noon	En Route/Motorcade
Noon–1:00 p.m.	Senior Citizens Lunch and Rally
	Bixby Park–Band Shell
	Long Beach
1:00–1:15 p.m.	Press filing

The reporters began to wake up as they walked into the chilly Studio 22 at CBS. There was a bank of telephones, hastily hooked up on a large worktable in the middle of the studio, and six or seven reporters made credit card calls to bureau chiefs and home offices. Dick Stout of *Newsweek* found out he had to file a long story and couldn't go to San Francisco later in the day. Steve Gerstel phoned in his day's schedule to UPI. Connie Chung dictated a few salient quotes from McGovern's breakfast speech to CBS Radio.

A loudspeaker announced that the interview was about to begin, so the reporters sat down on the folding chairs that were clustered around a monitor. They didn't like having to get their news secondhand from TV, but they did enjoy being able to talk back to McGovern without his hearing them. As the program started, several reporters turned on cassette recorders. A local newscaster led off by accusing McGovern of using a slick media campaign.

"Well, I think the documentary on my life is very well done," McGovern answered ingenuously. The press roared with laughter. Suddenly the screen of the monitor went blank—the video tape had broken. The press started to grumble.

"Are they gonna change that first question and make it a toughie?" asked Martin Nolan, the Boston *Globe*'s national political reporter. "If not, I'm gonna wait on the bus." Nolan, a witty man in his middle thirties, had the unshaven, slack-jawed, nuts-to-you-too look of a bartender in a sailors' cafe. He grew up in

Dorchester, a poor section of Boston, and he asked his first tough political question at the age of twelve. "Sister, how do you *know* Dean Acheson's a Communist?" he had challenged a reactionary nun in his parochial school, and the reprimand he received hadn't daunted him from asking wiseacre questions ever since.

The video tape was repaired and the program began again. The interviewer asked McGovern the same first question, but Nolan stayed anyway. Like the others, Nolan had sat through hundreds of press conferences holding in an irrepressible desire to heckle. Now was the big chance and everyone took it.

"Who are your heroes?" the newscaster asked McGovern.

"General Patton!" shouted Jim Naughton of the *Times.*

"Thomas Jefferson and Abraham Lincoln," said McGovern.

"What do you think of the death penalty?" asked the newscaster.

"I'm against the death penalty." There was a long pause. "That is my judgment," McGovern said, and lapsed into a heavy, terminal silence. The press laughed at McGovern's discomfiture.

By the time the interview was over, the press was in a good mood. As they filed back onto the buses, the normal configurations began to form: wire service reporters and TV cameramen in the front, where they could get out fast; small-town daily and big-city daily reporters in the middle seats, hard at work; McGovern staffers in the rear seats, going over plans and chatting. Dick Stout and Jim Naughton held their tape recorders to their ears, like transistor junkies, and culled the best quotes from the TV interview to write in their notebooks. Lou Dombrowski of the Chicago *Tribune,* who looked like a hulking Maf padrone, typed his Sunday story on the portable Olympia in his lap. The reporters working for morning newspapers would have to begin to write soon, and they were looking over the handouts and their notes for something to write about.

So it went. They went on to another interview in another chilly studio, at NBC. This time the reporters sat in the same studio as McGovern and the interviewer, so there was no laughter, only silent note-taking. After the interview there were phones and typewriters in another room, courtesy of the network. Only a few men used them. Then to Bixby Park for a dull speech to old people and a McGovern-provided box lunch of tiny, rubbery chicken parts. Another filing facility, this one in a dank little dressing room in back of the Bixby Park band shell. While McGovern droned on about senior citizens, about fifteen reporters used the bank of twelve phones that the McGovern press people had ordered Pacific Telephone to install.

At every stop there was a phone bank, but the reporters never rushed for the phones and fought over them as they do in the movies. Most of them worked for morning papers and didn't have to worry about dictating their stories over the phone until around 6 p.m. (Eastern Standard Time).* Earlier in the day they just called their editors to map out a story, or called a source to check a fact, or sometimes they called in part of a story, with the first paragraph (the "lead") to follow at the last moment. There was only one type of reporter who dashed for the phones at almost every stop and called in bulletins about everything that happened on the schedule. That was the wire service reporter.

If you live in New York or Los Angeles, you have probably never heard of Walter Mears and Carl Leubsdorf, who were covering McGovern for the Associated Press, or Steve Gerstel, who covered him for the United Press International. But if your home is Sheboygan or Aspen, and you read the local papers, they are probably the only political journalists you know. There are about 1,700 newspapers in the U.S., and every one of them has an AP machine or UPI machine or both whirling and clattering and ringing in some corner of the city room, coughing up stories all through the day. Most of these papers do not have their own political reporters, and they depend on the wire-service men for all of their national political coverage. Even at newspapers that have large political staffs, the wire-service story almost always arrives first.

So the wire services are influential beyond calculation. Even at the best newspapers, the editor always gauges his own reporters' stories against the expectations that the wire stories have aroused. The only trouble is that wire stories are usually bland, dry, and overly cautious. There is an inverse proportion between the number of persons a reporter reaches and the amount he can say. The larger the audience, the more inoffensive and inconclusive the article must be. Many of the wire men are repositories of informa-

*The reporters who worked for afternoon papers, such as the Washington *Star,* the Philadelphia *Bulletin,* or the Boston *Evening Globe,* had a much rougher schedule. Their deadline was between six and eight in the morning, and they usually wrote their stories late at night, when everyone else was having supper or drinking. Having gone to bed late, they then had to be up to inspect the first handouts and to cover the first event, just in case there was something important to file in the last few minutes before their papers went to bed. If a reporter from a morning paper missed an early morning event, he had the rest of the day to catch up on it.

tion they can never convey. Pye Chamberlain, a young UPI radio reporter with an untamable wiry moustache, emerged over drinks as an expert on the Dark Side of Congress. He could tell you about a prominent Senator's battle to overcome his addiction to speed, or about Humphrey's habit of popping twenty-five One-A-Day Vitamins with a shot of bourbon when he needed some fast energy. But Pye couldn't tell his audience.

In 1972, the Dean of the political wire-service reporters was Walter Mears of the AP, a youngish man with sharp pale green eyes who smoked cigarillos and had a nervous habit of picking his teeth with a matchbook cover. With his clean-cut brown hair and his conservative sports clothes he could pass for a successful golf pro, or maybe a baseball player. He started his career with the AP in 1955 covering auto accidents in Boston, and he worked his way up the hard way, by getting his stories in fast and his facts straight every time. He didn't go in for the New Journalism. "The problem with a lot of the new guys is they don't get the formula stuff drilled into them," he told me as he scanned the morning paper in Miami Beach. "I'm an old fart. If you don't learn how to write an eight-car fatal on Route 128, you're gonna be in big trouble."

About ten years ago, Mears' house in Washington burned down. His wife and children died in the fire. As therapy, Mears began to put in slavish eighteen-hour days for the AP. In a job where sheer industry counts above all else, Mears worked harder than any other two reporters, and he got to the top.

"At what he does, Mears is the best in the goddam world," said a colleague who writes very non-AP features. "He can get out a coherent story with the right point on top in a minute and thirty seconds, left-handed. It's like a parlor trick, but that's what he wants to do and he does it. In the end, Walter Mears can only be tested on one thing, and that is whether he has the right lead. He almost always does. He watches some goddam event for a half hour and he understands the most important thing that happened—that happened in public, I mean. He's just like a TV camera, he doesn't see things any special way. But he's probably one of the most influential political reporters in the world, just because his stuff reaches more people than anyone else's."

Mears' way with a lead made him a leader of the pack. Covering the second California debate between McGovern and Humphrey on May 30, Mears worked with about thirty other reporters in a large, warehouse-like press room that NBC had furnished with tables, typewriters, paper and phones. The debate was broadcast live from an adjacent studio, where most of the press watched it. For the reporters who didn't have to file immediately, it was something of a social event. But Mears sat tensely in the front of the press room, puffing at a Tiparillo and staring up at a gigantic monitor like a man waiting for a horse to begin. As soon as the program started, he began typing like a madman, "taking transcript" in shorthand form and inserting descriptive phrases every four or five lines: HUMPHREY STARTED IN A LOW KEY, or McGOV LOOKS A BIT STRAINED.

The entire room was erupting with clattering typewriters, but Mears stood out as the resident dervish. His cigar slowed him down, so he threw it away. It was hot, but he had no time to take off his blue jacket. After the first three minutes, he turned to the phone at his elbow and called the AP bureau in L.A. "He's phoning in a lead based on the first statements so they can send out a bulletin," explained Carl Leubsdorf, the No. 2 AP man, who was sitting behind Mears and taking back-up notes. After a minute on the phone Mears went back to typing and didn't stop for a solid hour. At the end of the debate he jumped up, picked up the phone, looked hard at Leubsdorf, and mumbled, "How can they stop? They didn't come to a lead yet."

Two other reporters, one from New York, another from Chicago, headed toward Mears shouting, "Lead? Lead?" Marty Nolan came at him from another direction. "Walter, Walter, what's our lead?" he said.

Mears was wildly scanning his transcript. "I did a Wallace lead the first time," he said. (McGovern and Humphrey had agreed near the start of the show that neither of them would accept George Wallace as a Vice President.) "I'll have to do it again." There were solid, technical reasons for Mears' computer-speed decision to go with the Wallace lead: it meant he could get both Humphrey and McGovern into the first paragraph, both stating a position that they hadn't flatly declared before then. But nobody asked for explanations.

"Yeah," said Nolan, turning back to his Royal. "Wallace. I guess that's it."

Meanwhile, in an adjacent building, *The New York Times* team had been working around a long oak desk in an NBC conference room. The *Times* had an editor from the Washington Bureau, Robert Phelps, and three rotating reporters watching the debate in the conference room and writing the story; a secretary phoned it in from an office down the hall. The *Times* team filed a lead saying that Humphrey had apologized for having called McGovern a "fool" earlier in the campaign. Soon after they filed the story, an editor phoned from New York. The AP had gone with a Wallace lead, he said. Why hadn't they?

Marty Nolan eventually decided against the Wallace lead, but NBC and CBS went with it on their news shows. So did many of the men in the room. They wanted to avoid "call-backs"—phone calls from their editors asking them why they had deviated from the AP or UPI. If the editors were going to run a story that differed from the story in the nation's 1,700 other newspapers, they wanted a good reason for it. Most reporters dreaded call-backs. Thus the pack followed the wire-service men whenever possible. Nobody made a secret of running with the wires; it was an accepted practice. At an event later in the campaign, a New York *Daily News* reporter looked over the shoulder of Norm Kempster, a UPI man, and read his copy.

"Stick with that lead, Norm," said the man from the *News.* "You'll save us a lot of trouble."

"Don't worry," said Norm. "I don't think you'll have any trouble from mine."

2:00–2:45 p.m.	*Fullerton Junior College*
	321 East Chapman, Fullerton
2:45–3:00 p.m.	*Press filing*
3:00–3:30 p.m.	*En Route/Motorcade*
3:30–3:40 p.m.	*Load Aircarft*
	Depart Orange County Community
	Airport
4:45 p.m.	*Arrive Oakland, California*
5:00–5:40 p.m.	*En Route/Motorcade*
5:40–6:45 p.m.	*Private dinner*
6:45–7:30 p.m.	*Rest—San Francisco Hilton*
7:30–8:30 p.m.	*En Route/Motorcade*
8:30–9:15 p.m.	*McGovern for President Rally*
	St. James Park, San Jose
9:15–10:00 p.m.	*En Route/Motorcade*
10:00–10:45 p.m.	*Private meeting*
10:45–11:15 p.m.	*En Route/Motorcade*
11:15 p.m.	*Arrive San Francisco Hilton*

At Bixby Park, Walter Cronkite showed up and rode on the press bus to Fullerton Junior College. Most of the reporters were quite dazzled and wanted to know why Cronkite was around. "He wants to be one of the guys and get a feel for something outside

Moscow," Connie Chung explained. Fred Dutton, Gary Hart and Bill Dougherty of the McGovern staff had joined the bus too. They were singing football songs and hymns in the back seats. In fact, things were getting chummy as hell. Shirley MacLaine was sitting in Marty Nolan's lap. Gary Hart was cracking up with the men from *The New York Times* and *Newsweek.* Bill Dougherty was chatting with David Schoumacher of CBS.

"I'd like to lock up the candidate," Dougherty confided.

"Like to take the vote right now, huh?" said Schoumacher.

Fullerton Junior College looked like a large complex of parking garages. The sweltering gym was packed with kids who treated McGovern as if he were Bobby Kennedy. The cameramen surrounded McGovern as he fought his way to the platform and the kids tried to push through the cameramen. The heat and commotion energized reporters as they squatted around the platform. When McGovern began to speak, they made frantic notes, although he said nothing new. Gradually they wound down.

"If there is one lesson it is . . ." said McGovern.

Carl Leubsdorf put up his finger. "I know what it is," he said to Elizabeth Drew of PBS. "Never again."

"It is that never again . . ." said George.

By the end of the speech no one was taking notes. As deadlines began to loom for the big-city daily reporters, the early afternoon euphoria began to give way to grumpy sobriety. Walter Cronkite went back to Los Angeles because his back was bothering him and he needed to rest. The rest of the press flew to Oakland.

The schedule began to go to hell. Instead of going to San Francisco, the bus took the press to an airport hotel called the Oakland Inn, where McGovern was going to have a hastily scheduled press conference with some black ministers. The press went to a small function room in the motel that had phony wood paneling on the walls and gold vinyl chairs. While reporters began to munch at the Danish lying on a small table at the rear, or worked at the five typewriters on a large table pushed up against a side wall, the cameramen set up in the front. Soon there was an outcry from the print press. "Do *you* want to go to a press conference where we stand behind the cameras?" James Doyle of the Washington *Star* asked Adam Clymer of the Baltimore *Sun.*

Doyle found Kirby Jones, McGovern's press secretary, and chewed him out. Jones made some excuses.

"Yeah," said Doyle, "but you're *never* organized at these press conferences."

Jones shrugged and walked away.

The press had to sit behind the cameras for the press conference, which was short and dull. As the reporters were getting up to stretch, Kirby Jones and Gordon Weil, another McGovern aide, began to pass the word that the Field Poll results were out: McGovern was twenty points ahead.

It was the only hard news of the day. Harry Kelly of Hearst, Steve Gerstel of UPI, and James Doyle all headed for the typewriters and began to hunt-and-peck. Pye Chamberlain, Curt Wilkie, and about twenty other reporters headed for the four pay phones in the hall outside the function room. People were getting testy. Carl Leubsdorf of the AP leaned over Jim Doyle's shoulder, took a good look at Doyle's lead and then asked, "Hey, can I see?"

Doyle looked up and registered what was happening. "Jesus, no!" he exploded. "Fuck you! Get outa here!"

A few moments later Steve Gerstel sauntered over to Doyle and said, "Let me see your lead, Jim."

"You might as well," Doyle said unhappily. "The AP just catched it."

Leubsdorf walked by again on his way to the phones and patted Doyle on the back. "I like it," he said, and chuckled.

An hour went by, and everybody got a chance to file on the Field Poll. The scene began to look like a bad cocktail party. Haynes Johnson of the Washington *Post*, Elizabeth Drew of PBS, and Jules Witcover of the Los Angeles *Times* were doing Humphrey imitations. Kirby Jones was trying to get nine people to go in the helicopter to San Jose as "pool" reporters—that is, to write a report for all the reporters who could not fit in the chopper. The San Jose rally promised to be McGovern's major lunge for the Bobby Kennedy Chicano constituency, but no one wanted to go. San Francisco lay ahead, and it was a great restaurant town. Finally Jim Naughton, Marty Nolan, and a couple of camera crews signed up.

At 7:00, Kirby Jones announced another press conference—McGovern would read a statement on Nixon's Moscow trip. At 7:30, Jones announced that *he* would read the statement. There was a general groan. Kirby launched into a predictable text. "Stop the presses," said Haynes Johnson, shutting his notebook.

The campaign day was drawing to a dreary close. Had all the events taken place in a single room, the reporters would have been climbing the walls with boredom by mid-afternoon. It was the bus rides and plane flights, the sense that a small army was being efficiently deployed, that had given the day its pace, variety, and excitement. Yet the reporters seldom wrote about this traveling around, which was so important in forming their gut feelings about the campaign. The day had yielded its one easy story: McGovern was leading Humphrey by twenty points in the Field Poll. This statistic sounded somehow *right* to the reporters, for it jibed with their half-digested notion that the McGovern campaign was a juggernaut about to flatten Hubert Humphrey. And where had this notion come from? "They partly got it from the slickness of the McGovern press operation," said a reporter who was covering Humphrey in California. "When a reporter got to his room at night his bag was there. He got handouts telling him where the candidate was going to be the next morning and who he could interview at 2 A.M. if he needed to get a fast quote. And so pretty soon the reporter started saying to himself, half-consciously, 'If the press operation is this good, they must have a helluva voter registration operation!' The press didn't create the McGovern juggernaut, but they sure as hell *helped* create it."

On June 1, a normal campaign day, the reporters had gained no fresh insights into George McGovern; they had not gone out of their way to look for any. They had not tried to find out whether the large sums of money that were suddenly pouring into the campaign coffers had changed the candidate; or whether the prospect of the nomination, now so close at hand, was tempting him to bend on some of his more controversial stands; whether, as some of his detractors charged, he had a ruthless streak to match Bobby Kennedy's. "We spent tons of ink of that guy," one of the reporters later lamented, "and I'd be willing to bet that on the night he got the nomination we hadn't told anybody in the United States who the hell we were talking about, what kind of man he was."

CONTRASTS IN PRESIDENTIAL CAMPAIGN COMMERCIALS

L. Patrick Devlin

Perched high on the girders of a new building, a construction worker munches on a sandwich and listens to a voice telling him how many people will be on welfare and who will pay for it if a certain candidate gets elected. The flip of a channel reveals a balding man in his shirt sleeves listening to an old woman describe her financial plight and responding that it breaks his heart to see old people picking up stale bread in grocery stores, trying to stretch their paychecks.

These were but two of the many political ads that were seen by millions during the 1972 campaign. On the surface they may suggest little of the constrasting philosophies which generated them; but closer scrutiny of these and other ads reveal a great deal about the media campaigns of President Nixon and Senator McGovern.

Specifically, the purpose of this study is to examine the different approaches used by Nixon's and McGovern's spot commercials focusing on how the two campaigns had different view-points regarding the function, length, and type of televised campaign spots.

BACKGROUND

In order to place the 1972 spot commercials in their proper prospective, one must examine what preceded them.

From L. Patrick Devlin, "Contrasts in Presidential Campaign Commercials in 1972," *Journal of Broadcasting*, 19 (Winter 1973–74):17–26. Copyright © 1974 by *Journal of Broadcasting*. Reprinted by permission.

Image building became very important in the 1960s and led to the emergence of "image merchants" and media specialists. Television became the chief medium for this image building that almost no politician dared to be without. The manner in which the "image makers" sold their candidates was written about, analyzed, glorified, and criticized.[1]

Analysts were quick to credit television for much of the politician's success. 1960 was the year of the televised "Great Debates" with several analysts claiming that Kennedy won the election because of the impression he made in contrast to Nixon in these televised debates.[2] 1964 was the year of the campaign spot TV commercial with one analyst claiming that Johnson's "Daisy Girl" and Social Security Card spots were "masterpieces of political television."[3] And 1968 was the year of Nixon's format in which the candidate was interviewed by representative voters. This format, devised by Nixon's media consultants, was exposed and analyzed in Joe McGinniss's best seller, *The Selling of the President, 1968.*

Television also played a role in state as well as national campaigns. In 1966, Rockefeller's New York gubernatorial campaign spent millions of dollars on commercials "in which the Governor was neither seen nor heard."[4] In the 1970 primary elections two candidates—Ottinger in New York and Metzenbaum in Ohio—literally bought their way to notoriety and victory through TV commercials. Yet, neither Ottinger nor Metzenbaum won in the general election, and other "TV candidates," so called because of their emphasis on television commercials—Rockefeller in Arkansas, Cramer in Florida, Bush in Texas, Smith in Illinois, and Gross in New Jersey—all lost. Their loss was attributed, not to their excessive TV spending, but to their blunt and accusatory commercials, which attacked their opponents. The results of 1970 made many media specialists reappraise their approach and led one, Joseph Napolitan, a consultant for several Democrats, to comment in regard to future commercials, "We'll get away from slick spots now and go back to homey face-to-the-camera stuff, because it will seem new."[5]

New approaches were tried in 1972, but they didn't seem too effective. In the primaries, "homey face-to-the-camera stuff" was used by Lindsay's media consultant David Garth but wasn't very effective in Florida. Muskie's consultant, Bob Squier, tried to take the advice of DeVries in his book, *The Ticket Splitter,* by creating media events that would give the appearance of network news stories, but this technique wasn't too effective either. If anything, the 1972 primary elections seemed to be the year of the "inverse spending law"—the more spent on political advertising, the lower the vote. Mills in New Hampshire, Lindsay in Florida, McCarthy in Illinois, and Jackson in Wisconsin were all examples of this "law" at work.

Certainly 1972 was not the year of the media consultant, for as one analyst stated, "Political advertising, much vaunted and much heralded, played an embarrassingly insignificant role in the most complex and dramatic primary season in history."[6] The general election of 1972 saw the survivor of the crowded Democratic primary media field—Charles Guggenheim—take on the Republican "November Group," which had been formed expressly to muster maximum media expertise on the side of Richard Nixon.

In retrospect the 1972 general election produced little that was new. Both groups used techniques that had been successfully used before by them and others. Therefore, readers hoping to find that 1972 was unique will be disappointed. 1972 still merits examination, however, and it is the goal of this study to examine how and why spot-commercial techniques differed in the Nixon and McGovern campaigns.

1972 CAMPAIGN

Media Directors

It is helpful to begin by examining Nixon's and McGovern's media directors, for their backgrounds explain much about their contrasting approaches to political advertising.

Charles Guggenheim, McGovern's media director, was, first and foremost, a maker of documentary films. He took on political clients as a sideline. His accomplishments included five Academy Award nominations and two Oscars. He was best remembered in political circles for his film, *RFK Remembered.* Even though primarily a documentary film maker, Guggenheim was an experienced media consultant with well over 50 political clients to his credit. Some of his recent media campaigns had been those of Senators Mondale, Pell, Gore, Moss, Symington, Ribicoff, and Kennedy. He was also Robert Kennedy's media consultant during the 1968 primary campaign.

The November Group was formed for the express purpose of bringing together a group of talented people who were philosophically (not simply monetarily) committed to the reelection of Richard Nixon. The November Group was composed primarily of people with advertising agency experience. And whereas McGovern used one man, Guggenheim, to act as both a creative and administrative director of media, Nixon's campaign divided the roles. Peter Dailey was media director and Bill Taylor was creative director for the November Group. Both were advertising men, not film-makers, and both were political neophytes in the sense that neither had had previous experience in political campaigns and political advertising. Daily had worked on various automobile ads while at Campbell-Ewell, and Taylor had created numerous television ads and won Clios (the advertising industry's award for television ads) in 1967 and again in 1971.

Variations in Basic Approach

The central difference between the two media campaigns was their differing view of the function or purpose of their spots. The Guggenheim ads stressed the candidate's human qualities. "Our material never said 'McGovern said, McGovern did, McGovern went'," Peter Vogt, vice president of Guggenheim Productions stated. "The viewer participated by natural observation and our objective was to recreate who this human being was."[7] Charles Guggenheim stated of his purpose: "You try to communicate those qualities which made you believe in and respect this man—and you try to do that within this arbitrary time period. That's the beginning and the end of it."[8]

The November Group ads focused not so much on human qualities as on accomplishments of the President. "Nixon is a known quantity," Peter Dailey stated, "His strengths and weaknesses are known. Our job is to amplify and to clarify and to remind people of the accomplishments of our President."[9] In their anti-McGovern ads, the November Group sought "to communicate a message and an idea and our Democrats for Nixon material makes the point in a direct way. Our defense spot is graphic because a lot of people can't comprehend numbers. With a sweep of a hand we can demonstrate the consequences of a vote for McGovern."[10]

Guggenheim's spot commercials were clearly identifiable. His technique was to film candidates talking informally with voters in natural settings. His camera became an eavesdropper on the conversations between a candidate and voters. Guggenheim's major goal was to reveal who this human being was, and he wanted to make the TV viewer an observer-participant in a natural and real communication act.

The November Group spots did not have an identifiable stamp because they were varied to fit the idea they wished to get accross. Some spots were filmed footage of Nixon's trips to Russia and China, with an announcer telling of Nixon's accomplishments. These spots took on the characteristics of a David Wolper documentary using stock footage and a voice overlay. Others were production spots, such as a picture of McGovern turning around while his contradictory stands were stated or one of a hand sweeping toy warships off a table.

Spot Length

The two campaigns had differing attitudes toward the time it took to convey their points effectively. Guggenheim took the position that 60-minute political programs were better than 30-minute programs and that 5-minute spot commercials were better than 1-minute commercials. Put simply, his view was that it took time to honestly allow the viewer to get to know a candidate. Guggenhiem did spots, not because he wanted to do them, but because reality demanded that political spots be made for available media time periods and 1-minute time periods have long been the most readily available.

In contrast, because of his background with television commercials, Bill Taylor of the November Group was at home dealing with short 1- and 5-minute intervals. He claimed many "half-hour things aren't valuable or necessary."[11] He thought short spots got the point across better than longer spots because "most half-hour stuff is just plain boring."[12] As an example he stated, "How long does it take to say to young people, 'Richard Nixon gave you the vote, stopped the draft, and is winding down the war'?"[13] Taylor believed a great deal could be said in a limited amount of time, and he was at home stating ideas within short time frames. His point is similar to one developed by another advertising man, Jim Callaway, when he said, "30 seconds is a long time. Remember it took only seven seconds for Lyndon Johnson to say, "I shall not seek nor will I accept my party's nomination to be your President.' Everybody understood [that] ... 30 seconds is plenty of time if you know your business."[14]

Production Spots

There were also differences of attitude in the two camps toward what constituted the type of ad that best presented what needed to be communicated. For example, Guggenheim and the November Group had widely differing views toward production-spot commercials.

Guggenheim preferred not to make production spots. He stressed "real spots" because "there is a value involved. We feel it's honest and it's decent, and it's real and it's believable."[15] Taylor, on the other hand, was very much at home with production spots. For him creating ideas and then translating them into film and tape was his stock in trade. He stressed that an ad should convey an idea that swiftly and memorably informs a viewer about a candidate.

Guggenheim held that production spots bring "attention not to the candidate but to the image makers."[16] A production spot "is antithetical to a candidate coming across,"[17] and thus brings attention not to the candidate but to the medium or to the particular ad. Guggenheim preferred to use television as a medium of conveyance—an unobtrusive medium to bring the candidate to the voters. Taylor was less candidate-oriented and more idea-oriented. He liked production spots because they could be used to bring an idea to the viewer.

Final McGovern Ads

Late in the campaign Guggenheim produced a series of crawl commercials—words rolling on the screen as a voice read the words. These were "production" spots in that they deviated from his hallmark of film of real-life situations. They were motivated by the desire of the McGovern camp to make Richard Nixon more of an issue.

Guggenheim's work with McGovern had begun in 1962, he knew the candidate well, and McGovern and Guggenheim had established a relationship of trust and respect. Through the primary campaigns of 1972, as other candidates and media specialists were falling by the wayside, Guggenheim's work was consistent and generally well received.

However, when McGovern's general election campaign failed to catch on, all sorts of pressures for change were brought to bear. Larry O'Brien especially counseled for stronger and more negative spots to make Richard Nixon and his record more of an issue.

Guggenheim was called upon to make some negative spots but was not enthusiastic. His assistant stated "We are generally suspicious of negative spots. We have done them and in the Brown-Reagan campaign our anti-Reagan spots backfired. We believe in advocacy. Let someone else do the name calling. We don't want the campaign to degenerate into a pissing match."[18]

Although Guggenheim chose not to make spots that strongly attacked Nixon, one member of the November Group thought this was a crucial error. "I think he (Guggenheim) should have attacked from the outset and should have kept attacking," William Novelli stated. "Whenever Mr. Guggenheim was cited in the press as saying 'I think I'll never run a negative commercial,' I began to feel good about the campaign."[19]

Instead of blatant negative spots, Guggenheim developed subtle spots using a crawl technique. A commentator repeated words such as:

> Alfred C. Baldwin, a former FBI Agent, has stated this. He was hired by James McCord, Security Chief for both the Republican National Committee and the Nixon Campaign Committee. Mr. Baldwin was assigned to listen illegally to over 200 private telephone conversations—calls made by Democratic Chairman Lawrence O'Brien and others from tapped telephones in Democratic Headquarters at the Watergate. He sent reports on these conversations to William E. Tiemans, Assistant to President Nixon for Congressional Relations, at the White House.
>
> In 1968 Mr. Nixon said: "The President's chief function is to lead, not to oversee every detail but to put the right people in charge, provide them with basic guidance, and let them do the job."
>
> This message has been brought to you by the McGovern for President Committee.[20]

Guggenheim used the crawl technique because it was easy to produce and little used on television, but more importantly he used it because he thought the crawl was "clean, factual, and non-emotional."[21] He thus rationalized the crawl technique, even though production spots were not compatible with his philosophy. The drawback to the crawl technique was that it didn't have the visual reinforcement needed for television. Crawls were little used on television because, except as an appeal for money at the end of McGovern's half-hour televised speeches, they were generally ineffective.

This ineffectiveness created additional pressure for change in the McGovern camp. John Stewart, Director of Communications for the Democratic National Committee stated, "the crawl spots weren't any good; they gave you too much information. Charles [Guggenheim] misunderstood how spots work. With the crawl spots you would have to literally take notes to come away with what he wanted."[22] He went on to say,

> Guggenheim doesn't like spot commercials. As a result he makes very poor spot commercials. Due to Charles' idea that spots be honest and not cooked up, he presents them as simply and as honestly as one could present them. But nobody even talked about them. They were almost without comment, which is extraordinary in a presidential campaign. They were totally inoffensive. They didn't even get people mad. They didn't turn people on. They didn't turn people off. They just didn't do anything. They went right on by you.[23]

As a result of the pressure for more effective spots late in the campaign, Tony Schwartz, creator of the daisy girl anti-Goldwater commercial of 1964, was contacted to make some last-minute spots. He made five, only two of which were approved by McGovern to be aired. Those two commercials—a voting booth spot and a corruption spot—were only aired twice, and their effectiveness was restricted by the lateness of the campaign and their limited showing.

Final Nixon Ads

Pressures were also present in the Nixon camp, but outsiders weren't aware of them. By late August the November Group had created 27 pro-Nixon spots; by early October they produced three anti-McGovern spots. Although the public saw several five-minute spots on China and Russia, few of the other pro-Nixon spots were shown. A White House decision was made to show the three anti-McGovern spots more frequently, and toward the end of the campaign, as McGovern became the issue, these three ads were shown almost exclusively. Bill Taylor thought the decision unfortunate but realistic. He was proud of his pro-Nixon spots and thought they showed a dimension of the President the public should see.

DISCUSSION

Bill Taylor reflected on the approaches used by the November Group and Guggenheim:

> People vote for strength. Our ads showed how the President operates. The way Guggenheim did it wasn't effective. His ads had

McGovern all over the place. There were too many issues and the
candidate didn't have any answers. Take his ad on the unemployed.
And those 16 employed people are going to be unimpressed with
what McGovern says. Voters think of the nation and themselves not
other people.[24]

In the November Group ads the viewer got "the feeling of a
man in obvious control of the situation who can handle the affairs
of this country with great dignity,"[25] Peter Dailey stated.

With the Guggenheim ads the viewer saw a compassionate
candidate who listened to and communicated with voters but who
didn't have answers—or answers acceptable to the majority of
voters. "What you saw was what was there," Peter Vogt stated,
"and because McGovern was honest and open the viewer got what
he deserved."[26] But Guggenheim was able to capture the essential
human essence of his candidate and as one reporter stated,
"McGovern may be the first presidential campaigner who is more
real on television than he is in person."[27]

The political ads used by Nixon and McGovern were but one
of many influences on the outcome of the campaign. The contrasts in their political ads reflected differing philosophies toward
political commercials—differences that were evident in the type of
ads the public saw during the 1972 campaign.

NOTES

1. Ray Hiebert et al., ed., *The Political Image Merchants* (Washington,
   D.C.: Acropolis, 1971); Gene Wyckoff, *The Image Candidates* (New
   York: Macmillan, 1968); Joe McGinniss, *The Selling of the President,
   1968* (New York: Trident Press, 1969); Joseph Napolitan, *The Election
   Game* (New York: Doubleday, 1972); Robert MacNeil, *The People
   Machine* (New York: Harper & Row, 1968); Sig Mickelson, *The Electric
   Mirror* (New York: Dodd, Mead, 1972); Dan Nimmo, *The Political Per-
   suaders* (Englewood Cliffs, N.J.: Prentice-Hall, 1970).

2. Sidney Kraus, ed., *The Great Debates* (Bloomington, Indiana: Indiana
   University Press, 1962), pp. 256–260; Theodore H. White, *The Making
   of the President, 1960* (New York: Atheneum, 1961), p. 294.

3. Theodore H. White, *The Making of the President, 1964* (New York:
   Atheneum, 1965), p. 322.

4. Frederic Papert, "Good Candidates Make Advertising Experts" in Ray
   Hiebert et al., eds., *The Political Image Merchants* (Washington, D.C.:
   Acropolis, 1971), p. 97.

5. Christopher Lyndon, "TV Political Advertising Loses Magic," *New York Times* (November 5, 1970), p. 26.

6. Allan D. Gardner, "Sick Transeunt Media," *Politeia* I:11 (Summer 1972).

7. Interview with Peter Vogt, Vice President and Production Manager of Guggenheim Productions, Washington, D.C., November 11, 1972.

8. Victor S. Navasky, "The Making of the Candidate," *New York Times Magazine* (May 7, 1972), p. 79.

9. Interview with Peter Dailey, Media Director of the November Group, Washington, D.C., October 16, 1972.

10. Ibid.

11. Interview with Bill Taylor, Creative Director of the November Group, New York, N.Y., November 10, 1972.

12. Ibid.

13. Ibid.

14. Jim Callaway, "Let's Cut the Baloney about Political Advertising," *Politea* I:37 (Summer 1972).

15. Interview with Nancy Sloss, Time Buyer for Guggenheim Productions, Washington, D.C., October 11, 1972.

16. Vogt interview.

17. Ibid.

18. Ibid.

19. Statement by William Novelli, Consultant to November Group at Conference on Political Communication, University of Maryland, November 18, 1972, audio transcript.

20. Audio transcript of Guggenheim spot.

21. Vogt interview.

22. Interview with John Stewart, Director of Communications for the Democratic National Committee, Washington, D.C., November 16, 1972.

23. Ibid.

24. Taylor interview.

25. H. D. S. Greenway, "Nixon's T.V. Campaign: The Chief Executive on the Job," *Washington Post* (October 9, 1972), p. A2.

26. Vogt interview.

27. William Greider, "McGovern T.V. Ads: Picture of a Moderate," *Washington Post* (October 1, 1972), p. A3.

—18—

THE INSIDE OF THE OUTSIDE

Tony Schwartz

It has become popular to speak of political candidates as products which can be sold like soap, or formless creatures who need an "image" created for them by media specialists. Image-makers concern themselves with makeup, lighting, camera angles, wardrobe, visual backgrounds, etc. or how a candidate *looks* to a viewer. His outside appearance constitutes his "image." But this represents a serious misunderstanding of how television functions in relation to our senses.

The image-makers follow a classic pattern of using an older medium (film) as the content of a new medium (TV). We've witnessed this process many times. Telephone communication is filled with movies. Records are filled with performance, and radio is filled with records. However, the physical and structural characteristics of media exert greater evolutionary control over our ideas and institutions than the content we receive from them. Media extend our senses into the world about us and structure our ways of learning, understanding and communicating. Also, the introduction of a new medium may upset our sensory balance, thereby creating a new awareness of the world and new modes of behavior. It is futile to employ television and radio in a political campaign as an extension of print or film. Television and radio are received differently from film or print. Our senses expect electronically mediated information to be organized in a particular way, and our brain applies different patterns in making sense of this data.

The image people work with concepts like "charismatic," "handsome," "youthful," etc. And they strive to keep their candidate *moving*–through shopping centers, old age homes, schools, etc. They utilize visual information on television to communicate this image. Television is thus conceptualized as a vehicle for bringing the voters to the candidate, where they can see and experience his glorious image.

I believe it is far more important to understand and affect the inner feeling of a voter in relation to a political candidate, than to package an image which voters tend not to believe anyway. It would be more correct to say that the goal of a media advisor is to tie up the voter and deliver him to the candidate. So it is really the voter who is packaged by media, not the candidate. The voter is surrounded by media and dependent on it in his every day life functioning. The stimuli a candidate uses on the media thus surround the voter. It is part of his environment, his packaging.

UNDERSTANDING ELECTRONIC MEDIA

In assessing the reactions of voters to candidates on television, it becomes very clear that a person sitting in his home watching a political figure on his TV set four or five feet away wants to feel that the candidate is talking to him. A politician who typically speaks to large audiences, in a grandiose style, must adjust his speech scale for television or radio. Though he may be part of an audience totaling 10 or 20 million people, a TV viewer experiences the candidate as someone speaking in his home to one, two, or maybe five people gathered around the set.

Any situation in which a politician is filmed may potentially find its way to the television viewer or the radio listener. Thus, a politician on the street, shouting over the volume of traffic to 50 or 100 people, must understand that a home audience of 2 or 3 million listening to him that evening will be put off by his shouting. The home viewer's ear is, in effect, only four or five feet away from the politician's mouth. And there are no diesel trucks or air hammers in his living room.

When I work with a candidate, I encourage him to speak to small groups or single individuals on walking tours, so the personal quality of his voice will fulfill the expectations of a single person or small group listening to him on TV. And when I record a candidate for radio or TV spots, I sit next to him and ask him to talk to me, not the microphone. If he sounds like he's reading from a script or begins talking to the mike, I'll interrupt and say, "You know, I don't feel you're talking to me." Many politicians in a recording situation will talk either to an imaginary vast audience spread across a wide geographic area, or, "on behalf of themselves," i.e., as if their position had been challenged by a reporter and they were defending it. A home listener is not interested in a politician who formally expresses a position. To the average voter, "expressing a position talk" is what government officials do when they want to cover up something. A voter wants the candidate to talk *to* him, not *at* him; to use the medium not as a large public address system, but rather as a private *undress* system. Further, many politicians tend to organize their thoughts for a home listener the way they might for a group of lawyers. But the logic of the position they try to develop fails to impress the typical voter who has one thought in the back of his mind whenever he listens to a politician, "how do I feel about him?"

Traditionally, successful politicians are usually quite effective in tuning their speech for a face-to-face audience. They learn to interpret very subtle feedback from a crowd and adjust their style to maximize the impact. However, when they have to speak to a radio or TV home audience (non face-to-face), they often give a mechanical rendering of their feelings. Rather than adjust for a more intimate relation to the listener, they project for a larger audience.

When a politician is both speaking to a large face-to-face audience and being broadcast on radio, it would be wise to insure that his talk is properly framed for the home listeners who may number millions. Simultaneously, he must affect the large public audience and the private home listener.

There are two possible solutions to this problem. The first solution is not yet possible in the U.S., but it is used by Russian politicians. The largest convention hall in Moscow has several thousand seats. Each seat is equipped with its own speaker. Thus, a politician addressing a large public audience in the convention hall, while simultaneously speaking on radio or TV, can speak as if he were in the personal space zone of each listener. The convention hall listener and the home listener have approximately the same distance relation to the speaker. Any comparable American convention hall utilizes several large speakers to amplify a voice, not individual speakers at each seat. Thus, someone sitting in the audience may be twenty, thirty or a hundred feet from a source of amplified sound, while the home listener is only three or four feet from the speaker's mouth.

A practical solution to this problem for an American politician is to address the large public audience the way he normally would, and use an announcer to properly "frame" his speech for the home listener. At the beginning, end, and appropriate times during the speech, an announcer can remind the home listener, "we are listening to Senator Jones address the United Auto Workers Convention." In this way, the home listener changes his expectations of the candidate. Senator Jones is no longer talking to him. Rather, he is overhearing Senator Jones speak to the convention. Proper framing of the candidate is absolutely essential when a small piece of a public address is to be extracted for use in a political spot. Unless the home listener is told that the candidate was speaking to a large crowd when this segment was recorded, he will think the candidate is shouting at him. One example of misframing I remember, occurred in a spot for the late Adlai Stevenson. The commercial opened with the announcer's voice, "Adlai Stevenson will now speak to you about his views on foreign aid." This was followed by a recorded segment of Stevenson speaking to a huge crowd.

To some degree, a candidate frames his own speech. He tells us that he regards the listener as a member of a large audience in a phrase such as, "My fellow Americans across this great land of ours . . ." Or he frames a personal, one to one relation in a phrase such as, "Good evening, I appreciate the opportunity to come into your home tonight." Of course, tone of voice can support or contradict either of these frames.

It is much more important for a voter to feel the candidate than to see him. Despite all myths to the contrary, a candidate's physical appearance alone does not win him many votes. But looks can lose votes. Generally, candidates tend to *look* dishonest, but *sound* honest. This visual handicap is magnified by the fact that most situations where a voter is likely to see the candidate are detrimental to his visual presentation of self. Television in particular is very difficult to structure for effective visual communication of a candidate. The candidate usually has no feeling of who is looking at him; he doesn't know which camera is on; and the lighting typically puts him in a spotlight situation, not an interpersonal encounter. For these and other reasons, I tend to use the candidate much more on radio than television.

TASK-ORIENTATION

It's often argued that TV "wears out" a candidate. This is generally true, but only because most political advisers use an "advertising" or "campaign" approach in creating and running TV spots. They make only a few commercials, weeks or months in advance of showing them on TV, and run them over and over. Since the commercials are produced so far in advance, they can only touch on general problems, not specific issues of the day. And since the home public hears a candidate say the same irrelevant thing over and over, they get tired of him very quickly. A listener doesn't want to hear a candidate frozen on film saying the same thing. He expects the candidate to tell him something new all the time. And he feels, why can't the candidate speak to me live? Video tape, combined with a task-orientation approach, can satisfy the public's demand for a fresh candidate. Video tape commercials can be assembled in hours, instead of days, and a producer can create a number of spots on issues of immediate relevance, with minimal cost.

There are some themes and issues that may be central to an election period and, therefore, can be repeated. Such a commercial should be a work of art that grows with multiple viewings. This all but eliminates a simple "candidate talking" format. In its place, a symbolic approach counterpointing auditory and visual information is more likely to stand up. If a voter is going to see the commercial several times, he should be able to get more into it and more out of it each time he experiences it.

Candidate "wear out" can take two forms: saturation wear out from too much exposure of the candidate, as discussed above; and fuse blow out. Mario Procacino, a candidate for mayor of New York City a while ago, blew out the receptivity fuses of people listening to him on radio, or listening and viewing on television. He was hotter than our personal media fuses could take. Every appearance on TV was like a performance at Madison Square Garden before 20,000 people without a microphone. He should be advised to run for mayor of Havana—where people generally watch TV in public, some distance from the set.

A candidate's announcement that he is running for office presents a special media problem. The broadcaster may cut a twenty minute speech to one minute for the evening news. His message is not only cut to 5% of its original length, it is edited by someone who does not have the candidate's interests in mind. It makes sense, therefore, to use a forty-five to fifty second speech when announcing one's candidacy. This way the speech will be covered in its entirety on the evening news. And the candidate, not the media, will be structuring how his position is presented to the public. Too, it recognizes the importance of electronic media. The home audience will no longer be given secondary status behind the live public audience. At the same time, people actually in the audience need not be disappointed by his short speech. A new format can be developed for such occasions in which famous personalities and other politicians can supplement the program, with the candidate topping the bill.

Another interesting media problem is the disclaimer at the end of political spots. All political commercials are required to have a legal label at the end, stating who paid for the message. Naturally, there is a conflict, or separation, between the candidate's interest in communicating an effective political message, and the government's requirement of a label. The intent of the disclaimer is to frame the spot as a paid, partisan message. The problem for a media specialist is to minimize the negative effects of the label (from the candidate's point of view) without violating the law. A solution I have employed for some time is to integrate the label as part of the spot, rather than let it stand as a tag pasted on at the end. The name of the committee which pays for the spot is arbitrary. However, the official title must be exactly duplicated in the disclaimer.

Some people might use *Committee for the Election of Senator Jones* or *Senator Jones Campaign Committee.* I've used the title, *A Lot of People Who Want Bob Jones in the Senate.* This legal committee title can then be integrated into the commercial by a phrase such as, "And that's why this message was brought to you by . . ."

See how the two versions might affect you:

A) Political spot ends . . .
    Announcer: "Paid for by the Senator Jones Campaign Committee."

B) Political spot ends . . .
    Announcer: "And that's exactly why this message was brought to you by a lot of people who want Bob Jones in the Senate."

The second version implies that any Jones supporter "puts his money where his mouth is!"

The San Francisco Alioto campaign illustrates a very important principle in media campaigning. In the early part of the campaign, we emphasized Alioto's personal feelings about a wide range of social problems. These were very low keyed spots designed to show voters that he was a man of deep feelings. Later in the campaign, our spots become highly competitive: counterpointing Alioto's specific stand on an issue with other candidates; building up his record, and attacking the record of other candidates; and asking the voter to support him. We tried to give the voter concrete reasons why he should vote for Alioto, and motivate him to perform a specific act of behavior . . . pulling the Alioto lever in the voting booth. This same kind of commercial would have been all wrong at the beginning of the campaign. If we tell someone why he should vote for a candidate and ask him to do so, seven or eight weeks before the election, we are asking him to perform the impossible. He can't vote until election day. It's like a midnight commercial on the Johnny Carson show which instructs us to "run right down" to the corner drugstore for some aspirin.

In the early part of a campaign we simply want the voter to think about the candidate and the issues. As the campaign proceeds, we can focus on specifics—why someone should support the candidate or why a given problem is important to the voter. Only in the last weeks should we ask voters to come out for the "one day sale." In this way we don't create frustration in a potential voter.

RESONANCE IN POLITICAL ADVERTISING

People tend to read ads for products they already own. The function of political advertising then, may be characterized as organizing or confirming the feelings of two groups who already own (or believe in) many of the products (approaches to solving social problems) a candidate is selling. The first group is the campaign workers and people who are planning to vote for the candidate. Their attitudes can be reinforced by political advertising. The second group consists of those people who share certain of the candidate's feelings about social problems. Advertising can reveal the candidate's feelings to those who inherently share these beliefs. The realization of an identity between their feelings and the candidate's can provide a strong motivation to vote for the candidate. (We should not overlook the fact that a voter has *four* ways to vote—for or against either of two candidates.)

It's very hard to change fixed beliefs. Hence, political advertising is not likely to change strongly held attitudes or convince a conservative Republican to vote for a liberal Democrat. However, most political decisions result from an interaction of many feelings and beliefs, often covering a wide spectrum of social philosophies. For example, there are many people who express a generally negative political attitude about a candidate, but agree with many of the positions he expresses. One such individual might be someone who traditionally votes for party X but shares party Y's feelings that the economy can be strengthened. If you can evoke these feelings deeply, you may be able to change his overt voting behavior.

Television is an ideal medium for surfacing feelings voters already have, and giving these feelings a direction by providing stimuli which may evoke the desired behavior. The reportage commercial which shows a candidate moving about and talking to people is not very effective for this purpose. I believe television spots function well as moving posters for a candidate, i.e., create auditory and visual stimuli that can evoke a voter's deeply held feelings. Indeed, the best political commercials are similar to Rorschach patterns. They don't tell the viewer anything. They surface his feelings and provide a context for him to express these feelings.

The real question in political advertising is, *how to surround the voter with the proper auditory and visual stimuli to evoke the reaction you want from him, i.e., his voting for a specific candidate.*

A commercial I created for President Johnson in 1964 illustrates my point. The spot shows a little girl in a field counting petals on a daisy. As her count reaches ten, the visual motion is frozen and the viewer hears a countdown for an atomic blast. When the countdown reaches zero, we see a nuclear explosion and hear President Johnson say, "These are the stakes, to make a world in which all God's children can live, or to go into the darkness. Either we must love each other or we must die." As the screen goes to black at the end, an announcer says, "On November 3rd, vote for President Johnson."

The "Daisy" spot was shown only once, on *Monday Night at the Movies,* but it created a huge controversy. Many people, especially the Republicans, shouted that the spot accused Senator Goldwater of being trigger happy. *But nowhere in the spot is Goldwater mentioned.* There is not even an indirect reference to Goldwater. Indeed, someone viewing the spot today will not perceive any illusion at all to Goldwater. They why did it bring such a reaction in 1964? Well, Senator Goldwater had stated previously that he supported the use of tactical atomic weapons. This mistrust was not in the "Daisy" spot. It was in the people who viewed the commercial. The stimuli of the film and sound evoked these feelings and allowed people to express what they inherently believed.

Probably the smartest thing Goldwater could have done at this time was to agree with the attitude of the commercial and offer to help pay for running it. This would have undercut the sensational effect of it and possibly won him many votes.

Political advertising involves tuning in on the attitudes and beliefs of the voter and then affecting these attitudes with the proper auditory and visual stimuli. If our research shows that most people feel one Vice Presidential candidate is clearly superior, we don't have to hit them over the head with this information in order to make it work for us. We might simply list their names on a card and ask, "Who is your choice to be a heartbeat away from the Presidency?" In this way, you surface attitudes (held by many) in a way that can produce the desired effect. Commercials which attempt to *tell* the listener something are inherently not as effective as those which attach to something that is already in him. We are not focused on getting things across to people as much as *out* of people. Electronic media are particularly effective tools in this regard because they provide us with direct access to someone's mind.

PAID AND NON-PAID MEDIA

A major problem of political candidates is to structure the effects of non-paid media, such as news, word of mouth, editorials, etc. A candidate gets more free time than paid time in a campaign. In my work I try to use paid media (political spots) to put non-paid media in context. I do not see them as unrelated to each other. If there is a lot of news about the candidate, and you don't feel it is accurately framed by the newscaster, station or newspaper, you can put in a proper frame by use of paid media.

Let me cite an example outside political campaigning. Con Edison, a large Eastern power utility, is constantly receiving bad press because of power failures. However, the same people who hear this news have also heard, at other times, that Con Edison's repeated attempts to build new plants are constantly being rejected. Well, Con Edison could put those two pieces of news together in paid spots and thereby give the power failure a reason for happening . . . a proper context. Later, when a person hears of a new power failure, he is likely to associate it with news of plants being rejected. Paid media has taught him how to attach two pieces of information in his environment. Con Edison can in this way make an ally of the public, rather than an enemy.

Paid media can also be used to introduce new information into the environment, for recall later on. An incumbent can take a position on a given problem and use paid media to convey his stance to the public. Later, when running for reelection, he can recall this position in his advertising. He can use the public's earlier experience of him as support in his current campaign. Similarly, a non-office holder can use paid media before the campaign to communicate his position on a problem that is currently very important. He thus establishes himself as an authority on the problem or champion of a cause. This can be recalled later when he announces his candidacy.

Within a campaign, we can utilize people's experience by integrating early spots into later spots. For this reason, some of my commercials in a campaign are often a montage of the first ones. Usually I can evoke people's full experience of the earlier commercials by using bits and pieces from them, properly designed. This makes use of a principle of perception . . . that people most readily understand things they've seen and heard before. This also prevents the negative effects of hearing the same thing over and over again.

I also apply this principle in use of a candidate's name. It is a standard rule of mine that whenever a candidate's name appears in print, either in newspaper ad or as graphics in a TV spot, it should look exactly as it will in the voting booth. This includes both the formal name and the type face.

RESEARCH AS X-RAY

Most advertising research investigates whether people understand the message told by a commercial, and if they retain it. Good political research seeks out attitudes in the environment and then judges a political spot by the way it affects these attitudes. I was introduced to this approach by Joseph Napolitan, whom I regard as the best political campaign strategist in the world. Joe has taught me the value of task-orientation in political and product advertising. He never researches the commercials; instead, he researches only the problems and the effect of media on the problems. Commercials must enter a complex world of attitudes and behavior ending in sale. A political spot does the same and only has meaning to the extent it affects behavior at the voting end. There is no way you can test a commercial in isolation to see how it will function in the everyday world. A political spot is broadcast into an environment rich with interaction . . . people are talking to friends about a candidate, reading and watching news, listening to other candidates' spots, etc. This is where a commercial must function, not in a theatre testing environment. A person does not listen to a political spot in isolation and then decide who he'll support, based on this single input. Therefore, the commercials must function as part of the environment. They must interact with all the elements present in a person's environment and produce the desired behavioral effect. The people listening are actually part of the content of any commercial. Their feelings and beliefs interact with the commercial stimuli in creating any attitudinal changes. Viewers are not a target of communication, but actually a work force.

Curiously, while I've created thousands of spots for commercial products, advertising agency research never provided me with information I could use in designing a commercial. Napolitan's task-oriented research carefully analyzes a candidate's problems and identifies for me those problems which can best be solved through electronic media. It works as an X-ray for me. I'll then create a commercial for each specific problem. Most political advertising, especially agency spots, works on the "let's think of some good ideas for commercials" principle. However, we always use research as a rudder for creating commercials, and this produces very different results.

After knowing the specific problem we want to solve and understanding the environment our spot must function in, we can use media as stimuli, not content. This enables us to utilize our audience as a work force which our paid paid media affects, rather than as a target our paid media must hit.

The political poll is a way to measure attitudes and concerns of people in the environment. It can provide raw data that is valuable only to someone who can analyze it honestly and critically. As an X-ray, it is a great tool if it is read correctly. For instance, we often deal with an LOP factor—that is, a favorable response on a poll often means the candidate is the Least Objectionable Politician. "Politician" is a negative word and tends to group with others like "landlord," "tax collector," "meter maid," "salesman," etc., in the public's eye. If one accepts this view, the logical task of the media specialist is to make his candidate the least objectional politician in the race. Many Presidential campaigns have been organized with this specific task as the major goal.

Research also reveals that issues are relatively unimportant. As long as pollsters ask voters whether the economy, defense spending, or transportation deserves the most attention, we can only obtain a list of the relative importance among various issues. But if issue-oriented questions are mixed with inquiries about personal qualities of the candidates in a single poll question, the relative unimportance of issues is revealed in a startling way. The following is the result of a poll taken in 1969 and 1970 by Mike Rowan in several states.

Question: If you were to see a TV program about a candidate running for Governor, what would you like to know or feel about him?

Answers broke down this way:

That he is honest, a man of conviction 47%
That he is a hard worker 27%
That he is an understanding, compassionate man 14%
That he is a capable, qualified person 9%
That he is a good person, familistic, warm 7%
That he is a leader, bold 5%
That he is a bright, intelligent man 4%
That he is a man who perceives the vital issues 3%
No response 8%

No one should interpret this as meaning that people are not concerned about issues ... all our research reveals that people are *consumed* by issues. The point here is that when it comes time to choose the person to be elected, voters are looking for the man best capable of dealing with the issues. Most of the problems he'll face in office don't arise until after the election. Issues in the campaign are typically a list of past problems. So it is personal qualities, like honesty or integrity, which tell a voter whether the candidate will be able to handle problems when they arise in the future. Understanding this, the task of a media specialist is not to reveal a candidate's stand on issues, so much as to help communicate those personal qualities of a candidate which are likely to win votes.

The campaign slogan—a carry-over of print's historical role in political campaigns—has little relevance in task-oriented political advertising. Print fostered a long range "program" approach to campaigning. The time lead needed in organizing, producing and distributing printed materials, e.g., pamphlets, billboard ads, posters, etc., required a great deal of guess work about the problems that would emerge during the campaign. The slogan was an attempt to focus on a central, overriding issue that would serve as a theme for the entire campaign.

The task-oriented use of electronic media enables the candidate to deal with campaign problems on a fire-fighting basis—to tune media to needs (feedback), to go deep rather than broad. On a given day people may feel that the candidate is anti-labor (e.g., the day after the president of the United Auto Workers attacked him in a speech), or that car safety is the most important issue facing the county (e.g., the day after G.M. announces it is recalling one million cars to correct defects). The long range "program" campaign cannot deal with these specific problems that arise on a day-to-day basis. A task-oriented campaign can create overnight a commercial which relates to a problem that has just arisen. For example, I received a call one afternoon from Napolitan in Massachusetts. A problem had just come up and he wanted a spot to handle it immediately. I designed a commercial, called an announcer in Los Angeles, who had the recorded material on a plane to me in hours, edited the material and made several copies that evening, and it was on the air the following morning. The quicker we respond to a problem, the greater are our chances of achieving a desired effect. Too, this utilizes a principle McLuhan described to me some time ago: "Instant information creates involvement in depth."

Also, a task-oriented approach to buying radio and TV time allows us to reach the specific audience for whom a spot will be most relevant. This involves a careful analysis of the people who listen to radio or watch television at various times. Time buying in most advertising agencies is detached. They purchase air time for a

candidate's media the same way regular product time is bought
... on a bargain basis. Packages of air time are purchased with
little or no thought given as to which people may be reached by a
specific political spot.

Time buys should be tuned to specific problems. The first time
I worked with Ruth Jones, an independent time buyer who has
worked on some of our campaigns, I was delightfully shocked
when she asked to hear the spots before she bought air time for
them. It may seem terribly obvious that a time buyer should do
this, but in all my years of creating commercials for products, no
agency time buyer ever discussed the commercials with me to
determine how we could best reach those people the spot would
affect.

There are a host of considerations in time buying. An afternoon radio program with light music will attract more older
people than a late night rock program, and is therefore a better
environment for placing a spot about social security. However, we
can buy time with a good deal more sophistication than simply
correlating the demographic characteristics of a program's audience with the subject matter in a given spot. We can pinpoint the
hours when people are driving to and from work in their cars (and
the programs drivers listen to most), and affect them with the
sound they sit in. These spots can be designed for car listening.
The physical characteristics of sound can be equalized to maximize their impact in a car environment. Similarly, we can alter the
characteristics of a spot if we know it will be heard by people
primarily in kitchens, or living rooms, or outdoors, or any other
environment. I designed commercials in a Gubernatorial race specifically for beach listening. The spots were played on Labor Day
weekend during the afternoon. We knew that seventy percent of
the people listening to radio at this time would be at the beach.

Task-oriented time buying also permits us to match or count-
erpoint the mood of the commercial with the mood of the person
listening to our spot. For example, the mood of a person listening
to radio in the morning *versus* afternoon *versus* evening will be
quite different. Radio and television serve different functions at
different times of the day. A person may use radio to cheer him
up in the morning, to provide company in the afternoon, and to
tranquilize him late at night. The design of a political spot should
relate to the way it will be used in a person's life. For example, if
we were in a person's home at these times of day, we would alter

the way we speak to him, in order to heighten the effect of what we say. A political spot should function in the same way. It should speak to a person in a way that reaches him.

MUNICATION AND COMMUNICATION

It is generally recognized that the near instantaneous speed of electronic communication has greatly increased the flow of information to the public. Nonpaid media such as news and paid political media are disseminated to a vast audience, at great speed, and with extraordinary efficiency. However, the flow is essentially in one direction. The public cannot easily feed back their opinions, suggestions, and objections. The President can at any moment reach the entire nation via television. But a member of the public cannot reach him, except through an inefficient letter or a vote once every four years. This is not a healthy situation for a "participatory democracy."

Rather than condemn electronic media as a corrupting force in politics (a futile, as well as incorrect position), I suggest that we have not even begun to explore the potential of electronic media in creating two-way political communication. The two-way potential of cable networks, and the current availability of telephone as a feedback line to radio or TV, establishes a realistic basis for town meetings that include an entire city, state, or even the nation. Similarly, we can use two-way cable or the telephone to instantly poll vast segments of the population on important problems.

Electronic communication does not signal the end of democracy. Rather it offers the potential of genuine democracy in a nation of two hundred million people.

PART FIVE

CAMPAIGN ETHICS
AND REFORM IN
THE NEW-STYLE ERA

Ethical considerations in the new campaigning have been transformed in recent years from concern by some critics over possible manipulation by computers, misuse of polls, and distortion in advertising to a more basic concern over how persons and groups gain access to, and operate within, the American election system. In earlier periods of the new campaigning, there was a latent feeling that the shift to newer forms of organization and techniques, particularly broadcasting, was making campaigning so expensive that access to office was limited to the privileged.[1] Recent elections, which have demonstrated the overwhelming financial superiority one candidate can have over another, and a related domination of the airwaves by contestants, seem to have made these concerns manifest. It began with the adoption of the first new national-campaign reform legislation in nearly a half-century. Then, in its first run came the events known as Watergate, including illegal campaign activities, illegal contributions, violations of campaign spending laws, systematic misuse of technology, use of funds in a manner that suggested influence peddling, and virtually no change in the inequities that the first legislation was to remedy.

A feeling of outrage over improper electioneering was sufficiently widespread to engender a longlasting wave of reform of the election process.

At the root of these reform issues is the new style of campaigning. As the party has given way to the personal organization, consultants, polls, computer usage, broadcasting, and other advertising, money has become the key to unlocking the tools of the modern campaign. To be sure, money is a resource that tends to cumulate with other key resources such as partisan support, volunteers, personal notoriety, group support, and key-issue positions, but to move from this base to widespread public support requires the ability to gain access to the channels where the public is likely to be—and it is no longer at torchlight parades, rallies, and behind campaign trains. Reaching the channels of access is less likely to be through ongoing political parties, but rather through direct acquisition of expertise, technology, and the means of communication. Indeed, there are some who believe that "technocracy," including campaign technology, has already begun the displacement of party as a meaningful alternative in elections.[2] It is not that these new techniques and approaches have brought on illegal campaigning for the first time. The smear, the fake letter, the political spy, the distorted fact, the theft of documents, the sabotage of an opponent's campaign, and the malicious prank date back to the earliest campaigns.[3] It is that the newer ways of competing for office without heavy reliance on the ongoing and representative party and its more seasoned politicians have created what are considered to be inequities and unfair modes of using the electoral system. These threaten the system of elections and thus there is public concern for preserving that system through reform.

Of major concern in the new campaign reform era are: the ethical use of polls, computers, and advertising; unfair campaigning and in particular—illegal use of intelligence; equal access to broadcasts; and finance reform, including reporting, disclosure, spending limits, and public financing of campaigns.

POLLS, COMPUTERS, AND ADVERTISING

The use of private polls and the influence of public polls have come under criticism from time to time as unwise political practices and unfair public information. Most criticism centers around the use of private polls by candidates to discern issues or over various effects of publicly reported polls, such as the leaking of private polls or other political effects of published polls.

A popular complaint of polls is that candidates use them to discern those issues uppermost in the minds of citizens and then use these issues in parrot-like fashion as the basis of their campaign, changing their positions to conform to public wishes. While this undoubtedly occurs from time to time, it is rarely to the identification of the two or three issues on most people's minds that polls look, but rather, to much deeper information such as to which groups are the key issues they already know about most important. The evidence of politicians' reversing their positions after a poll finding is rare. When critics cite these instances, they tend to forget that some politicians often read the polls as hostile to their views and maintain their views in spite of the poll results. Moreover, critics tend to forget that a politician's view and a constituent's often can be similar, or that other courses are open, such as persuading the public to the candidate's point of view or ignoring the issue. In other words, there is no formula whereby a politician reads a poll and automatically adopts an issue position.

Moreover, pollsters and others have argued that every politician tries to be representative by discerning opinion, and polling is the most scientific and accurate way of doing this. Since politicians respond to unscientifically discerned pressures, what is wrong with responding to accurately sampled pressures? Politicians should have the same right as other persons to find out what people think of them and which of their accomplishments are known and which are not. Nevada Senator Howard Cannon found in a campaign poll that Nevadans did not particularly regard aviation or air travel, an issue that he regarded as important, as important to their state. Using his position in the Congress as a recognized aviation leader, he launched a campaign to demonstrate the importance of the aircraft industry and air travel to his constituents. While some may feel such poll following is unwise and even should be regulated, any move to curtail a politician's freedom to poll election preferences will inevitably curtail his right, or any citizen's right, to investigate the public temper on any issue, from the taste of toothpaste to key issues.[4]

A more serious concern is the leaking of distorted poll results for the purposes of political advantage. One of the most famous such cases occurred on the eve of President Johnson's withdrawal from the 1968 race. Pollster Archibald Crossley was hired by an anonymous client to conduct a survey of preferences in three large industrial states and a few interviews in a single county of New Hampshire that is ordinarily four to seven points more Democratic than the state. The study showed Johnson behind Nixon by one percentage point but ahead of other Republicans. Contrary to the agreement with the pollster, the results were leaked to the Drew Pearson (now Jack Anderson) column, which reported they "proved that Johnson was ahead of Republicans in New York and Pennsylvania and leading them in an unnamed 'bell-weather' county in New Hampshire." There have been a number of other cases where polls have been similarly distorted or leaked to gain political advantage, and as in this case, rarely are the samples, methods, locations, or other relevant information fully disclosed.

The main reason why there is concern over the public exposure of poll data relates to their political effects. News-coverage attention is said to follow a candidate's standing in the polls, with the largest travelling news corps following the candidates with the largest poll tallies. The McGovern forces complained that they were not taken seriously early in the campaign by the news media because of their low standing in the national polls, even though they were gaining momentum through other demonstratable means, such as funds raised, organizational strength, and delegate counts. Polls also can have an effect on major contributors, inasmuch as many want to put their "smart money" only on those who have a chance to win. Thus, in Presidential races, the published polls can be important inside campaign weapons, and, in other campaigns, it often becomes important for the candidate to show major contributors a private poll demonstrating either that the candidate can win or that he is gaining on his opponent. Polls even have a form of legal standing, since Secret Service protection to Presidential aspirants is provided on the basis of a certain minimum standing in the public polls. But the most important political concern is over whether or not polls can be used to have a bandwagon effect, swaying party convention delegates and voters to go along with who is ahead and looks like a likely winner. Candidates frequently do use polls as campaign bandwagon weapons: they advertise their lead in the polls or their standing as the only contender of their party who demonstrates in trial heats that they can defeat the opposition party's candidate or they demonstrate that, contrary to the published poll or the opponent's poll, their own private poll shows that the race is very close. The obvious intent in all cases is to use the poll as an indicator of electability from which other campaign resources, including electoral support, will follow. The relative success of using polls to increase political support is still open to question, with the conflicting evidence that this technique has some effect,[5] little effect,[6] or a reverse effect, that is, it leads voters to support the underdog or trailing candidate.[7]

The reason why there is so much concern over the use and misuse of polls is that most members of the public have little knowledge of good and bad polling and the news media who report their results and findings have taken little effort to sift out competent and incompetent polls and pollsters. Leo Bogart has stated the issue very well:

> Agitation to have polls investigated generally starts from the premise that there are terrible secrets to be uncovered, when in fact the pollsters' perennial problems of theory, method, and technique are familiar to their own fraternity and can be communicated to others with little difficulty. Incompetence and bias in polling characteristically are encountered outside the ranks of the survey research profession, which can only enforce its code of ethics within its own membership. The troubles with the public polls are essentially the troubles with the news media, which too often cannot distinguish between good and bad surveys, which interpret or on occasion misinterpret them, which give them prominence and invest their findings with oracular portent. But any investigation of press handling of the polls would merely uncover evidence of the larger and more significant ineptitude or disinterest with which the media too often report expert findings in the domain of social science.[8]

Attempts at regulation of polling have centered around these issues. Representative Lucian Nedzi of Michigan has for some years unsuccessfully sponsored a Truth-in-Polling Act, which would require news media reporting standards that include: (1) identity of the survey's sponsors; (2) a description of the sample, its size, and percentage of refusals; (3) an indication of the allowance that should be made for sample error; (4) a report on which results are based on a subcategory or low response portion of the sample; (5) a statement of technique (i.e., interviews conducted in person, by telephone, by mail questionnaire, or on street corners); and (6) a statement on the timing of interviews, putting them in context with relevant events.[9] These proposed regulations are similar to the code of ethics in existence for organized professional pollsters.

Critics of the new campaigning have also argued that it is manipulative, especially in its use of polls and computers. The charges usually leveled are that, in what is defended as "rational campaign planning," political consultants use machines to prey on an unsuspecting electorate to find out what the voters want, and consultants then tailor their candidate to voter wishes. Meanwhile, they paint the opponent as something less than what the polls tell them is a desirable candidate. Campaign decision making is based on computer output rather than on perception of human needs, it is charged; machines are used to replace personal contact while creating the impression that they are every bit as personal. James Perry claims that such attempts to machine-manipulate voters are unethical:

> If they so desire, these new managers—acting rationally from their point of view all the while—can play upon the voters like virtuosos. They can push a pedal here, strike a chord there. And, presumably they can get precisely the response they seek. . . . In Michigan five good Democratic congressmen were turned out of office by five faceless Republicans, thanks to superior techniques. Robert Griffin, a conservative, was made to appear a moderate. And G. Mennen Williams was pushed by the new technology far to the left of where he actually stood. From a Republican management point of view, it was all quite rational. . . . In Arkansas surely it was rational to gull thousands of voters with computer-printed "personal" letters from Winthrop Rockefeller.[10]

These charges have formed the not-so-subtle storyline of political novels. Among them are *The Golden Kazoo* by John Schneider, in which a "perfect candidate" is selected and handled by an advertising firm, and *The 480* by Eugene Burdick, about a Presidential candidate whose issue positions and personal style are established by computer.

Consultants often claim that their formula for assisting candidates is simply a more efficient management of a serious political enterprise. They claim that what they are really doing is making the old politics—scheduling, canvassing, literature distribution, communicating with voters, and getting-out-the-vote—more systematic. Their claim is similar to those who advocate economy and efficiency in business and government. They merely offer efficient means of deciding how much time a candidate should spend in a given area, what the predispositions of voters are, and how particular messages can be communicated in a cost-effective fashion. Voters are not manipulated by the computer, they claim: the same information stored in the precinct captain's memory or card file is simply stored more accurately on computer tape.

Nor do political consultants particularly accept the notion that the machine dehumanizes politics. What machines do, in the era of large constituencies and ineffective parties, is make it possible to keep records and perform routine chores that volunteers once performed. Rather than keeping volunteers in campaign headquarters stuffing envelopes, the organization can free them for more meaningful and rewarding tasks. Recent candidate efforts to use volunteers to make personal contacts with voters have been made possible by the assistance of the computer with record keeping and list making, but the inputs have been supplied by people and the outputs tend to be people-assisting devices.

Perhaps the most long-standing attack on the new techniques of campaigning has come from those critics both inside and outside the advertising field who oppose the use of advertising techniques. Critics of mass-media campaigning argue that as the advertising men have taken over the business of formulating images, the true nature of the candidate and the issues he stands for are lost in the fine points of production and technique. As Stanley Kelley, Jr., has charged, "public relations men too often use the techniques of mass communication, potentially so powerful as methods for spreading knowledge, to destroy character, to deceive, and to distort." Kelley argues that in modern campaigns the admen use an important process in a democracy—discussion—for evil purposes.[11] The most serious deception and distortion comes, to most critics, from the adaptation of advertising techniques in short advertising formats, such as in display themes and radio and television spots. To advertising executives like John E. O'Toole of Foote, Cone and Belding, spots of less than five minutes are inappropriate for presenting a candidate to a voter and they open the door to Madison Avenue image-maker approaches symbolized by one-liners like "Our job is to glamorize them and hide their weaknesses," "If I had only three weeks for a campaign I would pick a pretty boy," and "He was a beautiful, beautiful body and we were selling sex."[12] Many of O'Toole's colleagues apparently agree with him. A panel of 408 advertising executives once indicated that 71 percent believed that political advertising does overstep the bounds of truth and good taste.[13]

There are abundant examples of advertising campaigns being used to distort or avoid the discussion process. During one of New York Senator Javits' campaigns, transit cards were displayed on buses, stating, "Another busload of Senator Javits' supporters."

Nelson Rockefeller's ad agency, Jack Tinker and Partners, was accused in one election of writing commercials showing his support of organized labor and higher education, when, in fact, his record indicated that in the previous year he had vetoed an important minimum wage bill and had killed free tuition at state universities.[14] Perhaps the best-known distortion commercials are two from the 1964 Presidential campaign. They are now held up as examples of deception in media campaigning. The Johnson camp produced a spot that shows a little girl picking daisies in a field. As she plucks the petals she counts, while on the soundtrack a male voice counts backwards from ten to zero, after which the scene is rent with an atomic explosion. "These are the stakes," says the voice of Lyndon Johnson. "To make a world in which all of God's children can live, or go in the dark. We must either love each other, or we must die." This commercial was an obvious attempt to underscore the charges of nuclear irresponsibility against Senator Goldwater. The Goldwater camp produced a commercial showing a series of news clips of race riots, dope peddling, alcoholism, and crime, backed by a sound track that attempted to link the Johnson administration and the moral decay pictured. The Goldwater camp was accused of being racist because many of the news pictures included blacks. Both commercials met with considerable public outcry and the campaign organizations quickly withdrew them from circulation. Critics argue that these two commercials stand as monuments to the process of commercial media distortion.[15]

The mass media deal with appearances, and as these appearances begin to transgress reality, the process of campaign discussion is destroyed, says Stanley Kelley.[16] The practice of using paid time means that the candidate himself can structure the message—including the subject matter, the facts, and the visual images—to paint the best possible picture of his candidacy. There is little opportunity for the public to check the facts or to see the subject matter in the entire context of campaign issues; most important, the opposing candidate cannot rebut. In other words, Kelley charges that modern campaigning is devoid of meaningful campaign debate.[17] The advertising-media-oriented campaign relies, rather, on gimmicky slogans or catch-phrases to get the attention of the public. The campaign slogan, theme, and symbol have replaced the discussion of issues by candidates, because the advertising man has no confidence in the public's ability to listen to campaign discussion.[18]

No one, of course, is willing to defend the practice of using commercial advertising to distort, and few will admit to it. The late Adlai Stevenson once said, "This idea that you can merchandise candidates for high office like breakfast cereal—that you can gather votes like boxtops—is, I think, the ultimate indignity to the democratic process." William Murphy, an executive of one of the largest advertising firms involved in political work, is representative of the admen. He feels that the slick production techniques used to sell products have no place in the campaign.[19]

The obvious question is, therefore, when are consultants selling candidates like soap or cereal, and when are they merely offering the candidate and his issue positions to the public? The team from the Tinker Agency that put together Rockefeller's commercials defended itself by claiming that people did not know his record, and it had to be presented in a way that would not turn off the public:

> Some elements of it were too complicated and the reason they took the form they did (without Rockefeller) was that we just wanted to dramatize, draw attention to the record. The man was already established. I understand they were the talk of upstate New York. They were very factual, they were not a phony image-making attempt. Rockefeller built 12,000 miles of roads. The usual way of stating that is to say he built three times as many as Harriman. We said they'd stretch all the way to Hawaii.[20]

Obviously, there is a difference of interpretation as to which practices amount to distortion of the discussion process and which do not. Admen generally agree that candidates should not be sold like soap, and none of them is willing to admit that he is engaged in this process.

Admen and media consultants traditionally defend themselves by claiming that they use short creative messages because their earlier experiences with longer formats in which issues were discussed led to massive viewer inattention. Recent research has indicated that viewer attention to political commercials is greater with specific information than with mere image presentation[21] and that commercials can increase the issue information level of voters.[22] Moreover, media consultants like to point out that campaign advertising is not the only media vehicle with which they work. They also encourage candidates to use uncontrolled media and personal media. Uncontrolled mass-media formats include newscasts, talk shows, debates, news panel shows, newspaper stories, and newspaper editorials. Personal (and more traditional) media include campaign organization contacts, party organization contacts, political discussions with friends and coworkers, and group membership discussion. A substantial body of literature on voting behavior indicates that these media are at least as important as commercial messages in formulating voter choices.[23]

UNFAIR CAMPAIGNING AND UNFAIR USE OF INTELLIGENCE

Even though breaching the principles of what is considered to be ethical campaigning has been a part of American campaigning for a long time, it appears to have become considerably more visible in recent years, and this exposure has revealed some very systematic and sometimes illegal practices. If the number of complaints reported to the nonpartisan Fair Campaign Practices Committee is any index, "dirty politics" reached its peak in 1972, when the largest single number of unfair campaign tactics complaints (eighty-four for Presidential, congressional, and gubernatorial) were filed. Perhaps as a reaction to a sort of post-Watergate morality, the number of unfair charges did taper off markedly (fifty-one) in 1974, although some argue that this decline is not due to more ethical campaigning but rather, to the one-sidedness of races, which lessen last-minute charges and smears. But it is the Watergate-related "dirty tricks" and illegal intelligence that attracted so much attention to this subject. For the first time, there was uncoverage of systematic sabotage and clandestine activities.

Polling is but one form of legal intelligence activities. In addition, campaigners use: monitoring of speeches, advertisements, and newscoverage; insights from friendly reporters; mailings, literature, and other documents distributed by the opposition; information from canvassing and from the political grapevine. Nixon's CREEP had an extensive legitimate public-information-gathering network that fed this type of information into the White House "Attack Group," made up of Haldeman, Erlichman, Colson, and others.

Because of an apparent mistrust of public sources, a sense of insecurity about the election, suspicions of FBI reports of the motivations or their opponent's behavior, or some unexplained reason, these men tried to find out exactly what was going on in the enemy camp by engaging in illegal intelligence activities. Thus, they designed a series of clandestine operations including spying, bugging, and sabotage to be carried out by a group of operatives called "plumbers." Observers have suggested that they had four basic missions in mind: (1) to identify opposition supporters to add them to an "enemy list," whose members were designated for denial of government preferments; (2) to get information about opposition strategies not available from public sources; (3) to search for "plots," such as in the relationships between Democrats and anti-war demonstrators, leakers in the bureaucracy, or hostile members of the press, and to find any "dirt" the Democrats had on the Republicans and whether or not Democratic Chairman Lawrence O'Brien had any information on a criminal charge of an illegal payoff to International Telephone and Telegraph, a former law client of his; and (4) to find usable information to discredit the opposition camp or any of its key members.[24] As is well known, the plumbers were apprehended at the Democratic National Headquarters in the Watergate Apartment complex while trying to install an electronic listening device—in turn setting off a whole series of Congressional investigations, criminal court proceedings, civil suits, an impeachment proceeding, and, ultimately, the resignation of President Nixon.

In the course of the investigations it became clear that specific campaign actions were taken on the basis of information gathered. For example, admitted campaign saboteur Donald Segretti engaged in activities such as sending letters on Muskie stationery making false accusations, hiring poster bearers to carry signs indicating that Muskie supported (controversial) busing in the Florida Primary, sending a letter on Muskie stationery accusing Senators Jackson and Humphrey of sexual misconduct, placing ads harmful to Muskie in newspapers and on the radio, arranging for many pickets, and hiring a plane to fly over the 1972 Democratic Convention center with a trailer reading "Peace, Pot, Promiscuity: Vote McGovern."[25] Other Segretti sabotage efforts included fake telephone calls, canceling schedules that were to continue, ordering services in the name of a campaign, jamming communications, generating phony telegrams and letters to the editor, and getting unkempt people with McGovern buttons to behave rudely to the President so that he could make an example of them. It has also been alleged but not proven that the famous Muskie letter to the *Manchester Union Leader*, referring to French-Canadians in a derogatory manner as "Canucks," and the leaking of information about Senator Thomas Eagleton's mental treatment came from the same sabotage forces. Some of these activities were not new to campaigning. A Democratic prankster named Dick Tuck has been playing tricks on Nixon for years, such as putting on an engineer's cap and signaling a train to depart while Nixon spoke from the rear platform or getting a number of obviously pregnant women to carry signs with Nixon's campaign theme, "Nixon's the One." Tuck has operated on his own and his tricks have been undertaken in a more humorous vein. What shocked people was that the Segretti dirty tricks were a part of an organizational warfare system in which one group used unethical and illegal tactics to systematically destroy the other; they had no place in an election campaign where they could subvert the free election process.

Intelligence gathering and dirty tricks contributed to a post-Watergate atmosphere that brought on attempts both legal and extralegal to cleanse the political process. In an interesting twist, the 1974 elections engendered unfair campaign tactics relating to who was the most upright claimant on the office: candidates began to claim their honesty and political purity, which engendered a new concern for innuendoes of dishonesty and invidious comparisons with one's opponent.

EQUAL ACCESS TO BROADCASTING

As broadcasting has become an important component of campaigning, there naturally has been considerable concern over access to the airwaves. Access normally comes through news coverage of campaign events, stimulation of news coverage through production of audio and video news tapes, purchase of spot announcements or program time, and acceptance of offers of free time provided by stations. The problems of access are legion: not many races receive much news attention and some receive none; purchase of time requires money and the stations must have the time available, few stations offer free time and stations are required to adapt to a legal framework which has served to inhibit access to candidates.

The Federal Communications Act contains an "equal-time" provision (section 315) that requires that if one candidate for any elective office at any level purchases or receives free time, equal access must be provided for the other candidate(s). At one time, the equal-time provision included news coverage, but, since 1959, appearances by candidates on news programs have been excluded from the equal-time provision. The Federal Communications Commission altered the equal time provision in 1975 to allow a network or local station to judge whether to cover a news conference or debate. If the broadcaster feels that news worthiness dictates coverage, the media would not be restrained by knowledge that every other candidate for a particular state, local or federal office, whether bonafide or fringe, could demand and receive equal time. However, stations must adhere to a "fairness doctrine," which requires that reasonable opportunity be afforded for discussion of conflicting views of public importance. As tested in the courts, the doctrine, however, does not guarantee the right of reply to public officials. The doctrine is applicable to "noncampaign" broadcast appearances and newscasts involving the discussion of controversial issues. When the campaign begins, legally qualified candidates then come under the equal-time provisions.[26]

It is generally agreed that the equal time provision in practice has inhibited the discussion of campaign issues; some have labeled it a no-time requirement. The practical effect of the law has been to deny free broadcast time to major candidates or to force free time to be shared with fringe candidates, and the practice has been to not offer time. However, it is not only the law that inhibits access. Even where there are only two major candidates in a race, the practice of commercial stations granting of free time is rare. Some say this is the broadcaster's strategy to get Congress to repeal the equal-time provision. The rule was repealed once in 1960 to allow Kennedy and Nixon to debate without the networks having to offer time to other candidates, but since that time it has been back in effect, until the 1975 change. As a result of this rule, some very fringe candidates, including one "lone wolf," had to be given free national-network exposure time in the 1972 programs surrounding the New Hampshire and California primaries. More frequently, that rule combined with no legal requirement of providing free time must be seen as the reason why very little free broadcast access to discussions of campaign concerns exists.

Since news appearances and news conferences are excluded from the fairness doctrine, there is considerable concern over the campaign advantage this gives incumbents. An incumbent in a high-visibility office can draw much more extensive news coverage over a long period of time than their opponents can ordinarily expect. An executive official such as a mayor, governor, or the President can receive almost daily news coverage of his activities. There has been recent concern, for example, over the fact that a President's overseas foreign policy trips make hours of televised news, while the other candidates are at the mercy of money raisers for paid commercial time. During the Nixon Presidency years, the Democrats challenged the virtually unlimited access of Presidents to speak on the air, charging that the immense power over public opinion exercised by the President when he uses the broadcast media to seek support for his policies requires equal time for the opposition. They lost this appeal because the Federal Communication Commission claimed that the President's talks are contributions to an informed citizenry. The FCC has guaranteed automatic reply when: (1) a person's honesty, character, or integrity is attacked, (2) a broadcast licensee endorses a certain candidate in an editorial; or (3) a political party is given time to present its views.

Attempts by the Democrats as the party out of power to gain access to broadcasting through paid time have further refined the doctrine. When the Democrats attempted to purchase network time to appeal for funds to reduce their debt, CBS refused them time on the basis of their policy of not selling time for discussion of controversial issues. The FCC ruled in favor of the Democrats for fund raising but said the networks could refuse to sell time for the broadcast of controversial issues. A U.S. Court of Appeals rule overturned the FCC's controversial issue rule, stating that broadcast advertising had a great potential for enlivening and enriching the debate of public issues. In a related issue, the Republicans petitioned the FCC for program time refused by CBS to reply to a Democratic program, which had been given to them to balance Nixon's messages on Indochina. The FCC granted the time to the Republicans, but the Federal Appeals Court said this would amount to two chances for the President's party and thus refused equal time.

The solutions to these problems of access have come through various proposals to legally require broadcasters to grant time to candidates. In practically every other democratic nation but the United States, both radio and television broadcasting time is free to all political parties and is allocated according to their electoral strengths. During the 1974 British elections, for example, the Labor and Conservative Parties each received five broadcasts of ten minutes each and the Liberals four broadcasts of ten minutes, with various minor parties receiving lesser amounts. All broadcasts were aired during prime time on all available channels.[27] American proposals to provide broadcast time come in many forms: (1) repeal of section 315 providing for equal time, (2) paid time available to candidates at a discount, (3) limited broadcast time purchased by the federal government, (4) grants of free time modeled after the

British system, and (5) spending limits and public financing within the existing system of equal time.[28]

Proponents of relaxing or repealing the equal-time provisions have met with little success in using these alternative proposals to ensure fair access to the campaign airwaves by candidates, despite an atmosphere of reform. Both pre- and post-Watergate public policy dialogue has centered on limiting the purchase of time by candidates. Repeal of the equal-time provision has not had serious Congressional discussion in over a decade.

FINANCE REFORM

The high cost of the new style of campaigning has led to a parallel concern over who has access to political office. Is office seeking limited to the very wealthy or the officeholder who can manipulate the means of turning on the key resources as long as the new techniques cost so much and parties cannot supply the necessary funds? In other words, the key reform issue has become "Have the new means of seeking office precluded or limited certain types of office seekers and thereby affected our means of electing officials?"

Attention to high-cost campaigns has often centered on the wealthy office seekers, a concern that began with the Kennedy family's supporting their family members' tries for office. More recently, Norton Simon spent $1,350,000 of his own money to try—unsuccessfully—for a California Senate nomination. Richard Ottinger once spent $3.9 million of his and his family's money to try to move from the U.S. House of Representatives to the Senate, and he lost. The most familiar example of personal family largese is Vice-President Nelson Rockefeller's attempts at office. It is estimated that the candidate and his family have contributed around $25 million to advance his political career.

These examples indicate that rich persons can and do use their personal and family fortunes to advance their political careers. It has led some to advance the argument that only the rich candidate can acquire sufficient campaign resources to wage a new-style campaign. The unfolding of recent American politics suggests that this is not the case. Along with the rich men who have sought and held office have been many men of relatively modest means—Richard Nixon, Hubert Humphrey, George McGovern, Gerald Ford, and many candidates for Senator, Governor, or Congressman. Among the 1976 Democratic Presidential contenders are men of comfortable but relatively modest means—Wallace, Udall, Bayh, Harris, and Jackson.

What is more important than sheer wealth is the total amount of support a candidate can garner. Many candidates of relatively modest means can muster organizational, popular, and financial support sufficient to withstand the onslaught of the wealthy. Richard Nixon has taken the Presidential nomination away from Nelson Rockefeller twice on the strength of party support. Thus, against the list of rich and successful candidates one must also list the rich and unsuccessful: Rockefeller, Stuart Symington, George Romney, and William Scranton, who sought the Presidency, plus Simon, Ottinger, and others like them. Undoubtedly, they lacked a favorable distribution of nonfinancial resources. Well into the 1972 primary season, George McGovern was not the candidate with the most money, but he had other forms of support.

A parallel concern has been the advantages that accrue with incumbency, particularly financial advantages. The holder of office has a number of political advantages, including greater experience at campaigning and knowledge of the constitutency, the use of one's office and staff for campaign purposes, greater news exposure, and the use of office for public-relations purposes in the inter-campaign period. But it is the advantage the incumbent has over his opponent in raising money for campaigns that raises concern over whether or not a challenger ever has a chance in the face of the big money that follows officeholders. In the 1972 and 1974 Congressional elections, House and Senate incumbents of either party far outspent their opponents. Nixon's ability to amass over $55 million was also testimony to the power of incumbency. Yet, when incumbents get in close races, the money advantage narrows considerably or vanishes, again suggesting that the various electoral forces actually are at work together. Also, it is clear that those who wish to limit the power of incumbency by limiting the amounts raised tend to hurt nonincumbents more, since they generally need to spend money to become known.

Why then has there been so much concern over reform of the ways we finance our election system? It is not only because of the advantages of the rich or the officeholder but also because of the way funds have been raised through large contributions from the wealthy and economically powerful and because of the widespread and systematic abuse of the system. The very high cost of campaigning, ranging from expenditures of $110 million to select a President in 1972 to state legislative races that sometimes exceed $100,000 in cost, have raised concern that money has led to certain political inequities that are not in the interest of free democratic elections.

Pre-1970's regulation of finance, however well intentioned, were not very effective. Federal and state laws generally set out to: (1) set ceilings and limits on expenditures to meet the rising costs and disparities; (2) prohibit the contributions of certain special interests, such as corporations and interest groups, in order to spare candidates from obligations to them, and limit the size of individual contributions; (3) provide the public with information through reporting and disclosure; and (4) prevent government workers from being forced to contribute to political campaigns.[29] Expenditure limits were unrealistic and were circumvented, usually through the proliferation of committees. The same dodge was generally used by individual large contributions. Where federal law limited contributions of $5,000 to a single committee, a Presidential candidate could be supported by fifty state committees and a host of other special group committees. Interest-group contributions were circumvented by the formation of special political-action committees, which could legally contribute to campaigns. Reporting and disclosure was easy to hide because of the many committees reporting, vague and overgeneralized reports, and little reporting in the news.

The heavy personal outlays by wealthy candidates, the large amounts of funds required to wage a modern campaign, reliance on large contributions, widespread knowledge of systematic circumvention of the law and flagrant violations of the law created a recent climate of spending reform. Support of Presidential campaigns through a voluntary income-tax-form check-off was passed in 1971 but delayed until the 1976 election.[30] The Federal Election Act of 1971 was passed, and its regulations tended to be more of the same. And as observers like Adamany have pointed out, its first test in 1972 led to more violations—more visible—of the same sort: illegal corporate contributions; the widespread "laundering" of money, i.e., transfering money to a third party source so as to conceal the identify of the contributor; the solicitation of funds from sources such as the dairy industry and ITT, which suggested influence peddling; as well as the continuation of large contributions, but through circuituous methods.[31]

Thus, the Federal Government and the states have attempted another wave of reform through law, working at more equal access and diminishing the effect of money. The states are now experimenting with various means of reform, including limitations on spending, more specific reporting and disclosure, matching public grants for small contributions and, in eight states, public financing of elections (through a tax-form-check-off in seven of them). In 1974, new federal legislation was passed that again created hope for reducing the inequities in political spending and for plugging the loopholes. Included in this bill are provisions for public funding of Presidential campaigns, matching funds and incentives for small contributions, financial support and incentives for political parties, limits on larger contributions, centralization of fund reporting, and stricter enforcement.[32] These reforms are all in the early experimental stage. It remains to be seen which will work and which will indeed solve the problems of money in politics and access to office.

In "Financing National Politics," David Adamany provides an introduction to the problems of political finance and then investigates the political implications of national finance reform. Special emphasis is placed on the Federal Election Campaign Act of 1974, which includes public financing of Presidential campaigns. David W. Adamany is a professor of political science at the University of Wisconsin-Madison and has authored three books and numerous articles on campaign finance. He has also been active in civic affairs and government, and he is currently on leave from Wisconsin, serving as Secretary of the Wisconsin Department of Revenue.

Herbert Alexander provides an overview of the major trends in state reform of campaign financing, including new disclosure laws, expenditure limits, contribution limits, tax incentives, and public financing of campaigns. The states have traditionally been testing grounds for many new governmental policies, programs, and regulations, and they are beginning to regain this role in regard to reforming the American campaign system. Herbert E. Alexander, a political scientist, is Executive Director of the Citizen's Research Foundation, which specializes in the field of political finance. He has published numerous books and articles on campaign finance and is considered to be the leading authority on campaign finance, broadcasting, and politics.

"A Memo to the Ervin Committee" was written by Stephen Hess just before former Senator Ervin's Select Committee to investigate Watergate and other campaign practices was to report on their findings. Hess urged the Committee to consider that the lack of ethics in recent campaigns may well be due to the non-party-oriented impermanent nature of their organizations and stressed that the strengthening of parties should not be ignored in their recommendations. Stephen Hess is a Senior Fellow at the Brookings Institution. He has served on the staff of two Presidents and has authored a number of books on American politics.

Herbert Alexander's "Watergate and the Electoral Process" analyzes the role of Watergate in engendering campaign reform and discusses various public policy reforms and their likely effect on elections. Dr. Alexander is less than sanguine about some of the more popular reforms, both in terms of their ability to reform and in terms of their effects on the way candidates are elected.

NOTES

1. See, e.g., Herbert E. Alexander, "Communications in Politics: The Medium and the Message," *Law and Contemporary Problems* 34 (Spring 1969): 255–77.

2. John S. Saloma, III, and Fredrick H. Sontag, *Parties: The Real Opportunity for Effective Citizen Politics* (New York: Random House, 1972), pp. 342–52.

3. Bruce Felknor, *Dirty Politics* (New York: Norton, 1966); *New York Times,* October 23, 1972, p. 26.

4. Leo Bogart, *Silent Politics: Polls and the Awareness of Public Opinion* (New York: John Wiley & Sons, 1972), p. 41.

5. Charles K. Atkin, "The Impact of Poll Reports on Candidate and Issue Preferences," *Journalism Quarterly* 46 (Autumn 1969).

6. Harold Mendelsohn and Irving Crespi, *Polls, Television and the New Politics* (Scranton, Pa.: Chandler, 1970), ch. 3.

7. Mervin D. Field, "The Role of Public Opinion Polls" (Speech presented to the American Psychological Association, 1968).

8. Bogart, *Silent Politics,* p. 41.

9. Andrew J. Glass, "Pollsters Prowl Nation as Candidates Use Opinion Surveys To Plan '72 Campaign," *National Journal* 3 (August 14, 1971): 1698.

10. James M. Perry, *The New Politics: The Expanding Technology of Political Manipulation* (New York: Clarkson N. Potter, 1968), pp. 213–214.

11. Stanley Kelley, Jr., "Afterthoughts on Madison Avenue Politics," *Antioch Review* 17 (June 1957): 176.

12. John E. O'Toole, "And If Elected, Here's What I'd Do About Political TV Spots" (Speech presented to the San Francisco Ad Club, November 1971).

13. "Do Agencies Belong in Politics?" *Printers Ink* 270 (March 25, 1960): 51.

14. Richard Donnelly, "How TV Turned a Race Around," *Television Magazine* 23 (December 1966): 64.

15. For a more complete account of the events surrounding these commercials, see Pete Hamill, "When the Client is a Candidate," *New York Times Magazine*, October 25, 1964.

16. Kelley, "Madison Avenue Politics," p. 176.

17. Stanley Kelley, Jr., *Political Campaigning: Problems in Creating An Informed Electorate* (Washington, D.C.: Brookings, 1960), ch. 2.

18. Kelley, "Madison Avenue Politics," p. 182.

19. Donnelly, "How TV Turned a Race Around," p. 64.

20. *Ibid.*

21. Charles K. Atkin et. al., "Quality Versus Quantity in Televised Political Ads," *Public Opinion Quarterly* 37 (Summer 1973): 209–224.

22. Thomas E. Patterson and Robert D. McClure, "Television News and Televised Political Advertising: Their Impact on the Voter" (Paper presented at the National Conference on Money and Politics, February 1974).

23. E.g., Bernard Berelson, Paul F. Lazarsfeld, and William N. McPhee, *Voting* (Chicago: Univ. of Chicago Press, 1954), chs. 3–7; Angus Campbell, et al., *The American Voter* (New York: John Wiley & Sons, 1960), chs. 3, 6, 8, and 12; Walter DeVries and V. Lance Tarrance, *The Ticket Splitter* (Grand Rapids, Mich.: Eerdmans, 1972), ch. 4.

24. The Ripon Society and Clifford W. Brown, Jr., *Jaws of Victory* (Boston: Little, Brown, 1974), p. 110.

25. *Congressional Quarterly* (October 6, 1973): 2630.

26. Alexander, "Communications In Politics"; Communcations Act of 1934, 47–U.S.C.–315 (1964); Communications Act of 1959, 73 Stat. 5-57, amending 47 U.S.C.–315 (1964); *Congressional Quarterly* (January 29, 1972); National Association of Broadcasters, *Political Broadcast Catechism* (Washington, D.C.: NAB, 1973).

27. For the impact of broadcast time on campaigns, see Penn Kimball, "British Elections: The Old Boys on the Bus," *Columbia Journalism Review* 13 (May/June 1974): 28–32.

28. Alexander, "Communications in Politics," pp. 270–75.

29. Herbert E. Alexander, *Money in Politics* (Washington, D.C.: Public Affairs Press, 1972), pp. 83–84.

30. "Campaign Fund Tax Check-off Gains in Users," *Congressional Quarterly Weekly Report* (July 6, 1974): 1742–44.

31. For a discussion of the 1971 impact on campaign techniques, see Jonathan Cottin "Political Spending Law Will Have Impact on Candidates, Business, Labor," *National Journal* 4 (February 12, 1972).

32. See: Yorick Blumenfeld and Bruce Freed, "Campaign Spending in Europe and America," *Editorial Research Reports* 40 (October 1974): 767–784; Robert Walters, "Campaign Spending Reform Loopholes," *National Journal* VII (January 11, 1975), p. 67; *Congressional Quarterly* (October 12, 1974):2865–70.

—19—

FINANCING NATIONAL POLITICS

David W. Adamany

A DEMOCRATIC PERSPECTIVE

George Washington's account books reveal that in his 1757 race for the Virginia House of Burgesses from Fairfax County he spent money generously for the "customary means of winning votes"—namely rum, punch, wine, beer, and cider. Two decades later James Madison was denied re-election to the Virginia legislature because he refused to make such expenditures.[1] The "problem" of money in American politics antedates the Republic, and in Western civilization its roots are found in ancient Greece where campaigns for the ecclesia were influenced by massive political spending.

Surely there must be available policy responses to so hoary a public problem. But waves of reform, in the nation and the states, have failed. Like other policy making, it has too often proceeded from specific scandals, unaccompanied by a broader democratic perspective. Campaign money in 1972, now tucked neatly but wrongly under the general rubric "Watergate", is once more the scandal. But again, where is the perspective?

The issue is essentially one of popular consent and of accountability of government to the people. Democracy involves not only equal voting by each citizen, but a congeries of other requirements.[2] There is neither consent nor accountability unless legally equal voters have information about the issue and candidate alternatives which face them, unless they can advance new alternatives

Prepared for this volume. An earlier version was delivered as "How Shall We Finance Our National Elections" at the 1974 Western Political Science Association Convention, Denver, Colorado, April, 1974.

that better suit their preferences, and unless they can discuss the information and alternatives with their fellow citizens. Only votes cast after such a process meet the requirements of consent; and only governors who must face the people in such a process are accountable.

From a democratic perspective, the most acute issues of campaign financing involve the presentation of information, the scheduling of alternatives, and the discussion of the merits of policies, governors, and candidates. Massive campaign organizations, mass communications media, the touring candidate, and the stumping of his surrogates are modern means for presenting information, scheduling alternatives, and discussing their merits. Indeed, despite the carnival atmosphere of much campaigning, virtually all American electioneering in some measure wins voter attention for public affairs, presents information, schedules alternatives, and discusses the merits of candidates, officeholders, and issues. But these are costly activities in a large society, and it is here that the campaign dollar is the indispensibale nutrient of consent and accountability.

To foreshadow the ensuing discussion, the issues may be somewhat more precisely stated. First, do we spend enough money on campaigns to supply information, present alternatives, and discuss their merits, so that the ordinary citizen may cast his vote for candidates and platforms that square with his own preferences? Second, do we distribute the money we spend for campaigning in a way that promotes these processes of consent and accountability throughout the political system?

Third, do our means of raising the money for these purposes treat all those wishing to provide information, schedule alternatives, and discuss them in an equal—or at least a "fair"—manner? Here is one of the most difficult questions for the linkage process. To make consent and accountability possible, must all views be heard equally? Or should they be heard proportionately to the number of their supporters, as they might be if speakers were randomly recognized in a town meeting?

Fourth, do our means for raising campaign money give some individuals and groups influence over governors disproportionate to their equally weighted votes, so that the electoral constituency is counterbalanced in some measure by a money constituency that provides the cash for making appeals to the voters? Conversely, does officeholding allow incumbents to obtain campaign resources, including money, not in equal or fair measure, but as a consequence of their power over persons and institutions vulnerable to governmental regulation? These questions go well beyond bribery and extortion to differential access at the seat of government and to the sociology of differential participation of individuals, groups, and institutions in public life.

Finally, do our present political finance arrangements encourage broad participation by citizens? From one perspective public participation is significant because it weds citizens to the political system, promoting stability. But the vantage points, focussing on the individual, are more pertinent for democratic government, which stresses the equality and self-determination of individuals. Each act of participation, including financial giving, stimulates interest in politics and leads finally to more effective citizen control over government. Further, political participation has been praised, both by classical theorists and by modern "radicals", as a means for improving the intellectual and moral development of individuals, for increasing the sense of dignity and self-worth. Participation in political finance is, then, but a small piece in completing the colossal puzzle of individual roles in democratic politics and society.

CAMPAIGN SPENDING IN AMERICA

Running for Office

For the political hopeful, campaign costs have become awesome. In 1952, national Republican committees spent about $6.6 million in the general election, mainly to support General Eisenhower's candidacy. Democratic and labor committees spent about $5.3 million. Outlays remained about the same in 1956: Republican committees spent $7.8 million while Democratic and labor committees spent $4.8 million.[3] At nineteen and twenty cents per vote cast, these two presidential elections fit a pattern that stretched back at least to 1912.[4] With some variations in particular presidential years, a nineteen cent per vote total outlay for all national level committees was usual.

In 1960, however, the lid blew off. Republican committees spent $10.1 million and Democratic and labor committees spent $10.6 million.[5] By 1964, national level committee costs had risen to $16 million on the Republican side, and $9.5 million by Democrats and labor.[6] Republican national committees pushed the ante to $25.4 million in 1968, while Democrats and labor reported spending $13.5 million.[7] George Wallace's third party added $7.2

million to campaign costs. More than sixteen months after the 1972 election, national committee totals are still obscure, thanks primarily to the avalanche of information loosed by the Federal Election Campaign Act of 1971. The Nixon-Agnew ticket spent at least $50 million in the general election, excluding other Republican national level committees; and George McGovern distinguished himself as the most expensive loser in presidential politics by spending $38 million in the general election.[8]

Total presidential campaign costs are more elusive than general election outlays because legal reporting requirements and news coverage have been more nominal in the pre-convention sweepstakes. One commentator has set 1964 primary and general election expenditures by all presidential candidates at $60 million, and 1968 outlays at $100 million.[9] The 1972 presidential politics bill will surely rise above $115 million.[10]

Campaign costs for other offices are also increasing sharply. A survey of House and Senate races in 1970 estimated total primary and general election campaign costs at $71.6 million.[11] Common Cause has put congressional outlays reported under the 1971 Act at $77.2 million, but additional millions were undoubtedly spent before the law went into effect on April 7, 1972.[12]

Campaign expenditures in specific contests may better tell the story of the financing problems faced by candidates. In 1968 Kentucky Democrat Katherine Peden spent $76,300 in her unsuccessful race for the United States Senate; in 1972, Walter Huddleston, running on the same ticket in the same state, spent $658,600 to win a seat in the nation's most deliberative body. Ms. Peden's 1968 opponent, Senator Marlowe Cook, spent $101,600 in 1968, and former Governor Louis Nunn spent $603,600 to lose to Huddleston in 1972. In California, Democrat Pierre Salinger spent $416,000 in his 1964 general election race for the United States Senate; but six years later Democrat John Tunney spent $1.3 million. It cost George Murphy, who had spent $910,000 to vanquish Salinger in 1964, $1.9 million to suffer defeat at Tunney's hands.

In the mid-1950's Alexander Heard estimated that a typical statewide campaign in New York would cost $1 million;[13] in 1970, Nelson Rockefeller showed how far costs could rise by spending nearly $9 million to win a fourth gubernatorial term. Similarly, Heard's estimate of $100,000 to $150,000 for statewide campaigning in Oregon has been outdated by the Common Cause report that Senator Mark Hatfield spent $299,600 to win re-election against former Senator Wayne Morse, whose campaign cost $251,900. In a sparsely settled state, such as Montana, Heard estimated campaign costs in the 1950's at $40,000 to $60,000. In 1972, Senator Lee Metcalf's successful re-election bid cost $136,600, while his challenger, Henry Hibbard, spent $286,700.

Campaigns for the House of Representatives have received little attention through the years, but they have mainly followed the general pattern of campaign costs. In 1968, Democratic congressional candidates in Connecticut spent an average of $53,300,[14] while Republican contenders averaged $53,600. Four years later the Democratic average had climbed to $74,400 and Republican average to $86,800. In Wisconsin, Democratic contenders averaged $17,500 in 1966,[15] and $31,000 in 1972, while spending by Badger state Republican candidates rose from $29,600 to roughly $41,000. A California study sets average general election expenditures for both Democratic and Republican contenders at $9,900 in 1958 and $24,700 in 1970.[16] Common Cause has reported that average outlays in all congressional contests in 1972 were $47,500 by Democrats and $49,600 by Republicans.

Many House seats are uncontested, while many others are noncompetitive; and low spending in these districts tends to obscure how costly congressional campaigning can be. In 66 races won by less than 55 per cent of the vote, however, the average cost to the winner was $107,400 and to the loser, $101,200. At least thirteen House candidates spent more than $200,000 in 1972.

The pattern of campaign spending may be characterized by a study showing that in campaigns for President, Senator, Representative, Governor, and state legislator in seven states and the United States, costs in the late 1960's were increasing between ten and ninety per cent *annually* for various offices in various locales. The average *yearly* increases were 33 per cent. Politicians, it concluded, must "calculate that, from one biennial election to the next, they must raise half again as much as their most recent election effort."[17]

Why Costs Rise

Often it is these precipitous increases in dollar costs, rather than the absolute spending level, that cause concern among voters, journalists, and politicians. The main reasons for rising campaign expenditures are not found in some special wickedness of American politicians, however, but rather in the economic, social, and political environment.[18] Examined in this context, rising campaign costs appear necessary, albeit alarming.

Larger electorate. Campaign spending increases as the electorate expands. There were 98.3 million persons of voting age in 1952 and 139.6 million in 1972. Politicians are paying for the post-war baby boom and for the democratic extension of the franchise to the young in the Twenty-Sixth Amendment and to racial minorities in the Voting Rights Acts of 1965 and 1970. The cost of a first class letter to 41 million additional voters is staggering; and expenses for bumper stickers, brochures, and mass media also follow the voting population.

Price levels. Inflation takes its toll on politicians as on the rest of us. The Consumer Price Index was five per cent higher in 1964 than in 1960, eighteen per cent higher in 1968, and forty-one per cent higher in 1972. Over two decades, the Index has risen fifty-eight per cent. Recent inflation as high as nine per cent foretells even sharper increases in campaign costs. Further, most goods and services politicians must buy suffer price increases even higher than the standard Index. Mass media advertising rates and air fares are obvious examples.

Changing technology. New communications media and other technology advances send campaign costs soaring. The onset of radio and then of television spurred campaign spending. Special production teams and skilled filmmakers to produce radio and television materials as sophisticated as those used commercially were the next step. Public opinion polls, to guide the candidate's issue strategy and his media tactics, impose still further costs. In 1972 President Nixon brought to the national scene the "personalized" letter campaigning that had been used in some city and district races. Elaborate phone banks, manned by paid operators, obtain information from voters months before the election. These data are then transferred to computer cards or tapes. The computer summons up names of certain categories of voters—e.g., Catholics, union workers, conservatives—and "types" a letter personally addressed to each. Postage costs top off this mechanical attempt to reintroduce the personal contact vote solicitation once done by the old-time precinct captain. While spending for old technologies may decline somewhat as new campaign methods are introduced, the available evidence suggests that displacement of costs is far from complete.

Constituency size. The geographical size of constituencies adds further costs, especially when taken with changed modes of travel. Nationwide campaigning—now including Hawaii and Alaska—by jet plane is far more expensive than the front porch campaigns or even the systematic city-by-city whistle stops of an earlier day. The one-man one-vote rule for congressional and legis-lative districts increases the number of far flung districts in sparsely populated regions. Further, media, small aircraft, and large distances combine to revise campaign methods: the optimum strategy is now to travel by plane for brief appearances in many media centers and thereby command radio, television, and print coverage in many states or many regions of the same state. The cost in travel and advance work is enormous. Also, in geographi-cally sprawling districts, such as sparsely populated House dis-tricts, spending may rise for staff, multiple headquarters, auto-mobile transportation, and other organizational activities.

Decline of parties. The decline of traditional party organiza-tions sends costs upward. The reliable year-in, year-out ward organization got voters registered, tallied their pre-election prefer-ences, persuaded them about candidates and issues, and took them to the polls. Now candidates must painstakingly and expensively build citizen organizations for each new campaign, or they must pay workers to get these tasks done. Even the guerrilla armies of Eugene McCarthy and George McGovern, which lived largely off the land as they moved, required huge supporting budgets for transportation, food, literature, headquarters, telephones, poll lists and district maps, and other similar expenditures.

Competition. Intensifying electoral competition, too, raises the financial ante. Candidates and their friends will spend more money in districts and circumstances where prospects of victory are promising. Partisans, regular givers, and new givers make new or greater contributions when a race is close. Interest groups, big contributors, and party leaders are also sensitive to the "realities" and will invest in close contests.

In the modern era competition has spread. As Republicans have broken open the once Solid Democratic South, outlays in senatorial and congressional races in the former Confederacy and Border have shot upward. Democrats, in turn, have become equal competitors in the Midwest and Plains, staunchly Republican since the Civil War, and more recently in the once-impenetrable Republican white collar suburbs. Decay of the Roosevelt New Deal coalition has made presidential contests more competitive. And in a time of "emerging" or "real" majorities,[19] when politicians struggle with social and economic issues for the loyalties of vast blocs of shifting voters, expenditures are likely to become truly heroic. Americans have always praised competitive electoral politics; but that virtue, it turns out, has a high price tag in campaign dollars.

Reform. The democratic impulse, too, looses high costs. When nominations were made by party caucuses or conventions, a candidate had only to appeal to a small number of persons. These delegates were reasonably well informed, so the process of persuasion entailed small costs. The convention system has now been abandoned in most states; and the selection of national convention delegates occurred in primaries in twenth-three states in 1972, with many more likely to move to that or some equally expensive grassroots caucus system. Candidates must now wage full-scale appeals to the electorate twice: first to seek the nomination in a primary, and second to compete for office in the general election. Further, popular discontents and the declining hold of traditional party clubs on nominations are likely to spur large numbers of primary contenders. Overall, the reform of nominating procedures has generated massive new political costs, and the trend cannot be expected to abate.

The availability of money. Political spending rises when money becomes available to support more vigorous campaigns. And candidates will seek out and use every available dollar, for the frenzy of campaigning spawns the view that extra dollars need to be spent to appeal to one group or another, to raise this or that new issue, and to answer the opposition's attacks. Aspirants, even in hopeless districts, see ways to win elections if only the resources can be found to woo "critical" vote blocs.

In the modern era money has become more available. The past decade has witnessed a large number of personally wealthy figures seeking office. They command not only their own resources, but those of families, business associates, and friends. Their lavish expenditures raise the ante for their opponents. The 1968 presidential nomination campaign was beset by inflation as other candidates tried to keep up with the Kennedys and Rockefellers.

Individuals and groups wanting to maintain their standing in politics must, in turn, spend more to make an impact as money becomes more available from others. Newcomers who spend lavishly also raise the stakes for established groups. Agricultural and medical groups have spewed money into campaigns recently, and all others must redouble their efforts. The personally wealthy, especially those with "new money", who have entered politics as patrons rather than candidates have also raised the stakes dramatically. In the 1972 Nixon-Agnew campaign more than $16 million was contributed by givers of $50,000 or more, an unprecedented outpouring of big gifts that laid the groundwork for a presidential effort more than doubling the expenditures of any previous canvass.

The multiplication of these factors in many races has fattened the nation's total politics bill. Greater spending by each of many candidates obviously up the total national campaign expenditure. The large number of offices contested in the United States contributes to the overall campaign bill. No other nation has our Jacksonian, long ballot tradition. Because we elect 524,000 local, state, and national officials, the pressure for campaign funds is much greater than in countries where the available funds can be concentrated in races for relatively few offices.

The Politics Bill

Reporting of campaign expenditures is problemmatic at best. Nonetheless, samples of estimated expenditures have over the years been converted into nationwide projections of the total political bill. The best estimates, by Alexander Heard and Herbert E. Alexander, have put campaign costs for all nomination and election contests at $140 million in 1952, $155 million in 1956, $175 million in 1960, $200 million in 1964, and $300 million in 1968.[20] Estimates for 1972 are not yet complete, but $425 million is a close approximation. These totals reflect the sudden spiraling of costs in individual campaigns since 1960. While campaign costs edged up forty-three per cent from 1952 to 1964, they have escalated 113 per cent since then.

The outlay for each vote cast went from $2.27 in 1952 to $2.38 in 1964, but rose sharply to $5.66 in 1972. Even using the eligible electorate as a base, to acknowledge that it is the potential voters and not the actual voters that candidates woo during campaigns, the cost went from $1.40 per voting age person in 1952 to $1.75 in 1964, and then abruptly to $3.04 in 1972.

The Distribution of Spending

Recitation of per voter expenditures is misleading, of course. Money is not spent evenly to woo voters in different districts or by different candidates. Campaigning is not as vigorous in some locales as in others. And the availability of money differs from race to race.

First, spending in competitive contests far outstrips expenditures in noncompetitive constituencies. Outlays in "safe" congressional districts, where the winner garnered seventy per cent or more of the vote, averaged $46,200 in 1972. Where margins were sixty-five to seventy per cent, spending averaged $58,300; and sixty to sixty-five per cent, $85,500. In close districts, expenditures were substantially higher: where margins were fifty-five to sixty per cent, $128,200; and where they were fifty to fifty-five per cent, $208,400.[21]

Second, incumbents substantially outspend challengers, primarily because they have greater fund-raising resources. Incumbent Democratic Representatives outspent their Republican challengers by an average margin of $50,000 to $33,600 in 1972; Republican incumbents led Democratic challengers by an average margin of $51,900 to $30,300. Where no incumbent was running, average Democratic outlays were $90,100 and average Republican spending, $90,000. Winners in these districts averaged $104,100 to $75,800 for losers.[22]

Third, Republicans have usually outspent Democrats, especially in presidential, senatorial, and gubernatorial races. In House contests, however, incumbency rather than party seems the dominating factor.

Fourth, personally wealthy candidates usually outspend their opponents. So do those who appeal to certain major economic or ideological groups. Candidates who win support from segments of the business and financial communities or from union labor hold an edge in campaign funding. In recent years those who have touched certain emotion-laden issues or ideologies have been rewarded with outpourings of money. We will return to these funding patterns when considering the sources of campaign money.

Fifth, candidates for highly visible offices tend to spend more than aspirants for less salient policy-making posts. The contrast between expenditures for executive and for legislative offices is particularly important. Candidates for nomination and election to the Presidency spent approximately $115 million in 1972. One-third of the United States Senate seats were also at stake, and spending there was $26.4 million. Projected to the full Senate, expenditures would have been somewhat more than $78 million. House contests cost a total of $40 million in 1972.[23] The same pattern of executive office dominance in campaign spending occurs at the state level. In Wisconsin, Democrats spent $439,200 to nominate and elect a governor in 1970, but only $68,900 for one-half the state senate seats and $211,000 for all state assembly posts. Republican gubernatorial expenditures were $513,300, while senatorial contenders spent $81,400 and representative hopefuls, $241,400.[24]

Contrary to some earlier projections by scholars, the urban or rural composition of a district apparently is not a sixth factor bearing on levels of spending. A study of 460 California assembly candidates, 152 state senate aspirants, and 217 congressional contenders in 1966, 1968, and 1970 revealed a slight statistical correlation between urban-rural differences in assembly district spending and none at all in races for the other two offices.[25]

Campaign Spending in Perspective

Both the dollar totals and the escalation of costs shock the public and bewilder politicans. But from a democratic perspective campaign costs in America are modest, and perhaps too small. If every citizen paid his share of $425 million, the effects would be virtually unfelt. The $3.04 required quadrennially to pay for campaigns for all local, state, and national offices amounts to 48 minutes' wages for the average production worker. All political spending comes from Personal Income, and we devote only .045 per cent to campaigning—the same as in 1968, when we allocated .044 per cent.

Nor do our campaigns burden us more than citizens of foreign nations. Only the United Kingdom and Australia boasted a smaller campaign cost burden in the early 1960's, when scholars calculated per vote expenditures as a share of the hourly wages of production workers in eight nations.[26] A more recent comparison put per vote costs in Sweden at four times the American outlay.

The escalation of campaign spending in recent decades is also not the danger signal that orators and journalists too often portray. National Personal Income has risen faster than political costs since 1952: 267 per cent compared with 204 per cent. Even the massive upturn in political spending from 1968 to 1972 only slightly outran our ability to pay; the 42 per cent increase in campaign outlays was almost matched by a gain of 36 per cent in Personal Income. And the share of earnings that an average production worker would commit to politics if costs were spread evenly has declined slightly, from fifty-one minutes in 1952 to forty-eight minutes in 1972.

Political costs must be seen in perspective. Campaigning alerts citizens to politics, poses policy alternatives, fuels criticism of government, and projects information about candidates. Not only is it necessary for consent and accountability, it also imposes an important check upon governmental arrogance. Our Constitution embodies the principle of institutional checks and balances, but as our politics have become democratic, by the involvement of the mass public, voting has become an additional and perhaps most important check upon government. But the essential ingredient in electoral checking is the presence of a viable opposition that is well enough funded to challenge the conduct of office-holders.

Despite abuse heaped upon the "ignorant" public by pollsters and social scientists, recent studies show that Americans have opinions on the major issues of the day and usually vote for candidates who share their opinions, that they can make effective retrospective judgments on the conduct of government, and that they switch parties or stand pat consistent with their approval or disapproval of party performance.[27] In elections, then, we decide questions of war and peace, levels and burdens of taxation, allocations of spending, civil rights, civil liberties, the future of our environment, and others necessarily faced by government in modern industrial societies. Yet in 1964 we spent on presidential politics only one-tenth what was spent on spectator sports. The $300 million total politics bill in 1968 was twenty-five per cent less than General Motors and Proctor & Gamble spent on peddling their wares, and sixteen per cent less than tobacco manufacturers spent pushing poison.[28]

If there are any complaints about campaign spending, they are: we do not spend enough on politics. And we do not distribute what we spend very well. If congressional campaigns in competitive districts cost each candidate roughly $100,000, then it is clear that the $38,000 spent by winners and $70,000 spent by losers in safe districts is not enough to guarantee competitive elections that give voters choices.[29] Piling money into the marginal districts is a good strategy for party leaders, special interests, and others concerned about winning. But it is a poor strategy for democratic citizens. Choices must be available in the most rock-ribbed Republican and Democratic areas as well as in marginal locales. If the incumbent cannot be defeated this time, a vigorous opposition will nonetheless make the public aware of his voting record and conduct. Such criticism heightens an incumbent's sensitivity to district wishes. And the "law of anticipated reactions" tells us that he becomes wary that next time, perhaps in the primary, his record may bring him down.

Further, concentrating money in executive office contests also makes sense from a strategic perspective, but not from a theoretical one. One factor contributing to executive might in America is the relative obscurity of legislators. The extensive campaigning of executive office candidates, compared to the more puny efforts of legislative contenders, informs voters of executive personalities and programs. If the legislature is to compete for power, and thus to check it, races for senator and representative must show more vitality, win greater public attention, pose clearer choices, and result in popular mandates. Generous campaign funding, spread to all districts and for all offices, is crucial, then, both for responsive government and for limited government.

MONEY FOR POLITICS

The Sociology of Giving

The highest participation of Americans in political financing occurred in 1960, 1964, and 1972, when twelve per cent gave to a candidate or party committee.[30] In some presidential years, however, support may be substantially lower, as demonstrated by eight per cent participation in 1968, ten per cent in 1956, and four per cent in 1952. Congressional years witness the same disinterest by contributors as by voters, with five per cent giving in 1958, nine per cent in 1962, and eight per cent in 1966. The 1972 participation rate is particularly disappointing, since media, mail, and personal appeals for funds reached an all-time high. Thirty-four per cent of Americans acknowledged being asked for campaign money in 1972, but the twelve per cent participation was the same as in 1960 and 1964 when only fifteen per cent were asked.[31]

Like other kinds of political activism, campaign giving is predominantly a middle and upperclass passtime. Only four per cent of families with incomes under $4,000 contributed in 1972, while thirty-two per cent of families with incomes of $20,000 or more did so. Political financing came from only five per cent of the grade school educated, but from twenth-eight per cent of college graduates.[32]

Why is the American majority silent in campaign giving? Why doesn't John Q. give a buck to support his party? By his own testimony, responding to the Twentieth Century Fund poll on campaign financing, the foremost reason (twenty per cent) is that too much money is already being spent in campaigns. Another fourteen per cent complained that their small contribution wouldn't make a difference. Seven per cent protested that they didn't trust the way politicians would spend their money. Only four per cent cynically said that the outcome of elections doesn't make any difference.

Big Gifts and Small

Scrutiny of campaign financing tends to confirm the distress of those who don't give because their small contribution wouldn't make a difference. Big givers dominate American politics. Only four of fourteen major party presidential nominees since 1948 have received more than half their money in contributions under $500.[33]

From 1952 to 1960, givers of $10,000 or more numbered about one hundred in each presidential year, with gifts totalling $1.6 to $2.3 million. In 1964 their number rose slightly to 130, but total gifts remained about the same, at $2.2 million. The 1968 campaign was a watershed: the number of $10,000 givers jumped to 424 and their total contributions exceeded $12.2 million.[34] 1972 was an orgy of big money. Big givers could now be defined at the $50,000 level, and the Nixon-Agnew drive wooed 124 such givers who anted up $16.8 million. The McGovern campaign had few similar givers: preliminary studies have identified thirteen contributors of $50,000 or more, who accounted for $2.4 million.

Even in less expensive congressional campaigning, big givers are important.[35] More than twenty-nine per cent of individual gifts were in sums of $500 or more, totalling $12.2 million. House candidates received $6.9 million in such gifts and Senate candidates $5.3 million. Another $9.5 million in congressional campaigns were from individual contributions of $100 or more, scarcely "small" gifts. And still another $16.5 million was received from committees and associations, primarily established special interests. In all, 38.2 million of congressional campaign funds came from sources that would not ordinarily be defined as "grass roots" givers.

A special breed of big money is the rich man's contributions to his own campaign. The Rockefeller family has the reputation for funding most of its political ventures—in New York, Arkansas, and West Virginia—primarily from personal funds. The Kennedys prefer to raise money from others, but they spend their own money lavishly when necessary.[36] Milton Shapp, Howard Metzenbaum, Richard Ottinger, Howard Samuels, Pierre DuPont IV, and H. J. Heinz III come quickly to mind as politicians advantaged by great personal wealth. In an era when most money in politics is tainted or believed by the public to be tainted, the self-financing rich man has a certain appeal. "I don't need to take money from any special interest," he says. And the public's refrain is, "He's too rich to be bought." The sordid in American political finance has enthroned a new class of political grandees, and it has subtly reimposed the means test for office discredited more than a century ago by the Jacksonian movement.

The McGovern campaign and three others in recent years—the McCarthy, Wallace, and Goldwater canvasses—present the other face of political giving. Each was funded primarily from small gifts. Eugene McCarthy's presidential nomination drive drew as many as 150,000 small givers, and a handful who made very large contributions. In 1964 Goldwater stimulated 650,000 small contributions to party and presidential campaign committees. George Wallace reported that eighty-five per cent of the $6.7 million received for his 1968 presidential drive was raised from as many as 750,000 givers of less than $100.[37] And George McGovern's nomination and election campaigns raised as much as $30 million from more than 600,000 givers of less than $100. How narrow is the American political finance constituency can be no better illustrated than by comparing the general belief that McGovern's 600,000 contributors were a swelling from the grassroots with the simple fact that the eligible electorate in 1972 numbered 139.6 million.

Whether race relations, war, or crime in the streets, what these four "broadly" financed campaigns have in common is a deeply divisive and emotional issue that for many people also ties into larger ideological commitments. Candidates stirring deep issue or ideological sentiments among relatively small, but intense and polarized, segments of the population might be rewarded with avalanches of small contributions. Moderates, by contrast, find mass fund raising almost impossible. Their constituencies are not sufficiently aroused to commit money to politics. They leave moderate candidates to raise funds, if at all, from traditional partisan and interest group sources.

Interest Group Giving

Since the Roosevelt Revolution a fairly clear pattern of interest group contributing has emerged. Manufacturers, bankers, stockbrokers, and other financial and business interests have generally preferred the Republicans. Union labor has been consistently friendly to the Democrats. Others, especially those directly reliant upon government contracts or regulation, have been switch-hitters, playing to whichever side might advance prospects and to both sides if necessary. Oil companies, construction firms, truckers, and brewers are prominent among these switch-hitters. Organized crime, too, makes contributions and plays both sides.[38] In recent years, doctors have played a large role in politics, fighting national health insurance, Medicare, and other advances of government into financing or regulating medicine. Agricultural cooperatives broke through in 1972 as important, influential, and well-publicized political moneybags.

Millions of dollars of interest group money cannot be traced, because it is transferred as services or goods, because it is spent through hundreds of nonreporting local or state committees, and because it is laundered through party committees before reaching candidates. Even the visible tip of the iceberg alerts us to the massive role of special interests in political finance, however. One commentator has shown that leaders of thirteen economic groups—such as the American Bar Association, American Medical Association, American Petroleum Institute, and American Iron and Steel Institute—gave $751,900 in 1956, $493,500 in 1960, $468,200 in 1964, and in excess of $1.3 million in 1968.[39] Republicans have commanded these funds by margins as high as 98 per cent in 1956 and 88 per cent in 1968.

In 1968 officers and directors of the twenty-five largest contractors with the Pentagon, the Aeronautics and Space Administration, and the Atomic Energy Commission together with the twenty-five largest corporations on *Fortune* magazine's list of the 500 largest industrial firms gave $1.5 million in sums of $500 or more.[40] In 1972, their gifts soared to $3.2 million. Like other businessmen, these company officials strongly preferred the Republicans. Eighty-three percent of these funds went to the GOP in 1968 and 86 percent in 1972.[41]

Two studies by Representative Les Aspin also show the magnitude of special interest giving to the Committee for the Re-Election of the President. Contributions by officials of the one hundred largest Department of Defense contractors totalled $5.4 million. All but fourteen companies made gifts. Campaign contributions by 413 directors, senior officials, and stockholders of 178 leading oil and gas companies totalled almost $5 million.[42]

Like agricultural, professional, and business groups, labor is a major source of political money. But unlike the others, its political spending for in-house programs of political education, training, and activation are greater than its direct campaign contributions. Money for these purposes is drawn largely from membership dues and is never reported as political expenditures. Labor's efforts in a presidential year may involve 200,000 canvassers, telephone operators, and poll watchers, 10,000 telephones, and a hundred million pieces of literature.

Union dollar efforts are also staggering. In 1956, seventeen national labor committees reported spending $2.2 million. By 1964, thirty-one committees spent $3.7 million. The herculean labor effort of 1968 featured thirty-seven committees making total disbursements of $7.1 million.[43] A preliminary analysis of 35 labor committees spending more than $25,000 and reporting in Washington revealed union expenditures of $14.8 million in 1972. In several states labor contributions account for twenty percent of campaign funds in hotly contested gubernatorial, senatorial, and congressional campaigns.[44]

Motives and Money

The search for campaign financing policies is not aided by oversimplifying the role of money in politics.[45] Money may, of course, purchase votes in legislative bodies and decisions in the executive branch. But such bribery is rare. It may purchase jobs or preferments; and, again, such direct transactions seldom occur. Money may be extracted from public employees, government contractors, and regulated businesses; but such direct extortion is infrequent.

The impact of money is far more subtle. Big contributors get on the list because they have demonstrated "good will" toward officeholders. An appeal for money need involve no direct threat to those reliant upon government. The pressure is implicit. The president of American Airlines, explaining his company's illegal gifts to the Nixon re-election bid warned that "a large part of the money raised from the business community for political purposes is given in fear of what would happen if it were not given."

The most important effect of campaign contributions is distributing access to officeholders.[46] The contributor seeks no commitment during the campaign, but his large gift allows him more easily to win an appointment in the officeholder's hectic schedule. Arguing his side of the case, presenting his version of the facts, giving his analysis of the politics of the issue vastly advantages the contributor in persuading an official on critical policy issues. Usually the campaign staff, not the candidate, raises the money. But this is no immunization against unequal access. Contributor access to staff is as important as to officeholders. The staff controls the officeholder's daily schedule. Further, it does much of the policy work, makes recommendations, and sets the tone on key issues. Staffers who know that in the next campaign they will again be going hat in hand to contributors are likely to treat givers' interests sympathetically as they govern.

Access to the electoral arena is equally important.[47] Contributions play an essential role in policy making because they allow certain candidates and viewpoints to make themselves known. Without money even this first step cannot be taken. Access to the electorate, like access to officeholders, depends largely on campaign contributions.

These motives for campaign giving must not, however, obscure a host of others that are less objectionable.[48] Many citizens give because of a high sense of citizen duty. Others do so to befriend a candidate and share his prestige. Still others contribute from personal friendship. Some want inconsequential things: an invitation to a White House dinner, a Christmas card from the Senator, acceptance of an invitation to the contributor's home. For a few the motivation is entirely nonpolitical: a corporation manager may contribute because he was asked to do so by the company vicepresident who determines his promotions and pay.

Whatever the motivation, however, two facts are clear. Those who do contribute win access both to officeholders and to the electorate for their points of view. Since all citizens do not give, since those who do are not a cross-section, and since givers contribute very unequal sums, different individuals and groups have very different access. Second, the officeholder and his staff often feel implicitly committed to give whatever special treatment is not grossly inconsistent with conscience and electoral standing to those who contributed in the past and will be approached to contribute in the future. Even this slight presumption in favor of contributors diminishes official responsiveness to the whole public.

Contributions in Perspective

The democratic case for private campaign contributions is that giving allows citizens to participate in the electoral process and that it is a form of expression about issues, candidates, and events. Further, contributing, like any other political activity, may be a means for showing intensity of sentiment in an electoral system whose outcomes are based upon equally weighted votes.

Practice falls far short of theory here as elsewhere in nation-state democracy. Very few citizens participate in financing campaigns. Indeed, most hold that campaign giving is a means of improperly influencing governmental decision making. Sixty-five per cent of those surveyed in the Twentieth Century Fund poll said that big gifts were made in whole or part for various reasons of personal gain. The nongivers distrust the amounts, uses, and sources of money and despair that their participation will have any impact.

Those who do contribute do not all mirror the general population. Rich men finance their own campaigns or the campaigns of others. Powerful economic interests—unions, business, professions, agriculture—pour money into politics. The well-off and the well-educated dominate giving. And in certain circumstances, several hundred thousand ideologues, of right or left, fuel a candidacy with an outpouring of modest contributions.

Inflation, technology, a larger electorate, vigorous competition and similar factors impose new demands for campaign funds on candidates. And they, in turn, must go to relatively narrow financing constituencies to find those dollars. At the least, they must shape their programs and appeals to the money constituencies as a precondition to wooing the electoral constituency. At the worst, funds are raised by bribery and extortion. Even the special access of contributors to officeholders is difficult to defend, for it imposes a toll upon the historic right to petition the government.

Finally, there simply is not enough money. The private financing constituencies neither raise enough money nor distribute what is raised to support vigorous competition in all races for all significant policy making offices.

IN SEARCH OF REFORM

In the aftermath of Watergate, Congress passed the Federal Election Campaign Act of 1974.[49] The new law embodies principles of campaign finance regulation that have been tried time and again in American politics: limiting spending, restricting contributions, full disclosure of money in politics, and independent enforcement. In addition, Congress provided for public financing of presidential campaigns—a new approach in America, but one which had been tried in many foreign democracies. Despite the Act's sweeping provisions, it illustrates many of the weaknesses and pitfalls of reform legislation.

Limits on Spending

The Act limits spending by presidential candidates to $10 million in nomination races and $20 million in general elections. No candidate may spend more than twice the senatorial limit in any state. Senate candidates may spend the greater of 8 cents times the voting age population or $100,000 in primaries and 12 cents times the voting age population or $150,000 in general elections. House candidates are limited to $70,000 in each primary and general election. Additional outlays up to 20 percent of these spending limits may be made to raise funds.

National party committees can spend an additional two cents times the voting age population to support their presidential candidates; national and state party committees can separately spend up to two cents per eligible voter to aid their Senate and House candidates, with a minimum allowance of $20,000 and $10,000 for those races. All expenditures by a candidate must be channelled through a single committee, so that the spending limit can be easily applied. But individuals or groups operating independently may spend up to $1,000 to support candidates. The spending limits are adjusted in each election to conform to changes in the consumer price index.

These provisions illustrate the difficulty of regulating campaign spending. First, it is impossible to know how much ought to be spent in campaigns. The $10 million presidential primary limit is more generous than most candidates have spent in the past; but the $20 million general election limit is much lower than either Nixon or McGovern spent in 1972. Few believed that the McGovern campaign was lavishly financed. In any case, do we want to put a lid on how much talking a candidate can do to spell out his programs, criticize his opponent, and draw attention of the voters?

The congressional spending limits illustrate another side of the problem. While they are generally high by past standards, the House limits are far below the spending that actually occurred in a handful of the hottest contests in 1972. It is doubtful whether any limits can be set that will take into account the great variation in campaign circumstances from one district to another—the number of voters, the density of the population, the strength of parties and interest groups; the availability of mass media for campaign advertising, the degree of competitiveness, the existence of nomination as well as general election races, the visibility and importance of deeply felt issues, the traditions of the district, and many others.

Spending limits are very difficult to enforce. Do expenditures supporting a candidate, but made outside his campaign organization, count against his spending limit? If so, such independent expenditures could very quickly diminish a candidate's own opportunity to spend money to emphasize the issues he believes are important. Even more troublesome are expenditures which do not support any candidate, but which might affect elections. Should spending by independent citizens or groups opposing a candidate be counted against his opponent's spending limit? Whose spending limit is affected by expenditures which only mention a candidate, but neither endorse or censure him? And what about expenditures—such as those by the National Rifle Association or "right to life" (anti-abortion) groups—which discuss issues on which candidates have well defined positions, but which do not mention any candidate by name?

Many believe that spending limits are an unconstitutional restriction on the freedoms of speech and association.[50] To prevent evasion of spending limits, the Act requires that money be channelled through the candidate's campaign committee. Otherwise interest groups, parties, and separate campaign committees would simply take over the financing of a candidate's canvass when he reached his spending limit. But the central campaign committee imposes a form of censorship; citizens can spend money to express their opinions about candidates only if the candidate approves.[51] Further, when some citizens have contributed or spent money through the candidate's committee up to the spending limit, other citizens are entirely cut off from spending any money to express their views.

Congress tried to avoid these issues by allowing independent citizens and committees to spend up to $1,000 outside the candidate's campaign committee. Even this solution falls short, however. When a citizen contributes $1,000 to the candidate's committee, his money can be pooled with other contributions and used for expensive activities, such as television promotions. Outside the committee, it can be spent only in $1,000 amounts. This favors those who act through the candidate's committee, and it restricts the freedom of those acting independently.

The 1974 Act's spending limits include a serious discrimination against some candidates. The special two cent per voter spending allowance for national and state party committees favors partisan candidates over independents. And it may also discriminate against the congressional candidate of a state party—such as the Conservative Party of New York—who can benefit from the two cent allowance for state parties, but who does not belong to a national party which can spend the additional two cent allowance on his behalf.

Most important, spending limits do nothing to solve the problem that most candidates in most districts have too little money to wage vigorous campaings. The need for strong competitive elections, in which candidates can present their programs and criticize the opposition, is overlooked by expenditure ceilings.

Limits on Contributions

The 1974 Act limits an individual's contributions to any federal office candidate to $1,000 in each nomination and election contest and restricts his annual gifts to all federal office candidates to $25,000.[52] A candidate's contributions to his own campaign cannot exceed in nomination and election contests together $50,000 for president, $35,000 for senator, and $25,000 for representative. Political committee gifts are limited to $5,000 to each federal office candidate in each nomination and election contest. Contributions from union dues and corporation treasuries continue to be prohibited.[53]

Contribution limits are an important step toward reducing the influence of big money and special interest money in American politics. They can never be perfect, of course. A contributor might give the maximum contribution to his favored candidate and then give additional money to his political party, knowing that it too will aid the candidate. Many officials of a single company or industry may make contributions up to $1,000 maximum, and together their gifts represent a significant political force. Similarly, many different union groups may make contributions up to the $5,000 limit, and together they advance labor's influence in politics.

The $10,000 total limit on individual gifts will help curb many gifts by the same giver. But there is no limit on multiple gifts by political committees. Congress could achieve the same result by limiting the percentage of funds a candidate could accept from all other organizations.

If contribution limits restrict the influence of monied interests, they do not achieve other important goals. They do not provide enough money to wage vigorous campaigns. Indeed, they may dry up sources of money needed for political activity. Nor do they distribute money more evenly to all races for all offices.

Full Disclosure

The favorite approach of modern reformers has been full disclosure of the sources, amounts, and uses of money in politics. Its advocates argue that publicity about contributions and expenditures will discipline candidates by increasing the political risk of voter retaliation against those who misuse campaign money.[54] Some also argue that full information about campaign money will awaken citizens to the true cost of elections and will encourage more people to contribute to campaigns.[55]

The 1974 Act builds on the sweeping full disclosure provisions of the Federal Election Campaign Act of 1971.[56] Together they require candidates and political committees to disclose total contributions, expenditures, loans and other transactions. The name, address, occupation, and principal business place of each contributor over $100 must be revealed; and those receiving expenditures of more than $100 must be reported. Money must be channelled through a candidate's principal campaign committee to make information more easily available. Funds must be handled through a single depository bank account to simplify auditing of campaign finances. Reports must be filed before and after each election, quarterly, and annually.

These rules provide ample information about money in politics.[57] But claims that full disclosure will clean up campaign financing seem hopelessly optimistic. First, to obtain truly full disclosure reports must be made as near the election as possible. But to obtain publicity for political finance practices, to alert and arouse the public about misconduct, takes relatively a long time. Second, full disclosure requires complete reporting. But complete reporting is unwieldy. The Federal Election Campaign Act of 1971 is the most complete disclosure law in any American jurisdiction. It generated more than 500,000 pages of reports in 1972, and more than a year after the election a full statement of contributions and expenditures was still not available from the supervising government officials.

Third, citizens should be skeptical about a technique of regulation that rests on the good will of the mass media. Media may carry political finance stories or not; they may give them prominence or not; and they may repeat and interpet the mass of data for public use or not. Anyone who has read Ben Bagdikian's study of early newspaper reaction to Watergate will come away with second thoughts about full disclosure: Nixon-endorsing newspapers buried the story, while McGovern-endorsing papers highlighted it.[58] Local media, dominant in congressional campaigns, are likely to even more effectively conceal or feature political finance disclosures that confirm their editorial preferences.

Fourth, there is the public's ability to know. We long ago learned that voters cannot reasonably be expected to absorb and interpret complex or technical information—such as long lists of contributions and expenditures. Whatever success American electoral politics enjoys proceeds from the simplification of choices by party designation, by ideological label, by broad statements of issues, by retrospective judgment, by voter attention to that which is truly important and highly salient. The intricacies of political financing do not meet these requirements.

Fifth, even if the public could intelligently focus on political financing practices, what choice would they have? The present arrangements for campaign funding link both parties and all candidates to big givers, special interest contributors, and other narrow constituencies. No candidate is likely to give up such arrangements in order to woo a small margin of voters who comprehend and care about the political finance issue. And one who did would simply not raise the money to carry the campaign financing issue to the voters.

Finally, disclosure fails because it treats political financing as a high priority issue. It is not. Can a voter who approves a candidate's stand on foreign policy, race relations, civil liberties, economic and welfare programs, and the "Social Issue" be expected to vote for the opposition because he disapproves his candidate's funding sources? To put it directly, would a 1972 voter who wanted "peace with honor" in Viet Nam, who thought civil rights had proceeded too fast, who disapproved of abortion and amnesty and acid, who favored a hard-line against crime in the streets and disorders on the campuses have voted for George McGovern in order to punish Richard Nixon for taking $16 million in contributions over $50,000, some of it illegally from corporations and most of it from those self-interested in the conduct of the government?

At the very most, full disclosure may occasionally affect an election outcome where financing abuses are flagrant and few other differences occur between candidates. It may, however, serve a most important inter-election function by allowing the public, press, and opposition to compare an official's conduct with the sources of his campaign funds, looking for potential or actual contributor influence over public policy.

Enforcement

The 1974 Act creates a Federal Election Commission consisting of the Senate Secretary and House Clerk, serving ex officio without vote, and of six appointed members. Two are named by the President; two are appointed by the President Pro Tem of the Senate and two by the Speaker of the House, upon the recommendation of the majority and minority leaders in the respective houses. No pair of members may be from the same political party. Commissioners must be confirmed by a majority vote of both houses.

The Commission is given power to supervise the full disclosure provisions of the law, but the Secretary and Clerk continue to receive campaign finance reports of candidates for the respective houses. The Commission is given authority to investigate reported or apparent violations, to give advisory opinions about the meaning of the law, and to adopt rules and regulations. It may seek civil remedies to prevent or correct violations of the law. And it may report apparently wilful violations to the Justice Department for criminal prosecution.

The creation of an independent enforcement agency is a long step toward reform. In the past, even strong laws have been undermined by the reluctance of elected officials to open the pandora's box of campaign law enforcement. They often feared that prosecutions would catch members of their own party as well as the opposition. Often there was no requirement that those who received campaign finance reports notify prosecutors of violations. And frequently the laws were so unreasonable or so ridden with loopholes that effective prosecution would have been unfair or impossible.

Although the new Commission is a step forward, it is not fully independent and does not have a full complement of enforcement powers. Congress wanted to retain influence over the agency to protect itself from too vigorous enforcement. In no other regulatory agency do congressional leaders appoint members. And for no other federal post must both houses of Congress confirm nominees. Some believe that these rules violate the separation of powers, in which the President names executive officers, and the Senate's prerogative to confirm. Another objection to the appointment system is that minor party and independent candidates might not receive fair treatment before commission members named upon the recommendation of the leaders of the two major parties in Congress.

Congress has also hobbled the commission's power to make rules and regulations. Unlike any other federal regulatory agency, the commission must submit its proposals to each house, and either may veto them by majority vote within 30 days. In addition, Congress refused to allow the commission power to bring criminal prosecutions against wilful violators. The Senate adopted such a provision, because the Justice Department was historically so lax in upholding campaign finance laws. But the House refused to go along.

TOWARD REFORM: PUBLIC FINANCING

Conventional reforms have merit only when combined with a substantial element of public financing. Low contribution limits may curb the influence of big and special interest donations. Full disclosure has limited uses for revealing flagrant financing practices during campaigns and assessing official conduct between elections. Independent enforcement is essential both to uphold the law and to maintain the confidence of citizens and candidates in financing regulations. Expenditure limits, on balance, appear inconsistent with the need for vigorous electioneering in widely varying situations, unenforceable, and unconstitutional. Public financing provides enough money for vigorous competition, obtains those funds from an "untainted" source, and can be distributed to campaigns for all offices in all districts. Questions of who is eligible for public grants and how much they are eligible for are the main barriers to workable public financing of campaigns.

The 1974 Act provides public financing for presidential general elections, nominating contests, and national party conventions. Major party general election candidates are given the option to receive the full spending limit ($20 million) in public funds or to accept private contributions instead. Major party candidates seeking a presidential nomination may receive matching grants for each individual contribution up to $250, after qualifying by raising $5,000 in such contributions in each of 20 states. Each candidate's matching grants are limited to $5 million—half the statutory spending limit of $10 million. Major parties may draw $2 million in public funds to pay for their national nominating conventions.

Minor parties are eligible for proportional participation in all public funding formulas. Their grants are calculated as the percentage of major party subsidies that their vote in the past election was of the average major party vote. New parties as well as minor parties may qualify for post-election public financing on the same basis if their vote in a current election entitles them to larger grants than would their polling in the prior election.[59]

All public grants for campaigns are financed from the one dollar income tax check-off. Citizens indicate on their income tax forms whether they wish to allocate one dollar of taxes to the Presidential Election Campaign Fund. The Act establishes priorities for payments from the Fund, with all funds necessary for nominating conventions and general election grants set aside in that order and with nomination matching grants taken from any balance remaining in the Fund. If citizens check off too little money to meet the Act's commitments, the Secretary of the

Treasury is responsible for setting up a fair allocation system. All grants from the Fund are adjusted to conform to changes in the consumer price index.

In several aspects, the 1974 Act takes long strides toward reform. Public financing, coupled with low contribution limits, curbs special interest money while stimulating vigorous competition. Extension of public financing to primaries and nominating conventions as well as to general elections recognizes the potential for financing abuses in selecting party nominees and the special effectiveness of money in primary campaigns where voters do not have party labels on the ballot to guide them. The proportional financing of new and minor parties acknowledges the potential that they will become major contenders and honors their historical roles as vehicles for new ideas, voter protest, and charismatic leaders.

In other ways, however, the Act falls short of respecting the realities of American politics and campaign financing. Most important is the Act's failure to publicly finance congressional campaigns. Presidential candidates funded fully with tax dollars may use their awesome influence to solicit and channel private money for Senate and House races. This already happens in midterm elections, reaching a zenith in Mr. Nixon's White House, where key staffers secretly directed money in 1970 to help the President's friends in Congress and punish his enemies. The deployment of even greater presidential influence in financing campaigns, in both midterm and presidential elections, will increase the President's clout in Congress and further undermine the already badly eroded separation of powers.

A shift in public confidence is also likely when presidential candidates are "cleanly" funded with tax money and congressional aspirants are still dependent on "tainted" private fund sources. Finally, of course, public financing of presidential elections makes candidates both more responsive and more visible to the public. Congress, meanwhile, remains in a shadowland, where financial undernourishment of challengers makes it less accountable to voters in elections and less visible to citizens.

Basing eligibility for presidential general election grants on past election results will produce distortion and unfairness in American politics. These are aggravated by the requirement that new party and independent candidates must wait until after the votes are counted before receiving public grants, while others receive theirs for use during the campaign. Under these rules, formerly significant parties whose support has decayed may none-theless claim full grants in later elections; the Whig party after 1852, the Bull Moosers in 1916, and the Wallace American Inde-pendents in 1972 come easily to mind as examples. By contrast, newly emerging parties or independent candidates, with strong citizen support in an election, may not receive grants in a timely or useful fashion. Neither the Bull Moosers nor the American Inde-pendent Party would have received public grants during the cam-paign when it made its impressive showing.

The Act's provision for post-election grants to new candidates or parties making a strong showing at the polls allows them, at best, to pay off election debts. But most insurgent parties will not be able to borrow large sums during the campaign, so post-election grants will do them little good in wooing votes. Indeed, the Act's limit of $1,000 on loans as well as contributions throws up a barrier to such borrowing by new parties and candidates.

The matching grant system for nominations seems to address many of these issues by basing public financing on a current rather than a past index of support. But the index is support by contribu-tors, not by voters. And the $250 level for matchable grants appears to promote substantial inequality among citizens. Ironi-cally, each citizen equally can allocate only one dollar to the Presidential Election Campaign Fund; but in the distribution of these dollars, citizens trigger very unequally grants to candidates. A $250 contributor directs a like amount to his preferred candi-date while a one dollar contributor sends only a single public dollar to his favorite. The $250 maximum for contributions count-ing toward the eligibility threshold creates similar inequalities. A mere 4,000 of these donors qualify a candidate for matching grants, but it would take 100,000 one dollar contributors to achieve that result.

The requirement that a candidate raise $5,000 in each of 20 states to become eligible for nomination matching grants is ap-parently intended to discourage favorite sons or regional candi-dates. This is a doubtful goal, since these contenders have sometimes emerged as national leaders after starting in their home areas. Particularly, it discriminates against governors, whose initial constituencies for the presidency are likely to be local rather than national. In addition, the 20 state rule ignores the distribution of voters in favor of a peculiar "state equality" theory of presidential politics. The Constitution does not require a candidate to carry, or even to run in, 20 states in order to be elected President. Indeed, the electoral votes of the eleven largest states are sufficient for victory.

Nomination financing raises an inter-party distributional problem. Is it fair for a party with a heated nomination contest to draw most or all of the matching money? Since all the party's hopefuls are likely to campaign against the opposition party, especially against a sitting opposition party President, the nomination grants have general election implications. Yet during the nomination stage, one party's contenders will claim vastly more of the available public funding than will the uncontested or weakly contested nominee of the other party.

Finally, the Act finances candidates, but it does not provide funds for political parties. This may upset delicate balances in American politics. Several studies have found a "specialization of functions" in political finance.[60] Candidates spend money for self-promotion, especially in media, and for staff activities related to campaigning. Party groups register voters, get out the vote, recruit candidates, and perform essential interelection tasks. While state party committees spend for planning, coordination, publicity, and candidate promotion, local groups spend money for canvassing, registration, and getting out the vote. By financing candidates, but not parties, Congress has given a higher priority to some specialized political activities rather than others.

In addition, many commentators have argued that strong parties are necessary.[61] They draw officeholders together to support a common program and push it through the complicated governmental process. Party provides a bridge between the President and Congress; it overcomes the separation of powers to allow cooperation between members of the same party in competing branches of government. And parties, it is said, hold candidates to the platform which is offered to the people and which they endorse in elections. Yet financing candidates, but not parties, weakens the role of parties—making candidates even more independent of the common party program and platform.

AFTERTHOUGHTS

Public financing is plainly necessary to support vigorous campaigning without reliance on large gifts and special interest money. But the formulas in the 1974 Act fall short. Public financing must apply to congressional as well as presidential races, to parties as well as candidates, and to both parties and candidates according to a current index of popular support rather than past election results.

A provocative alternative relies on vouchers, and combines them with fixed grants.[62] A nationwide voter registration system would be necessary, and such a system has already been endorsed by the Senate and has excellent prospects in the House. A voucher for each campaign for president, senator, and representative could be put in the hands of each voter. The collection of vouchers would trigger flat or proportional grants. For instance, each candidate who collected either a fixed number or a fixed percentage of vouchers would be entitled to a flat grant. Those who collected a smaller number would receive a proportion of the flat grant equivalent to the proportion their vouchers were of the higher threshold. This combined system would create a current index of support as citizens allocate their vouchers during the campaign, but it would also guarantee adequate money for campaigns because flat grants could be set high enough to support vigorous electioneering.

Such a plan could be adapted to party support as well. Vouchers could trigger flat and proportional grants to national party committees. Since national committees do not have grassroots organizations, they would presumably work out formulas to share grants with state and local committees in proportion to the vouchers collected. This division of grants would preserve the delicate power balances that exist between national, state, and local party organizations. At the outset, party grants could be large enough to support party headquarters operations and some additional activity related to candidate recruitment, research, getting out the vote, and inter-election opposition to incumbents in those districts held by the other party.

Public opinion in recent years has overwhelmingly endorsed public financing of campaigns. Congress, too, has shown approval. The 1974 Act adopts the principle, but it does not base public financing on current measures of voter preference and it does not respect significant power balances in American politics. The principle is here to stay; a voucher system may prove workable in practice.

NOTES

1. George Thayer, *Who Shakes the Money Tree?* (New York: Simon and Schuster, 1973), p. 25.

2. The discussion of consent and accountability that follows draws heavily on Robert A. Dahl, *A Preface to Democratic Theory* (Chicago: University of Chicago Press, 1956); and on Austin Ranney and Willmoore Kendall, *Democracy and the American Party System* (New York: Harcourt, Brace and World, Inc., 1956), chs. 2 and 3.

3. The 1952 and 1956 figures are from Alexander Heard, *The Costs of Democracy* (Chapel Hill: University of North Carolina Press, 1960), p. 20.

4. Herbert E. Alexander, *Money in Politics* (Washington: Public Affairs Press, 1972), p. 79. Also, Herbert E. Alexander, *Financing the 1968 Election* (Lexington, Mass.: Heath Lexington Books, 1971), p. 4.

5. Herbert E. Alexander, *Financing the 1960 Election* (Princeton: Citizens' Research Foundation, 1962), p. 10.

6. Herbert E. Alexander, *Financing the 1964 Election* (Princeton: Citizens' Research Foundation, 1966), p. 8.

7. Alexander, *Financing the 1968 Election,* p. 2.

8. Estimated presidential campaign expenditures for 1972 are based upon reports of the Office of Federal Elections released under the Federal Election Campaign Act of 1971 and on press reports of expenditures prior to the effective date of the Act on April 7, 1972.

9. Alexander, *Financing the 1968 Election,* p. 3.

10. Estimates by the author. The figures released by the Office of Federal Elections confirm that figure, but estimates of pre-April 7 spending may push it substantially higher.

11. Alexander, *Money in Politics,* pp. 24–25.

12. The author is grateful to Common Cause for making available to him a complete copy of the "Common Cause Study of 1972 Congressional Campaign Finances." Portions of the study have been published in U.S. Congress, Senate, Committee on Rules and Administration, Subcommittee on Privileges and Elections, Hearings on *S. 1103, S. 1954, S. 2417,* 93d Congress, 1st Sess., 1973, pp. 96–111; *Congressional Quarterly Weekly Report,* Vol. 31, Number 38, September 22, 1973, pp. 2515–2517; and *Congressional Quarterly Weekly Report,* Vol. 31, Number 48, December 1, 1973, pp. 3130–3137.

13. Estimates in this paragraph of campaign expenditures in the mid-1950's are found in Heard, *op. cit.,* p. 425.

14. Connecticut congressional spending for 1968 is from David Adamany, *Campaign Finance in America* (Scituate, Mass.: Duxbury Press, 1972), p. 27. Reports of 1972 spending are from the "Common Cause Study", *op. cit.*

15. Wisconsin congressional spending for 1966 is from David Adamany, *Financing Politics* (Madison: University of Wisconsin Press, 1969), p. 65. Reports of 1972 spending are from the "Common Cause Study", *op. cit.*

16. John R. Owens, *Trends in Campaign Spending in California, 1958-1970: Tests of Actors Influencing Costs* (Princeton: Citizens' Research Foundation, 1973), p. 64.

17. Adamany, *Campaign Finance in America*, pp. 43–44.

18. The main studies of campaign cost variables are Heard, *op. cit.*, pp. 380–387; Adamany, *Financing Politics*, pp. 61–107; and Adamany, *Campaign Finance in America*, pp. 51–78. An important statistical analysis of the significance of the variables is Owens, *op. cit.*, pp. 70–80.

19. Kevin Phillips, *The Emerging Republican Majority* (New Rochelle, New York: Arlington House, 1969); Richard Scammon and Ben Wattenberg, *The Real Majority* (New York: Coward-McCann, Inc., 1970). See also Walter DeVries and V. Lance Tarrance, *The Ticket-Splitter* (Grand Rapids: William B. Eerdmans, 1972).

20. For 1952 and 1956, see Heard, *op. cit.*, pp. 7–8. For 1960, 1964, and 1968, see Alexander, *Financing the 1968 Election*, p. 1. The 1972 figure is the author's estimate.

21. "Common Cause Study", *op. cit.*

22. *Ibid.*

23. *Ibid.*

24. These figures were obtained from the Governor's Study Committee on Political Finance. For other Wisconsin campaign finance expenditure and receipt estimates, see Governor's Study Committee on Political Finance, *Final Report* (Madison, 1974), pp. 1–33.

25. Owens, *op. cit.*, pp. 76–77.

26. Arnold Heidenheimer, "Comparative Party Finance: Notes on Practices and Toward a Theory", *Journal of Politics*, Vol. 25 (November, 1963), pp. 796–97. Also, Adamany, *Financing Politics*, pp. 53–57.

27. The literature refurbishing the tarnished image of the American voter includes V. O. Key, Jr., *The Responsible Electorate* (New York: Vintage Books, 1968); Gerald M. Pomper, "From Confusion to Clarity: Issues and American Voters, 1956–1968", *The American Political Science Review*, Vol. 66 (June, 1972), pp. 415–428; Richard W. Boyd, "Popular Control of Public Policy: A Normal Vote Analysis of the 1968 Election", *The American Political Science Review*, Vol. 66 (June, 1972), pp. 429–449; Philip E. Converse, *et. al.*, "Continuity and Change in American Politics: Parties and Issues in the 1968 Election", *The American Political Science Review*, Vol. 63 (December, 1969), pp. 1095–1101.

28. Thayer, *op. cit.*, p. 274.

29. "Common Cause Study", *op. cit.*

30. Surveys for 1968 and earlier years are reported in Alexander, *Money in Politics*, pp. 335–336. The 1972 data are from the Twentieth Century Fund Poll of Campaign Finance taken by the National Opinion Research Center for the Twentieth Century Fund Project on Public Financing of Elections. The author is co-director of the project.

31. The 1960 and 1964 figures are found in Alexander, *Money in Politics*, pp. 335–336. The 1972 figures are from the Twentieth Century Fund Poll on Campaign Finance.

32. The 1972 figures are from the Twentieth Century Fund Poll on Campaign Finance. Earlier studies show the same upper class bias in campaign contributions. See Herbert E. Alexander, *Responsibility in Party Finance* (Princeton: Citizens' Research Foundation, 1963), p. 25. Also, Adamany, *Campaign Finance in America*, p. 197.

33. Alexander, *Financing the 1968 Election*, p. 163.

34. *Ibid.*, pp. 167–168.

35. "Common Cause Study", *op. cit.*

36. Fascinating details of family financing by the Rockefellers and Kennedys are found in Thayer, *op. cit.*, pp. 157–164.

37. On the Goldwater campaign, see Alexander, *Financing the 1964 Election*, pp. 44, 160.

38. The basic pattern of modern campaign giving is described in Heard, *op. cit.*, pp. 120–129, and ch. 7. See also Alexander, *Money in Politics*, chs. 9 and 10. Descriptions of the business link to Republicans and the labor commitment to Democrats in state politics are John P. White and John R. Owens, *Parties, Group Interests and Campaign Finance: Michigan '56'* (Princeton: Citizens' Research Founcation, 1967); Adamany, *Financing Politics*, ch. 6; Adamany, *Campaign Finance in America*, pp. 136–155.

39. Alexander, *Financing the 1968 Election*, pp. 181–185.

40. *Ibid.*, pp. 185–187.

41. Herbert E. Alexander, "G.O.P.'s Big Bankrollers of 1972," *New York Times*, September 3, 1974, Section 3, Business and Finance, p. 1.

42. For a summary of 1972 expenditures and contributions by selected interest groups, see *Congressional Quarterly Weekly Report*, Vol. 31, No. 11, March 17, 1973, pp. 568–588.

43. Alexander, *Financing the 1968 Election*, p. 194.

44. Greenhill, *op. cit.* Also, White and Owens, *op. cit.* Adamany, *Campaign Finance in America*, pp. 139–141 and Adamany, *Financing Politics*, p. 205.

45. The complex motivations of campaign contributors have been considered by Heard, *op. cit.*, pp. 68–84. See also William Buchanan and Agnes Bird, *Money as a Campaign Resource: Tennessee Democratic Senatorial Primaries, 1948–1964* (Princeton: Citizens' Research Foundation, 1966), pp. 77–81.

46. Delmer D. Dunn, *Financing Presidential Campaigns* (Washington, Brookings Institution, 1972), pp. 19–25. Also, Heard, *op. cit.*, pp. 84–94.

47. Dunn, *op. cit.*, pp. 11–14. For the view that a serious contender must raise a basic threshold of funds and that most can do so, see Buchanan and Bird, *op. cit.*, p. 90.

48. Heard, *op. cit.*, pp. 64–84. Thayer, *op. cit.*, pp. 125–129, 280–281.

49. The Federal Election Campaign Act of 1974, Public Law 93-443, 93d Congress, 2d Sess., 1974. A review of state and federal campaign finance laws is Office of Federal Elections, *Analysis of Federal and State Campaign Finance Law* (Washington, 1974).

50. An early state supreme court decision held spending limits were constitutional when applied to a candidate, but they could not also restrict spending by other citizens. This ruling caused most campaigns to be financed by "voluntary" committees, which by legal fiction were not directed by the candidate. See *State ex rel. LaFollette v. Kohler*, 200 Wis. 518 (1930). More recently, the Washington Supreme Court struck down that state's expenditure limits in a closely reasoned opinion that seemed to condemn any spending restrictions. *Bare v. Gorton,*–Wash. 2d–, 526 P. 2d 379 (1974).

Most legal commentators agree that expenditure limits are unconstitutional. See, for example, Joel L. Fleishman, "Freedom of Speech and Equality of Political Opportunity: The Constitutionality of the Federal Election Campaign Act of 1971," *North Carolina Law Review*, Vol. 51 (1973) pp. 434–479. Also, Martin H. Redish, "Campaign Spending Laws and the First Amendment," *New York University Law Review*, Vol. 46 (November, 1971), pp. 907–924. An opposite view is expressed in "Common Cause Memorandum on the Constitutionality of Contribution and Expenditure Limitations," (Washington, 1973), pp. 15–21.

51. This so-called "central treasurer" system for regulating campaign expenditures has been condemned by the two courts that have considered it. *State v. Pierce*, 163 Wis. 615 (1916); *American Civil Liberties Union v. Jennings*, 336 F. Supp. 1041 (1973) (three-judge court).

52. Most commentators agree that Congress can, within its authority to regulate elections, restrict campaign contributions that threaten the integrity of elections. Albert J. Rosenthal, *Federal Regulation of Campaign Finance: Some Constitutional Questions* (Princeton: Citizens' Research Foundation, 1972), pp. 20–25. Fleishman, *op. cit.*, pp. 442–445; "Common Cause Memorandum," *op. cit.* A somewhat different view is that contributions might be restricted within the congressional power to enforce the equal protection of the laws guaranteed by the Fourteenth Amendment. Marlene Arnold Nicholson, "Campaign Financing and Equal Protection," *Stanford Law Review*, Vol. 26 (April, 1974), pp. 815–854. At least one law professor believes, however, that any restriction on campaign contributions is a curtailment of political freedom and therefore a violation of the First Amendment. Ralph K. Winter, Jr., "Money, Politics and the First Amendment," in *Campaign Finances: Two Views on the Political and Constitutional Implications* (Washington: American Enterprise Institute, 1971), pp. 59–62.

53. Corporations and unions apparently have a constitutionally guaranteed right to spend money to communicate with stockholders and members on any political subject. *United States v. Congress of Industrial Organizations*, 335 U.S. 106, 121 (1948).

54. Herbert E. Alexander, *Money, Politics, and Public Reporting* (Princeton: Citizens' Research Foundation), p. 7.

55. Twentieth Century Fund Task Force on Financing Congressional Campaigns, *Electing Congress* (New York: Twentieth Century Fund, 1970), p. 15.

56. For an excellent discussion of the Act, see Jeffrey M. Berry and Jerry Goldman, "Congress and Public Policy: A Study of the Federal Election Campaign Act of 1971," *Harvard Journal on Legislation*, Vol. 10 (February, 1973), pp. 331–356. Also Alexander, *Money in Politics*, pp. 305–311.

57. One commentator has argued that only very large contributions, posing a plain danger of corrupting the political system, can be subject to disclosure laws. Other disclosure provisions would run afoul of the First Amendment freedoms of speech, association, and privacy. Winter, *op. cit.*, pp. 62–65.

Courts have, however, tended to uphold sweeping disclosure laws and to grant the legislature wide discretion in setting the amounts that must be disclosed. *Burroughs v. United States*, 290 U.S. 534 (1934) (upholding the Corrupt Practices Act of 1925); *United States v. Harriss*,

347 U.S. 612 (1954) (upholding the Federal Lobbying Act); *Stoner v. Fortson*, 369 F. Supp. 704 (1974) (three-judge court) (upholding a Georgia law requiring disclosure of contributions of $100 or more).

58. Ben H. Bagdikian, "The Fruits of Agnewism," *Columbia Journalism Review*, Vol. 11 (January/Fedruary, 1973), pp. 9–21.

59. Major parties are defined as those receiving more than 25 percent of the vote in the past election, and minor parties are those receiving between 5 and 25 percent of vote in the prior balloting. New parties are those which polled less than 5 percent.

60. Heard, *op. cit.*, pp. 387–399. David Adamany, *Campaign Funds as an Intraparty Political Resource: Connecticut, 1966–1968* (Princeton: Citizens' Research Foundation, 1972), esp. pp. 33–51.

61. E. E. Schattschneider, *Party Government* (New York: Holt, Rinehart, and Winston, 1942); American Political Science Association, Committee on Political Parties, "Toward A More Responsible Two-Party System," *American Political Science Review,* Vol. 44 (September, 1950), Supplement; David S. Broder, *The Party's Over* (New York: Harper and Row, 1971).

62. This proposal is elaborated in David Adamany and George Agree, *Political Money: A Strategy for Campaign Financing in America* (Baltimore: Johns Hopkins Press, 1975), esp. ch. 11.

—**20**—

CAMPAIGN FINANCE REFORM:
WHAT IS HAPPENING
IN THE INDIVIDUAL STATES?

Herbert E. Alexander

In recent years, Americans have come to look to the federal government for major initiatives in reform legislation. Since the days of Franklin Roosevelt's New Deal, it has seemed that the lead in formulating economic and welfare legislation, and in such diverse areas as education and housing and health and antipoverty programs, has come from Washington. One reason that we tend to focus on the federal government is that it is easier to keep track of what is going on in Washington than it is to monitor developments in 50 state capitals.

Yet in the area of campaign finance reform, our natural tendency to look first to Washington would cause us to miss much of the action. Not, perhaps, since the turn of the century or the progressive era have the states served as such busy laboratories of reform as they have during the past two years in changing the regulations by which political campaigns are financed.

The Congress started the new reform movement in 1971–72, when two laws were enacted: the Federal Election Campaign Act of 1971, and the Revenue Act of 1971. The former brought much more comprehensive and detailed disclosure of political campaign fund receipts and expenditures, and improved procedures for enforcement of the election law. The latter provided tax incentives for political contributions and a tax dollar checkoff; these will be explained shortly. The states soon began to move rapidly toward reform, and now have outpaced the Congress which, at this writing, is moving very slowly in the second round of reform. At the National Governors' Conference in June, 1974, a resolution was adopted in support of full disclosure of receipts and expenditures, alternative means of campaign funding, and independent enforcement procedures. In the two years since the Presidential election, the Congress has not enacted any substantial election legislation; in that same period 35 of the 50 states have passed such laws. Twenty-two states have enacted such measures in 1974 alone. Most of the laws have been enacted through the legislative process. There are, however, two states where political reform was achieved through a ballot initiative. In 1972 the voters of the state of Washington passed Initiative Measure No. 276 and in 1974 California voters approved Proposition 9.

There has been so much activity that it is difficult to keep up with what the states have been doing. It is no longer sufficient simply to check the states' election laws to keep current; one must now delve into tax law, where provisions for checkoffs and tax incentive are codified, and into administrative law, where restrictions on contributions by state contractors may be found. The states have been coming to the realization that political finance is not a small area of the law which can be kept neatly segregated; they are coming to learn that the ways campaigns are financed affect the whole of our political and electoral processes.

Because the answers to the knotty problems of campaign financing are not as self-evident as some reformers think, and the goals which are thought desirable are sometimes conflicting and even contradictory, this burst of activity at the state level is a heartening development. Justice Brandeis called the states laboratories of reform, and in the area of political finance, the experiments which can most appropriately be performed in such laboratories are most needed. Some state enactments will doubtless be proven unwise, as have some pre-1972 state finance regulations. Others may be declared unconstitutional; in fact the new laws have been challenged in Washington, Georgia, New Jersey and other states. Barring unconstitutionality some changes may prove to work better than their proponents or opponents expect. Some which have been passed into law in some states seem not to have occurred to legislators at the federal level, or would have no chance of passage in the Congress. As Brandeis suggested, the advantage of state experimentation is that mistakes made in a few states will not significantly harm the entire nation, and at the same time successes at the state level can serve as models for imitation, both in other states and, to the extent they are applicable, at the federal level.

MAJOR TYPES OF EXPERIMENTATION

A brief look at the major types of experimentation will not permit us to review all state change. Focus will be on those laws which seem most promising, or most unusual, or to indicate the possibilities of change which may not be appreciated by observers of the federal level.

Disclosure

A basic requirement is full disclosure of campaign income and expenditures. Without such knowledge, the voter cannot make an intelligent choice on election day. Disclosure may not prevent large contributors from exerting undue influence on the political process or on governmental decisions, but it should help to discourage such practices. That is why full and frequent disclosure is a keystone of the model state statute on campaign finance reform which J. Paul Molloy and I have drafted for the Citizens' Research Foundation, entitled *Model State Statute: Politics, Elections and Public Office.* A few states have been far ahead of the federal government with respect to disclosure. The federal law prior to 1972 contained many loopholes and disclosure was limited. But as long ago as 1951, Florida passed a comprehensive "sunshine law," resulting from revelations about politics made at the Kefauver Committee hearings.

Currently, only four states have no reporting or disclosure requirements at all: Idaho, Illinois, Louisiana, and North Dakota. There is, however, growing sentiment in all of them for reform measures. Only two years ago, nine states had no such regulations. Fully 31 of the states now require disclosure of contributions and/or expenditures before as well as after elections. Naturally, this is an integral part of the need for disclosure; if you do not learn what disclosure tells until after the election, you can hardly use that information as a basis for your vote. Another integral part of disclosure is the need for an independent election commission to receive the required reports, to audit them, and to determine if there are violations. The federal government does not have such a commission although many proposals to establish one have been made; reports are currently made to three supervisory officers, the Secretary of the Senate, the Clerk of the House, and the Comptroller General, all of whom are accountable to the Congress. But 12 states do have election commissions independent of either the executive or legislative branches, with powers of investigation, subpoena, or the holding of hearings. Two other states have election commissions with lesser powers. The commissions are nonpartisan, and are an attempt to replace partisan elected officials, such as Secretaries of State, who traditionally were repositories of campaign fund reports, but whose partisanship did not make them ideal enforcers.

The states to watch most closely are those which have given their election commissions strong powers, including the power to assess penalties. New Jersey's Election Law Enforcement Commission has been in operation through a major election year. More recently the New York State Board of Elections has been given the same powers. The California measure was part of Proposition 9, the initiative proposal which, despite heavy opposition from business and labor, was passed with 69 percent of the vote. Among its many other provisions, Proposition 9 sets up a Fair Campaign Practices Commission to receive detailed reporting from campaigns, and gives the commission the power to assess fines of up to $10,000 or three times the amount of an illegal contribution. It will be interesting to observe how the experiment works out in the laboratory that is our most populated state.

Campaign expenditure limits

The inspiration for many state laws limiting campaign expenditures has been their high and rising costs. Clearly, few voters want a wealthy candidate or campaign to be able to "buy" an election. But there is a less generally recognized countervailing goal. It costs money to run a campaign which will effectively reach voters in this age of mass media and public apathy. There is danger that expenditure limits which are set too low will prevent candidates, especially candidates challenging well-entrenched incumbents, from getting their messages across. If limits are too low they may be circumvented, and in any case may favor incumbents who are better known and may not need to spend heavily just to achieve name recognition.

Such has been the experience with limits like Alabama's, which allows gubernatorial candidates to spend only $50,000. Similarly, Indiana, a state where many public employees are assessed percentages of their salaries by political party organizations, purports to limit gubernatorial spending to $25,000; Wisconsin sets a $20,000 limit on gubernatorial contests. These limits are circumvented by such means as the creation of multiple committees in the support of the same candidate. What they mainly accomplish is increased public cynicism.

Perhaps the most unrealistic absolute limits are those in some states, such as the Dakotas, which limit candidates to spending a percentage of the salary of the office they are seeking. Since salaries in these sparsely-populated states are low, allowed spending may be only a few thousand dollars. One might expect such unrealistic limits to be regularly exceeded, and the law unlikely to be enforced. Most politicans seek such offices because they have some deeply held convictions about what they can accomplish, not for their munificent salaries.

More realistic limits on spending have been established more recently in other states. Florida allows gubernatorial candidates to spend $600,000; Kansas, $500,000; Minnesota, $600,000. Rhode Island, a state in which party organizations dominate politics, allows gubernatorial candidates to spend $400,000 in the general election, but only $100,000 in the primary. Not surprisingly, since the 1930s, the candidate endorsed by the Democratic Party leadership has usually won his primary; but competition has sometimes been spirited in general elections.

Probably the most rational way to set limits is to base them, as many states have, on the total voting population, or on voting-age population. By gearing spending to these figures, these states have enacted built-in escalator clauses, allowing at least some increase in spending as the electorate or the population grows. Since campaign costs are rising rapidly, the federal law and some states make at least some allowance for inflation by tying limits to the cost of living index.

As these laws are implemented, it will be interesting to compare the way they affect politics in states with low limits and those with high limits. The amount allowable per voter varies from 4¢ each for a primary election or a general election in Michigan to 75¢ each for a primary or general election in Wyoming. The amount per person ranges in Arizona and Ohio from 10¢ in either a primary or general election to 16¢ in a primary and 24¢ in a general election in Alaska. Calculating from the 1970 census or the

1972 election results, these limits range from $49,524 in New Hampshire to $1.00 million in Ohio, almost 4 million in New York. Some limits seem unrealistically low, $273,926 in Michigan, and $133,509 in Maryland, but we will at least have the opportunity to measure the variations in the states. Additionally, three states have placed upper limits on media spending, from $100,000 in Utah to $500,000 in Massachusetts for gubernatorial candidates, as the federal law does, without attempting overall ceilings.

Contribution limits

A less popular reform in the states is the placing of limits on contributions by individuals or groups to campaigns. Most of the 15 states which have individual contribution limits restrict the amounts given to the $3,000 figure mandated by federal gift tax law, which has been habitually circumvented by the proliferation of committees in support of a single candidate. The states' limits for contribution to any one candidate range from $600 in New Jersey to $5,000 in New Hampshire, Oklahoma, and West Virginia, with just one exception: the huge $150,000 overall limit in New York—a limit which affects only the wealthiest individuals. New York also limits a candidate's contributions to his own campaign to one percent of total permitted expenditure, and members of his family to an aggregate of five percent of the total. Some of these laws attempt to plug the gift tax loophole by prohibiting multiple contributions to multiple committees supporting the same candidate. Their success or failure in this endeavor will be well worth watching.

Curiously, New York and Maryland rescinded prohibitions on corporate contributions which are forbidden under federal law and in 35 states, a step which may be seen as either an invitation to corruption or as a concession to reality. Only five states prohibit labor union contributions to political activity, which is a wide disparity considering that federal law treats corporations and unions alike by prohibiting contributions from either.

To the extent that contribution limits effectively put a lid on the size of campaign contributions, we can expect to see a spate of litigation in the next few years. Many people, by no means all of them large contributors, believe that such laws abridge an individual's constitutional right under the First Amendment to support the candidate of his choice to the maximum extent he desires. That claim must be taken seriously, yet however the courts decide it, there is the public policy question of the potential danger in laws which, however well intended, have the effect of diminishing political participation. We may very well see conflicting judicial decisions on this issue in various jurisdictions, which may ultimately have to be settled by the United States Supreme Court. But at the same time as this litigation is going on, we will be able to observe how strict contribution limits actually work, whether they effectively reduce the influence of large contributors or whether money simply will seek new channels and make its way, tortuously but effectively, into campaigns. Similar attacks on the constitutionality of candidate expenditure limits are also to be expected.

WHAT ABOUT CAMPAIGNS THAT ARE UNDERFINANCED?

In the opinion of some observers, large contributions by a few individuals present a lesser problem than that so many individuals contribute nothing at all. For every campaign that is overfinanced, as President Nixon's 1972 campaign surely was, there are dozens of campaigns which are underfinanced and the candidates are never able to afford to get their messages across to the voters. The long ballot, with simultaneous federal, state, and local elections in many jurisdictions means that many candidates cannot raise sufficient dollars to be able to buy adequate exposure to the electorate. If we do not want more large contributions, then we must create some incentives or set up some system to get larger numbers of small contributions.

Unfortunately, most of the ways campaigns and candidates have found to do this on their own are themselves expensive. Candidates like Barry Goldwater in 1964 and George McGovern in 1972 were able to raise major shares of their campaign treasuries through direct mail appeals; but direct mail is itself expensive, and in some cases costs the candidate more than it brings in.

The Tax System as Incentive

There are other means of raising small contributions from many contributors, and some of them operate through the income tax system. The federal government now allows taxpayers to channel $1 of their tax money, $2 on a joint return, to a fund for presidential campaign spending. The federal system also allows taxpayers to claim one half the amount of contributions up to $12.50

credit on individual and $25 on joint returns. Alternatively, a taxpayer can take a deduction for the full amount of contributions up to $50 on a single return or $100 on a joint return.

Among the states, the deduction is the most popular device, and is available in 11 states—but not all states have income taxes. Only two states, Oregon and Minnesota, provide tax credits and the amounts are the same as that permitted by the federal system. Considering the comparatively low rate of state income taxes, these are worth much more to taxpayers than are deductions.

The tax credit is a more powerful incentive, because the taxpayer does not simply reduce the amount of income on which the tax must be paid, but reduces the amount of taxes payable. Thus the states which allow credits are in effect subsidizing, albeit indireclty, political campaigns to the extent contributions to these campaigns are eligible for the credit.

The checkoff device, now employed by the federal government, is also utilized by five states. Here the state, on direction of the taxpayer, actually relinquishes $1 of the amount of tax due, either to a general campaign fund from which the money is allocated according to formula, as in Montana, or to the party organization as in Iowa, Minnesota, Rhode Island, and Utah. In Minnesota and Rhode Island, a taxpayer can alternatively check off money for a non-partisan general fund. The fact that this money goes to parties rather than to candidates may well help to strengthen the often atrophied party organizations around the country, another example of an experiment that may produce worthwhile results.

A device used in two states that has not yet been suggested at the federal level is the tax surcharge. Under this plan, the taxpayer's liability is increased by $1 (in Maine) or $2 (in Maryland) and that money would be given to a fair campaign financing fund. Since many state income taxpayers receive refunds from withheld taxes, in practical terms this would mean simply reducing the refund by a dollar or two. Yet at the same time, the state would not be deflecting tax money which would otherwise go to its general fund.

DIRECT PUBLIC FINANCING OF ELECTIONS

The states have been as slow as the federal government in providing a system of direct public financing of elections; in fact, Louisiana's recently passed constitution prohibits such a reform. Nevertheless, two states have enacted matching fund proposals. In Maryland, starting with the state elections of 1978, each $1 of private contributions up to $50 would be matched by $3 of state money. In New Jersey, starting in 1977, gubernatorial candidates would be eligible, after raising an initial $40,000 in small sums, for $2 of public funds for each $1 of private funds they raise up to $600. These matching incentive programs have the advantage of avoiding rigid formulas to determine how much each candidate gets, which is particularly difficult when it comes to primaries or minor party candidates. These decisions are made, in·effect, by ordinary contributors, and those soliciting contributions will be able to tell potential donors they contact that a contribution costing $1 to them is worth $3 or $4 to the campaign. Whether this will prove a valuable incentive for giving will not be demonstrated in these states until 1977 and 1978, although there is time for other states to enact such reforms for 1976.

CONCLUSION

Some people, looking at this burst of activity in the states, may see only chaos, the potential of 50 different systems. Certainly, it is difficult to keep up with the various laws. Nevertheless, to the extent there is chaos, it is creative chaos. The states are taking positive actions to eliminate abuses in the political financing process. Some will work better than others. Some will fail or be evaded or not enforced. But all will provide valuable experience for the nation as we seek to cleanse and improve our system of elections.

-21-

A MEMO TO THE
ERVIN COMMITTEE

Stephen Hess

At last the Senate Watergate Committee has called off its public hearings and decided to get on with the business of writing its report. Senate Resolution 60, authorizing the Select Committee, charged it with recommending new laws, if needed, "to safeguard the integrity or purity of the process by which Presidents are chosen."

Since television permitted the American people to have the same data as the seven Senators who served on the committee, it is not presumptuous for us to advise Sen. Ervin and his colleagues on what they should report.

As the events of Watergate relate to the presidential selection process, they include the wiretapping and burglary of the Democratic National Committee, organized and executed by operatives of the Nixon campaign; a series of Nixon committee efforts to sabotage contenders for the Democratic nomination, presumably designed to increase George McGovern's chances of being nominated; and illegal contributions to and expenditures by the Nixon organization. Other events, possibly of even greater consequences to the governance of a democratic society, have become enmeshed in the scandal, but should have been outside the scope of an inquiry into how Americans choose their Presidents.

Watergate, the Senate Committee should conclude, was primarily a failure of individuals who should have been conscious of

From Stephen Hess, "A Memo to the Ervin Committee," *Wall Street Journal*, March 25, 1974, p. 14. Reprinted with the permission of the *Wall Street Journal*, copyright © by Dow Jones & Company, Inc., 1974.

acting illegally and should have known the possible consequences of their actions. That these were men who held high trust and upon whom society had lavished honor might cause us to ask how representative they are of the nation that produced them. If indeed they are like us, then we must find ways to contain ourselves. But a free society pays a price for assuming its own immorality. "Should we have a law against red wigs? A law compelling search of all suitcases for $100 bills?" asks Meg Greenfield, of the *Washington Post*. "There are certain limits to what we can expect the written laws to do for us and certain dangers in trying to write laws that will cover and control every possible aspect of human malfeasance."

LAWS AND CONDUCT

The prescription to prevent future Watergates is not likely to be additional laws or even stiffer penalties. Stiffer penalties will reflect the seriousness that society attaches to aberrant behavior, but there is little assurance that this would have deterred those involved in the crimes of 1972. Society proscribes through law a negative code of conduct—"thou shalt nots"—and enforces them through its legal system. The legal system is not designed to reward those who keep the law nor can it in most cases prevent those who wish to from breaking the law.

Even if Watergate is viewed as a failure of men, it may be that politics can cause people to act more immorally than they might in other pursuits. There is no reason to believe, for example, that the bright young men who appeared before the Ervin Committee were not good husbands, good parents, or didn't otherwise conduct themselves in an exemplary manner.

Jerry Bruno, a leading Democratic advance man, once wrote, "When you're part of a political campaign, the stakes are as high as they come. . . . I think sometimes it's what fighting a war or playing a pro football game is like." The analogies are apt. Modern warfare is often a suspension of morality, often in the name of morality; pro football is a sport in which infractions of the rules are penalized by loss of yards, rarely by banishment, so that breaking the rules becomes a calculated risk, rather than a moral stigma.

Moreover, it is in the nature of the ad hoc staffing arrangements of presidential campaigns to temporarily remove the participants from their "real" worlds in which they individually abide by the codes of conduct of whatever occupations engage them. This does not mean that all citizens leave their morality at home when they enter a presidential campaign; only a very small number do. But, almost without exception, they do see the world of politics as different, less enduring. And for some this makes a difference in their conduct.

Under the existing system, candidates seeking a presidential nomination propose themselves, raise their own funds, and build their own organizations. When a person wishes to run for President he must very quickly recruit a staff from among friends and others who are in a position to drop what they are doing and devote themselves to his cause for periods of up to a year. Personnel are often loaned by corporations, law firms, advertising agencies, newspapers, labor unions, and trade associations. The rich often loan themselves. The young are available and do not cost much.

After the conventions, the winning candidates' personal staffs become the nuclei of the campaign organizations. These people, who are responsible for conducting the most important free election in the world, are generally amateurs in that politics is not their profession, despite varying degrees of experience. It is worth recalling the statement of Harvard Professor Richard Neustadt, made in a somewhat different context: "The presidency is no place for amateurs."

The process of conducting a presidential campaign raises questions about individual and group ethics in an election system that lacks a professional memory. Professionalism, by definition, includes a set of standards by which one is judged and upon which depends one's status. High standards of conduct are strengthened by, if not dependent upon, continuing relationships. Yet continuity is exactly what is absent from the organization of presidential campaigns.

Instead we have devised a system that tends to divorce the presidential candidates from the political parties they represent. Television has encouraged this. So have election laws. So have legions of campaign consultants, who now can supply candidates with the services that they once received from their party organizations. So too has the predominance of foreign affairs, a special concern of Presidents, but traditionally one that has been treated with bipartisan detachment.

Primarily, though, this is a product of a prevailing of American attitude. We have scorned the professional politician and glorified a form of political Cincinnatus, the citizen-soldier who drops his plow to wage war for his candidate. Running as a Republican or a

Democrat is no longer an unalloyed asset and so, in many cases, the candidates have chosen to run away from their parties. "I'm not going to ask anybody here to vote on November the 8th because of the party label that I happen to wear," said Richard Nixon in 1960. One by-product of this attitude is that the permanent party committees at the national level are anemic creatures, little more than the caretakers that keep the files, convene the conventions and dispense routine services.

A SORROWFUL REMINDER

Watergate provides a sorrowful reminder of how much we miss by not having a strong two-party system with a professional code of ethics for those who participate in the political process. Running presidential campaigns under the centralized control of the parties' national committees would not produce the millennium. Our parties practice a type of accommodation politics that is not well suited to injecting creativity into public debate. But it is highly unlikely that the Republican National Committee would seriously consider breaking into the Democratic National Committee, or vice versa, if only for the reason stated by David S. Broder in "The Party's Over": "Our political parties are old, and they expect to be in business a long time. Neither of them has any great temptation to kick down the walls, or to pursue tactics when temporarily in power that will invite revenge from the opposition when it (inevitably) returns to power."

It is doubtful that our political parties could ever regain the central position in our system that they held in the 19th Century. Government has replaced the parties as dispenser of social services, patronage is no longer an attractive enough lure to recruit political workers, other forms of entertainment and voluntary associations now compete with the parties on unequal terms, and television gives the voters increased opportunities to get information and judge candidates outside of the party context.

But the parties do have it within their power to regain control of presidential campaigns. For they have one lever without which no candidate could expect to become President, a major party line on the voting machines. It is high time presidential contests were again run by the parties, rather than by individual political entrepreneurs. This is what I hope that the Ervin Committee will report.

—22—

WATERGATE AND THE ELECTORAL PROCESS

Herbert E. Alexander

I

Occasionally, a public issue surfaces which relates to the basic fibers of our democratic system, and whose resolution further translates the democratic theory of 1776 into actual practice. Such were the issues of black and woman suffrage, of the civil and voting rights movements. The series of events known as Watergate and other recent disclosures such as the Agnew resignation, have produced many issues relating to our democratic system, but none are more profound than those relating to the electoral process. The problem is how to apply democratic principles to elections in an age of media politics seemingly dominated by an atmosphere of dollar politics. The electoral process presents perhaps a classic case of conflict between the democratic theory of full public dialogue in free elections and the conditions of an economic marketplace. It is idle to posit an unabridgeable First Amendment Right to unrestricted electioneering, but in determining regulation it is necessary to choose between—or strike a happy balance between—protecting the integrity of the electoral system and making laws that give candidates or government administrators discretion to prohibit free speech, or that have a chilling effect on citizen participation.

From Herbert E. Alexander, "Watergate and The Electoral Process" (paper delivered at a Conference of the U.S. Senate Select Committee on Presidential Campaign Activities and the Center for the Study of Democratic Institutions, Santa Barbara, California, December 1973).

The prevalence of corrupt practices and criminal actions in the 1972 Presidential election could provide the impetus for broad political reform that would extend and expand citizen participation in the governing processes. Remarkably, most of the reform proposals would tend to restrict and limit popular electoral participation rather than to enlarge it. It is unsettling for some of us who have advocated reform to find ourselves in the awkward position of advising caution in considering some well-intentioned proposals which entail massive changes from American tradition. Many of these reforms would have uncertain impact upon our political structure, and it is essential to consider carefully their possible consequences before they are implemented. Any proposals that would heavily invest government with functions traditionally in the private sector should be looked at with a healthy skepticism. Public policies adopted in immediate reaction to scandal may not have been given the measured thought desirable when major change is contemplated. We are faced with the dilemma of needing reform but not knowing precisely the form reform should take.

The 1972 Presidential election demonstrated the slippage of some governmental officials into illegal acts that could have harmed irreparably the most sensitive of democratic processes—free and unfettered elections. The 1972 Republican Presidential campaign provides documentation for almost every corrupt practice imaginable. It marked the culmination of years of neglect and of failure to be sufficiently concerned about the ways elections and campaigns were conducted.

The Federal Election Campaign Act of 1971 (FECA) preceded rather than followed the scandals of Watergate, which is notable considering that so many observers had said for so long that only serious scandal would bring reform. The Bobby Baker and Tom Dodd cases may be considered causal, but reform came before the greatest of all recent scandals, Watergate, because of the persistence and leadership of a very few Members of Congress. Once legislation reached the floors of the Senate and House, pressure to be recorded in favor became overriding. Before the FECA, a tradition of disclosure dated back to 1910, but inadequacies in the predecessor Federal Corrupt Practices Act, and a parallel inadequacy in enforcement, led to an habitual failure of many to take certain election laws seriously.

At all levels of government, too many electoral statutes have invited criminal offenses while doing little to discourage them. For too many years, in too many jurisdictions, too many candidates, election workers, and enforcement authorities have tended to wink at certain election laws, to make loose and strained legal interpretations designed to assist friends and opponents alike, to keep the rules of the game agreeable to fellow politicians. Unrealistic laws, particularly those regulating public finance, invited noncompliance. Laws that fail to take into account the clear needs for funds or the high stakes in winning elections, lead readily to noncompliance.

Peel away the acts of eavesdropping and sabotage in the Watergate and related abuses, and the root of the problem was money. The Republicans had too much money and thus had the flexibility to indulge themselves in ventures leading to Watergate. A campaign with a lean budget does not engage in such activities. The Nixon campaign had so much money that it indulged in overkill, spending $55 million, much more than was necessary to defeat Senator McGovern and a substantially greater amount than any other Presidential campaign had spent in American history. The Nixon campaign had no real need to take money in cash or from questionable sources. There was no need to keep cash in safes. The excess money could have been used to assist Senatorial and Congressional candidates in their campaigns and in that way to help strengthen the Republican Party.

But as overwhelming and distressing as the money scandals have been, many potential dangers just as serious exist in the entire electoral process—from the ways we register voters to the modes and means of campaigning, to the ways we nominate and vote for the candidates and then count the votes. While there is disillusionment with the ways we nominate and elect our President and Vice President, the problems go deeper. Serious questions need to be asked about other aspects of the electoral process: about open primaries in which there are candidates too numerous for the voters to appraise; about cross filing; about the ways Presidential and other nominating conventions are financed; about electoral administration; about the tremendous numbers of elected officials—by all counts, more than 500,000; about judicial elections; about ballot issues and propositions.

We must be concerned now about diminished confidence in the electoral process, and accordingly, we must examine every aspect of that process in terms of increasing levels of confidence, participation, relevance and efficacy. Some of these problems cannot be addressed at this conference because they must be considered by state and local governments, but they are nevertheless crucial parts of what should be our national concern.

To identify one critical underlying fault, American politics have become excessively candidate-oriented. The abuses of the 1972 campaign and its aftermath are in essence the culmination of parallel trends more closely related than many realize: the lessening importance of political parties, the decline of the Cabinet, the changing role of the White House staff. The electoral process encourages loyalty to the man, not to the party and its program. This undermines the party and leads to emphasis on the candidate's own organization, the apotheosis of which was the Committee for the Re-election of the President, responsible and responsive to the candidate, perhaps, but to no one else—not to voters, not even to contributors, and certainly not to the party of which the candidate was the nominee. Just as we have a rule of law and not of men, we should take steps to encourage, both in the electoral and governing processes, a rule of party and not of men.

The Republican National Committee and the Democratic National Committee do not control the presidential campaigns. The candidate committees that are created are often at odds with the party committees. This fragments loyalty, centering the election around the candidate, and once he is elected, sets the stage for a Presidency independent of party, so egocentric that power resides overwhelmingly in the incumbent, subject to his idiosyncrasies and character, and need not be shared with either a party, or a Cabinet, or a responsible White House staff.

Observers have long known that the American system of private financing of politics had its share of secret money, unreported money, extorted money, corporate money, laundered money, foreign money, tax-free money. Yet few have recalled Bobby Baker getting a cinch amendment introduced in the Senate, which posed a threat to the savings and loan industry, then promising to kill it in return for cash contributions. Or the allegations about contributions made to the President's Club during the Johnson Administration in return for government contracts. Or the low-key Justice Department prosecutions of 18 corporations in 1968-71 for violating the federal prohibition of use of corporate funds, in some cases by their permitting public relations and advertising agencies to falsify bills to them for work actually done for candidates. Such known instances were only occasionally revealed, and most often occurred at the state and local levels. In 1972, in contrast, an incumbent's Presidential campaign was conducted, at the top of the system, replete with abuses relating to fund raising, handling, and spending, all now or about to be documented in court proceedings and in Congressional testimony under oath. The possibilities of convictions are overwhelming, the instances of misdeeds, unsettling, the scandals, seemingly unending.

Although political financing in the United States had long been undemocratic, with a strong tendency toward corruption, the system survived because for many years it managed to provide sufficient funds. Also, it served the purposes of certain special interests. Nevertheless, the system has come increasingly under attack, not only because of past corruptions, but because it has been failing to provide funds adequate to the needs in many campaigns. The increased incidence of deficit financing in the past decade is striking evidence of this failure.

The cynicism of the electorate in the pre-election phases of Watergate is as frightening as the abuses of the Nixon campaign. The confirmation to many citizens that politics is corrupt and that such abuses are politics as usual illustrates misunderstandings which will be difficult to correct.

Perhaps corrupt practices and government lawlessness have helped to create perceptions among many elements of the population that all politicians are crooks and deceivers. Perhaps Watergate and the Agnew case have reinforced that view among many. But in addition, it has been in the best interests of some of those accused to make it appear that guilt is so universal among politicians that the opposition or others would have done the same thing if they had the chance. According to one Louis Harris poll, 73 percent felt that "dirty campaign tactics exist among Republicans and Democrats, and the Nixon campaign people were no worse than the Democrats except they got caught at it." Fifteen percent disagreed and twelve percent were not sure.[1] While these attitudes may change with later developments, no doubt many want to believe that our political system is hopelessly corrupt. At the same time, many have come to believe that the traditional system of private financing of politics is hopelessly corrupt and must be changed.

One lesson to be learned is that having too much money for campaigns is as harmful as having too little. I would not have expected the Republican Presidential campaign to engage in fund-raising extortion, given the more reliable Republican financial constituency, the Democratic defections among large contributors, the traditional Republican efficiency in raising funds, and the ex perience their finance personnel had gained in the 1968 Nixon campaign. The Democrats, reeling from a large debt carried over since 1968 and a chronic shortage of funds, have always seemed more vulnerable to special interest demands in return for contributions. It is ironic that while the Republicans criticized the Democrats for adopting delegate quotas at their convention, they used corporate and industry quotas in raising funds. It is also ironic that the Republicans, the traditional exponents of private financing of politics, did more through their excesses and abuses in 1972 to create an atmosphere conducive to public financing, than all the lobbies or Democrats could have achieved alone.

Public attention is further focused upon political finance due to the Agnew resignation. But the cumulative impact of Watergate and related plumber missions, the milk industry contributions, IT&T, Vesco, convictions of federal officials for campaign irregularities, and the illegal corporate contributions is devastating. This crest of public concern provides an opportunity to enact electoral reform, an opportunity we cannot afford to misuse.

Before tackling the specifics, a few systemic fundamentals should be considered.

II

In a pluralistic, democratic society like that of the U.S., it is natural that individuals and groups with abundant economic resources will try to use their wealth to influence the course of government. While money is a common denominator in shaping political power, other ingredients are vital as well: leadership, skill, information, public office, numbers of voters, public opinion.

Much of the public debate about the high cost of campaign expenditures is misguided. The nation's total budget for party and electoral politics in 1968 was approximately $300 million, only slightly higher than the advertising budget of Proctor & Gamble. This expenditure is smaller than comparable costs in most other democratic nations. This country can easily afford to spend more money, if necessary, to ensure an equitable, competitive and democratic electoral system.

Money is but one element in the equation of power. In the broadest sense, government is legitimized, and its future course largely determined, at the ballot box. People, not dollars, vote. But dollars help shape both voter behavior and governmental decisions. Individuals or groups with wealth use it to achieve policy goals, by attempting to influence nominations or elections by promoting candidates with congenial views; or to influence public officials. When wealthy persons seek to translate their economic power into political power, one of their tools may be financial contributions.

The American system of government is rooted in the egalitarian assumption of "one man, one vote," but, like all democracies, it is confronted with an unequal distribution of economic resources. The attempt to reconcile the inequalities lies at the base of the problem of money in politics. Many political philosophers from Aristotle on have regarded property or economic power as the fundamental element in political power. In a sense, broadly-based political power, as effected through universal suffrage, was conceived and has been used to help equalize inequalities in economic resources. But that promise is compromised if special interests get undue preferment from candidates and parties forced to depend on them because alternative sources of adequate funds are not available.

Coincident with the extension of the franchise and the democratization of the institutional framework, the economic element that makes for political power—wealth—has been increasingly concentrated. The great industrial, financial, labor, and other interests not only vie to dominate economic life but they also seek to master the political environment. They do this in many direct and indirect ways—directly through lobbies and the contribution of money, indirectly through access to the public in both election and non-election activities.

Money is convertible into other resources, including both the buying of goods and human energy and skills. But the obverse is also true, for other resources in turn can be converted into political money, through use of rights pertaining to public office, for example, in awarding contracts and jobs, in controlling the flow of information, in making decisions. Skillful use of ideology, issues, and the perquisites and promises of office attract financial support to political actors, in legitimate forms as contributions or dues, or in illegitimate ways as scandals have from time to time illustrated.

The underlying concerns about money in politics can be summarized as follows: the costs of political campaigning will make money the crucial factor in determining who will hold political office and will prevent the candidacy of qualified citizens without adequate financial resources or backing; high costs of campaigning will force candidates to accept financial support that will make them beholden and will enable a few persons or groups with financial means to gain access to and perhaps control of the political processes; the power of government will be used unfairly, through employment practices, threats or changes in policies, or use of the airwaves or mails, to favor one party or candidate over another.

The disproportionate influence of special interest group contributors raises basic questions about the relationship of the economic substructure to that of the political superstructure in a pluralistic democratic society. To develop a model system which is practical and enforceable we need to further explore questions such as: Is a new concept and definition of corrupt practices required? When does a political contribution or gift become a bribe? Is systematic campaign soliciting equivalent to a conspiracy to extort funds? Do incumbents so completely dominate the collections of campaign funding to prevent truly competitive elections?

The exploitation and abuse of political power revealed in the Watergate disclosures have prompted new reform proposals designed mainly to impose more stringent restrictions on the use of money, or to supplant private financing with government funding. This can be called the politics of fervency, and it leads inevitably to the politics of exclusion rather than to the politics of competition.

Electoral ground rules inherently favor the resources and skills of some groups and individuals over those of others. Assets are not distributed equally among groups in their ability to contribute campaign funds, to provide volunteer workers, to obtain media coverage, to influence public opinion by endorsement, and to reach opinion leaders. In a pluralistic society, therefore, certain groups are better able to influence the electoral and governing processes, due largely to the resources which they can mobilize on behalf of a candidate or party.

Carleton Sterling has criticized the reformer's ideal as seeking "... a direct dialogue between candidates and voters both free of outside influences."[2] Politics without the influence of interest groups is idealistic only in the sense that it is not realistic. Politics can be improved but it cannot be sterilized and purified to the degree reformers dream. Politics is about people, their ideas, interests, and aspirations. Since people seek political fulfillment partly through groups, a politics in which supportive groups are shut out or seriously impaired is difficult to envisage. Too many ideas and interests of value to society would get lost without the organized participation of groups in electoral politics. Some groups with few members participate mainly through their wealth. Since people and groups differ, conflict occurs, but in a political arena in which government sets the rules and the players are expected to play by them. The government, however, is also a player, and the only failsafe guarantee against its dominance lies in the ability of groups and interests in society to articulate their demands, to coalesce, and to oppose government with resources they command.

Watergate illustrates the ability of an incumbent administration to use its power to subvert the rules of the game. Accordingly, we should be certain to impose effective restraints on the government's administration of election laws. Guarantees must be provided to ensure that the flagrant abuses of 1971–72 are not repeated in different forms through misuse of discretionary power to favor one party or assist incumbents, or to stifle new movements. Especially troublesome are some formulas for government funding in which the government in power can gain control over the funding of its opposition. Automatic mechanisms are essential so that little or no element of control or discretion is involved. Long-term funding through trusts is crucial so that in case government funds are not appropriated oppositions are not left without assured resources and with no means to raise privately the funds necessary for effective campaigning.

If we stipulate that the rules of the game now favor big interests with abundant financial resources, then the rules can be altered. The most simplistic alteration is to restrain their political activity by limiting their participation in the electoral process, and that means limiting the amounts of their political contributions. The course of limiting excessive contributions levels is not as easy as some would make it appear, for money has a way of carving new channels. So long as economic interests are subject to governmental actions, they will find alternative methods of seeking influence. There are, however, legitimate indirect ways to modify the influence of the big interests without stifling a healthy electoral competition. If limitations are adopted, they should be as high as possible, at threshold levels compatible with public confidence that the integrity of the system is being preserved. With or without limits on contributions, efforts should be made to provide alternative sources of funds so that politicians need not rely to the extent some do now on large contributions from special interests. With or without such limits, the rules can be revised to maximize resources which non-monied organizations have in abundance, such as volunteer workers, small contributors, and voters.

Other indirect means of regulating dominant interests also exist, and are preferred ways to diminish their power than are low limits that in effect exclude some from meaningful electoral participation. For example, it is desirable to enact more meaningful disclosure of lobbying, and provide better means of monitoring and publicizing that activity. With proper lobbying regulation, civic organizations could be permitted to lobby for legislation under similar restraints to those which govern corporations, labor unions, and trade associations. Monitoring the Washington scene is expensive. Less secrecy and a more open decision-making process in both the Executive and Legislative branches, and a better publicizing of times and places of hearings and meetings, of governmental studies and regulatory agency rulings, would better enable civic organizations representing important public issues, to participate more fully and more effectively in the decision-making process.

Several other indirect means of restraining special interests come to mind: (1) Improve conflict of interest laws; (2) Minimize by statute special interest representation on regulatory commissions; (3) Reassess the guidelines for movement of representatives of special interests into government positions, and of government employees into related jobs in the private sector; (4) Improve government procurement procedures and policies relating to the awarding of government contracts, particularly in professional services such as consulting engineers and architects.

Thus through improved monitoring and disclosure of the various relationships between private interests and government, might the seemingly undue influence of big interests be diminished without unduly restricting their electoral participation. Electoral participation by special interests provides an important safety valve in the political system, and should not be restricted more than is necessary, compatible with public confidence. A free, flexible, healthy society can withstand more give and play in the system than many give it credit for. A sense of balance and equilibrium between competing forces in society is difficult to achieve, and government can weight the balance to favor smaller and unorganized and weaker players. This would make for a more competitive, vibrant society than one in which special interests are inordinately restricted.

By definition, the pluralist system of competition in free elections entails unequal distribution of influence because resources are unequal. The goals of reform should be to expand the diversity of interest groups which compete to influence elections in the contest for power. Competition should be encouraged, not discouraged. If some interests are dominant, countervailing interests should be built up.

Limitations on special interest contributions to candidates are more easily enforced against issue-oriented citizens groups soliciting many small contributions from the general public, than they are against large corporations or labor unions or trade associations which are better structured to proliferate their committees, each of which can contribute up to the limit. For example, every labor union local can have a political action arm contributing to favored candidates, whereas other groups are not spread geographically and cannot organize as many state and local affiliates. I refer to the National Committee for an Effective Congress, Americans for Constitutional Action, League of Conservation Voters, and other similar groups. Moreover, limitations on expenditures affect groups such as these because any expenditures on behalf of a given candidate—whether incurred in mail solicitation or as a direct contribution—qualifies as an expenditure within the candidate's limit, and in a strict system of enforcement, such expenditures must be authorized by the candidate.

On the other hand, corporations and certain groups can mobilize numerous individual large contributors from among their officers and directors, each of whom can legally contribute as much as a large organization composed of thousands of members whose small contributions are aggregated into a single larger one.

Thus the impact of contributions limits affects individuals, corporations, unions, and public interest groups in varying ways. Setting identical limits for individuals and committees equates one wealthy person with a large organization which aggregates many small contributions.

These are typical of the practical political considerations which limits on contributions entail, and they do not touch on the more thorny consitutional and public policy questions regarding limits.

The agruments favoring limitations on spending are readily summarized: that money has come to affect the democratic ideal of equality of opportunity for public office, that the man of little or no wealth increasingly finds it difficult to enter public life, that the well-financed candidate has an unfair advantage and with a media blitz may win, that the ill-financed candidate has too little chance to win nomination or election or may obligate himself to special interests in order to meet the competition of mounting costs. All these arguments are verities to some extent although no comprehensive studies of the incidence of either wealthy or better financed candidates securing nomination and election have been done to my knowledge. Limitations, in theory, would narrow the range of spending, and this would tend to reduce the imbalances that sometimes exist in financial aspects of campaigning. Limitations, in theory, would diminish the need for funds, and this would tend to reduce the need or temptation to accept contributions with strings, explicit or tacit, attached.

The arguments against limitations are more complex, and their brunt is that if limitations are not effective, then they are illusory and breed disrespect for the law, and if they are effective, then they may inhibit free expression.

The President's Commission on Campaign Costs asserted its belief that both overall and partial limitations were unenforceable while full disclosure is a better way to control both excessive contributions and unlimited expenditures. The Commission stated: "The imposition of 'realistic ceilings' or 'segmental limitations,' the latter designed to limit expenditures for certain purposes, e.g., broadcasting, which has been urged by some, would only create a false impression of limitation. Moreover, there is doubt whether individuals could be prohibited from making certain expenditures, instead of contributions if the latter were effectively limited, in view of constitutional guarantees of freedom of expression."[3]

Partial limitations applying only to the communications media are contained in the FECA. Whatever their merits, such partial limitations, particularly those relating to broadcasting, are more readily enforceable, because of the federal power to regulate broadcasting and because of the limited number of larger purchases that are made in the communications media. But it gets progressively harder to keep track of what a candidate or his supporters are spending on such easily manufactured items as bumper stickers or other printed materials; anyone with an offset machine is a printer. The requirement to issue certificates for each outlay becomes burdensome for both the campaign organization and particularly for the seller of goods and services. The concept that all expenditures in excess of $100 must be certified gives the central campaign committee an increment of power to prevent outsiders from participating and seems an overreaction in that it will inhibit voluntarism in ways that may not be salutary.

A decision of the U.S. District Court (D.C.) has already declared unconstitutional certain implementation and enforcement procedures of the FECA with regard to limitations on political advertising in newspapers, magazines, and on television.[4] The implications of the decision are uncertain, as is its future if appealed to the Supreme Court. The decision raises sufficient questions to ponder the efficacy of expenditure limits applicable to other than federal candidates and their authorized committees. Without the possibility of effective enforcement against issue-oriented, personal, or negative political advertising, which the decision in effect struck down, it is questionable whether any purpose would be served by such limits when they can be readily bypassed.

Even given strong and effective enforcement, the implementation of overall limitations is most difficult. There are many openings for disbursement to support a candidate: (1) through party, labor, business, professional, or miscellaneous committees, if not through candidate committees; (2) through direct disbursements by the candidate, his family, or other individuals (not channeled through organized committees); (3) through issue organizations such as peace groups and gun lobbies. In the circumstances that money will likely carve new channels, limitations can readily become unenforceable and thus a mockery. The regulation of political finance has been marked too often by lack of serious enforcement. There is little point in enacting legislation that is likely to be unenforceable without changing the modes of campaigning or without infringing upon First Amendment rights.

Strict enforcement would require that paid or published endorsements by labor unions, other groups, or individual supporters fall within the candidate's limitation. Constitutionally, an effective limitation would give candidates discretion to prohibit free speech by empowering them to refuse to authorize certain expenditures by potential supporters. For example, a group seeking to publicize its support of a candidate may determine that the most effective way to reach the public will be through a broadcast endorsement. To prohibit such a broadcast might be construed in the courts as the same thing as prohibiting free speech—on the theory that an expenditure for speech is substantially the same thing as speech itself, because it is necessary to reach large audiences, and is therefore protected by the First Amendment. The same theory may apply to an individual who seeks to advertise his support of a candidate. The constitutional issue is how far the Congress may go in protecting the purity of elections without abridging freedoms guaranteed under the First Amendment. The judicial presumption might be against enforced surrender of rights unless justified by the existence and immediate impendency of danger to the public interest. One wonders whether the courts would find the use of money in elections sufficiently dangerous to justify, in effect, giving the candidate discretion to prohibit speech—or even in effect limiting the candidate's own speech over an effective medium.

The ways the courts have affected other electoral issues—reapportionment, voting rights, the 18-year old vote, I suspect they would ultimately opt in favor of more rather than less speech, especially in political matters. There may, of course, be years of uncertainty and contradictory opinions, as in obscenity cases.

Admitting that Congress can legislate to protect the purity of the electoral process, should not the burden be on those proposing or enacting such laws to prove that damage to the integrity of the process is being done under the present system? How can such evidence be gathered to be presented in a court of law?

The amount of any limitation must be arbitrary because political exigencies change and what was spent in one campaign in one year or place may be inadequate for another. There are so many variations in regions, campaign practices, and costs in a country as heterogeneous as the United States that fair uniform limits are difficult to achieve. What happens when a candidate has carefully programmed his spending to stay within the limit, and a new allegation is made which needs answering on television, but he cannot adequately catch up with the original headline without violating the limit? If limits are too high, they may spur spending to that level. If limits are low, they invite forms of evasion—such as channeling funds to committees that attempt to influence opinion on issues helpful to a given candidate or to committees that speak out against an opponent rather than for a candidate. If limitations are too low, they fail to recognize political necessities.

One reason that costs are relatively high is that in some areas party identification may be diminishing, and there is certainly more ticket splitting, so candidates think advertising can effectively get their names before potential voters. Gallup polls show that between 25 and 30 percent of respondents consider themselves independents, and the figure has risen in recent years. A Gallup poll shows that as many as 54 percent say they have split their tickets. Many voters now get their perceptions less from traditional means, such as family or party allegiances, than from the media, particularly the broadcast media, in the form of both news and advertising. Many major campaigns, particularly those of challengers in primaries, are won mainly by means of identity campaigning over the broadcast media. To artificially limit these modes of campaigning is to tend to disadvantage the challenger who is not as well known as the incumbent or the celebrity. The challenger may well have to spend more on the broadcast or other media to get recognized across the state; it may take several years of exposure before announcement. The reformer challenging the party organization may well have to spend more.

Of course, the ability of the challenger to spend more is only theoretical unless he raises enough to spend more, or unless he is wealthy. Leaving these possibilities open serves as a safety valve to permit challenges when entrenched interests or policies become unbearable. The opportunity for anti-establishment or peace or black or whatever candidates to challenge successfully is essential to responsible and responsive government.

A Common Cause study has suggested the fund-raising advantages Congressional incumbents have, by showing that incumbents spent substantially more than challengers in 1972. Common Cause failed to note how many incumbents first won election by outspending their incumbent opponents before the 1972 FECA limitation on amounts candidates and their immediate families can spend went into effect. The number of millionaires in the Senate is testimony in that regard. But if Common Cause is correct, the policy issue is whether to limit amounts that can be spent by or on behalf of candidates or to diminish the hidden and obvious advantages of incumbency. Serious attention should be paid to the perquisites of office, which are more apparent in Presidential campaigns but are perhaps as influential in Senatorial and Congressional campaigns. Perquisites include matters such as: adequate salary; use of the franking privilege; available broadcast facilities for taping programs; the equal opportunity provisions which allow delay in announcing candidacy in order to continue to qualify for free broadcast time; adequate representational allowances to permit legitimate travel to state or district; the roles of White House and Congressional staffs paid for by government but working largely on campaign matters.

Limitations do achieve some narrowing of disparities in spending between candidates, but in reality they do little to spread competition because they do not provide funds to the needy, they only hold down spending by the affluent. More important, they reduce the ability of well-financed challengers to contest effectively against strong and established incumbents. The ability to beat a well-entrenched incumbent whose seniority makes him a committee chairman able to stop legislation, and who cannot be defeated excepting by massive effort, is important in Congressional campaigns.

One can argue that if the political system is to be kept open and responsive to challenge, then limitations are undesirable because they tend to favor the status quo. The rates of successful challenge against Congressional incumbents are rather low. Limitations reinforce the advantages incumbents already have.

One of the key goals of the political system should be a more highly competitive system, because that helps to make the system more responsive. Limitations tend to reduce opportunities for voters to learn something about candidates, but even more significant, ceilings reduce opportunities for voters to learn something about politics, that is, that the political season is here and an election is coming up. Electioneering helps to structure and politicize society, and this is periodically essential to the smooth functioning of a democracy. Moreover, the stimulation provided by election campaigns probably impacts differentially, having more effect in arousing the more lethargic Democratic majority than the more highly educated Republicans whose turnout is consistently higher proportionately.

To oppose limitations is not necessarily to argue that the sky is the limit. In any campaign there are saturation levels and a point where spending no longer pays off in votes per dollar. Common sense dictates that only marginal benefits can be derived from unlimited spending. An essential way to deal with fund imbalances and undesirable sources of funds is to maintain meaningful disclosure and publicity laws.

A comprehensive and effective public reporting system helps to control excessive spending and undue reliance on large contributions from special interests, but it is well to remember that the availability of money for a given campaign may be an inherent effect of our democratic and pluralistic system—either the constitutional right to spend one's own money or to financially support candidates with congenial viewpoints or a manifestation of popularity. This is not to say that monied interests do not sometimes take advantage of a candidate's need for funds, or that candidates do not sometimes become beholden to special interests. They do, but that is part of the price we pay for a system in which the candidate arranges his own financing, and most often he cannot rely on the party or on a broad-based financial constituency for adequate financing.

The case for greater competition in an open political system with a safety valve to permit effective challenge must be balanced against the case for delimiting the advantages of wealth in the political process. This is a matter of values but also of presumed constitutional rights to be weighed in the balance. Permitting unlimited use of money by candidates and their supporters does violence to our sense of fairness and of the democratic ideal of equality of opportunity, but it also offers the possibility of enlarging the dialogue by encouraging the voicing of varying points of view and also of increasing the possibility of competition for public office. In fact, throughout the Twentieth Century, the Republicans have consistently had more money at their disposal in Presidential elections; clearly, Democratic victories have been possible despite Republican financial superiority.

Limitations on campaign expenditures, when combined with a limitation on contributions, make for an unhealthy squeeze on political campaigning. If the candidate cannot accept larger contributions, he must seek to broaden his financial base, which is desirable in any case. Under present circumstances, without government assistance, there are very few promising alternative ways to raise big money in small sums. Mail drives, televised appeals for funds, newspaper ads, are all expensive ways to raise money. If only Presidential, Senatorial and Congressional candidates, as well as related party committees, were each to try to organize widespread solicitation by these means, the costs would be prohibitive, and many such efforts would fail. Literally dozens of appeals would be directed at the same people, the activists on mailing lists, or the supporters who listen to political broadcasts. If federal candidates tried to broaden the base by attracting more contributors in the $100-$500 range, each would need more fund-raising events—such as dinners and cocktail parties—and again the competition to reach the affluent activists would be fierce and ultimately unproductive for many candidates.

The three most successful small contributor drives in Presidential politics were the Goldwater campaign in 1964, the Wallace campaign in 1968, and the McGovern campaign in 1972—each a factional or fringe candidate. Whether a centrist candidate could attract sufficient numbers of small contributors to sustain a Presidential campaign is debatable. Nixon attracted large numbers of small contributors in 1972, but the circumstance and the size of the landslide make prediction impossible for other centrist candidates.

Under a system of limits on both contributions and expenditures, the costs of competitive wider solicitation by mail or fund-raising events would dig deeply into allowable expenses for many candidates. A successful mail drive costs 30 percent of gross, so it costs $5 million to raise $15 million, leaving perhaps too little for effective campaigning for votes. The strategy of some advocates of reform is to achieve such a squeeze, to the point where campaign funds will be inadequate, and then incumbents will want to vote for government subsidies.

If ceilings on contributions are enacted, it is important to provide alternatives simultaneously, in order to achieve the best public policy posture: lessened dependence on large contributions but government assistance or encouragement of other means to help make up the dollar gap. The history of American regulation of political finance has been that, one after another, traditional sources of political funds were cut down without provision for new sources to take their place. Now, limitations on private giving should not be enacted without providing alternative sources.

To set contributions limits without providing new sources would be especially harmful to certain categories of candidates. For example, a black candidate in a low-income district, who cannot raise sufficient funds in his own constituency to mount an effective campaign against an entrenched party machine or a white-dominated power structure in a Southern State, will need other sources of funds, either large contributions from wealthy contributors, or governmental assistance. For another example, a limit on contributions helps incumbents who can raise sufficient money from supporters knowing that challengers will not be able to outspend them; the reformer candidate cannot raise funds up to the spending limit because the wealthy liberals who would give him more are prohibited from doing so. In Presidential politics, the effort to stake out an independent posture—for example, Humphrey in 1968, trying to distance himself from both the Chicago Convention and the Administration—can be costly, so the ability to beg or borrow to try to turn an unfavorable situation around, should not be unduly restricted.

Strong competition among various interests and groups in society, each trying to generate widespread support in elections, is essential to the vitality of our pluralist society, our system of free elections, and the freedoms of the First Amendment which guarantee the right to organize and to try to persuade others. It took five or more years to effect a change in American policy toward Vietnam, and a good deal of the strife took place in election campaigns. The so-called "peace movement" attracted scores of millions of dollars into the electoral process because people felt strongly about their beliefs. Present or future issues as vital as American policy in the Middle East is currently, will continue to arise; small groups such as Jews or oil interests will feel the need to influence elections. It is inadequate to be permitted to run ads in newspapers espousing given causes; people get involved much more readily when they see an opportunity to help elect government officials who see things their way. Elections are where the action is.

Elections are also where the tuning devices are the most sensitive, the calibrations the finest. Watergate and the Agnew resignation undoubtedly have made many large contributors and special interests wary of giving large sums again; if the calls for public funding emanating from some of these sources are more than lip-service, many large contributors would like to be relieved of future duty. With full disclosure under the FECA, and with high risk in violating the law, more should ponder why it is urgent to limit at uncertain levels that are bound to hurt some candidates, that are certain to be challenged in the courts, and that are really unnecessary so long as there is full and timely disclosure. We now have levels of disclosure previously thought impossible, with a public by now thoroughly conscious of the problems of money, with a vigilant media probing at high levels. The main reason to adopt limits is to raise public confidence in the electoral process: but in the long run, public confidence will not result from unenforceable limits that are harmful to various categories of candidates, or that may get struck down by the courts. Why insist on entering the thicket of judicial determination in an area as sensitive as elections, where the highest order of First Amendment rights should be encouraged?

III

Although numerous bills have been introduced that would provide for public subsidies in campaigns for federal office, and much rhetoric is heard for and against, scant attention has been paid to the implications of the various plans for the political system in general and the two-party system in particular. Questions of fairness, cost, administration and enforcement need to be asked, assumptions challenged, and understanding developed of the conditions that ought to be met if subsidies are to be provided. It is simplistic to expect that public financing is a panacea for the electoral system, or to believe that fundamental changes in the political structure or electoral processes will not result. Change is desirable, perhaps urgent, but further thought and dialogue are necessary to a better understanding of what impending changes may mean.

The main design difficulties in public funding are who should receive the subsidy, and how and when it should be made. Critics of public funding have charged that subsidies would not alter the pattern of private interest contributions, but would simply raise the costs of political campaigns and be a boon to the broadcasting and other advertising media, unless private funding were severely limited. However, limitations on private giving raise still more constitutional and public policy questions, as noted, and these must be considered part of the subsidy question.

Presumably, the goal of government subsidization is to help serious candidates, yet retain enough flexibility to permit opportunity to challenge those in power without supporting with significant tax dollars candidates merely seeking free publicity and without attracting so many candidates that the electoral process is degraded. Accordingly, the most difficult problems in working out fair subsidies are definitional: How define major and minor parties, and distinguish serious and frivolous candidates, without doing violence to equality of opportunity, or to "equal protection" under the Constitution? Any standards must be arbitrary, and certain screening devices must be used, based upon past vote, numbers of petitions, posting of money bonds, or other means. Some of these means require "start-up" funds or masses of volunteers to get petitions signed, and other plans, such as matching incentives, require popular appeal that can best be achieved through incumbency or years of exposure which also costs money.

The first federal experiment in public funding has been the Presidential campaign dollar checkoff. That law serves as a useful starting point for inquiry because it raises questions of whether a subsidy program should be linked to the tax system; should be optional for candidates to choose or not choose, at their discretion; and should be extended to prenomination campaigns for President and to Senatorial and Congressional candidates as well.

The most that can be said for the checkoff is that it is experimental, that it offers a symbolic means of political participation and legitimizes a subsidy by involving taxpayers' approval. However, it is risky to undertake subsidy programs based on popular support, for if taxpayers revolt, there is no guarantee of funds. Moreover, the checkoff can be considered discriminatory, because only taxpayers qualify, unless it is extended to permit those receiving social security or welfare payments to designate their dollars to be similarly checked off, or to add a dollar for that purpose. Further, it is doubtful that an optional choice for candidates to accept or reject the subsidy, is desirable, because subsidies should be uniformly applicable and acceptable to all significant participants.

The pre-nomination Presidential campaign is an aspect of the electoral process which public subsidies can alter dramatically. Circumstances to consider for purposes of public funding in Presidential campaigns include:

A movement to draft a potential nominee who had not announced his candidacy or participated in any primaries;

Dark horse candidates;

Favorite son and daughter candidates;

A candidate who loses a primary or two but insists his candidacy is viable and wants continued governmental assistance;

A candidate who does not expect to be nominated, but enters the contest in order to dramatize an issue, such as Representative McCloskey in the Republican Party in 1972.

Solutions to many of these contingencies may well be found, but these are kinds of activities that offer safety valves, which should not be closed without considerable scrutiny.

Because American politics is candidate-oriented, any subsidy program is complex. Giving money to candidates and not to parties could accelerate the demise of the two-party system. At present, without pre-nomination endorsement by parties, each candidate is on his own to get nominated; he collects his own money, builds his own organization, conducts his own media or grass-roots campaign. Once nominated, he may or may not campaign in close relationship to the party. He has developed a successful personal organization; why take chances by depending on weak party machinery.

The extent of candidate distancing from the party varies from area to area. When the candidate advertises or broadcasts, he features himself, projects his personality, perhaps not even identifying his party, in the hope of appealing to independents and ticket-splitters. He competes for money with the party, but under present circumstances, at least in campaigns for federal office, the party at the national, state, county, or local levels may well provide a portion of his funds. If government funding is provided, the candidate may need to rely less than at present on the party or on party identification. Would relationships between parties and candidates diminish further if candidates receive government financing without reference to parties? Would this, in turn, affect the cohering and unifying roles parties play? This is less of a problem in Presidential campaigns, because the party identification of the candidate is widely known. Yet the Nixon reelection example is instructive here too, because sources of funds independent of the party enabled the marked separation of his campaign from that of the Republican Party, to the detriment of both. When subsidies are extended to Senatorial and Congressional campaigns, however, reduced party loyalty would tend to fragment both majorities and minorities, perhaps leading to new factionalism and splinter parties. At the least, subsidies directly to candidates without reference to parties would lead to more independent-minded candidates on the ballot, and some would get elected. At a time when there is concern over Executive-Legislative relationships, when there is concern about Executive encroachment, any further splintering of Congress or of state legislatures would ensure the diminishing of the Legislative branch. Checks and balances would be more diffused. The parties can be an important part of the balancing act, and therefore need continuing relationships with their legislators.

Foreign experience with political subsidies is instructive. Puerto Rico has a partial subsidy worth studying because it operates in a political setting similar to that of the United States. But subsidies in European countries with parliamentary systems are made to political parties, not to candidates. In these countries, parties control the electoral campaigns, and candidates mobilize only limited supplemental support. In these countries, open primaries in which party candidates can be challenged do not exist.

In most of the nations with subsidies, governments fund the parties annually, not only at election time. This is supplemented by free broadcast time, again made to the parties and not to the candidates. Historically, at first most of the subsidies were given in small amounts to supplement resources already in the political process, and later increased when the system adjusted to the infusion of new funds. Excepting in Puerto Rico, in no country providing subsidies have ceilings been imposed on private contributions. In contrast, efforts are being made in this country to both limit and subsidize. Would that we knew the possibilities of doing both effectively, or the consequences of doing either ineffectively.

Both major political parties are in ferment and transition. Goldwater took the Republican Party out of the hands of the traditional Eastern Establishment and Nixon helped to expand Goldwater's base in the West and the South, and among the nouveau riche. Before Watergate, the social issues of the Nixon Administration were leading to opportunities for new coalitions— among the ethnics, blue collars, the New South—to reshape the Republican Party and to alter its traditional ties to big business.

From the first days, the Nixon Administration's domestic policy on some crucial issues has worked to the disadvantage of big business, whose support the Administration knew to be solid. Reduction of the oil depletion allowance, EEOC enforcement policies, and environmental regulations have convinced many big businessmen that they can no longer afford to rely upon the good intentions of any President or one political party. Watergate should sharpen this perception, and the corporate campaign fund extortion should further loosen ties between Republicans and big business.

Simultaneously, the McGovern Reform Commission and the McGovern Presidential nomination shook the power of the national Democratic power brokers. The Charter Reform Commission of the Democratic Party is considering a variety of approaches to restructure the party apparatus and procedures and to make it a more effective and significant electoral and governing institution. The post-McGovern climate could foster the rise of insurgent groups to recast and alter the influence of big labor in the Democratic Party—which complements the uncertainty of relationships of the Republican Party with big business. However, a basic inconsistency exists which some reformers have failed to recognize: democratic reforms mean higher political costs. Power to the people is expensive. It is inconsistent to give voters a choice in the selection of candidates, and not expect campaign costs to be substantial. In particular, primary campaigns are expensive, and the impact of money is greatest in the pre-nomination phase. Similarly, it is unrealistic to give more power to the party grass-roots without increasing costs for maintaining the party structure. This is an important reason why government funding must help the parties.

In the post-Watergate atmosphere, with the Presidency in turmoil, and the Congress too cautious, the parties could become the new anchors of a political system in which they are dynamic and relevant instrumentalities producing the best combination of national interest and local concerns. Recent works by Sundquist, Saloma and Sontag, and Broder,[5] all point ways to a regeneration of the political parties. Legislative reform can enhance and strengthen the parties, or it can serve to further their decline. Since money in politics is an immediate issue, the steps taken to reform it will be crucial in determining the direction of later restructuring of other aspects of the political system. Two recent signs are hopeful. Both are provisions of S.372, which has passed the Senate and is before the House. One would put each party's national committee in sole charge of coordinating Presidential campaign contributions and expenditures in the post-nomination period. I have long been concerned about both the separation of financial and political functions in campaigns and the separation of candidates from their sponsoring parties. Political parties are better instruments for financial accountability and responsibility than are ad hoc committees, and mixing political and financial functions ensures that political considerations will be paramount in structuring and executing the fund-raising program. The political operatives serve as a check upon the financial staff.

The other provision exempts certain national party committees—the national committees and the Senatorial and Congressional campaign committees of the major parties—from limitations but state and local party committees are subject to the same limits as are any other campaign committees. This throws the balance in favor of national as against state and local party committees. Nationalizing politics is desirable as long as the party organizations at the grass-roots know and approve moving in that direction. The same argument applies to federal funding of campaigns: money should be funnelled through the party to the extent possible—but not without wide understanding of what is happening and approval through National Party Conventions or Commissions.

Thus far, the roles of business and labor leaders in reform efforts are ambiguous. Both big business and big labor are increasingly unable to engender public confidence, which creates a vacuum that could be filled by an anti-institutional campaign against the vested interests because they are perceived as being the perpetrators of corruption and lawlessness. Certainly the business community has been damaged by Watergate and the Agnew resignation. Ironically, the image of the greedy businessman as the corrupter, seeking favors from the politicians, has been somewhat changed. When extortion is involved, the businessman becomes the victim, not the perpetrator. Richard E. Neustadt observes that "We now are in a period of antipolitical politics, with journalists and politicians playing to their own sense of successive, cumulative, public disillusionments. Watergate feeds the mood."[6] Organized groups such as Common Cause and Public Citizen, while leading the anti-institutional, anti-political politics, will one day realize that lobbying and public influence has its limitations; then they will add political action arms, educate their members as labor did, and then be sorry they so restricted electioneering.

Many business and labor leaders are publicly supporting government funding of campaigns while quietly working behind the scenes to repeal Section 611 of the FECA, which prohibits government contractors from contributing and raises questions about the legality of some political action committees of both labor and business. Whether there will be follow-through on support of public funding, or some are merely paying lip-service to the idea, when the crunch comes and labor or business muscle is desired to influence major governmental decisions affecting them, then the rules of the traditional system may not seem so bad after all. On the other hand, no doubt many large contributors, particularly businessmen, would be relieved if a new system put fewer political demands on their pocketbooks. And some labor leaders realize they can never match the dollars that the business and financial communities can muster.

Electoral regulation should recognize the legitimate concern of labor and management with public policy. There is nothing inherently immoral or corrupting about a corporate or labor dollar, any more than any other private dollar, apart from responsibilities to stockholders and members. Nonetheless, the 1972 elections do demonstrate the means by which collection and distribution mechanisms of special interest groups can be unhealthy and corrupting, and other collection systems have to be considered.

Special interest domination of electoral politics at the state level is considered by many to be a national scandal. While no single state has been shattered by a Watergate, abuses similar to those which recently occurred in New Jersey and Maryland are no doubt common. The thrust of governmental decentralization as exemplified by revenue sharing has resulted in considerably greater special interest involvement in elections and in lobbying at the state and local level, because that is where more of the money and the action is now. State governments are only beginning to better regulate special interest involvement by experimenting with reform in the regulation of political finance, lobbying, conflict of interest, and government secrecy. In regulating political money, four states now have independent election commissions, and four states now have forms of tax checkoffs, while eleven provide tax credits or deductions for political contributions. Several states have adopted or are in the process of adopting so-called "Sunshine Laws" designed to open up the system by moving away from secrecy and toward the right of the public to know in the election and decision-making processes. In several states where the legislatures would not enact reform, move fast enough, far enough or at all, reformers are using the initiative route, seeking public approval through ballot propositions. The Citizens' Research Foundation currently has in preparation a Model State Statute, and its most significant aspect is the concept embodied in its title: "Model State Statute on Politics and Public Office," which goes beyond elections and seeks to reach political aspects of incumbency.

Of the various subsidy proposals that could be linked to the tax checkoff if desired, matching incentives would seem to solve more problems and achieve more goals than any other formulation. Matching incentives combine the traditional system of private contributions with government assistance. For decades there have been efforts to broaden the financial base of politics; matching incentives go in that direction because the amount of the subsidy is triggered by the numbers of contributions, giving incentive to the party, committee, or candidate to concentrate efforts on expanded solicitation. The matching incentive provides an important argument for the solicitor in persuading the potential contributor that a small contribution, perhaps $10 or $25, will mean twice that amount of money for the campaign since the government will match at least part of the gift. Combined with tax credits or deductions for the contributions, as federal law now provides, there is further incentive to the giver, who can make a personal tax claim on his federal tax return the following year.

The amount and the recipients of the matching subsidy are determined by citizens in making their contributions, rather than by an arbitrary formula set by the Congress. One weakness is that capable and deserving candidates who are not well-enough known to attract a large number of contributors will benefit very little from the plan. On the other hand, the popular and effective challenger who can attract broad-based support will be able to mount a significant campaign and, because of the added margin provided by the matching funds, compete strongly, even against an incumbent. Working on the basis of popular selection, the matching incentives formula encourages responsible opposition while screening out unrealistic candidates. Accordingly, it becomes feasible to extend eligibility for the subsidy to Presidential candidates in both pre- and post-nomination periods, and to Senatorial and Congressional candidates also in both election periods. Matching incentives may be more palatable to incumbents than alternative subsidies which provide support for any challengers who qualify at the ballot, and therefore present the threat of a well-funded opposition. With matching incentives, an opponent is only as well-funded as his popular appeal in raising contributions.

Matching incentives encourage a broadening of the financial base, and get and keep people in the habit of giving. Matching incentives provide most insurance for the future because of their link to private giving; in case subsidies are not appropriated or sufficiently checked off, people have not gotten out of the habit of giving out of their own pockets. Matching incentives also effectively screen out candidates in both the pre- and post-nomination periods, because candidates who are not popular get little if any financial support.

While matching incentives will infuse more money into the system, the demands for funds could become great with no end in sight, because matching incentives do nothing to restructure the political system. Only a system emphasizing government subsidies to parties, perhaps on a matching basis, will satisfy long-term needs. Anything less is short-term patching, essentially encouraging the status quo and politics as it is now, but with government funds added. Matching incentives serve that short-term purpose well. But in the long run, problems are not solved by merely pumping more money into the system.

Whether or not government policy provides dollar assistance for politics, or seeks to limit either contributions or expenditures, an essential cornerstone of regulation must be disclosure on a continuous, comprehensive, detailed and timely basis. The integrity of the political process is protected when politicians and interests are held accountable by virtue of their being required to reveal their financial transactions. They are less likely to undertake sharp practices when the risks are high in being found out. Alert administration and serious enforcement are crucial. The public must be able to evaluate the uses of money in politics, whether or not public funds are used. Disclosure should be based upon the right of the public to know the sources of financial and other forms of support for candidates and parties.

A major reason for creating a Federal Elections Commission is to isolate as much as possible from political pressures the functions of receiving, auditing, tabulating, publicizing and preserving the reports of political and campaign receipts and expenditures required by law. An agency that is neither part of the Executive nor the legislature, but a new one with a new mandate, would be an ideal means for building confidence in the administration of the political fund reporting system. The Commission should be established, and be provided with the subpoena and enforcement powers which the law does not give the supervisory officers currently receiving the campaign fund statements.

A Federal Elections Commission would have responsibility for campaigns for all federal offices and should be required to make timely public reports on political funding before elections as well as after. A Federal Elections Commission would combine information from campaigns for all federal offices in ways that would avoid the present duplications of information on spending by committees supporting candidates for more than one office, giving a truer picture of where political money comes from and where it goes. Despite the increased availability of data about sources of funds and items of expenditure since the Federal Election Campaign Act went into effect, the annual tabulations of campaign spending information for 1972 will be unnecessarily confusing and duplicative because of the overlapping jurisdictions in reporting funds under the present law.

Under present proposals, the Federal Elections Commission would be solely the body to administer and enforce the disclosure laws. Other important functions, however, should be considered, either as additional responsibilities for the Commission, or better, in a Congressionally-chartered private organization designed to achieve purposes beyond disclosure.

For example, Watergate has pointed up the desirability of a governmental or neutral organization to serve for the exchange of intelligence information for use by opponents. Candidates' daily schedules, copies of speeches, white papers, brochures, campaign advertising, lists of fund raisers and contributors, schedules of fund raising events, if freely available for public inspection, would obviate the apparent felt need for information about the opposition party and candidate. It would also lead to more responsibility in preparing information and more accountability for its content.

Such an agency could also monitor political mailings, particularly the use of the franking privilege by incumbents, set guidelines for the legitimate use of government facilities by incumbents and perform other such functions.

A federally-chartered nonpartisan organization could work full-time with the parties with the responsibilities of encouraging broadly-based fund raising, assisting registration and election-day drives, and responding when asked to help or monitor other campaign activities. As a byproduct, the organization could serve as a catalyst or a neutral meeting ground for joint undertakings—such as bipartisan appeals or competitions between fund-raising groups—either to encourage wider participation, to reduce costs, to arrange joint broadcasts, or even voluntarily to limit certain spending. The organization could finance internships that help train personnel for professional party work, leadership, and public service in politics. Candidate fellowships could assist those whose personal resources are necessarily limited and who could not otherwise take time from their usual work to run for public office. Such an organization could be financed readily if the political parties tithed one percent of gross receipts each year, or if foundations, corporations and labor unions were permitted to contribute.

One of the necessary functions of the organization would be to help fulfill a continuing commitment to some forms of private financing of politics. We need to devise or better utilize effective solicitation and collection systems. To do so, we must begin to pay more attention to the mechanics of who asks for, how we ask for, and how we receive political money. It is not enough to legislate tax or matching incentives; action to improve solicitation and collection systems is essential to make them work. The political party, of course, is the most desirable collection agency, and my concept goes beyond funding party committees and extends to funding candidates' campaigns as well. Another important collection system occurs through associational networks existing in membership groups, although some of these are now in disrepute. Labor unions, dairy cooperatives, trade associations, or professional groups can solicit effectively because of two characteristics: they have large groups of like-minded persons, and they have ready-made channels for communicating with their memberships. Whether in person, at meetings, through field men, or even by mail if combined with a newsletter or other communication, they have internal and therefore cheap means of asking for political money. There is no doubt that this can be done on a nonpartisan basis, without coercion, if the national leadership properly addresses the problem. Still other collection systems with real bipartisan potential exist at places of employment, and these can be extended to include large organizations, such as universities, as well as corporations and other businesses. With proper safeguards, even government employees can be asked to contribute.

No solicitation and collection system—whether door-to-door, union or other membership organization, payroll withholding, or mass mail—will satisfy financial needs to all candidates. Barring a system in which all money is contributed to and distributed by a party choosing all candidates, campaigners will continue to seek funds separately. But labor, trade association, and corporate bipartisan fund-raising drives have special advantages: they cost the parties or candidates hardly anything and the costs to the sponsoring organizations are minimal.

In the post-Watergate atmosphere, mere exhortation and a call for honesty in politics will not suffice. While public attention focuses on reform, it may be possible to make structural changes that will recast public institutions into supportive instruments to help mobilize energies into constructive channels. Indeed, it may be possible to harness public dissatisfaction with a call for a Newer Politics buttressed by restructured or new institutions. The theme could be one of new respect for election laws and for ethical campaigning. But this requires structuring administrative and enforcement processes in such ways that deviant behavior becomes too risky. The theme could accentuate voter-candidate contact, new incentives to encourage citizen participation in the electoral process, and an open environment in which public policy alternatives can be debated fully and freely. This will entail new approaches to concepts of equal time, equal opportunity, and fairness. The new book of Newton Minow and co-authors[7] should serve as a starting point for debate on how to achieve wider dissemination of varying viewpoints; noteworthy and commendable is the proposal for opposition party response time, which the National Committee would control, to Presidential broadcasts. Clearly, free speech, new ideas, public dialogue are inadequate unless hooked to an amplification system only the mass media can provide. Government for the people means government for those able to make themselves heard. American democracy can be defined as government for those most effectively heard. Talk may be cheap but not on radio and television.

Other indirect forms of government assistance need consideration as well. Apart from the many proposals for free or discounted use of both commercial and public airwaves, government can provide campaign services through assuming greater responsibility in registering voters, cheaper or free mailing rates, voters' pamphlets, in whatever ways will diminish tolls for candidates and parties and thereby remove some financial pressures from them.

Watergate and the Agnew resignation provide an unmistakable impetus for electoral reform. Haste and the politics of fervor are not good approaches to reforming the electoral machinery. Change must be approached judiciously and the implications of reforms clearly understood. While considering electoral reforms it may be useful to remember one of the sayings of Benjamin Franklin, "They that can give up essential liberty to obtain a little temporary safety deserve neither liberty nor safety."

AN AFTERTHOUGHT

If limitations on contributions or expenditures are felt necessary to restore public confidence in the electoral process, and a constitutional formula for such ceilings can be devised, then one adaptation from the English system of regulation merits consideration as a means of strengthening the political parties. The idea would be to limit severely amounts candidates can receive and spend, but not limit at all amounts the parties can receive and spend, even on behalf of these candidates. That would force candidates to seek and accept party help. Further thought would have to be given to the applicability, if any, of this notion in the pre-nomination period. Possibilities do exist of pre-nomination party endorsement of candidates whom the party has helped financially, or of challenge primaries as utilized in Connecticut, where the party convention nominates but losing candidates who have received sufficient convention support can call for an open primary; party financing is then justified to carry out the convention decision.

NOTES

1. Louis Harris, "Nixon Should Not Resign as a Result of Watergate," *Chicago Tribune*, May 8, 1973.
2. Carleton W. Sterling, "Control of Campaign Spending: The Reformers' Paradox," *American Bar Association Journal*, 59 (October, 1973), p. 1153.
3. *Financing Presidential Campaigns*, Report of the President's Commission on Campaign Costs, (April, 1962), p. 17.
4. *American Civil Liberties Union, Inc., et al v. W. Pat Jennings, et al*, Civ. A. No. 1967-72, U.S. District Court, District of Columbia, November 14, 1973.
5. James L. Sundquist, *Dynamics of the Party System* (Washington, D.C.: The Brookings Institution, 1973); John S. Saloma III and Frederick H. Sontag, *Parties* (New York: Alfred A. Knopf, 1972); David S. Broder, *The Party's Over* (New York: Harper & Row, Publishers, 1971).
6. Richard E. Neustadt, "The Constraining of the President," *The New York Times Magazine*, October 14, 1973, p. 117.
7. Newton Minow, John Bartlow Martin, and Lee Mitchell, *Presidential Television* (New York: Basic Books, 1973).

INDEX

Adamany, David W., 376, 379-414
ADP (Automatic data processing)
    See Electronic data
    processing
Advance men, 31, 56, 104-22
    crowd-building, 109, 110, 313
    manual for, 108-9
Advertising agency, 101, 102
    "anchor and loan plan," 97, 99
    charges, 32-33, 36
    functions in political campaign,
        53-56, 90-91, 102-3
        pros and cons, 96-97, 103
        working under pressure, 99-103
    revenues, 87, 88
    staffing, 97-99, 102
    techniques, 92-94, 365
Advertising campaign:
    good taste, 93, 365
    theme-centered, 130-31
Aggregate electoral data, 129, 139,
    150
    analysis of, 198-200
    case study, 212-22
    hard data vs. poll, 198
    manipulating data, 207-12
    precinct boundary limitation,
        202-4
    problems, 200-204, 207-8, 210-12
    sample precincts, 201
    selection of data, 204-6
    sources, 202
Agnew, Spiro T., 242, 428, 432, 433,
    446, 452, 458
Agranoff, Robert, 56, 123-41, 150,
    198-223
Ailes, Roger, 268
Alaska pipeline, 14
Alexander, Herbert E., 376, 377,
    387, 415-23, 428, 459
America Votes, 202
American Association of Advertising
    Agencies (AAAA), 89
American Association of Political
    Consultants, 158

American Federation of Labor-
    Committee for Industrial
    Organizations (AFL/CIO)
    policy, 17
    Committee on Political Education
        (COPE), 17, 188, 189
    data processing project, 150,
        162, 167, 170, 188-97
    security measures, 192-93
    uses of data, 196-97
American Independent Party, 118,
    407
American Voter, The (Campbell et
    al.), 19
Americans for Constitutional Action,
    438
Auxiliary committees, 81 (*see also*
    Campaign committees)
Azbell, Joe, 267-68

Backstrom, Charles H., 150, 198-223
Bailey, Deardourff & Bowen, 53
Barabba, Vincent P., 150, 224-36
Billboards, 34, 41, 293
Black leaders, 18
Blacks in South, 20
Bogart, Leo, 363
Brandeis, Louis D., 416
British party system, 127, 372, 458
Brooke, Edward, 145
Bruno, Jerry, 425
Burnham, Walter Dean, 22
Business: (*see also* Contributions,
    corporations)
    aid to Republicans, 394-95
    Watergate and, 452-53
Buttons and gadgets, 34-35, 259 (*see
    also* Specialized media)

Cable tv (CATV), 271, 358
Cahill, William, 243, 246, 247
California Fair Campaign Practices
    Commission, 418
"Campaign American Style" (*CBS
    Reports*), 89

Campaign committees, 108, 131-32, 375
  as contributors, 393
  laws governing, 398-404
  proliferation, 375
Campaign ethics and reform, 359-78
  finance reform in states, 415-23
  post-Watergate concerns, 428-59
Campaign expenditures *See* Campaign finance; Campaign spending; Fund raising
Campaign files, 164-83
  biographical, 180-81
  campaign worker data, 173-76
  constituent-voter, 164-69
  correspondence, 169-71
  financial, 171-73
  political research and issues, 176-80
Campaign finance, 133-34, 444 (*see also* Fund raising; Presidential Election Campaign Fund)
  crucial, 391
  direct public financing, 422-23
  money for politics, 391-98
    concerns about, 434-35 (*see also* Campaign ethics and reform)
    limits on contributions, 436-39
    limits on expenditures, 439, 441
    motives for giving, 395-97
    overfunding, 1972, 430, 432
  present situation, 402-3
  public financing, 376, 404-8
    alternatives, 409
    difficulties, 447-48
    eligibility, 406-7, 447
    in foreign countries, 449-50
    matching incentives, 453-55
    vs. party funding, 449
  reform, 360, 375, 398-404
    disclosure, 401-3, 405, 439, 443, 446, 455-56
    in states, 376, 415-25
    limits to giving, 400-401
    spending limits, 398-400, 439, 441
Campaign finance reform laws, 29, 359, 375, 376
Campaign laws, 68, 80-81, 359, 375 (*see also* Campaign finance reform laws)
Campaign literature, 36
Campaign management, 23-25, 30, 31, 127-28, 130-32 (*see also* Professional campaign management)
  computer technology, 158 (*see also* Electronic data processing)
  devices, 138
  major phases, 153-54
  using aggregated data analysis, 212-14, 218-22
Campaign planning, 51-53, 85, 128 (*see also* Fund raising; Media)
Campaign research, 5, 27, 37, 50, 51, 144
  cost, 36
  in Minnesota DFL case, 129-30
  party investment in, 137-38
  task-oriented, 353-54, 356
  use of EDP, 176-80
Campaign resources, 140, 145-46, 360, 433 (*see also* Campaign finance; Fund raising)
  availability of money, 386-88, 430, 444 (*see also* Campaign ethics and reform, post-Watergate concerns)
  basic needs, 18-19, 39
  other than money, 436
Campaign schedule, 132, 176 (*see also* Critical Path Method)
Campaign slogan, 356, 366
Campaign spending, 375, 381-91
  in competitive contests, 385-86, 388
  expenditure limits, 418-20, 436-39 (*see also* Campaign finance, reform)
  in highly visible contests, 389
  in other countries, 389
  reported expenditures, 387-88
  rising costs, 383-88
Campaign strategy, 17, 36-42, 52, 129, 131-32, 154
  area-based, 200
  suggestions from data, 214, 221-22
  tactics, 154
Campaigning, new style, 3-4, 18-20, 25, 36-39, 41-42, 128
  causes, 7
  education in, 130-32
  high cost, 28-36, 128, 136, 138, 359, 374, 375, 434-35
  illegal activities, 359, 360 (*see also* Campaign ethics and reform; Watergate)

importance of media and money,
259, 360
manipulative, 363-64
questions about, 43, 359
unfair, 368-70
Candidate:
announcing candidacy, 348-49
biography, 180
building staff, 426
challenger, 374, 442, 443, 445
education in techniques, 130-32
expenditures, 286, 386-87
laws affecting, 398, 418-20
limits on, 438, 439
"have not," 124, 126, 136-38, 374,
404, 445
image, 28, 36, 245-46, 335 (*see
also* Image-makers)
independent, 124, 400, 404, 407,
442, 446
laws on contributions, 400-401
(*see also* Campaign finance)
major speech, 111
manager, 50, 310-18 (*see also*
Campaign management; Pro-
fessional campaign management)
modest means, 373-74
organization, 14-16, 23
costs, 29-30, 385
personality, 6, 21, 22, 41, 63, 92
assets and liabilities, 52, 54
personal-contact campaigning,
302-5
sincerity, 300-302
on tv, 41, 262, 263, 270, 286,
316
vs. the issues, 300-301, 355-56
selection:
parties and, 11, 13, 427
responsibility for, 69, 355-56
test of competency, 264, 270
underfinanced, 421-22, 439
voting record, 181
wealthy, 373-75, 386, 388, 393,
418
Candidate-centered campaign, 4-7, 9,
13, 42, 43, 136, 139, 431,
448-49
Candidate-issue positions, 13, 14, 21,
22, 54, 93, 251-54, 264, 270,
367
Cantril, Albert H., 151, 237-58

Census, 172, 178
Census Users' Guide, 178
Charter Reform Committee of
Democratic Party, 450
Chartrand, Robert Lee, 149-50,
153-87
Chavez, Cesar, 122
Citizens Research Foundation, 28,
376, 417
Model State Statute, 453
Civil rights, 20, 21
"Code of Ethics for Political Cam-
paign Advertising" (AAAA),
89
Commercials, 94 (*see also* Television
spots)
Commission on Campaign Costs in
the Electronic Era, 88 (*see
also* President's Commission
on Campaign Costs)
Committee for the Re-election of the
President (CREEP) *See*
Nixon, Richard M.
Committee on Political Education
(COPE) *See* American Fed-
eration of Labor (AFL/CIO)
Communication:
ad agency with candidate, 100-101
mass media and voter, 264-65,
350-58
organization, 101
Comptroller General, 179
Computer Campaign Services, 158
Congressional campaigns:
giving, 391-93
spending, 382, 390-91, 442
Congressional Information Service,
179
Congressional Quarterly, 272, 285-
95, 300-309
Connally, John, 290
Constituency, 150, 303, 380, 385
Consumer Price Index, 384
Contributions (*see also* Campaign
ethics and reform; Labor)
corporations, 9-10, 375, 394-95,
397, 420, 431, 450
limits on, 420-21, 436, 438
sources, 440
Contributors:
greatest support, 391
large, 68, 374, 375, 387, 392, 417,
436-37

Contributors (*continued*)
laws affecting, 400-401
enforcement, 440
motives of, 395-97
polls effect on, 362
small, 376, 392, 393-94, 421, 445,
454
tax checkoff, 375, 376
Convention delegates, 12, 13, 180,
386
Coolidge, Calvin, 26
Cottin, Jonathan, 56, 104-22
County election data, 202, 212
Critical Path Method (CPM), 52-53,
176, 191, 192
Crouse, Timothy, 272, 320-33

Dailey, Peter H., 3, 289, 290, 337,
342
Daley, Richard, 6, 38, 80
Danforth, John C., 79-86
Data Processing Support at DNC,
163
Deardourff, John, 300, 301, 303,
306
DeCarlo, John P., 117-19
Decision Making Information, Inc.,
150, 158, 178
Democracy, 60, 358, 379, 458
consent and accountability, 380
free elections and, 429
participation in, 381, 428, 457-58
Democratic National Committee:
break-in at Watergate, 369
on McGovern commercials, 340-41
services to candidates, 125-26
EDP, 162-64, 168-69, 172, 176
study of wage and price control,
257
voter identification, 148
Democratic Party:
changes in, 450-51
convention, 369
platform, 14
Democrats for Nixon, 4, 15, 289,
290, 337
de Sola Pool, Ithiel, 180, 183, 262
Devlin, L. Patrick, 272, 334-43
DeVries, Walter, 20, 153, 158, 308,
336
Direct mail, 27, 29, 30, 41, 291
computerized, 170, 189, 305
costs, 32, 36, 170, 445
in fund raising, 147-48, 421

lists, 147
technology, 149, 384
use of P.I.P.S. in, 230, 236 (*see
also* Precinct Index Priority
System)
Discussion, 365, 366, 368, 380
fairness doctrine and, 371, 372
Documentary film, 27, 278, 283,
289
Donnelly, Richard, 4
Durant, Dr. Henry, 237

Eagleton, Thomas, 22, 369
Economic issues, 75, 257, 287 (*see
also* Tax issues)
Effects of Mass Communication
(Klapper), 264
Eldersveld, Samuel, 260
Election commissions, 417-18, 453
Election data analysis, 31-32
Electoral process, 430, 436
Electorate, 195, 214, 384, 393
Electronic Data Processing (EDP),
154-55 (*see also* Campaign
research; Direct mail; Infor-
mation storage)
deciding specifics, 161
justification for, 157-58, 179-80,
364
uses, 156, 196-97, 305, 384
*Electronic Data Processing and Poli-
tics* (Nichols), 162
*Electronic Data Processing for the
Political Executive* (RNC),
162
Ervin Committee *See* Campaign
ethics and reform; Watergate
Ethics of campaign "selling," 89-93
Evry, Hal, 31

Face the Nation, 315
Fair Campaign Practices Committee,
368
Federal assistance programs, 178
Federal Communications Act, 370
equal time, 370-71
Federal Communications Commis-
sion (FCC), 29, 310, 372
equal access, 370-73
fairness doctrine, 310, 371
Federal Corrupt Practices Act, 429
Federal Election Commission,
403-4, 455, 456
Federal Election Campaign Act,

1974, 286, 290, 376, 398, 401, 455
media limits, 439, 440
pros and cons, 406-9
Section 611, 452
Federal Election (Reform) Act, 1971, 29, 375, 382, 401, 402, 415, 429
Federal gift tax law, 420
Fisher, Harry N. D., 55-56, 79-86
Florida, reform law, 417
Franklin, Benjamin, 458
480, The (Burdick), 364
Fund raising, 68, 134, 380, 397-98
(*see also* Campaign finance; Campaign resources)
abuses *See* Watergate
costs, 444-45
EDP in, 171-73
emotional issues, 393-94
full disclosure of receipts and expenditures, 416-48, 429, 439, 443, 455
party, 127, 128
by special membership organizations, 457

Gallup organization, 146, 151, 242
Gardner, Allan, 268
Garfield, James, 238
Garth, David, 268, 307, 335
Golden Kazoo, The (Schneider), 364
Goldwater, Barry, 18, 22, 244, 256-57, 450
Daisy commercial, 352, 366
fund raising, 393, 445
on Vietnam, 316
Gosnell, Harold F., 3, 259
"Governmental competence," 7
Grasso, Ella, 11
Grecian History (Joy), 80
Gubernatorial candidates, 33, 407
Guggenheim, Charles, 267, 285, 287, 290, 302, 307, 308, 336-42

Hammond, Jay, 14
Handbook of Practical Politics (Van Riper), 160
Hardesty, Rex, 150, 188-97
Heard, Alexander, 382, 383, 387
Hess, Stephen, 376, 377, 424-27
House candidates, 33, 383
House of Representatives "Special Report . . . on a Computer-

ized Addressing and Mailing System," 169-70
Humphrey, Hubert, 16, 446
advancing, 107-11
campaign costs, 33, 35
control over campaign, 91, 109, 105-7, 109, 110
debate with McGovern, 328-29
polls, 145, 146

Illinois campaign, 291-92
Image-makers, 344-45, 356
advice to candidate, 345-50
candidate overexposure, 348
critics of, 365
task-oriented approach, 353-56
two-way communication, 358
use of paid and free media, 352-54, 366
videotaped commercials, 348
Incumbents, 9, 380-81, 435, 443
advantages, 16, 38, 125, 169, 299, 314, 371, 374
expenditures, 388, 418, 442, 443
guidelines for, 456
perquisites, 442-43, 456
U.S. Senators, 169, 442
voting record, 181, 391
Independent voters, 20, 21, 449
Information gathering, 51, 129, 132, 143-52, 154, 173 (*see also* Campaign research)
"hard" and "soft" data, 129-30
for key decisions, 158
types of information, 144, 148-51
Information sharing, 70, 181
Information storage, 148, 155, 156
basic files, 160
management and maintenance, 160, 181
practical questions, 160-61
retrieval, 160
Information systems, 143-51
Information technology, 148, 154-61
future of, 183-84
industry assistance, 167
special data service organizations, 178-79
state political organization aid, 167
Institute for International Social Research, 251
Institute for Social Research, 179
Intelligence activities, 368, 456 (*see also* Nixon campaign)

Interest groups, 16-17, 150, 434
  as collection and solicitation
    agents, 457
  contributions of, 375, 387, 394,
    395, 434, 435, 438, 440,
    443-44 (*see also* Contribu-
    tions, corporations)
  power shift, 153
  reforms, 438, 440
  restraints on, 436-37
  in state politics, 453
  support, 39
Inter-University Consortium for
    Political Research, 179, 202
Issues, 93 (*see also* Candidate-issue
    positions)
  in commercials, 94, 366-67
  contributions and, 393-94
  controversial, 371-372
  developing, 129, 133
  polling and, 146, 149, 151, 238-42,
    360-61, 363-64
Issues and Answers, 315, 316

Johnson, Lyndon B., 314, 318
  Daisy commercial, 335, 341, 351-
    52, 366
  speech on Vietnam, 299
  withdrawal, 361-62
Jones, Ruth, 357
Joy, James R., 80

Kelley, Stanley, Jr., 49, 264-65, 271-
    72, 277-84, 365, 366
Kennedy campaigns, 39, 313
  financial support, 373, 393
Kennedy, Edward, 315
Kennedy, John F., 22, 318
  debates, 260, 335, 371
  1960 campaign, 14-15, 180
Kennedy, Robert, 88, 91, 333
  issues, 95
  media consultant, 336
  media coverage, 313-16, 318
  use of tv, 94-95, 269
Kimball, Penn, 10
King, Coretta Scott, 120-21
King, Martin Luther, 80
Klapper, Joseph, 264
Kopelman, Arie, 90-91, 93, 98, 100,
    103

Labor [*see also* American Federation
    of Labor (AFL/CIO) COPE]
  aid to Democrats, 16, 17, 394

contributions prohibited, 420
  influence of, 450-51
  labor committees, 395, 438, 440,
    452
  political education, 395
  Republican party platform and, 14
Lazarsfeld, Paul F., 264, 280
League of Conservation Voters, 438
Lobbying interest, 452
Lobbying regulation, 437 (*see also*
    Interest groups)
Local government campaigns, 69 (*see
    also* Minnesota DFL cam-
    paign)
Long ballot, 421
Long formats, 96

McCarthy, Eugene, 147, 316, 393
McCloskey, 448
McGovern, George:
  advancing for, 112-16
  budget, 35
  campaign costs, 33, 145, 382
  debate with Humphrey, 328-29
  direct mail, 147
  efficiency, 333
  endorsements, 120, 122
  film biography, 287
  fund raising, 286-87
  image, 22, 38, 263, 342
  in nonprimary states, 12
  in primary states, 8, 112, 119, 262
  issues, 14, 286-88
  media, 12, 28, 30, 94, 112, 146,
    286
  media director, 337
  organization, 15-16
  poll advice, 145, 332, 362
  press corps coverage, 320-33
  Reform Commission, 450
  small gifts to, 393, 445
  strategy, 112
  voter identification effort, 148
Machine Politics (COPE), 170, 173
Machine Politics: Chicago Model
    (Gosnell), 3, 259
Machine-run politics, 364-65
McLuhan, Marshall, 25, 267, 356
MacNeil, Robert, 272, 310-19
Madison, James, 379
Mail Advertising Corp. of America
    (MAC), 167
Mannes, Marya, 87
"Manual of Political Campaign Ad-
    vertising," 89, 91-92, 94, 96

Market Opinion Research, 25
Marttila, John, 301-2
Mass communication techniques, 10,
    23 (*see also* Media; Radio;
    Television)
Mass media:
  accessibility, 11, 18-19, 43
  costs, 32-35
  dependence on, 50, 62, 259
  size of audience, 265
Matching grants, 405, 407
Matching incentives, 453-55
Matt Reese & Associates, 53, 304
Mears, Walter, 327-29
Media: (*see also* Mass media)
  electronic, 5-6, 25-28, 62, 344-45,
    358
  "event," 27-28, 31, 64, 105, 109,
    262, 270, 272, 311-18 (*see
    also* News media; Press)
  markets, 6, 42, 105, 139
  media-oriented campaign, 39-41,
    52, 94, 269
    changes due to, 261-64, 366
    costs, 35-36
    effects on voters, 264-65, 269
    trends in 1970s, 269-71
  "mix," 139, 270
  personal, 367-68
  specialist, 266-68, 345 (*see also*
    Guggenheim, Charles; Napoli-
    tan, Joseph; Schwartz, Tony)
  uncontrolled, 310-18, 367
Meet the Press, 315, 316
Merrill Research Associates, 158
Meyner, Robert, 243, 246-47
Microform systems, 155
Minnesota DFL campaign, 1968,
    124, 127-40
Minnesota Republican State Central
    Committee, 126-27
Minor parties, 404, 405, 406
Minority party candidate, 85-86, 442
    (*see also* Danforth, John C.)
Minow, Newton, 88, 458
Model State Statute: Politics, Elec-
    tions and Public Office, 417,
    453
Movie star candidates, 63
Murphy, George, 63
Muskie, Edmund, 369

Napolitan, Joseph, 9, 51, 303, 335,
    354
  pre-election media blitz, 305-6, 356

National Commission on Technol-
    ogy, Automation and Eco-
    nomic Progress, 161
National Committee for an Effective
    Congress, 438
National party committees, 125,
    130, 139, 409, 427, 431, 451
  computerized information, 162-64
  limits on spending, 398 (*see also*
    Campaign finance; Campaign
    spending; Contributors)
  research divisions, 176-77
National party conventions, 13, 386,
    405
Nedzi, Lucian, 363
New Hampshire campaign, 292-93,
    362
New politics, 10-42
  new experts, 23-25
News media, 30, 71, 84, 260-61,
    362, 370-71 (*see also* Media,
    "event")
  reaction to Watergate, 402
  reporting poll results, 363 (*see also*
    Polling)
News releases, 84
News-style commercials, 64, 268-69,
    271, 285
News wire services, 327, 330, 332
Newspaper advertising, 34, 36, 261,
    292, 293
Newtòn, Carroll, 281-82
Nichols, Edward J., 162
Nixon, Richard M., 257, 282, 317,
    369
  campaigns, 9, 244-45, 260, 335
    (*see also* Presidential cam-
    paign, 1972)
  big money, 374, 403
  computerized mailings, 384
  media directors, 337
  November Group, 3, 33, 286,
    289, 336-42
  polls and, 146
  radio, 272, 296-99
  strategy, 38-39, 288
  telephone, 35, 279
  tv spots, 90
  voter identification canvass, 148
Committee for the Re-election of
    the President (CREEP), 9,
    15, 16, 289, 368, 431 (*see
    also* Watergate)
  contributions to, 395
  Finance Committee, 15

Nixon, Richard M. (*continued*)
    illegal activities, 9-10, 15, 368-
        70, 424-25
    competency image, 22, 342
    effect on party, 449, 450
    North Carolina race, 294

O'Brien, Lawrence, 14-15, 339, 340,
    369
Opinion research *See* Polling
Oregon race, 294-95
Ottinger, Richard L., 307, 335, 373,
    393
Outdoor and transit advertising, 36,
    84

Packaging of candidates, 87-103
Partisan falloff, 220-21
Party (*see also* Democratic National
    Committee; Democratic
    Party; Republican National
    Committee; Republican
    Party)
    campaign manager, 50 (*see also*
        Candidate, manager)
    changes in, 18-19, 259-60
    decline of party voting, 19-23, 41,
        43
    demise of parties, 10-19, 65, 360,
        385
    demise of political machine, 199
    future of, 137-40, 427, 451
    loyalty, 19-22, 43
        vs. candidate loyalty, 138-39,
            427, 431
    organization:
        Kennedy-O'Brien approach, 15
        mobilizing role, 136, 140, 408
        new role in Minnesota campaign,
            127-36
        as resource, 38
        reform rules, 13
        reinforcers, 41
    role in candidate selection, 11, 13,
        43, 459
    role in communication, 5-6
    role in new campaigning, 56, 123-
        41
    role in planning, 17-18, 128
    role on the issues, 13-14, 124
    services and the new politics,
        125-27
        to candidates, 124, 374, 449,
            458-59

    to state legislature candidates,
        127-36
    specific services offered, 128
    support of modest-means candi-
        date, 374, 449
    traditional functions, 7, 124, 260,
        408
Party committees, 394, 401, 408,
    419, 420 (*see also* National
    party committees)
Party competition, 23
Patronage, 18, 50, 109, 124, 427
Pell, Claiborne, 8-9, 290-91
People's Choice (Lazarsfeld), 264
Perquisites of office, 442-43, 456
    (*see also* Incumbent)
Personal income, 389-90
Personal income tax checkoff, 375-
    76, 405
Phinney, Michael, 111
Pitchell, Robert, 7, 50
Plurality, 210
Political communication (*see also*
    Communication; Media), 72-
    76, 350-51, 367-68
    candor in, 73-75
    good taste, 365, 367
Political consultants, 8-9, 25, 126,
    300, 364 (*see also* Profes-
    sional campaign manage-
    ment)
    history of profession, 60-67
    professional pride, 76-78
    role, 59-78
    new role, 67-71, 77-78
Political subsidies *See* Public financ-
    ing
Political Surveys and Analysis, 151
Political system in U.S., 59-60, 360,
    375 (*see also* Campaign ethics
    and reform; Democracy;
    Watergate)
    dangers in, 430
    effect of broadcast media, 88-89,
        359 (*see also* Media; Televi-
        sion)
    participation in, 381
    political elective offices, 387
    public attitude, 432
    threat to, 360, 367, 370
Politics, 62, 65, 66, 74
    costs seen in perspective, 389-91
    financing, 379-409, 432 (*see also*
        Campaign finance; Reform in

politics)
private financing, 431, 432
major concerns, 360, 375
Polling, 37, 38, 64, 126, 127, 133,
        147, 151
abuses, 360-61
addressing the issues, 251-54
code of ethics, 363
costs, 31
effects on campaign, 145-46, 362
firms, 146
incompetence and bias, 363
key role, 144-45, 237, 362
leaks, 361-62
reading the poll, 21-22, 354-55
sharing information, 70
types of information, 146-47
uses, 237-58
    candidate recognition, 242-43,
        362
    on the issues, 238-42, 361
    opponent weakness, 254-57, 364
Pollster, 24, 126, 127
Population, 178
mobility, 153, 166-67, 203
Precinct activity, 259-60
Precinct data, 201-7, 210
ranking, 212-13
Precinct Index Priority System
        (P.I.P.S.), 224-36
Precinct walking list, 174, 188, 189
President: (see also Incumbent)
access to media, 372
candidates for, 11-12, 250, 364
limits on spending, 398
public financing for, 398, 405, 448
Presidential campaign, 1972, 4, 21,
        22, 53 (see also names of
        candidates)
announcement of candidacy, 262
broadcast spending, 26, 33
corrupt practices, 429 (see also
        Campaign ethics and reform;
        Nixon, Richard M., Commit-
        tee for the Re-election of the
        President)
costs, 28, 382, 389, 392
media audience, 260-61
polls, 250
primaries, 336
television commercials (Nixon-Mc-
        Govern), 334-43
Presidential election:
1952, 1956, 1960:

costs, 381, 382
1964: 22, 366, 390
    Daisy commercial, 335, 341,
        351-52, 366
1968: 20, 26, 56, 88, 392
Presidential Election Campaign Fund
        Fund, 405-6, 407, 421, 448
Presidential nominating process, 11-
        13
polls, 21-22, 250
primaries, 11, 12, 336, 386, 430
    costs, 33, 387
    Nixon tv spots, 90
    polls, 146
public funding, 448, 451
reform, 386
Presidential Television (Minow), 458
President's Commission on Campaign
        Costs, 439
Press, 61-62, 65, 70
relations with, 70-71, 84-85
traveling news corps, 272, 362
Press conference, 108, 271, 283
Press corps, Presidential campaign,
        320-33
Professional campaign management,
        5, 7-9, 49-56, 60, 124, 426
        (see also Political con-
        sultants)
campaign manager, 49, 50, 51, 61
training for, 456
Professional Public Relations and
        Political Power (Kelley), 49
Public relations, 85, 135
counselor, 23-24, 49

Radio, 34, 36, 298
audience, 260, 261, 297-98, 357-
        58
free, 312, 458
use in New Hampshire, 292-93
use in Presidential campaign, 296-
        98
Reagan, Ronald, 54, 63
Reeves, Richard, 305
Reform in politics, 10, 66-67, 360,
        370, 373, 435 (see also Cam-
        paign ethics and reform;
        Campaign finance, public fi-
        nancing)
legislation, 68, 359
safeguards needed, 436-38
unfair tactics complaints, 368
Revenue Act of 1971, 415

Reinforcement, 264, 265-66, 350
Republican Convention, 1972, 262-63
Republican National Committee, 17, 427
  education in EDP, 162, 163
  service to candidates, 125-26, 162
  use of EDP, 172
Republican Party: (*see also* Goldwater, Barry; National party committees; Nixon, Richard M.)
  changes in, 449, 450, 451
  1972 platform, 14
  voter canvass, 167
RFK Remembered (film), 336
Rhode Island race, 290-91
Rockefeller, Nelson:
  campaign for President, 12-13, 93 316
  campaigns for governor, 5, 6, 33, 92-93, 249-51, 306, 335, 382
  family contributions, 373, 393
  issues, 239-40, 248, 256-57, 313
  record, 366, 367
  tv strategy, 4
Rockefeller, Winthrop, 167-68, 294, 335, 364
Roll, Charles W., Jr., 151, 237-58
Romney, George, 145, 312

Schneider, John, 364
Schwartz, Tony, 266-67, 272-73, 290, 341, 344-58
Scientific Political Services, 158
Secret Service, 107, 362
Selling of the President, The (McGinniss), 335
Senate candidates, 33, 391, 398
Separation of powers, 404, 406, 408
Setting of campaign, 37
Shafer, Raymond, 245-46
Shapp, Milton, 9, 13, 306, 393
Simulation, 183
Singer, William, 6-7
Social research findings, 39
Sorauf, Frank, 7, 123
Sorenson, Theodore C., 183
Southern Democrats, 17-18
Specialized media, 259, 439-40
Spencer, Walter Troy, 56, 87-103
Spencer-Roberts, 25, 30, 53-54
Stans, Maurice, 15
Stevenson, Adlai, 367

Stewart, John, 340-41
"Sunshine Laws," 453
Survey Research Center, 19, 20-22

Taft, Robert, Jr., 174
Tax incentives, 415-16
Tax issues:
  sales vs. income tax, 252-56
  tax checkoff, 375-76, 405, 416, 421-22, 448, 453
  tax credit, 422, 453, 454
Tax laws, 416
Tax surcharge, 422
Taylor, Bill, 337-38, 341-42
Technology, 18-19, 43, 64, 123, 124, 136, 137, 154, 360
  costs, 384-85
Telephone, 269-70, 303-5, 384
  feedback, 358
Television, 6, 87-89, 261, 351
  audience, 260, 280, 367
  cost, 30, 33-36, 62
  credibility, 40, 311
  distortion of truth, 366
  early use, 60-62, 271, 277-79
  equal time provision, 278, 310, 317 *(see also* Federal Communications Act; Federal Communications Commission)
  formats, 270-71, 279, 283, 367
  half-hour show, 96
  making politics entertaining, 281-82, 317
  Neilsen ratings, 281
  network-controlled time, 277-78, 316-17
  networks' data banks, 202
  New York City stations, 313, 318
  paid time, 278-83
  projection of candidate image, 262-64, 300-309, 335, 365
  public affairs programs, 315-16
  time factors, 315
  uncontrolled programs, 310-18
  visual variety, 279, 314
Television spots, 268, 271, 278-79, 282, 283, 287, 291, 292, 365
  Alioto campaign spots, 350
  crawl commercials, 339, 340-41
  Daisy, 335, 341, 351-52, 366
  disclaimer, 349
  Nixon spots, 90
  Rorschach patterns, 351
Ticket Splitter, The (DeVries), 336

Ticket splitting, 42, 205-6, 268-69, 442, 449
Time buying, 356-57
Tinker, Jack, 4, 92-93, 366, 367
Travel expenses, 35, 36, 385
Treyz plan, 270
Truth-in-Polling Act, 363
Tuck, Dick, 369-70
Twenty-sixth Amendment, 384

U.S. Constitution, 390, 399
  First Amendment right, 420, 428, 439-41, 444, 446, 447
  Twenty-sixth Amendment, 384
U.S. Senate, 169, 442
U.S. Supreme Court decisions, 179

Van Riper, Paul, 160
Vietnam war, 63, 251-52, 287, 288, 446
  Goldwater, 316
  Nixon-Johnson speeches, 299
"Visual," 105 (see also Media, "event")
Volunteers, 15, 64, 150, 176
  computer aids, 174, 365
  dropoff in, 304
  recruiting, 30, 138
Vote splitters, 20-21 (see also Ticket splitting)
Vote switchers, 244
Voter contact activities, 26, 132, 148, 260, 365
Voter Decides, The (Campbell et al.), 20, 21
Voter falloff, 220
Voter lists, 166-67, 173, 190-91, 193
Voter location and registration, 168, 174, 194-96
  national system, 409
Voters, 380
  attitudes, 350-51, 353-54
  ethnic, 290
  tv as stimulus, 351-52, 354
  undecided, 280, 281
  unregistered, 195-96
Voting, 153, 381, 390
Voting Rights Acts, 384
Voucher plan, 409

Wallace, George, 21, 32, 74, 329, 381
  crowd building, 117, 119
  media format, 267-68
  Oregon primary, 119
  RNC study, 163
  schedule, 117-18
  small gifts to, 393, 445
Washington, George, 379
Watergate, 9-10, 15, 65-66, 72, 340, 359, 368, 369, 379 (see also Campaign ethics and reform; Campaign finance; Nixon, Richard M., campaigns)
  electoral process and, 428-59
  reaction to, 272, 304, 377, 446, 452
  Select Committee to Investigate, 376, 424-27
Weiner, Sanford, 55, 59-78, 272, 302, 305, 307-8
West Virginia race, 293-94
Whites in South, 20
Witcover, Jules, 272, 296-99

Year 2000, The (Kahn and Weiner), 156